CASES IN COLLECTIVE BARGAINING
AND INDUSTRIAL RELATIONS
A Decisional Approach

CASES IN COLLECTIVE BARGAINING AND INDUSTRIAL RELATIONS

A Decisional Approach

STERLING H. SCHOEN
Professor of Management

RAYMOND L. HILGERT
*Professor of Management
and Industrial Relations*

*Both of the Graduate School
of Business Administration,
Washington University,
St. Louis, Missouri*

1978   Third Edition

Richard D. Irwin, Inc.   Homewood, Illinois,   60430
Irwin-Dorsey Limited   Georgetown, Ontario   L7G 4B3

Third Edition

5 6 7 8 9 0 ML 5 4 3 2 1 0

ISBN 0-256-02002-7
Library of Congress Catalog Card No. 77–089789
Printed in the United States of America

PREFACE

This third edition provides a convenient but relatively extensive set of cases in a variety of union-management problem situations. The book is probably most appropriate as a supplementary book in basic or survey courses in collective bargaining, labor economics, and industrial relations. However, the collection of cases is of sufficient magnitude that the book would be suitable for advanced courses or case courses in the field of collective bargaining and labor relations.

A major objective is to provide a means by which students can apply principles, concepts, and legal considerations that they have learned in realistic decision situations and confrontations between labor and management. We have used the cases in seminars and classes, and have found them to be challenging and fascinating learning instruments.

The cases are representative of the types of problems that continue to confront management and labor unions. Cases such as these test analytical ability in dealing with challenging human relations and union-management situations in a way useful even for students who do not have a management or labor relations career in mind.

In an effort to reflect the impact of recent trends, we have collected representative cases dealing with problems that focus upon current and contemporary issues. Thirty-five of the 65 cases in this third edition, or somewhat more than 50 percent, are new to this collection. We have retained 30 cases from the first and second editions in order to provide continuity and balance, and because these cases are "timeless" in the evaluation of union-management relations.

Part One of the book presents a collection of cases heard by the National Labor Relations Board and restructured from published reports of the NLRB and court decisions. Our intent has been to describe each situation from the perspective of impartial writers reporting the facts and issues of the case. The case format has been developed as follows: the background information of the case is first presented, including relevant legal issues; the position of the union(s) or person(s) is stated; and the position of the management or company is stated. An introductory discussion and important and substantive sections of the Labor Management Relations Act (as amended) are included at the outset of Part One to enable students to become familiar with the provisions of the act which are applicable throughout the cases.

We believe that the legal obligations and responsibilities of unions and management under the Labor Management Relations Act continue to be among the most dynamic and important areas of collective bargaining today. Case studies such as those in the first section enable the student to appreciate the nature of this act, its application in numerous union-management situations, and the duties and legal obligations of management and union representatives to carry out their bargaining responsibilities in good faith.

Part Two consists of cases adapted from grievance-arbitration decisions. We are grateful to the Bureau of National Affairs, Inc., William Beltz, Executive Editor, for permission to adapt certain published cases from *Labor Arbitration Reports.* Here, too, the approach has been to restructure these actual arbitration cases in a convenient format. The highlights and issues of each case are provided through relevant background information, including the contractual clauses, rules, practices, and the like, which are pertinent. Principal arguments of the union and management sides are then presented. Cases in this part demonstrate complexities and controversial areas, which continue to manifest in the ongoing relationships between management and union personnel. We also have included a brief introductory discussion of the major considerations involved in grievance-arbitration procedures from which these cases emanate.

For both the NLRB and labor arbitration cases—which have not been selected with any intent of presenting "good" or "bad" or "right" or "wrong" union-management practices—the student should ask, "What are the problems or principal issues?" "What is at stake between the parties?" "What is justice or equity in the situation?" "What does the law require?" "What does the contract say on the issue(s)?" "How have previous NLRB decisions or previous labor arbitration decisions handled similar circumstances?" These types of questions, and the more specific questions we have developed at the conclusion of each case, urge students toward a depth analysis of issues. Decisions of the NLRB, the courts, and labor arbitrators for these cases are included in an Instructor's Manual. It has been the authors' experience that most students want to compare their decisions and approaches with those of authorities in the field.

Index and classification tables are included in each section of the book prior to the cases. These tables briefly cite the major issues of each case; for the NLRB cases, legal provisions are indicated. Selected bibliographies are also provided for more detailed reading in areas that either directly or indirectly are involved in the cases and materials in both sections of the book.

Although we cannot recognize everyone who has had a part in developing this book, we wish particularly to acknowledge the work of our research assistants at Washington University, Patrick Mathis, Terry Smith, and James Pandjiris, who were involved in researching case materials and in case manuscript development. James Craft of the University of Pittsburgh, Thomas A. Noble of the University of North Alabama, and Donald Goodman of Niagara University reviewed some of the case materials and offered numerous helpful suggestions.

Further, we acknowledge with many thanks, the cooperation of Deans Karl Hill and Nicholas Baloff of the Graduate School of Business Administration of Washington University. They provided us support in several ways, including granting us the services of Ruth Scheetz of the Washington University staff, who again typed the entire manuscript as she did for the previous edition.

December 1977   STERLING H. SCHOEN
                                                                            RAYMOND L. HILGERT

CONTENTS

PART II.   Problems in Union Management Relations

CASES

PART ONE

Legal Aspects of Collective Bargaining

NATIONAL LABOR RELATIONS BOARD CASES

Introduction to

THE LABOR MANAGEMENT RELATIONS
ACT (LMRA)

This introductory section will briefly introduce the principal provisions of the Labor Management Relations Act of 1947 as amended. A partial text of this act follows this introductory section. For even more analytical understanding of the provisions of the act and its applications, a selected bibliography for reading is included at the end of this introductory section. It also is recommended that the student of collective bargaining and industrial relations contact a regional or national office of the National Labor Relations Board to obtain various NLRB publications which explain detailed principles and procedures involved in administration of the law. For example, a publication included in the bibliography entitled, "A Layman's Guide to Basic Law Under the National Labor Relations Act," is prepared by the Office of the General Counsel of the NLRB; this booklet is very helpful in understanding many of the day-to-day activities of the Board and some of its most recent thinking.

The Labor Management Relations Act of 1947, also known as the Taft-Hartley Act in recognition of the principal congressional authors of the law, is the principal labor legislation governing the "rules of the game" of collective bargaining for the private sector of the United States economic system.[1] The LMRA of 1947 constituted a major amendment and revision of the National Labor Relations (Wagner) Act of 1935. The act since has been amended a number of times (1951, 1958, 1959, 1969, 1973, 1974), with the most recent amendments being focused upon health care institutions. As it stands today, the act is the fundamental legislative basis for the majority of union-management

---

[1] The Railway Labor Act of 1926 (as amended) governs collective bargaining in the rail and airline industries. Although the Railway Labor Act is not widely applicable and some of its provisions are considerably different from those in LMRA, its premises and procedures were drawn upon by the framers of the National Labor Relations (Wagner) Act of 1935, upon which the act of 1947 subsequently was based. The student is encouraged to study the provisions of the Railway Labor Act, as well as a history of labor laws in the railroad industries, which led to the passage of the Railway Labor Act of 1926.

relationships in the United States.[2] The Labor Management Relations Act is an extremely complex document in and of itself. Of even greater complexity, however, is the body of administrative laws and decisions which has evolved over the years of its existence in hundreds of thousands of union-management case situations. The act is constantly being tested, evaluated, and reevaluated by the NLRB, the courts, and by the Congress of the United States, in the light of changing times, new confrontations, and new decisions. It is not the purpose of this section to completely interpret the act nor to present it in its entirety. Rather, selected parts of the act will be discussed to underscore the major elements of the act governing the collective bargaining process. An understanding of these parts of the act should provide sufficient insights on which various aspects of specific union-management cases may be analyzed.

EXCERPTS AND COMMENTS ON THE TEXT OF THE LABOR MANAGEMENT RELATIONS ACT, 1947, AS AMENDED

Section 1. The Statement of Findings and Policy

The Labor Management Relations Act begins with a statement to the effect that industrial strife interferes with the normal flow of

---

[2] One of the major developments in contemporary labor relations has been at the federal government employee level. Executive Order 10988 originally signed by President Kennedy in 1962 was replaced by Executive Order 11491 issued by President Nixon in 1970. Subsequently, Executive Orders 11616 and 11636 issued by President Nixon in 1971 and Executive Order 11838 issued by President Ford in 1975 amended Executive Order 11491. These orders have provided for federal employees union representation and collective bargaining rights. Executive Order 11491 as amended closely parallels the LMRA in many fundamental areas, with most of its provisions strikingly similar to various provisions in LMRA governing union-management relations in the private sector. Of course, federal government employees do not have the right to strike, and a number of key areas remain outside of the scope of bargaining in the federal sector. For example, most wages, and certain working conditions are set by Congress, and a number of areas of employee concern are handled under Civil Service regulations. Nevertheless, Executive Order 11491 is a major development in collective bargaining in the United States. The authors have chosen not to include any cases from the federal sector in this part of the text. However, numerous cases have been decided under Executive Order 11491 which have drawn heavily for precedent and policy from decisions of the National Labor Relations Board in the private sector. Included in the bibliography at the end of this introductory section are a number of sources to consult for public sector bargaining law, cases and decisions.

The United States Postal Service, however, was brought under partial coverage of the LMRA through enactment of the Postal Reorganization Act of 1970 (Public Law 91–375). This law granted the National Labor Relations Board jurisdiction over the United States Postal Service for various aspects of bargaining unit determination, unfair labor practices, bargaining procedures, and related matters.

commerce. The purpose of the act is to promote the full flow of commerce by prescribing and protecting rights of employers and employees and by providing orderly and peaceful procedures for preventing interference by either with the legitimate rights of the other.

Also included in this statement of public policy is that the labor law of the land is designed to regulate both unions and employers in the public interest. The act encourages the right of employees to organize labor unions and to bargain collectively with their employers as a means of balancing bargaining power. At the same time, the act encourages union and employer practices which are fundamental to the friendly adjustment of industrial disputes, with the objective of eliminating some union and employer practices which impair the public interest by contributing to industrial unrest and strikes.

The National Labor Relations Board, which is the federal agency administering the act, has consistently interpreted this section to mean that the public policy of the United States is to promote and encourage the principle of unionism.

Section 2. Definitions

This section of the act defines various terms used in the course of the act, and also outlines the coverage of the act. By its terms, the act does not apply to employees in a business or industry where a labor dispute would not affect interstate commerce. In addition, the act specifically states that it does not apply to the following:

Agricultural laborers, as defined by the Fair Labor Standards Act (Wage-Hour Law).

Domestic servants.

Any individual employed by one's parent or spouse.

Government employees, including those of government corporations or the Federal Reserve Bank, or any political subdivision such as a state or school district.[3]

Independent contractors who depend upon profits, rather than commissions or wages, for their income.

A later section (212) also exempts employees and employers who are subject to provisions of the Railway Labor Act.

---

[3] A number of states have laws to provide collective bargaining rights and procedures for state and local government employees, including teachers and employees of government operated health care facilities.

Supervisors are excluded from the definition of employees covered by the act. Whether or not a person is a supervisor is determined by authority rather than by title. The authority required to exclude an employee from coverage of the act as a supervisor is defined in Section 2(11) of the act.

The 1974 amendments to LMRA (Public Law 93–360) brought all private health care institutions, whether or not operated for a profit, under the coverage of the act. Section 2 (14) defines a private health care institution as, "any hospital, convalescent hospital, health maintenance organization, health clinic, nursing home, extended care facility, or other institution devoted to the care of sick, infirm, or aged person."

An *employer* is defined in the law as including "any person acting as an agent of employer, directly or indirectly."

The term *labor organization* means any organization, agency, or employee representation committee or plan in which employees participate and which exists for the purpose, in whole or in part, of dealing with employers concerning grievances, labor disputes, wages, rate of pay, hours of employment, or conditions of work.

Section 2 (12) defines the meaning of the term "professional employee" for which specific organizational rights are guaranteed in a later section.

Sections 3, 4, 5, 6. The National Labor Relations Board

Section 3 creates the National Labor Relations Board as an independent agency to administer the act. The NLRB consists of five members appointed by the President of the United States.

Section 3 also authorizes the appointment of a General Counsel of the Board, who is given supervisory authority over the Board attorneys and officers and employees in the regional offices of the Board.

Sections 4 and 5 outline certain compensation, procedural and administrative authorities granted to the NLRB by the Congress.

However, the key section is Section 6, which gives the Board authority to establish rules and regulations necessary to carry out provisions of the Labor Management Relations Act. *In effect, this section empowers the National Labor Relations Board to administer and interpret the labor law in whatever manner it deems appropriate to the situations encountered.*

In order to do this, the Board has developed various standards—for the most part, dollar sales or volume standards—by which it determines whether or not a business enterprise is deemed to be interstate commerce and thus covered under the provisions of the act.[4] The Board has developed detailed rules, policies, and procedures by which it determines appropriate collective bargaining units, holds representational elections, investigates labor disputes, and other such matters. *The National Labor Relations Board by its policies and rulings in effect can and does reshape the act, subject only to review of the federal courts.* The *Appendix* to this Introductory section will provide an overview to the general operations of the NLRB and the magnitude of those operations.

Section 7. Rights of Employees

This section is perhaps one of the most significant in the act. It guarantees employees the right to self-organization; to form, join, or assist labor organizations; to bargain collectively through representa-

---

4 For example, the NLRB has used a standard of $500,000 total annual volume of business to determine if a *retail enterprise* was considered interstate. For *non-retail businesses* the Board uses two tests: (a) direct sales to consumers in other states or indirect sales through others called outflow of at least $50,000 a year; or direct purchases of goods from suppliers from other states or indirect purchases through others called inflow of at least $50,000 a year.

Among the NLRB jurisdictional standards in effect since January 1, 1970, are the following:

Office buildings: Total annual revenue of $100,000 of which $25,000 or more is derived from organizations which meet any of the standards except the indirect outflow and indirect inflow standards established for nonretail enterprises.

Public utilities: At least $250,000 total annual volume of business, or $50,000 direct or indirect outflow or inflow.

Newspapers: At least $200,000 total annual volume of business.

Radio, telegraph, television, and telephone enterprises: At least $100,000 total annual volume of business.

Hotels, motels, and residential apartment houses: At least $500,000 total annual volume of business.

Transit systems: At least $250,000 total annual volume of business.

Taxicab companies: At least $500,000 total annual volume of business.

Associations: These are regarded as a single employer in that the annual business of all association members is totaled to determine whether any of the standards apply.

National defense: Jurisdiction is asserted over all enterprises affecting commerce when their operations have a substantial impact on national defense, whether or not the enterprises satisfy any other standard.

Private nonprofit universities and colleges: At least $1,000,000 gross annual revenue from all sources (excluding contributions not available for operating expenses because of limitations imposed by the grantor).

In addition, the NLRB has adopted other standards and policies which it uses in determining its jurisdiction depending upon various types of businesses and unique conditions involved. For example, in 1976, the NLRB changed its policy of exempting nonprofit, noncommercial and charitable institutions from coverage of LMRA. The Board asserted that it would use the same general revenue standards for these types of institutions to determine if an employer's operations "substantially affect interstate commerce" and thus should be subject to provisions of the act.

tives of their own choosing; and to engage in (or refrain from) certain other concerted activities for the purpose of collective bargaining or other mutual aid or protection.

Examples of employee rights protected by Section 7 are:

Forming or attempting to form a union among the employees of a company.

Joining a union.

Assisting a union to organize the employees of any company.

Going out on strike for the purpose of attempting to obtain improved wages, hours, or other conditions of employment.

Refraining from joining a union in the absence of a valid union shop agreement.

UNFAIR LABOR PRACTICES: EMPLOYERS

Employers are forbidden from engaging in the following types of unfair labor practices:

Section 8 (a) (1). To interfere with, restrain, or coerce employees in the exercise of rights guaranteed by Section 7;

Section 8 (a) (2). To demonstrate or interfere with the formation or administration of any labor organization or contribute financial or other support to it.

In this regard, the Board distinguishes between "domination" of a labor organization and conduct which amounts to little more than illegal "interference." When a union is found to be "dominated" by an employer, the Board will normally order the organization completely disestablished as a representative of employees. But if the organization is found only to have been supported by employer assistance amounting to less than domination, the Board usually orders the employer to stop such support and to withhold recognition from the organization until it has been certified by the Board as a bona fide representative of employees.

Section 8 (a) (1) constitutes a broad statement against interference by the employer; employers violate this section whenever they commit any of the unfair labor practices. Thus, a violation of Section 8 (a) (2), (3), (4), or (5) also results in a violation of Section 8 (a) (1).

Various acts of an employer may independently violate Section 8 (a) (1). Examples of such violations are:

Spying on union meetings, or on the activities of the union organizer.

Threatening to terminate credit at the company store or to force employees to move out of company housing if the union wins bargaining rights for employees.

Circulating antiunion petitions among employees.

Improving wages or other conditions of employment deliberately timed to undercut the union's organizing campaign.

Threatening to move the plant out of town or to close it if the union wins bargaining rights in the plant.

An employer violates Section 8 (a) (2) by engaging in activities such as:

Assisting employees in organizing a union or an employee representation plan by providing financial support, legal counsel, or active encouragement.

Conducting a "straw vote" to determine whether employees favor an inside union, as opposed to one affiliated with one of the national unions.

Signing a union security contract with an inside union to forestall an organizing drive by an outside union.

Exerting pressure on employees to join a particular union.

Permitting a union to solicit dues checkoff authorizations from new employees as they go through the hiring process.

Permitting officers of one union to leave their machines to solicit union members while denying officers of a competing union these same privileges.

Section 8 (a) (3). This section prohibits discrimination in hiring or tenure of employment or any term or condition of employment which tends to encourage or discourage membership in any labor organization. This provision, together with Section 8 (b) (2), prohibits the "closed shop," in which only persons who already hold membership in a labor organization may be hired. It also prohibits discriminatory hiring hall arrangements by which only persons who have "permits" from a union may be hired. However, a proviso of this section permits an employer and labor union to agree to a union shop where employees may be required to join a union after 30 days of employment. Some examples of types of discrimination in employment prohibited by this section would include:

Discharging or demoting an employee because he[5] urged fellow employees to join or organize a union.

Refusing to reinstate an employee (when a job for which he can qualify is open) because he took part in a lawful strike of a union.

Refusing to hire a qualified applicant for a job because he belongs to a union.

Refusing to hire a qualified applicant for a job because he does not belong to a union or because he belongs to one union rather than to another union.

Section 8 (a) (4). Employers may not discharge or otherwise discriminate against employees because they have filed charges or given testimony under this act. Examples of violations of this section are:

Refusing to reinstate an employee when a job he is otherwise qualified for is open because he filed charges with the NLRB claiming his layoff was based on union activity.

Demoting an employee because he testified at an NLRB hearing.

Section 8 (a) (5). It is an unfair labor practice for an employer to refuse to bargain collectively with the representatives of the employees. The meaning of "bargaining collectively" is more specifically outlined in Section 8 (d) of the act. Section 8 (d) has been interpreted in many ways, and it might be considered as the cornerstone for the basic philosophy of the act.

Examples of employer violations of this section are as follows:

Refusing to meet with representatives of a certified union because employees have threatened to go out on strike.

Insisting that the union withdraw its demand for a union shop before the company would enter negotiations over a contract.

Insisting that members of the negotiating committee of the union be composed of employees of the company.

Refusing to discuss an increase in the price of coffee served in the company cafeteria.

Granting a wage increase without consulting the certified union.

Refusing to supply the union negotiators with information concerning the incentive system.

---

5 In these and other examples provided by various official NLRB publications, it is understood that pronouns such as "he," "his," "him" are used in a generic sense and are not limited to a male interpretation.

UNFAIR LABOR PRACTICES: LABOR ORGANIZATIONS

The 1947 and 1959 amendments to the act made certain activities of labor unions unfair labor practices.

Section 8 (b) (1) forbids any activity on the part of a labor organization which tends "to restrain or coerce employees in the exercise of the rights guaranteed in Section 7." This includes activities such as the following:

Trailing or waylaying nonstrikers.

Mass picketing in such numbers that nonstrikers are unable to enter or leave the plant.

Threatening nonstrikers with bodily injury, or with loss of their jobs.

Committing or threatening acts of violence against nonstrikers on a picket line.

This section also prohibits a union from restraining or coercing an employer in the selection of a bargaining representative. For example, a union may not:

Demand that the employer hire only supervisors who are members of the union and give them power to negotiate grievances.

Insist that the employer include or exclude certain persons from his negotiating committee.

Section 8 (b) (2). The only way by which a union may cause an employer to "discriminate" against a union member (or nonunion member) is if such person has failed to "tender" periodic dues and initiation fees uniformly required as a condition of acquiring or retaining membership in the union, where a union shop agreement is in effect.

Section 8 (b) (2) bars a union from causing or attempting to cause an employer to discriminate against an employee in violation of Section 8 (a) (3). It also prohibits the union from attempting to cause an employer to discriminate against an employee to whom the union has denied or terminated membership, except where this action was taken by the union because the employee failed to "tender" the regular initiation fees and/or periodic dues. Examples of violations of this section are:

In the absence of a union security clause, demanding that the employer discharge an employee who is not a member of the union.

Demanding that the employer discharge an employee who was expelled from the union after refusing to pay a fine levied upon him for failure to attend union meetings.

Insisting upon a contractual clause which requires the employer to employ only members of the union or employees "satisfactory" to the union.

Section 8 (b) (3). A union may not refuse to bargain collectively in good faith with an employer, if the union is the duly authorized representative of the bargaining group. Examples of violations of this section are as follows:

Demanding that the company post a performance bond as a condition for bargaining.

Striking against an employer who has bargained, and who continues to bargain, on a multiemployer basis in an effort to force him to bargain separately.

Insisting upon the inclusion of an illegal clause, such as a "hot cargo" clause, in the contract.

Section 8 (b) (4). This section forbids secondary boycotts and certain types of strikes and picketing; it is an extremely complicated section. Secondary boycotts; sympathy strikes or boycotts to force recognition of an uncertified union; a strike to substitute another bargaining representative for one certified by the Board; strikes over so-called union jurisdictional disputes or work assignment disputes; and several other types of unfair acts—all are forbidden under this section. One proviso in Section 8 (b) (4) (D) permits informational picketing in various circumstances, so long as such publicity and informational picketing do not have the effect of inducing any individual employed by any person other than a primary employer to refuse to pick up, deliver or transfer goods or not to perform services at the establishment of the employer involved in the dispute.

The following union activities are considered to be unfair labor practices under this section:

Picketing a company after three of its four partners refused to comply with the union's demand that they become members [8 (b) (4) (A)].

Insisting that where final court action requires employees to handle goods at premises involved in a labor dispute, the employer must pay triple wages for the day or the entire tour of duty [8 (b) (4) (A)].

Picketing the premises of an employer to compel him to cease doing business with another employer who has refused to recognize the union [8 (b) (4) (B)].

Threatening an employer by telling him that his business will be picketed if he continues to do business with another employer whom the union has designated as "unfair" [8 (b) (4) (B)].

A union's directing its members not to pick up and deliver products from a plant where the drivers had voted to be represented by a different union which had received certification from the NLRB [8 (b) (4) (C)].

A union's engaging in a strike to attempt to force the employer to assign to it the job of installing metal doors, when the employer had assigned the work to the members of another union [8 (b) (4) (D)].

Section 8 (b) (5). A union may not require employees under a union shop agreement to pay an initiation fee which the Board finds excessive or discriminatory. The section states that the Board shall consider in determination of these types of fees the practices and customs of labor organizations in the particular industry and the wages currently paid to employees affected.

For example, a union violated this section when it took the following action with respect to its initiation fees:

A union raised its initiation fee from $50 to $500 when other locals of the same union charged from $10 to $200 and the starting rate for the job was $90 per week.

Section 8 (b) (6). This section prohibits what is commonly known as "featherbedding." Unions may not force an employer to pay or deliver or to agree to pay or deliver, any money or thing of value for services which are not performed or not to be performed. This section has been narrowly interpreted by the Board and does not include situations in which the work is performed, although it may be "unnecessary."

Section 8 (b) (7) is a complex provision prohibiting a union which has not been certified as the bargaining agent from picketing or threatening to picket an employer for the purpose of obtaining recognition by that employer or acceptance by his workers as their bargaining representative. Both recognitional and organizational picketing constitute unfair labor practices when: (*a*) the employer has recognized a certified union and a new representation election would be barred under the act; (*b*) an NLRB election has been conducted during the previous 12 months; or (*c*) a representation petition has not been filed with the Board "within a reasonable period of time not to exceed thirty days from the commencement of such picketing."

However, this section does not prohibit picketing for the purpose of truthfully advising the public (including consumers) that the company does not employ union members, nor have a contract with a union, unless the effect of the picketing is to interfere with deliveries, pickups, and other services required by the picketed employer.

Section 8 (e). This complicated provision forbids both labor organizations and employers to enter into agreements commonly known as "hot cargo" agreements. These are defined as agreements where the employer will not handle, use, sell, transport, or deal in any of the products of another employer as required or forced by the labor organization.

The act excepts both the construction and garment industries from the conditions of this section. In the construction industry the parties may agree to a clause which restricts the contracting or subcontracting of work to be performed at the construction site. Typically, the union and the employer agree that subcontracted work will go to an employer who has a contract with the union. A union may strike, picket, or engage in any other lawful activity in order to obtain such an agrement with the employer. A labor organization in the garment industry may not only strike, picket, or engage in other lawful activity to obtain such an agreement, but it may also engage in such activities in order to enforce it.

Section 8 (f) provides that a union and employer in the construction industry may enter into an agreement whereby employees must join the union not later than seven days after the date of hire, rather than 30 days, as provided in Section 8 (a) (3) for all other employers. The parties may enter into such an agreement without having first established the majority status of the union, as required in Section 9.

FREE SPEECH

Section 8 (c) of the act provides that the expression of any views, argument, or opinion shall not constitute or be evidence of an unfair labor practice "if such expression contains no threat of reprisal or force or promise of benefit." Examples of situations which this provision does not protect, and which would be ruled as unfair labor practices, are:

Where an employer has made an implied threat that the organization of a union would result in the loss of certain benefits for employees.

If an employer would threaten to close down a plant to move to another location, in the event of a union's winning an election.

A statement by a management official to an employee that the employee will lose the job if the union wins a majority in the plant.

THE MEANING OF COLLECTIVE BARGAINING

Section 8 (d) defines the meaning of collective bargaining as required from both parties by the act. This definition imposes a mutual obligation upon the employer and the representative of the employees

to meet at reasonable times and confer in good faith with respect to wages, hours, and other terms and conditions of employment or the negotiation of an agreement or any question arising thereunder and the execution of a written contract incorporating any agreement reached if requested by either party, but such obligation does not compel either party to agree to a proposal or require the making of a concession.

The duty to bargain thus covers all matters concerning rates of pay, hours of employment, or other conditions of employment. These are called "mandatory" subjects of bargaining about which the employer, as well as the employees' representative, must bargain in good faith, although the law does not require "either party to agree to a proposal or require the making of a concession." As determined by the NLRB, mandatory subjects of bargaining include but are not limited to such matters as pensions for present and retired employees, bonuses, group insurance, grievance procedure, safety practices, seniority, procedures for discharge, layoff, recall, or discipline, and the union shop. On "nonmandatory" subjects, that is, matters that are lawful but not related to "wages, hours, and other conditions of employment," the parties are free to bargain and to agree, but neither party may insist on bargaining on such subjects over the objection of the other party.

Section 8 (d) also requires that the parties to a collective agreement follow certain steps in terminating or modifying the agreement. Among these requirements are that the party wishing to terminate or modify a labor contract must notify the other party to the contract in writing about the proposed termination or modification 60 days before the date on which the contract is scheduled to expire. This party also must, within 30 days after the notice to the other party, notify the Federal Mediation and Conciliation Service of the existence of a dispute if no agreement has been reached by that time, and further notify at the same time any State or Territorial mediation or conciliation agency in the State or Territory where the dispute occurred.

The NLRB has interpreted this section to mean that employees who go on strike without following the prescribed steps for terminating or modifying the contract lose the protection of the law. They may not appeal to the Board if the employer disciplines or discharges them.

REPRESENTATIVES AND ELECTIONS

Section 9 of the act is a lengthy section which governs the procedural and legal requirements for the designation of representatives and election of union representatives.

Section 9 (a) provides that the union representative designated by a majority of employees appropriate for collective bargaining becomes the exclusive representative of the employees in bargaining. When a union majority representative has been chosen, it becomes illegal for an employer to bargain with anyone else. This section of the act provides three types of elections among employees:[6]

1. *Representation elections* to determine the employees' choice of a collective bargaining agent. These are held upon petition of an employer, employees, or a labor organization. Typically the NLRB will not hold an election unless the labor organization can show that at least 30 percent of the employees involved have indicated their support for the union.
2. *Decertification elections* to determine whether or not the employees wish to withdraw the bargaining authority of the union. These, too, are held upon the petition of the employees of the labor organization.
3. *Deauthorization polls* to determine whether or not the employees wish to revoke the authority of their union to enter into a union shop contract.

---

[6] The Board also conducts "expedited elections" in connection with Section 8 (b) (7) (C), and employer last-offer elections in connection with Section 209 of the act.

Section 9 (b) outlines in general terms the "rules of the game" for holding of NLRB elections. Included in the section is the designation for the Board to determine what group of employees constitutes an appropriate unit for bargaining. The appropriate bargaining unit may extend to one or more employers, to one or more plants of the same employer, or it may be a subdivision of a plantwide unit such as a unit of skilled craftsmen. It is up to the Board to consider similarities of skills, wages, working conditions; the history of collective bargaining in the company; the wishes of the employees; and any other factors which the Board may consider important in determination of the appropriate unit. In short, employees who possess common employment interests concerning wages, hours, and conditions of employment usually are grouped together in a bargaining unit.

The act specifically limits the Board in its determination of a bargaining unit in several ways. It may not include professional and nonprofessional employees in the same unit, unless a majority of the professional employees votes to be included in the unit. It also prohibits the Board from including plant guards in the same unit with other employees, and from certifying a union of guards if it also includes members who are not guards. The Board also may not use "the extent to which employees have organized" as the controlling factor in deciding the appropriate bargain unit.

Thus, Section 9 is one of the key sections which constantly confronts both unions and management in collective bargaining relationships, particularly in the formulative stages of a labor union in a company or plant.

SPECIAL PROVISIONS FOR HEALTH CARE INSTITUTIONS

Representation election procedures are the same for health care facilities as for other establishments.[7] Similarly, as to unfair labor practices, the health care area is covered by the same statutory provisions such as those which forbid employer or union discrimination against employees, failure to bargain in good faith, certain unlawful union picketing, and employer domination or support of a labor organization.

---

[7] In early 1975, the NLRB issued its guidelines for appropriate representational units in private health care institutions. In a series of cases—217 NLRB 131–138—these guidelines limit the number of bargaining units to avoid "proliferation" of units in health care organizations.

But with a goal of minimizing work stoppages at health care institutions and providing continuity of patient care, Congress in 1974 wrote into the act a new unfair labor practice—Section 8 (g). It prohibits a labor organization from striking or picketing a health care institution, or engaging in any other concerted refusal to work, without first giving the employer and Federal Mediation and Conciliation Service a 10-day notice of such action. The section specifies, "The notice shall state the date and time that such action will commence. The notice, once given, may be extended by the written agreement of both parties."

Additionally, a series of special provisions for the health care industry were added to Section 8 (d) of the act. These health care amendments call for special dispute-settling procedures. A 90-day written notice must be served by employer or union of intent to terminate or modify a collective-bargaining contract (30 days more than required by the act elsewhere). If the dispute continues, the Federal Mediation and Conciliation Service and similar state agencies must be notified at the 60-day point. If a dispute arises in bargaining for an initial contract, 30 days' notice must be given by the union to the employer, FMCS, and the appropriate agency. In either a contract termination-modification or initial contract dispute, under Section 213 of the act, the FMCS may, if disagreement continues, invoke a 30-day no-strike, no-lockout period and set up a fact-finding board to make settlement recommendations, while continuing its mediation-conciliation efforts.

All else failing, the 10-day strike or picketing notice must be given as required by Section 8 (g).

Section 19 of the act solely for health care institutions provides that an employee with religious convictions against joining or financially supporting unions may not lawfully be required to do so. However, under a valid union-security agreement, such an employee may be required to contribute funds equal to union dues and initiation fees to a nonreligious charitable fund.

PREVENTION OF UNFAIR LABOR PRACTICES

Section 10 is very important in that it outlines the procedural requirements and limitations which are placed upon the Board and interested parties in processing unfair labor practice cases. The Labor Management Relations Act is not a criminal statute. The NLRB's actions are designed to stop unfair labor practices and to restore situations to their "original states" which prevailed before the violations occurred, insofar as possible. The orders of the Board serve basically to remedy the situation, not to punish persons who may have violated its provisions.

Sections 10 (a), 10 (b), 10 (c), 10 (d) of the act outline the general procedures by which the National Labor Relations Board and its regional offices investigate, attempt to prevent, and/or remedy unfair labor practices. Generally, a complaint of an unfair labor practice must be filed with an office of the NLRB within six months of the date of the occurrence of the alleged unfair labor practice or representational case complaint. (As of 1977, some 44 regional and other field offices of the NLRB were located in major cities in various sections of the country.) When a complaint is received in the office of the Board, an agent will investigate the complaint to see whether formal proceedings are warranted. If the regional office of the NLRB is unable to resolve the issue, and the complaint warrants a full hearing, an Administrative Law Judge from the office of the General Counsel of the Board will be assigned to conduct a full, formal hearing to take testimony and examine the evidence. If the opinion of the Administrative Law Judge representing the Board is that the evidence presented is not sufficient to justify a finding that an unfair labor practice has been committed, the office of the Board will issue an order dismissing the complaint. However, if the Administrative Law Judge is of the opinion that an unfair labor practice(s) has occurred, he or she will make an appropriate recommendation and the Board, through its regional office, will issue an order accordingly. This order usually will require the person, union or company involved to cease and desist from the unfair labor practice(s) and to take affirmative action designed to remedy the effects of the unfair labor practice(s). Since the Labor Management Relations Act is not aimed at designating criminal penalties, these orders will be designed to restore equity to the situation on the assumption that such equity is necessary to guarantee rights protected under the act. Examples of affirmative actions required of employers are:

Disestablish a union dominated by the employer.

Reopen a plant closed in an attempt to thwart the employees' attempts at self-organization.

Offer to hire employees denied employment because of their pro-union attitudes or activities.

Offer to reemploy workers who were discharged for union activity;

reimburse the employees for all lost wages, including interest; restore full seniority and all other rights, including promotions, pay increases, pension privileges, and vacation rights, that would have been received had the discriminatory discharges not occurred.

Examples of affirmative actions required of unions are:

Notification to the employee and the employer that the union does not object to the reinstatement or employment of certain persons who were discharged or denied employment as a result of certain discriminatory actions by the union.

Order the union to refund dues and fees illegally collected, including interest.

Sign an agreement which had been negotiated with the employer.

Sections 10 (e) and 10 (f) provide the machinery for the legal enforcement of Board orders and for appeal for relief from Board orders by an employer or union who believes that an order has been issued in error. Normally, the first appeal from an order of the Administrative Law Judge will go to the full five-member NLRB itself in Washington, D.C. Further appeal, if any, can take the route of the federal judicial system, that is, to a federal district court, a federal appeals court, and perhaps ultimately to the United States Supreme Court. The large majority of cases, however, are not appealed to the federal courts, but are decided at Board regional office and/or national NLRB levels.[8]

Section 10 (j) provides for special injunction procedures designed to stop quickly certain union strikes and boycotts which may result in "irreparable harm" to the employer.

Section 10 (k) provides for special procedures for hearing and adjudicating jurisdictional disputes.

MISCELLANEOUS PROVISIONS

The remainder of the Labor Management Relations Act, although quite extensive in length, is not nearly so important to the duty to

---

[8] Statistically, about 70 percent of the unfair labor practice charges filed with the NLRB are dismissed by the regional offices of the Board or withdrawn by the parties. Of the remainder, about 80 percent are settled at the regional office level. Of the remaining 20 percent which are tried by an Administrative Law Judge, about two thirds are appealed to the full NLRB.

bargain collectively as are the provisions discussed to this point. Only brief mention will be made of the more salient miscellaneous provisions covered in the remaining sections which have not been mentioned previously.

Sections 11 and 12—Investigatory Powers and Penalties. As the name suggests, Section 11 outlines the legal powers of investigation given the NLRB by the Congress. Section 12 provides for penalties under the act.

Sections 13 to 18—Limitations. Sections 13 through 18 state a series of limitations which the act is not to be construed as interfering with or diminishing in any way. Section 13 guarantees that the right to strike is still a right not limited by the Labor Management Relations Act. Section 14 (a) permits supervisors to be members of a labor organization, but states that employers are not required to bargain with supervisors as part of labor organizations. Section 14 (b) permits so-called right-to-work laws in states where these laws are enacted. Specifically, Section 14 (b) allows states to ban union shop contracts if they so choose. (As of 1977, twenty states had right-to-work laws on their statute books. Organized labor is seeking to have Section 14 (b) repealed, which in effect would make these state laws banning the union shop illegal.)

Sections 201 through 205 create and outline the functions of the Federal Mediation and Conciliation Service and create a National Labor Relations Panel to advise the President on problems of industrial relations. The National Labor Relations Panel, consisting of representatives of management, labor, and the public, has not been active in recent years.

Sections 206 through 210 outline the National Emergency Strike provisions, giving the President power to intervene in those types of disputes which he deems to be national emergencies.

Section 301 provides that suits for violation of contracts between an employer and a union may be brought into the federal district courts. Unions are made responsible for the acts of their agents; however, money judgments assessed against a labor organization in a district court are only enforceable against the organization as an entity and not against individual members per se.

Section 303 makes strikes and boycotts enumerated in Section 8 (b) (4) illegal, as well as their being unfair labor practices. Employers may sue to collect damages for injury resulting from such strikes.

SUMMARY

The remaining provisions of the act are minor in nature but should be studied by the student of industrial relations. Certainly, the complexity of the Labor Management Relations Act is one which the student recognizes from both study and application in case situations. Only by extensive analysis of labor-management cases can the student come to understand and appreciate the intent and effectiveness of the act and its purpose to govern the duty to bargain collectively.

APPENDIX

Excerpts from the Informational Pamphlet, *The NLRB—What It Is, What It does**

Each fiscal year the NLRB receives more than 40,000 cases of all kinds. Some two thirds are unfair labor practice charges. Over the years charges filed against employers have outnumbered those filed against unions by about two to one. Charges are filed by individual workers, employers, and unions. The total flow of cases of all types filed with the NLRB has sharply increased in the last decade.

Since its establishment, the NLRB has processed more than 300,000 cases alleging violation of the act's prohibitions against unfair labor practices. And it has conducted more than 200,000 secret ballot employee self-determination elections in appropriate worker groups. Millions of employees have cast ballots in these elections—the 25 millionth voter entered the polling place in 1967.

What Is the Structure of the NLRB?   The NLRB has five Board Members and a General Counsel, each appointed by the President with Senate consent. The Board Members are appointed to five-year terms, the term of one member expiring each year. The statute specifies that the President shall designate one member to serve as Chairman of the Board. The General Counsel is appointed to a four-year term. Reappointments may be made; two of the six officials currently are serving second or third terms.

Headquartered in Washington, the NLRB has 31 Regional Offices and 13 smaller field offices throughout the country. Total Washington and field staffs number approximately 2,450.

The NLRB's judicial functions are separate, by law, from its prosecuting functions. The five-member Board acts primarily as a

---

* Published by the NLRB, Washington, D.C., 1974.

quasi-judicial body in deciding cases upon formal records, generally upon review from Regional Directors' or Administrative Law Judges' decisions. The General Counsel is responsible for the investigation and prosecution of charges of violations of the act, and he has general supervision of the Regional Offices.

Who Enforces Board Orders? The NLRB has no statutory independent power enforcement of its orders, but it may seek enforcement in the U.S. Courts of Appeals. Similarly, parties aggrieved by its orders may seek judicial review in the courts.

Annually, the U.S. Courts of Appeals hand down some 350 decisions related to enforcement and/or review of Board orders in unfair labor practice proceedings. Of these, about 85 percent affirm the Board in whole or in part.

How Do NLRB Procedures Work? Upon the filing of an unfair labor practice charge with an NLRB Regional Office, members of the professional staff of that office investigate circumstances from which the charge arises, in order to determine whether formal proceedings are warranted. Approximately one third of the unfair labor practice allegations are found, after investigation, to require legal disposition. In such a case, the Regional Office works with the parties in an attempt to achieve a voluntary settlement adequate to remedy the alleged violation. A very substantial number of cases are settled at this stage. If a case cannot be settled, then a formal complaint is issued, and the case is tried before an Administrative Law Judge.

NLRB Administrative Law Judges conduct formal hearings and issue decisions, which may be appealed to the five-member Board; if they are not appealed, the Administrative Law Judges' recommended orders become orders of the Board.

The NLRB's traditional emphasis on voluntary disposition of cases at all stages means that only about five percent of the unfair labor practice charges originally filed with the Regional Offices are litigated all the way through to a decision of the Board. Yet, despite the small percentage, the Board is still called on to decide almost 1,000 unfair labor practice cases and more than 400 representation cases each year.[9]

In representation election cases, the 31 Regional Directors have the authority to process all petitions, rule on contested issues, and direct elections or dismiss the requests, subject to review by the Board on

---

9 *Authors' Note:* In the fiscal year July 1, 1975–June 30, 1976, the NLRB received some 50,000 unfair labor practice charges and representational petitions. During this period, the NLRB issued 1,030 unfair labor practice decisions and 643 decisions involving representational cases.

limited grounds. The NLRB, through its Regional Offices, conducts some 9,000 representation elections a year in which more than half a million employees exercise their free choice by secret ballot.

SELECTED BIBLIOGAPHY

Aaron, Benjamin, and Meyer, Paul S.   "Public Policy and Labor-Management Relations," in *A Review of Industrial Relations Research,* vol. 2. Madison: Industrial Relations Research Association, 1971.

Abner, Willoughby.   "The FMCS and Dispute Mediation in the Federal Government." *Monthly Labor Review,* May 1969, pp. 27–29.

Abodeely, John E.   *The NLRB and the Appropriate Bargaining Unit,* Labor Relations and Public Policy Series, Report no. 3. Philadelphia: University of Pennsylvania, Industrial Research Unit, 1971.

A Layman's Guide to Basic Law under the National Labor Relations Act. Washington D.C.: Office of the General Counsel of the NLRB, U.S. Government Printing Office, 1971.

Allen, A. Dale, Jr.   "A Systems View of Labor Negotiations." *Personnel Journal,* February 1971, pp. 103–14.

Barrett, Jerome T., and Lebel, Ira B.   "Public Sector Strikes—Legislative and Court Treatment," *Monthly Labor Review,* September 1974, pp. 19–23.

Bloom, Gordon F., and Northrup, Herbert R.   *Economics of Labor Relations.* 7th ed. Homewood, Ill.: Richard D. Irwin, Inc., 1973.

Brinker, Paul A., and Taylor, Benjamin J.   "Secondary Boycott Analysis by Industry," *Labor Law Journal,* vol. 24, no. 10, October 1973.

Bunker, Charles S.   *Collective Bargaining: Non-Profit Sector.* Columbus, Ohio: Grid, Inc., 1973.

Clark, R. Theodore, Jr.   *Coping with Mediation, Fact Finding and Forms of Arbitration.* Chicago: International Personnel Management Association, 1974.

Cohen, Sanford.   *Labor in the United States,* 3d ed. Columbus, Ohio: Charles E. Merrill Publishing Co., 1970.

Cullen, Donald E.   *Negotiating Labor-Management Contracts* (Bulletin #56). Ithaca, N.Y.: New York State School of Industrial and Labor Relations at Cornell University, 1970.

Davey, Harold W.   *Contemporary Collective Bargaining.* 3d ed. Englewood Cliffs, N.J.: Prentice-Hall, Inc., 1972.

Dempsey, Joseph R., S.J.   *The Operation of Right-to-Work Laws.* Milwaukee: Marquette University Press, 1961.

Gerhart, Paul F.   "The Scope of Bargaining in Local Government Labor Relations." *Labor Law Journal,* August 1969.

Jackson, Louis, and Lewis, Robert, eds. *Winning NLRB Elections: Management's Strategy and Preventive Programs.* New York: Practicing Law Institute, 1972.

Kleingartner, Archie. "Collective Bargaining between Salaried Professionals and Public Sector Management." *Public Administration Review,* vol. 33, no. 2, March–April 1973, pp. 165–72.

Krawlewski, John. "Collective Bargaining among Professional Employees." *Hospital Administration,* Summer 1974.

Lowenberg, J. Joseph, and Moskow, Michael M. *Collective Bargaining in Government: Readings and Cases.* Englewood Cliffs, N.J.: Prentice-Hall, 1972.

Major Labor-Law Principles Established by the NLRB and the Courts (December 1964–February 1971). Washington, D.C.: The Bureau of National Affairs, Inc., 1971.

Mansour, M. A. *The Legal Rights of Federal Employees to Unionize, Bargain Collectively, and Strike.* Ann Arbor, Michigan: University Microfilms, Inc., 1970.

McCulloch, Frank W., and Bornstein, Tim. *The National Labor Relations Board.* New York: Praeger, 1974.

McGuiness, Kenneth C. *Silverberg's How to Take a Case Before the National Labor Relations Board,* 3d ed. Washington, D.C.: The Bureau of National Affairs, 1967.

Metzger, N., and Pointer, D. D. *Labor-Management Relations in the Health Service Industry: Theory and Practice.* Washington, D.C.: Science and Health Publications, Inc., 1972.

Morris, Charles, ed. *The Developing Labor Law.* Washington, D.C.: The Bureau of National Affairs, 1971.

Nesbitt, Murray B. *Labor Relations in the Federal Government Service.* The Bureau of National Affairs, Inc., Washington, D.C., 1976.

Oberer, Walter E., and Hanslowe, Kurt L. *Cases and Materials on Labor Law: Collective Bargaining in a Free Society,* St. Paul: West Publishing, 1972.

Pointer, Dennis D. "How the 1974 Taft-Hartley Amendments Will Affect Health Care Facilities." *Hospital Progress,* October–November 1974.

Richardson, Fred C. *Collective Bargaining by Objectives.* Englewood Cliffs, N.J.: Prentice-Hall, Inc., 1977.

Schlossberg, Stephen I., and Sherman, Frederick E. *Organizing and the Law: A Handbook for Union Organizers,* Rev. ed. Washington, D.C.: Bureau of National Affairs, 1972.

Simkin, William E. *Mediation and the Dynamics of Collective Bargaining.* Washington, D.C.: The Bureau of National Affairs, 1971.

Sloane, Arthur A., and Witney, Fred. *Labor Relations,* 3d ed. Englewood Cliffs, N.J.: Prentice-Hall, Inc., 1977.

Smith, Russell A., Merrifield, Leroy S., and St. Antoine, Theodore J. *Labor Relations Law: Cases and Materials,* 5th ed. Indianapolis: Bobbs-Merrill, 1974.

Stanley, David. *Managing Local Governments under Union Pressure.* Washington, D.C.: The Brookings Institution, 1972.

Stieber, Jack. *Public Employee Unionism: Structure, Growth, Policy.* Washington, D.C.: The Brookings Institution, 1973.

Swift, Robert A. *The NLRB and Management Decision Making.* Labor Relations and Public Policy Series, Report no. 9. Philadelphia: University of Pennsylvania, Industrial Research Unit, 1974.

The Labor Board and the Collective Bargaining Process. Washington, D.C.: The Bureau of National Affairs, Inc., 1971.

Wellington, Harry H. *Labor and the Legal Process.* New Haven: Yale University Press, 1968.

Williams, Robert E., Janus, Peter A., and Huhn, Kenneth C. *NLRB Regulation of Election Conduct.* Labor Relations and Public Policy Series, Report no. 8. Philadelphia: University of Pennsylvania, Industrial Research Unit, 1974.

Woodworth, Robert T., and Peterson, Richard B. *Collective Negotiations for Public and Professional Employees: Text and Reading.* Glenview, Illinois: Scott, Foresman and Company, 1969.

Zagoria, Sam, ed. *Public Workers and Public Unions,* New York: Prentice-Hall, Inc., 1972.

Partial Text of

THE LABOR MANAGEMENT RELATIONS ACT, 1947*

as amended by the Labor-Management
Reporting and Disclosure Act of 1959†
and by Public Law 93–360, 1974

[Public Law 101–80th Congress]
[Chapter 120–1st Session]

AN ACT

To amend the National Labor Relations Act, to provide additional facilities for the mediation of labor disputes affecting commerce, to equalize legal responsibilities of labor organizations and employers, and for other purposes.

Be it enacted by the Senate and House of Representatives of the United States of America in Congress assembled.

Short Title and Declaration of Policy

Section 1.   (a) This Act may be cited as the "Labor Management Relations Act, 1947."

(b) Industrial strife which interferes with the normal flow of commerce and with the full production of articles and commodities for commerce, can be avoided or substantially minimized if employers, employees, and labor organizations each recognize under law one another's legitimate rights in their relations with each other, and above all recognize under law that neither party has any right in its relations with any other to engage in acts or practices which jeopardize the public health, safety, or interest.

It is the purpose and policy of this Act, in order to promote the

---

* Also known as the Taft-Hartley Act. At the time of publication of this text, a bill was pending before the U. S. Congress designated as the Labor Law Reform Act of 1977. This legislation, if passed, would amend the Labor Management Relations Act in several places, particularly in certain procedural aspects governing union representational elections.
† Also known as the Landrum-Griffin Act, Public Law 86–257.

full flow of commerce, to prescribe the legitimate rights of both employees and employers in their relations affecting commerce, to provide orderly and peaceful procedures for preventing the interference by either with the legitimate rights of the other, to protect the rights of individual employees in their relations with labor organizations whose activities affect commerce, to define and proscribe practices on the part of labor and management which affect commerce and are inimical to the general welfare, and to protect the rights of the public in connection with labor disputes affecting commerce.

TITLE I—AMENDMENT OF NATIONAL LABOR RELATIONS ACT

Section 101. The National Labor Relations Act is hereby amended to read as follows:

Findings and Policies

Section 1. The denial by some employers of the right of employees to organize and the refusal by some employers to accept the procedure of collective bargaining lead to strikes and other forms of industrial strife or unrest, which have the intent or the necessary effect of burdening or obstructing commerce by (a) impairing the efficiency, safety, or operation of the instrumentalities of commerce; (b) occurring in the current of commerce; (c) materially affecting, restraining, or controlling the flow of raw materials or manufactured or processed goods from or into the channels of commerce, or the prices of such materials or goods in commerce; or (d) causing diminution of employment and wages in such volume as substantially to impair or disrupt the market for goods flowing from or into the channels of commerce.

The inequality of bargaining power between employees who do not possess full freedom of association or actual liberty of contract, and employers who are organized in the corporate or other forms of ownership association substantially burdens and affects the flow of commerce, and tends to aggravate recurrent business depressions, by depressing wage rates and the purchasing power of wage earners in industry and by preventing the stabilization of competitive wage rates and working conditions within and between industries.

Experience has proved that protection by law of the right of employees to organize and bargain collectively safeguards commerce from injury, impairment, or interruption, and promotes the flow of commerce by removing certain recognized sources of industrial strife and unrest, by encouraging practices fundamental to the friendly adjustment of industrial disputes arising out of differences as to wages, hours, or other working conditions, and by restoring equality of bargaining power between employers and employees.

Experience has further demonstrated that certain practices by some labor organizations, their officers, and members have the intent or the necessary effect of burdening or obstructing commerce by preventing the free flow of goods in such commerce through strikes and other forms of industrial unrest or through concerted activities which impair the interest of the public in the free flow of such commerce. The elimination of such practices is a necessary condition to the assurance of the rights herein guaranteed.

It is hereby declared to be the policy of the United States to eliminate the causes of certain substantial obstructions to the free flow of commerce and to mitigate and eliminate these obstructions when they have occurred by encouraging the practice and procedure of collective bargaining and by protecting the exercise by workers of full freedom of association, self-organization, and designation of representatives of their own choosing, for the purpose of negotiating the terms and conditions of their employment or other mutual aid or protection.

Definitions

Section 2.   When used in this Act—

(1) The term "person" includes one or more individuals, labor organizations, partnerships, associations, corporations, legal representatives, trustees, trustees in bankruptcy, or receivers.

(2) The term "employer" includes any person acting as an agent of an employer, directly or indirectly, but shall not include the United States or any wholly owned Government corporation, or any Federal Reserve Bank, or any State or political subdivision thereof, or any person subject to the Railway Labor Act, as amended from time to time, or any labor organization (other than when acting as an employer), or anyone acting in the capacity of officer or agent of such labor organization.

(3) The term "employee" shall include any employee, and shall not be limited to the employees of a particular employer, unless the Act explicitly states otherwise, and shall include any individual whose

work has ceased as a consequence of, or in connection with, any current labor dispute or because of any unfair labor practice, and who has not obtained any other regular and substantially equivalent employment, but shall not include any individual employed as an agricultural laborer, or in the domestic service of any family or person at his home, or any individual employed by his parent or spouse, or any individual having the status of an independent contractor, or any individual employed as a supervisor, or any individual employed by an employer subject to the Railway Labor Act, as amended from time to time, or by any other person who is not an employer as herein defined.

(4) The term "representatives" includes any individual or labor organization.

(5) The term "labor organization" means any organization of any kind, or any agency or employee representation committee or plan, in which employees participate and which exists for the purpose, in whole or in part, of dealing with employers concerning grievances, labor disputes, wages, rates of pay, hours of employment, or conditions of work.

(6) The term "commerce" means trade, traffic, commerce, transportation, or communication among the several States, or between the District of Columbia or any Territory of the United States and any State or Territory, or between any foreign country and any State, Territory, or the District of Columbia, or within the District of Columbia or any Territory, or between points in the same State but through any other State or any Territory or the District of Columbia or any foreign country.

(7) The term "affecting commerce" means in commerce, or burdening or obstructing commerce or the free flow of commerce, or having led or tending to lead to a labor dispute burdening or obstructing commerce or the free flow of commerce.

(8) The term "unfair labor practice" means any unfair labor practice listed in section 8.

(9) The term "labor dispute" includes any controversy concerning terms, tenure or conditions of employment, or concerning the association or representation of persons in negotiating, fixing, maintaining, changing, or seeking to arrange terms or conditions of employment, regardless of whether the disputants stand in the proximate relation of employer and employee.

(10) The term "National Labor Relations Board" means the National Labor Relations Board provided for in section 3 of this Act.

(11) The term "supervisor" means any individual having author-ity, in the interest of the employer, to hire, transfer, suspend, lay off, recall, promote, discharge, assign, reward, or discipline other em-ployees, or responsibility to direct them, or to adjust their grievances, or effectively to recommend such action, if in connection with the foregoing the exercise of such authority is not of a merely routine or clerical nature, but requires the use of independent judgment.

(12) The term "professional employee" means—

(a) any employee engaged in work (i) predominantly intellec-tual and varied in character as opposed to routine mental, manual, mechanical, or physical work; (ii) involving the consistent exer-cise of discretion and judgment in its performance; (iii) of such a character that the output produced or the result accomplished cannot be standardized in relation to a given period of time; (iv) requiring knowledge of an advanced type in a field of science or learning customarily acquired by a prolonged course of specialized intellectual instruction and study in an institution of higher learn-ing or a hospital, as distinguished from a general academic edu-cation or from an apprenticeship or from training in the per-formance of routine mental, manual, or physical processes; or

(b) any employee, who (i) has completed the courses of special-ized intellectual instruction and study described in clause (iv) of paragraph (a), and (ii) is performing related work under the super-vision of a professional person to qualify himself to become a professional employee as defined in paragraph (a).

(13) In determining whether any person is acting as an "agent" of another person so as to make such other person responsible for his acts, the question of whether the specific acts performed were actually authorized or subsequently ratified shall not be controlling.

(14) The term "health care institution" shall include any hospital, convalescent hospital, health maintenance organization, health clinic, nursing home, extended care facility, or other institution devoted to the care of sick, infirm, or aged person.

National Labor Relations Board

Section 3.   (a) The National Labor Relations Board (hereinafter called the "Board" . . . as an agency of the United States, shall consist of five . . . members, appointed by the President by and with the advice and consent of the Senate . . . for terms of five years each, excepting that any individual chosen to fill a vacancy shall be appointed only for the unexpired term of the member whom he shall succeed. The President shall designate one member to serve as Chairman of the Board. Any member of the Board may be removed by the President, upon notice and hearing, for neglect of duty or malfeasance in office, but for no other cause.

(b) The Board is authorized to delegate to any group of three or more members any or all of the powers which it may itself exercise. The Board is also authorized to delegate to its regional directors its powers under section 9 to determine the unit appropriate for the purpose of collective bargaining, to investigate and provide for hearings, and determine whether a question of representation exists, and to direct an election or take a secret ballot under subsection (c) or (e) of section 9 and certify the results thereof, except that upon the filing of a request therefor with the Board by any interested person, the Board may review any action of a regional director delegated to him under this paragraph, but such a review shall not, unless specifically ordered by the Board, operate as a stay of any action taken by the regional director. A vacancy in the Board shall not impair the right of the remaining members to exercise all of the powers of the Board, and three members of the Board shall, at all times, constitute a quorum of the Board, except that two members shall constitute a quorum of any group designated pursuant to the first sentence hereof. The Board shall have an official seal which shall be judically noticed.

(c) The Board shall at the close of each fiscal year make a report in writing to Congress and to the President stating in detail the cases it has heard, the decisions it has rendered, and an account of all moneys it has disbursed.

(d) There shall be a General Counsel of the Board who shall be appointed by the President, by and with the advice and consent of the Senate, for a term of four years. The General Counsel of the Board shall exercise general supervision over all attorneys employed by the Board (other than trial examiners and legal assistants to Board members) and over the officers and employees in the regional offices. He shall have final authority, on behalf of the Board, in respect of the investigation of charges and issuance of complaints under section 10, and in respect of the prosecution of such complaints before the Board, and shall have such other duties as the Board may prescribe or as may be provided by law. In case of a vacancy in the office of the General Counsel the President is authorized to designate the officer or employee who shall act as General Counsel during such vacancy, but no person or persons so designated shall so act (1) for more than forty days when the Congress is in session unless a nomination to fill such vacancy shall have been submitted to the Senate, or (2) after the adjournment *sine die* of the session of the Senate in which such nomination was submitted.

*   *   *   *   *

[Omitted: Sections 4 and 5—Compensation and offices of the NLRB.]

Section 6.   The Board shall have authority from time to time to make, amend, and rescind, in the manner prescribed by the Administrative Procedure Act, such rules and regulations as may be necessary to carry out the provisions of this Act.

Rights and Employees

Section 7.   Employees shall have the right to self-organization, to form, join, or assist labor organizations, to bargain collectively through representatives of their own choosing, and to engage in other concerted activities for the purpose of collective bargaining or other mutual aid or protection, and shall also have the right to refrain from any or all of such activities except to the extent that such right may be affected by an agreement requiring membership in a labor organization as a condition of employment as authorized in section 8(a) (3).

Unfair Labor Practices

Section 8.   (a) It shall be an unfair labor practice for an employer—

(1) to interfere with, restrain, or coerce employees in the exercise of the rights guaranteed in section 7;

(2) to dominate or interfere with the formation or administration of any labor organization or contribute financial or other support to it: *Provided,* That subject to rules and regulations made and published by the Board pursuant to section 6, an employer shall not be prohibited from permitting employees to confer with him during working hours without loss of time or pay;

(3) by discrimination in regard to hire or tenure of employment or any term or condition of employment to encourage or discourage membership in any labor organization: *Provided,* That nothing in this Act, or in any other statute of the United States, shall preclude

an employer from making an agreement with a labor organization (not established, or assisted by any action defined in section 8(a) of this Act as an unfair labor practice) to require as a condition of employment membership therein on or after the thirtieth day following the beginning of such employment or the effective date of such agreement, whichever is the later, (i) if such labor organization is the representative of the employees as provided in section 9(a), in the appropriate collective-bargaining unit covered by such agreement when made, and (ii) unless following an election held as provided in section 9(e) within one year preceding the effective date of such agreement, the Board shall have certified that at least a majority of the employees eligible to vote in such election have voted to rescind the authority of such labor organization to make such an agreement: *Provided further,* That no employer shall justify any discrimination against an employee for nonmembership in a labor organization (A) if he has resonable grounds for believing that such membership was not available to the employee on the same terms and conditions generally applicable to other members, or (B) if he has reasonable grounds for believing that membership was denied or terminated for reasons other than the failure of the employee to tender the periodic dues and the initiation fees uniformly required as a condition of acquiring or retaining membership;

(4) to discharge or otherwise discriminate against an employee because he has filed charges or given testimony under this Act;

(5) to refuse to bargain collectively with the representatives of his employees, subject to the provisions of section 9(a).

(b) It shall be an unfair labor practice for a labor organization or its agents—

(1) to restrain or coerce (A) employees in the exercise of the rights guaranteed in section 7: *Provided,* That this paragraph shall not impair the right of a labor organization to prescribe its own rules with respect to the acquisition or retention of membership therein; or (B) an employer in the selection of his representatives for the purposes of collective bargaining or the adjustment of grievances;

(2) to cause or attempt to cause an employer to discriminate against an employee in violation of subsection (a)(3) or to discriminate against an employee with respect to whom membership in such organization has been denied or terminated on some ground other than his failure to tender the periodic dues and the initiation fees uniformly required as a condition of acquiring or retaining membership;

(3) to refuse to bargain collectively with an employer, provided it is the representative of his employees subject to the provisions of section 9(a);

(4) (i) to engage in, or to induce or encourage any individual employed by any person engaged in commerce or in an industry affecting commerce to engage in, a strike or a refusal in the course of his employment to use, manufacture, process, transport, or otherwise handle or work on any goods, articles, materials, or commodities or to perform any services; or (ii) to threaten, coerce, or restrain any person engaged in commerce or in an industry affecting commerce, where in either case an object thereof is:

(A) forcing or requiring any employer or self-employed person to join any labor or employer organization or to enter into any agreement which is prohibited by section 8(e);

(B) forcing or requiring any person to cease using, selling, hanling, transporting, or otherwise dealing in the products of any other producer, processor, or manufacturer, or to cease doing business with any other person, or forcing or requiring any other employer to recognize or bargain with a labor organization as the representative of his employees unless such labor organization has been certified as the representative of such employees under the provisions of section 9: *Provided,* That nothing contained in this clause (B) shall be construed to make unlawful, where not otherwise unlawful, any primary strike or primary picketing;

(C) forcing or requiring any employer to recognize or bargain with a particular labor organization as the representative of his employees if another labor organization has been certified as the representative of such employees under the provisions of section 9;

(D) forcing or requiring any employer to assign particular work to employees in a particular labor organization or in a particular trade, craft, or class rather than to employees in another labor organization or in another trade, craft, or class, unless such employer is failing to conform to an order or certification of the Board determining the bargaining representative for employees performing such work:

Provided, That nothing contained in this subsection (b) shall be construed to make unlawful a refusal by any person to enter upon the premises of any employer (other than his own employer), if the employees of such employer are engaged in a strike ratified or approved by a representative of such employees whom such employer is required to recognize under this Act: *Provided further,* That for the purposes of this paragraph (4) only, nothing contained in such paragraph shall be construed to prohibit publicity, other than picketing, for the purpose of truthfully advising the public, including consumers and members of a labor organization, that a product or products are produced by an employer with whom the labor organization has a primary dispute and are distributed by another employer, as long as such publicity does not have an effect of inducing any individual employed by any person other than the primary employer in the course of his employment to refuse to pick up, deliver, or transport any goods, or not to perform any services, at the establishment of the employer engaged in such distribution;

(5) to require of employees covered by an agreement authorized under subsection (a) (3) the payment, as a condition precedent to becoming a member of such organization, of a fee in an amount which the Board finds excessive or discriminatory under all the circumstances. In making such a finding, the Board shall consider, among other relevant factors, the practices and customs of labor organizations in the particular industry, and the wages currently paid to the employees affected;

(6) to cause or attempt to cause an employer to pay or deliver or agree to pay or deliver any money or other thing of value, in the nature of an exaction, for services which are not performed or not to be performed; and

(7) to picket or cause to be picketed, or threaten to picket or cause to be picketed, any employer where an object thereof is forcing or requiring an employer to recognize or bargain with a labor organization as the representative of his employees, or forcing or requiring the employees of an employer to accept or select such labor organization as their collective bargaining representative, unless such labor organization is currently certified as the representative of such employees:

(A) where the employer has lawfully recognized in accordance with this Act any other labor organization and a question concerning representation may not appropriately be raised under section 9(c) of this Act.

(B) where within the preceding twelve months a valid election under section 9(c) of this Act has been conducted, or

(C) where such picketing has been conducted without a petition under section 9(c) being filed within a reasonable period of time not to exceed thirty days from the commencement of such picketing:

Provided, That when such a petition has been filed the Board shall forthwith, without regard to the provisions of section 9(c) (1) or the absence of a showing of a substantial interest on the part of the labor organization, direct an election in such unit as the Board finds to be appropriate and shall certify the results thereof: *Provided further,* That nothing in this subparagraph (C) shall be construed to prohibit any picketing or other publicity for the purpose of truthfully advising the public (including consumers) that an employer does not employ members of, or have a contract with, a labor organization, unless an effect of such picketing is to induce any individual employed by any other person in the course of his employment, not to pick up, deliver or transport any goods or not to perform any services.

Nothing in this paragraph (7) shall be construed to permit any act which would otherwise be an unfair labor practice under this section 8(b).

(c) The expressing of any views, argument, or opinion, or the dissemination thereof, whether in written, printed, graphic, or visual form, shall not constitute or be evidence of an unfair labor practice under any of the provisions of this Act, if such expression contains no threat of reprisal or force or promise of benefit.

(d) For the purposes of this section, to bargain collectively is the performance of the mutual obligation of the employer and the representative of the employees to meet at reasonable times and confer in good faith with respect to wages, hours, and other terms and conditions of employment, or the negotiation of an agreement, or any question arising thereunder, and the execution of a written contract incorporating any agreement reached if requested by either party, but such obligation does not compel either party to agree to a proposal or require the making of a concession: *Provided,* That where there is in effect a collective-bargaining contract covering employees in an industry affecting commerce, the duty to bargain collectively shall also mean that no party to such contract shall terminate or modify such contract, unless the party desiring such termination or modification—

(1) serves a written notice upon the other party to the contract of the proposed termination or modification sixty days prior to the expiration date thereof, or in the event such contract contains no expiration date, sixty days prior to the time it is proposed to make such termination or modification;

(2) offers to meet and confer with the other party for the purpose

of negotiating a new contract or a contract containing the proposed modifications;

(3) notifies the Federal Mediation and Conciliation Service within thirty days after such notice of the existence of a dispute, and simultaneously therewith notifies any State or Territorial agency established to mediate and conciliate disputes within the State or Territory where the dispute occurred, provided no agreement has been reached by that time; and

(4) continues in full force and effect, without resorting to strike or lockout, all the terms and conditions of the existing contract for a period of sixty days after such notice is given or until the expiration date of such contract, whichever occurs later:

The duties imposed upon employers, employees, and labor organizations by paragraphs (2), (3), and (4) shall become inapplicable upon an intervening certification of the Board, under which the labor organization or individual, which is a party to the contract, has been superseded as or ceased to be the representative of the employees subject to the provisions of section 9(a), and the duties so imposed shall not be construed as requiring either party to discuss or agree to any modification of the terms and conditions contained in a contract for a fixed period, if such modification is to become effective before such terms and conditions can be reopened under the provisions of the contract. Any employee who engages in a strike within any notice period specified in this subsection, or who engages in any strike within the appropriate period specified in subsection (g) of this section shall lose his status as an employee of the employer engaged in the particular labor dispute, for the purposes of sections 8, 9, and 10 of this Act, as amended, but such loss of status for such employee shall terminate if and when he is reemployed by such employer. Whenever the collective bargaining involves employees of a health care institution, the provisions of this section 8(d) shall be modified as follows:

(A) The notice of section 8(d) (1) shall be ninety days; the notice of section 8(d) (3) shall be sixty days; and the contract period of section 8(d) (4) shall be ninety days;

(B) Where the bargaining is for an initial agreement following certification or recognition, at least thirty days' notice of the existence of a dispute shall be given by the labor organization to the agencies set forth in section 8(d) (3).

(C) After notice is given to the Federal Mediation and Conciliation Service under either clause (A) or (B) of this sentence, the Service shall promptly communicate with the parties and use its best efforts, by mediation and conciliation, to bring them to agreement. The parties shall participate fully and promptly in such meetings as may be undertaken by the Service for the purpose of aiding in a settlement of the dispute.

(e) It shall be an unfair labor practice for any labor organization and any employer to enter into any contract or agreement, express or implied, whereby such employer ceases or refrains or agrees to cease or refrain from handling, using, selling, transporting or otherwise dealing in any of the products of any other employer, or to cease doing business with any other person, and any contract or agreement entered into heretofore or hereafter containing such an agreement shall be to such extent unenforceable and void: *Provided,* That nothing in this subsection (e) shall apply to an agreement between a labor organization and an employer in the construction industry relating to the contracting or subcontracting of work to be done at the site of the construction, alteration, painting, or repair of a building, structure, or other work: *Provided further,* That for the purposes of this subsection (e) and section 8(b) (4) (B) the terms "any employer," "any person engaged in commerce or in industry affecting commerce," and "any person" when used in relation to the terms "any other producer, processor, or manufacturer," "any other employer," or "any other person" shall not include persons in the relation of a jobber, manufacturer, contractor, or subcontractor working on the goods or premises of the jobber or manufacturer or performing parts of an integrated process of production in the apparel and clothing industry: *Provided further,* That nothing in this Act shall prohibit the enforcement of any agreement which is within the foregoing exception.

(f) It shall not be an unfair labor practice under subsections (a) and (b) of this section for an employer engaged primarily in the building and construction industry to make an agreement covering employees engaged (or who, upon their employment, will be engaged) in the building and construction industry with a labor organization of which building and construction employees are members (not established, maintained, or assisted by any action defined in section 8(a) of this Act as an unfair labor practice) because (1) the majority status of such labor organization has not been established under the provisions of section 9 of this Act prior to the making of such agreement, or (2) such agreement requires as a condition of employment, membership in such labor organization after the seventh day following the beginning of such employment or the effective date of the agreement, whichever is later, or (3) such agreement requires the employer to notify such labor organization of opportunities for employment with such employer, or gives such labor organization an opportunity to refer qualified applicants for such employment, or (4) such agreement specifies minimum training or experience qualifications for employment or provides for priority in opportunities for employment based upon length of service with such employer, in the industry or in the particular geographical area: *Provided,* That nothing in this subsection shall set aside the final proviso to section 8(a) (3) of this Act: *Provided further,* That any agreement which would be invalid, but for clause (1) of this subsection, shall not be a bar to a petition filed pursuant to section 9(c) or 9(e).

(g) A labor organization before engaging in any strike, picketing, or other concerted refusal to work at any health care institution shall, not less than ten days prior to such action, notify the institution in writing and the Federal Mediation and Conciliation Service of that intention, except that in the case of bargaining for an initial agreement following certification or recognition the notice required by this subsection shall not be given until the expiration of the period specified in clause (B) of the last sentence of section 8(d) of this Act. The notice shall state the date and time that such action will commence. The notice, once given, may be extended by the written agreement of both parties.

Representatives and Elections

Section 9.   (a) Representatives designated or selected for the purposes of collective bargaining by the majority of the employees in a unit appropriate for such purposes, shall be the exclusive representatives of all the employees in such unit for the purposes of collective bargaining in respect to rates of pay, wages, hours of employment, or other conditions of employment: *Provided,* That any individual employee or a group of employees shall have the right at any time to present grievances to their employer and to have such grievances adjusted, without the intervention of the bargaining representative, as long as the adjustment is not inconsistent with the terms of a collective-bargaining contract or agreement then in effect: *Provided further,* That the bargaining representative has been given opportunity to be present at such adjustment.

(b) The Board shall decide in each case whether, in order to assure to employees the fullest freedom in exercising the rights guaranteed by this Act, the unit appropriate for the purposes of collective bargaining shall be the employer unit, craft unit, plant unit, or subdivision thereof: *Provided,* That the Board shall not (1) decide that any unit is appropriate for such purposes if such unit includes both professional employees and employees who are not professional employees unless a majority of such professional employees vote for inclusion in such unit; or (2) decide that any craft unit is inappropriate for such purposes on the ground that a different unit has been established by a prior Board determination, unless a majority of the employees in the proposed craft unit vote against separate representation or (3) decide that any unit is appropriate for such purposes, if it includes, together with other employees, any individual employed as a guard to enforce against employees and other persons rules to protect property of the employer or to protect the safety of persons on the employer's premises; but no labor organization shall be certified as the representative of employees in a bargaining unit of guards if such organization admits to membership, or is affiliated directly or indirectly with an organization which admits to membership, employees other than guards.

(c)(1) Wherever a petition shall have been filed, in accordance with such regulations as may be prescribed by the Board—

(A) by an employee or group of employees or any individual or labor organization acting in their behalf alleging that a substantial number of employees (i) wish to be represented for collective bargaining and that their employer declines to recognize their representative as the representative defined in section 9(a), or (ii) assert that the individual or labor organization, which has been certified or is being currently recognized by their employer as the bargaining representative, is no longer a representative as defined in section 9(a); or

(B) by an employer, alleging that one or more individuals or labor organizations have presented to him a claim to be recognized as the representative defined in section 9(a);

the Board shall investigate such petition and if it has reasonable cause to believe that a question of representation affecting commerce exists shall provide for an appropriate hearing upon due notice. Such hearing may be conducted by an officer or employee of the regional office, who shall not make any recommendations with respect thereto. If the

Board finds upon the record of such hearing that such a question of representation exists, it shall direct an election by secret ballot and shall certify the results thereof.

(2) In determining whether or not a question of representation affecting commerce exists, the same regulations and rules of decision shall apply irrespective of the identity of the persons filing the petition or the kind of relief sought and in no case shall the Board deny a labor organization a place on the ballot by reason of an order with respect to such labor organization or its predecessor not issued in conformity with section 10(c).

(3) No election shall be directed in any bargaining unit or any subdivision within which, in the preceding twelve-month period, a valid election shall have been held. Employees engaged in an economic strike who are not entitled to reinstatement shall be eligible to vote under such regulations as the Board shall find are consistent with the purposes and provisions of this Act in any election conducted within twelve months after the commencement of the strike. In any election where none of the choices on the ballot receives a majority, a run-off shall be conducted, the ballot providing for a selection between the two choices receiving the largest and second largest number of valid votes cast in the election.

(4) Nothing in this section shall be construed to prohibit the waiving of hearings by stipulation for the purpose of a consent election in conformity with regulations and rules of decision of the Board.

(5) In determining whether a unit is appropriate for the purposes specified in subsection (b) the extent to which the employees have organized shall not be controlling.

(d) Whenever an order of the Board made pursuant to section 10(c) is based in whole or in part upon facts certified following an investigation pursuant to subsection (c) of this section and there is a petition for the enforcement or review of such order, such certification and the record of such investigation shall be included in the transcript of the entire record required to be filed under section 10(e) or 10(f), and thereupon the decree of the court enforcing, modifying, or setting aside in whole or in part the order of the Board shall be made and entered upon the pleadings, testimony, and proceedings set forth in such transcript.

(e)(1) Upon the filing with the Board, by 30 per centum or more of the employees in a bargaining unit covered by an agreement between their employer and a labor organization made pursuant to section 8(a) (3), of a petition alleging they desire that such authority be rescinded, the Board shall take a secret ballot of the employees in such unit and certify the results thereof to such labor organization and to the employer.

(2) No election shall be conducted pursuant to this subsection in any bargaining unit or any subdivision within which, in the preceding twelve-month period, a valid election shall have been held.

Prevention of Unfair Labor Practices

Section 10. (a) The Board is empowered, as hereinafter provided, to prevent any person from engaging in any unfair labor practice (listed in section 8) affecting commerce. This power shall not be affected by any other means of adjustment or prevention that has been or may be established by agreement, law, or otherwise: *Provided,* That the Board is empowered by agreement with any agency of any State or Territory to cede to such agency jurisdiction over any cases in any industry (other than mining, manufacturing, communications, and transportation except where predominantly local in character) even though such cases may involve labor disputes affecting commerce, unless the provision of the State or Territorial statute applicable to the determination of such cases by such agency is inconsistent with the corresponding provision of this Act or has received a construction inconsistent therewith.

(b) Whenever it is charged that any person has engaged in or is engaging in any such unfair labor practice, the Board, or any agent or agency designated by the Board for such purposes, shall have power to issue and cause to be served upon such person a complaint stating the charges in that respect, and containing a notice of hearing before the Board or a member thereof, or before a designated agent or agency, at a place therein fixed, not less than five days after the serving of said complaint: *Provided,* That no complaint shall issue based upon any unfair labor practice occurring more than six months prior to the filing of the charge with the Board and the service of a copy thereof upon the person against whom such charge is made, unless the person aggrieved thereby was prevented from filing such charge by reason of service in the armed forces, in which event the six-month period shall be computed from the day of his discharge. Any such complaint may be amended by the member, agent, or agency conducting the hearing or the Board in its discretion at any time prior to the issuance of an order based thereon. The person so complained of shall have the right to file an answer to the original or amended complaint and to appear in person or otherwise and give testimony at the place and time fixed in the complaint. In the discretion of the member, agent, or agency conducting the hearing or the Board, any other person may be allowed to intervene in the said proceeding and to present testimony. Any such proceeding shall, so far as practicable, be conducted in accordance with the rules of evidence applicable in the district courts of the United States under the rules of civil procedure for the district courts of the United States, adopted by the Supreme Court of the United States pursuant to the Act of June 19, 1934 (U.S.C., title 28, secs. 723–B, 723–C).

(c) The testimony taken by such member, agent, or agency or the Board shall be reduced to writing and filed with the Board. Thereafter, in its discretion, the Board upon notice may take further testimony or hear argument. If upon the preponderance of the testimony taken the Board shall be of the opinion that any person named in the complaint has engaged in or is engaging in any such unfair labor practice, then the Board shall state its findings of fact and shall issue and cause to be served on such person an order requiring such person to cease and desist from such unfair labor practice, and to take such affirmative action including reinstatement of employees with or without back pay, as will effectuate the policies of this Act: *Provided,* That where an order directs reinstatement of an employee, back pay may be required of the employer or labor organization, as the case may be, responsible for the discrimination suffered by him: *And provided further,* That in determining whether a complaint shall issue alleging a violation of section 8(a) (1) or section 8(a) (2), and in deciding such cases, the same regulations and rules of decision shall apply irrespective of whether or not the labor organization affected is affiliated with a labor organization national or international in scope. Such order may further require such person to make reports from time to time showing the extent to which it has complied with the order. If upon the preponderance of the testimony taken the Board shall not be of the opinion that the person named in the complaint has engaged in or is engaging in any such unfair labor practice, then the Board shall state its findings of fact and shall issue an order dismissing the said complaint. No order of the Board shall require the reinstatement of any individual as an employee who has been suspended or discharged, or the payment to him of any back pay, if such individual was suspended or discharged for cause. In case the evidence is presented before a member of the Board, or before an examiner or examiners thereof, such member, or such examiner or examiners, as the case may be, shall issue and cause to be served on the parties to the proceeding a proposed report, together with a recommended order, which shall be filed with the Board, and if no exceptions are filed within twenty days after service thereof upon such parties, or within such further period as the Board may authorize, such recommended order shall become the order of the Board and become effective as therein prescribed.

(d) Until the record in a case shall have been filed in a court, as hereinafter provided, the Board may at any time, upon reasonable notice and in such manner as it shall deem proper, modify or set aside, in whole or in part, any finding or order made or issued by it.

(e) The Board shall have power to petition any court of appeals of the United States, or if all the courts of appeals to which application may be made are in vacation, any district court of the United States, within any circuit or district, respectively, wherein the unfair labor practice in question occurred or wherein such person resides or transacts business, for the enforcement of such order and for appropriate temporary relief or restraining order, and shall file in the court the record in the proceedings, as provided in section 2112 of title 28, United States Code. Upon the filing of such petition, the court shall cause notice thereof to be served upon such person, and thereupon shall have jurisdiction of the proceeding and of the question determined therein, and shall have power to grant such temporary relief or restraining order as it deems just and proper, and to make and enter a decree enforcing, modifying, and enforcing as so modified, or setting aside in whole or in part the order of the Board. No objection that has not been urged before the Board, its member, agent, or agency, shall be considered by the court, unless the failure or neglect to urge such objection shall be excused because of extraordinary circumstances. The findings of the Board with respect to questions of fact if supported by substantial evidence on the record considered as a whole shall be conclusive. If either party shall apply to the court for leave to adduce additional evidence and shall show to the satisfaction of the court that such additional evidence is material and that there were reasonable grounds for the failure to adduce such evidence in the hearing before the Board, its member, agent, or agency, the court may order such additional evidence to be taken before the Board, its member, agent, or agency, and to be made a part of the record. The Board may modify its findings as to the facts, or make new findings, by reason of additional evidence so taken and filed, and it shall file such modified or new findings, which findings with respect to questions of fact if supported by substantial evidence on the record considered as a whole shall be conclusive, and shall file its recommendations, if any, for the modification or setting aside of its original order. Upon the filing of the record with it the jurisdiction of the court shall be exclusive and its judgment and decree shall be final, except that the same shall be subject to review by the appropriate United States court of appeals if application was made to the district court as hereinabove provided, and by the Supreme Court of the United States upon writ of certiorari or certification as provided in section 1254 of title 28.

(f) Any person aggrieved by a final order of the Board granting or denying in whole or in part the relief sought may obtain a review of such order in any circuit court of appeals of the United States in the circuit wherein the unfair labor practice in question was alleged to have been engaged in or wherein such person resides or transacts business, or in the United States Court of Appeals for the District of Columbia, by filing in such court a written petition praying that the order of the Board be modified or set aside. A copy of such petition shall be forthwith transmitted by the clerk of the court to the Board, and thereupon the aggrieved party shall file in the court the record in the proceeding, certified by the Board, as provided in section 2112 of title 28, United States Code. Upon the filing of such petition, the court shall proceed in the same manner as in the case of an application by the Board under subsection (e) of this section, and shall have the same jurisdiction to grant to the Board such temporary relief or restraining order as it deems just and proper, and in like manner to make and enter a decree enforcing, modifying, and enforcing as so modified, or setting aside in whole or in part the order of the Board; the findings of the Board with respect to questions of fact if supported by substantial evidence on the record considered as a whole shall in like manner be conclusive.

(g) The commencement of proceedings under subsection (e) or (f) of this section shall not, unless specifically ordered by the court, operate as a stay of the Board's order.

(h) When granting appropriate temporary relief or a restraining order, or making and entering a decree enforcing, modifying, and enforcing as so modified, or setting aside in whole or in part an order of the Board, as provided in this section, the jurisdiction of courts sitting in equity shall not be limited by the Act entitled "An Act to amend the Judicial Code and to define and limit the jurisdiction of courts sitting in equity, and for other purposes," approved March 23, 1932 (U.S.C., Supp. VII, title 29, secs. 101–115).

(i) Petitions filed under this Act shall be heard expeditiously, and if possible within ten days after they have been docketed.

(j) The Board shall have power, upon issuance of a complaint as provided in subsection (b) charging that any person has engaged in or is engaging in an unfair labor practice, to petition any district court of the United States (including the District Court of the United States for the District of Columbia), within any district wherein the unfair labor practice in question is alleged to have occurred or wherein such person resides or transacts business, for appropriate temporary relief or restraining order. Upon the filing of any such petition the court shall cause notice thereof to be served upon such person, and thereupon shall have jurisdiction to grant to the Board such temporary relief or restraining order as it deems just and proper.

(k) Whenever it is charged that any person has engaged in an unfair labor practice within the meaning of paragraph (4)(D) of section 8(b), the Board is empowered and directed to hear and determine the dispute out of which such unfair labor practice shall have arisen, unless, within ten days after notice that such charge has been filed, the parties to such dispute submit to the Board satisfactory evidence that they have adjusted, or agreed upon methods for the voluntary adjustment of, the dispute. Upon compliance by the parties to the dispute with the decision of the Board or upon such voluntary adjustment of the dispute, such charge shall be dismissed.

(1) Whenever it is charged that any person has engaged in an unfair labor practice within the meaning of paragraph (4) (A), (B), or (C) of section 8(b), or section 8(e) or section 8(b) (7), the preliminary investigation of such charge shall be made forthwith and given priority over all other cases except cases of like character in the office where it is filed or to which it is referred. If, after such investigation, the officer or regional attorney to whom the matter may be referred has reasonable cause to believe such charge is true and that a complaint should issue, he shall, on behalf of the Board, petition any district court of the United States (including the District Court of the United States for the District of Columbia) within any district where the unfair labor practice in question has occurred, is alleged to have occurred, or wherein such person resides or transacts business, for appropriate injunctive relief pending the final adjudication of the Board with respect to such matter. Upon the filing of any such petition the

district court shall have jurisdiction to grant such injunctive relief or temporary restraining order as it deems just and proper, notwithstanding any other provision of law: *Provided further,* That no temporary restraining order shall be issued without notice unless a petition alleges that substantial and irreparable injury to the charging party will be unavoidable and such temporary restraining order shall be effective for no longer than five days and will become void at the expiration of such period: *Provided further,* That such officer or regional attorney shall not apply for any restraining order under section 8(b) (7) if a charge against the employer under section 8(a) (2) has been filed and after the preliminary investigation, he has reasonable cause to believe that such charge is true and that a complaint should issue. Upon filing of any such petition the courts shall cause notice thereof to be served upon any person involved in the charge and such person including the charging party, shall be given an opportunity to appear by counsel and present any relevant testimony: *Provided further,* That for the purposes of this subsection district courts shall be deemed to have jurisdiction of a labor organization (1) in the district in which such organization maintains its principal office, or (2) in any district in which its duly authorized officers or agents are engaged in promoting or protecting the interests of employee members. The service of legal process upon such officer or agent shall constitute service upon the labor organization and make such organizations a party to the suit. In situations where such relief is appropriate the procedure specified herein shall apply to charges with respect to section 8(b) (4) (D).

(m) Whenever it is charged that any person has engaged in an unfair labor practice within the meaning of subsection (a)(3) or (b)(2) of section 8, such charge shall be given priority over all other cases except cases of like character in the office where it is filed or to which it is referred and cases given priority under subsection (1).

*   *   *   *   *

[Omitted: Sections 11 and 12—Investigatory powers of the NLRB.]

Limitations

Section 13.   Nothing in this Act, except as specifically provided for herein, shall be construed so as either to interfere with or impede or diminish in any way the right to strike, or to affect the limitations or qualifications on that right.

Section 14.   (a) Nothing herein shall prohibit any individual employed as a supervisor from becoming or remaining a member of a labor organization, but no employer subject to this Act shall be compelled to deem individuals defined herein as supervisors as employees for the purpose of any law, either national or local, relating to collective bargaining.

(b) Nothing in this Act shall be construed as authorizing the execution or application of agreements requiring membership in a labor organization as a condition of employment in any State or Territory in which such execution or application is prohibited by State or Territorial law.

(c)(1) The Board, in its discretion, may, by rule of decision or by published rules adopted pursuant to the Administrative Procedure Act, decline to assert jurisdiction over any labor dispute involving any class or category of employers, where, in the opinion of the Board, the effect of such labor dispute on commerce is not sufficiently substantial to warrant the exercise of its jurisdiction: *Provided,* That the Board shall not decline to assert jurisdiction over any labor dispute over which it would assert jurisdiction under the standards prevailing upon August 1, 1959.

(2) Nothing in this Act shall be deemed to prevent or bar any agency or the courts of any State or Territory (including the Commonwealth of Puerto Rico, Guam, and the Virgin Islands), from assuming and asserting jurisdiction over labor disputes over which the Board declines, pursuant to paragraph (1) of this subsection, to assert jurisdiction.

*   *   *   *   *

[Omitted: Sections 15, 16, 17, 18 relating to limitations.]

Individuals with Religious Convictions

Section 19.   Any employee of a health care institution who is a member of and adheres to established and traditional tenets or teachings of a bona fide religion, body, or sect which has historically held conscientious objections to joining or financially supporting labor organizations shall not be required to join or financially support any labor organization as a condition of employment; except that such employee may be required, in lieu of periodic dues and initiation fees, to pay sums equal to such dues and initiation fees to a nonreligious charitable fund exempt from taxation under section 501(c) (3) of the Internal Revenue Code, chosen by such employee from a list of at least three such funds, designated in a contract between such institution and a labor organization, or if the contract fails to designate such funds, then to any such fund chosen by the employee.

*   *   *   *   *

[Omitted: Sections 102, 103, 104 concerning effective dates of certain changes.]

TITLE II—CONCILIATION OF LABOR DISPUTES IN INDUSTRIES AFFECTING COMMERCE; NATIONAL EMERGENCIES

Section 201.   That it is the policy of the United States that—

(a) sound and stable industrial peace and the advancement of the general welfare, health, and safety of the Nation and of the best interest of employers and employees can most satisfactorily be secured by the settlement of issues between employers and employees through the processes of conference and collective bargaining between employers and the representatives of their employees;

(b) the settlement of issues between employers and employees through collective bargaining may be advanced by making available full and adequate governmental facilities for conciliation, mediation, and voluntary arbitration to aid and encourage employers and the representatives of their employees to reach and maintain agreements concerning rates of pay, hours, and working conditions, and to make all reasonable efforts to settle their differences by mutual agreement reached through conferences and collective bargaining or by such methods as may be provided for in any applicable agreement for the settlement of disputes; and

(c) certain controversies which arise between parties to collective-bargaining agreements may be avoided or minimized by making available full and adequate governmental facilities for furnishing assistance to employers and the representatives of their employees in formulating for inclusion within such agreements provision for adequate notice of any proposed changes in the terms of such agreements, for the final adjustment of grievances or questions regarding the application or interpretation of such agreements, and other provisions designed to prevent the subsequent arising of such controversies.

Section 202.   (a) There is hereby created an independent agency to be known as the Federal Mediation and Conciliation Service (herein referred to as the "Service) ... The Service shall be under the direction of a Federal Mediation and Conciliation Director (hereinafter referred to as the "Director"), who shall be appointed by the President by and with the advice and consent of the Senate. . . .

(b) The Director is authorized, subject to the civil-service laws, to appoint such clerical and other personnel as may be necessary for the execution of the functions of the Service. . . .

(c) The principal office of the Service shall be in the District of Columbia, but the Director may establish regional offices convenient to localities in which labor controversies are likely to arise. The Director may by order, subject to revocation at any time, delegate any authority and discretion conferred upon him by this Act to any regional director, or other officer or employee of the Service. The Director may establish suitable procedures for cooperation with State and local mediation agencies. The Director shall make an annual report in writing to Congress at the end of the fiscal year.

*   *   *   *   *

[Omitted: Section 202(d), which relates to the original creation of the FMCS.]

Functions of the Service

Section 203.   (a) It shall be the duty of the Service, in order to prevent or minimize interruptions of the free flow of commerce growing out of labor disputes, to assist parties to labor disputes in industries affecting commerce to settle such disputes through conciliation and mediation.

(b) The Service may proffer its services in any labor dispute in any industry affecting commerce, either upon its own motion or upon the request of one or more of the parties to the dispute, whenever in its judgment such dispute threatens to cause a substantial interruption of commerce. The Director and the Service are directed to avoid attempting to mediate disputes which would have only a minor effect on interstate commerce if State or other conciliation services are available to the parties. Whenever the Service does proffer its services in any dispute, it shall be the duty of the Service promptly to put itself in communication with the parties and to use its best efforts, by mediation and conciliation, to bring them to agreement.

(c) If the Director is not able to bring the parties to agreement by conciliation within a reasonable time, he shall seek to induce the parties voluntarily to seek other means of settling the dispute without resort to strike, lock-out, or other coercion, including submission to the employees in the bargaining unit of the employer's last offer of settlement for approval or rejection in a secret ballot. The failure or refusal of either party to agree to any procedure suggested by the Director shall not be deemed a violation of any duty or obligation imposed by this Act.

(d) Final adjustment by a method agreed upon by the parties is hereby declared to be the desirable method for settlement of grievance disputes arising over the application or interpretation of an existing collective-bargaining agreement. The Service is directed to make its conciliation and mediation services available in the settlement of such grievance disputes only as a last resort and in exceptional cases.

Section 204.   (a) In order to prevent or minimize interruptions of the free flow of commerce growing out of labor disputes, employers and employees and their representatives, in any industry affecting commerce, shall—

(1) exert every reasonable effort to make and maintain agreements concerning rates of pay, hours, and working conditions, including provision for adequate notice of any proposed change in the terms of such agreements;

(2) whenever a dispute arises over the terms or application of a collective-bargaining agreement and a conference is requested by a party or prospective party thereto, arrange promptly for such a conference to be held and endeavor in such conference to settle such dispute expeditiously; and

(3) in case such dispute is not settled by conference, participate fully and promptly in such meetings as may be undertaken by the Service under this Act for the purpose of aiding in a settlement of the dispute.

*   *   *   *   *

[Omitted: Section 205 which creates a national labor-management panel to advise the Director of FMCS.]

National Emergencies

Section 206.   Whenever in the opinion of the President of the United States, a threatened or actual strike or lock-out affecting an entire industry or a substantial part thereof engaged in trade, commerce, transportation, transmission, or communication among the several States or with foreign nations, or engaged in the production of goods for commerce, will, if permitted to occur or to continue, imperil the national health or safety, he may appoint a board of inquiry to inquire into the issues involved in the dispute and to make a written report to him within such time as he shall prescribe. Such report shall include a statement of the facts with respect to the dispute, including each party's statement of its position but shall not contain any recommendations. The President shall file a copy of such report with the Service and shall make its contents available to the public.

Section 207.   (a) A board of inquiry shall be composed of a chairman and such other members as the President shall determine, and shall have power to sit and act in any place within the United States and to conduct such hearings either in public or in private, as it may deem necessary or proper, to ascertain the facts with respect to the causes and circumstances of the dispute.

*   *   *   *   *

Section 208.   (a) Upon receiving a report from a board of inquiry the President may direct the Attorney General to petition any district court of the United States having jurisdiction of the parties to enjoin such strike or lock-out or the continuing thereof, and if the court finds that such threatened or actual strike or lock-out—

(i) affects an entire industry or a substantial part thereof engaged in trade, commerce, transportation, transmission, or communication among the several States or with foreign nations, or engaged in the production of goods for commerce; and

(ii) if permitted to occur or to continue, will imperil the national health or safety, it shall have jurisdiction to enjoin any such strike or lock-out, or the continuing thereof, and to make such other orders as may be appropriate.

*   *   *   *   *

Section 209.   (a) Whenever a district court has issued an order under section 208 enjoining acts or practices which imperil or threaten to imperil the national health or safety, it shall be the duty of the parties to the labor dispute giving rise to such order to make every effort to adjust and settle their differences, with the assistance of the Service created by this Act. Neither party shall be under any duty to accept, in whole or in part, any proposal of settlement made by the Service.

(b) Upon the issuance of such order, the President shall reconvene the board of inquiry which has previously reported with respect to the dispute. At the end of a sixty-day period (unless the dispute has been settled by that time), the board of inquiry shall report to the President the current position of the parties and the efforts which have been made for settlement, and shall include a statement by each party of its position and a statement of the employer's last offer of settlement. The President shall make such report available to the public. The National Labor Relations Board, within the succeeding fifteen days, shall take a secret ballot of the employees of each employer involved in the dispute on the question of whether they wish to accept the final offer of settlement made by their employer as stated by him and shall certify the results thereof to the Attorney General within five days thereafter.

Section 210.   Upon the certification of the results of such ballot or upon a settlement being reached, whichever happens sooner, the Attorney General shall move the court to discharge the injunction, which motion shall then be granted and the injunction discharged. When such motion is granted, the President shall submit to the Congress a full and comprehensive report of the proceedings, including the findings of the board of inquiry and the ballot taken by the National Labor Relations Board, together with such recommendations as he may see fit to make for consideration and appropriate action.

*   *   *   *   *

[Omitted: Section 211 which covers authorization for collection and dissemination of collective bargaining information by federal agencies, and Section 212 which exempts persons covered by provisions of the Railway Labor Act from the provisions of the LMRA.]

Conciliation of Labor Disputes in the Health Care Industry

Section 213.   (a) If, in the opinion of the Director of the Federal Mediation and Conciliation Service a threatened or actual strike or lockout affecting a health care institution will, if permitted to occur or to continue, substantially interrupt the delivery of health care in the locality concerned, the Director may further assist in the resolution of the impasse by establishing within 30 days after the notice to the Federal Mediation and Conciliation Service under clause (A) of the last sentence of section 8(d) (which is required by clause (3) of such section 8(d)), or within 10 days after the notice under clause (B), an impartial Board of Inquiry to investigate the issues involved in the dispute and to make a written report thereon to the parties within fifteen (15) days after the establishment of such a Board. The written report shall contain the findings of fact together with the Board's recommendations for settling the dispute, with the objective of achieving a prompt, peaceful and just settlement of the dispute. Each such Board shall be composed of such number of individuals as the Director may deem desirable. No member appointed under this section shall have any interest or involvement in the health care institutions or the employee organizations involved in the dispute.

* * * * *

[Omitted: Section 213(b) which provides for compensation for members appointed to a Board formed under Section 213(a).]

(c) After the establishment of a board under subsection (a) of this section and for 15 days after any such board has issued its report, no change in the status quo in effect prior to the expiration of the contract in the case of negotiations for a contract renewal, or in effect prior to the time of the impasse in the case of an initial bargaining negotiation, except by agreement, shall be made by the parties to the controversy.

(d) There are authorized to be appropriated such sums as may be necessary to carry out the provisions of this section.

TITLE III

Suits by and against Labor Organizations

Section 301.   (a) Suits for violation of contracts between an employer and a labor organization representing employees in an industry affecting commerce as defined in this Act, or between any such labor organizations, may be brought in any district court of the United States having jurisdiction of the parties, without respect to the amount in controversy or without regard to the citizenship of the parties.

(b) Any labor organization which represents employees in an industry affecting commerce as defined in this Act and any employer whose activities affect commerce as defined in this Act shall be bound by the acts of its agents. Any such labor organization may sue or be sued as an entity and in behalf of the employees whom it represents in the courts of the United States. Any money judgment against a labor organization in a district court of the United States shall be enforceable only against the organization as an entity and against its assets, and shall not be enforceable against any individual member or his assets.

(c) For the purposes of actions and proceedings by or against labor organizations in the district courts of the United States, district courts shall be deemed to have jurisdiction of a labor organization (1) in the district in which such organization maintains its principal offices, or (2) in any district in which its duly authorized officers or agents are engaged in representing or acting for employee members.

(d) The service of summons, subpena, or other legal process of any court of the United States upon an officer or agent of a labor organization, in his capacity as such, shall constitute service upon the labor organization.

(e) For the purposes of this action, in determining whether any person is acting as an "agent" of another person so as to make such other person responsible for his acts, the question of whether the specific acts performed were actually authorized or subsequently ratified shall not be controlling.

*　*　*　*　*

[Omitted: Section 302—Restrictions on payments to employee representatives.]

Boycotts and Other Unlawful Combinations

Section 303.　(a) It shall be unlawful, for the purpose of this section only, in an industry or activity affecting commerce, for any labor organization to engage in any activity or conduct defined as an unfair labor practice in section 8 (b) (4) of the National Labor Relations Act, as amended.

(b) Whoever shall be injured in his business or property by reason of any violation of subsection (a) may sue therefor in any district court of the United States subject to the limitations and provisions of Section 301 hereof without respect to the amount of the controversy, or in any other court having jurisdiction of the parties, and shall recover the damages sustained by him and the cost of the suit.

*　*　*　*　*

[Omitted are the following sections: Section 304—Restrictions on political contributions; Title IV—Creation of a joint committee to study and report on basic problems affecting labor relations and productivity.]

TITLE V

Definitions

Section 501.   When used in this Act—

(1) The term "industry affecting commerce" means any industry or activity in commerce or in which a labor dispute would burden or obstruct commerce or tend to burden or obstruct commerce or the free flow of commerce.

(2) The term "strike" includes any strike or other concerted stoppage of work by employees (including a stoppage by reason of the expiration of a collective-bargaining agreement) and any concerted slow-down or other concerted interruption of operations by employees.

(3) The terms "commerce," "labor disputes," "employer," "employee," "labor organization," "representative," "person," and "supervisor" shall have the same meaning as when used in the National Labor Relations Act as amended by this Act.

Saving Provision

Section 502.   Nothing in this Act shall be construed to require an individual employee to render labor or service without his consent, nor shall anything in this Act be construed to make the quitting of his labor by an individual employee an illegal act; nor shall any court issue any process to compel the performance by an individual employee of such labor or service, without his consent; nor shall the quitting of labor by an employee or employees in good faith because of abnormally dangerous conditions for work at the place of employment of such employee or employees be deemed a strike under this Act.

Separability

Section 503.   If any provision of this Act, or the application of such provision to any person or circumstance, shall be held invalid, the remainder of this Act, or the application of such provision to persons or circumstances other than those as to which it is held invalid, shall not be affected thereby.

Index to Cases for Part One

Case Number and Title	Principal Issues of Case	Principal LMRA Provisions Involved
16. Could the Employees Refuse to Cross Another Union's Picket Lines?	Interpretation of contract regarding rights of employees to refuse to cross another union's picket line.	8 (a) (1) Sect. 7
17. The Companies' Lockout during Negotiations	Employer's use of offensive lockout and temporary replacements during negotiations of a new contract.	8 (a) (1) 8 (a) (3)
18. The Challenge to the Arbitrator's Award	Challenge to arbitrator's award upholding discharge of employee who refused to be interrogated without a union representative being present.	8 (a) (1), Sect. 7
19. Withdrawal of a Traditional Christmas Bonus	Good faith bargaining concerning company's unilateral termination of a traditional Christmas bonus.	8 (a) (5), 8 (d)
20. The Offensive Sweatshirts	Discipline of employees wearing sweatshirts which offended company management during negotiating period.	8 (a) (1), 8 (a) (3)
21. A "Threat" to Picket, or "Cooperation" with a Neutral Employer?	Union statement that it might picket a plant of a company doing business with another company being struck by the union.	8 (b) (4) (i) (ii) (B)
22. The Picket Line and the Expulsion of the Union Members	Union members fined and expelled from union because of working for a non-union employer and crossing a union picket line; secondary boycott charges.	8 (b) (1) (A), 8 (b) (2), 8 (b) (4)
23. The Contract and the Mediation Services	Procedural requirements under the LMRA to notify mediation services.	8 (b) (3) 8 (d) (1), 8 (d) (3), 8 (d) (4)
24. Secondary Boycotting, or Free Speech and Acts of Conscience?	Refusal of union employees to accept deliveries from another struck company; statements of union business representative to influence union members.	8 (b) (4) (i) (ii) B, 8 (b) (4) (D), 8 (c), 10 (1)
25. The Employee Who Worked on Dr. Martin Luther King's Birthday	Union discrimination against employee who violated union policy regarding not working on birthday of Dr. Martin Luther King.	8 (a) (3), 8 (b) (2)
26. The Turncoat Union Members	Union fines imposed on members some of whom first resigned from union, who crossed picket lines during strike and returned to work.	8 (b) (1) (A), Sect. 7
27. Did the Union Fail to Properly Represent a Minority Employee?	Charges against both company and union by minority employee who was suspended and later discharged after filing charges with EEOC and the NLRB.	8 (a) (1), 8 (b) (1) (A)
28. Who Should Install the Concrete Planks?	Jurisdictional issue involving claim of two labor unions to disputed work.	8 (b) (4) (D), 10 (K)
29. Eligibility of Economic Strikers to Vote in a Decertification Election	Question of eligibility of employees engaged in an economic strike to vote in a decertification election conducted 12 months after beginning of strike.	9 (c) (3), 2 (3)

1. SHOULD NONEMPLOYEE UNION ORGANIZERS BE ALLOWED ON COMPANY PROPERTY?

COMPANY: *Scholle Chemical Corporation, Northlake, Illinois*

UNION: *Oil, Chemical, and Atomic Workers International Union, AFL–CIO*

BACKGROUND

The Scholle Chemical Company is located in a plant building within an industrial tract in the Chicago suburb of Northlake, Illinois, near the intersection of North Avenue and Railroad Avenue. North Avenue is a four-lane thoroughfare running east and west through Chicago and certain of its western suburbs. The speed limit is posted at forty miles per hour and the average daily traffic load in both directions is about 38,000 vehicles. Railroad Avenue is a private road owned by the Automatic Electric Company, the principal occupant of the industrial tract. Scholle owns an easement over Railroad Avenue which runs north of North Avenue, perpendicular to it, and dead-ends in Automatic Electric's parking lots. It is a paved, three-lane road with a posted speed limit of thirty miles per hour. Traffic control lights at the intersection of North and Railroad Avenues and traffic signs on Railroad Avenue itself are owned and maintained by Automatic Electric.

The Scholle plant is located on the west side of Railroad Avenue. The entrances to the plant itself, and to three adjoining company parking lots, face Railroad Avenue.

At the time of this case, Scholle employed about 350 people at its Northlake plant. None of the employees resided on the premises; approximately 27 percent of them resided in the town of Northlake itself; approximately 30 percent lived in suburban DuPage County; approximately 15 percent lived in Chicago; and the remaining 28 percent resided in suburbs other than Northlake or DuPage County.

Scholle's employees, as well as almost all of Automatic Electric's 11,000 employees, arrive and leave the premises by private automobile. An estimated 40 percent of Automatic Electric's employees use Railroad Avenue in entering or leaving the industrial tract. Shifts of the two companies overlap with the result that during the short period of time when the shifts change, it is almost impossible to distinguish Scholle employees from Automatic Electric employees.

In October 1969, organizers from the Oil, Chemical, and Atomic Workers Union began an organizational campaign aimed at Scholle employees. George Maddox,[1] a business representative of the union, met with two Scholle employees to discuss possible organization. The next day, Maddox and Howard Zager, another union representative, visited Scholle's plant. While standing near the main entrance, they attempted to speak with employees and distribute to them envelopes containing a handbill and union authorization card. However, Scholle's personnel manager, Thomas Grissom, informed the union representatives that Railroad Avenue was a private road and that all nonemployee solicitations and distributions on this private property were prohibited. Maddox and Zager then moved to the intersection at North Avenue and Railroad Avenue where they determined that because of the heavy traffic and the impossibility of ascertaining which of the passing cars contained Scholle employees, further handbilling would not be productive. Another attempt at handbilling was made on November 11th; but after about one hour at the entrance to the Scholle plant, only 120 handbills had been distributed.

On November 8, 1969 Maddox met again with two Scholle employees who brought him an old Christmas mailing list. The list was out of date and contained mainly supervisors' addresses. On November 21, 1969 Maddox wrote to the Scholle management requesting access to the plant entrances for distribution of leaflets. This request was rejected by the company on December 2, 1969. Later, Maddox wrote to Scholle requesting a list of names and addresses of all current hourly employees, but he received no response from the company.

On April 21, 1970 Maddox again attempted to handbill Scholle's employees after having been informed that Automatic Electric was on strike. After spending over two hours at the intersection during shift changing times, this effort also proved unsuccessful.

Maddox also attempted a mailing to Scholle employees. On Jan-

---

1 All names are disguised.

uary 28, 1970 he wrote to about 40 employees requesting assistance in compiling a current mailing list. On February 12, a mailing containing authorization cards and self-addressed envelopes was sent to 70 employees. Subsequent mailings to 150 Scholle employees and 220 Scholle employees were also attempted, again with the enclosed authorization cards and self-addressed envelopes. However, Maddox was unsure of the accuracy of either the employees' names or their addresses.

Subsequently, the union filed unfair labor practice charges against the company claiming that the Scholle company had interefred with, restrained, and coerced its employees in the exercise of their organizational rights in violation of Section 7 and Section 8(a) (1) of the Labor Management Relations Act by refusing to permit nonemployee union organizers to distribute leaflets and handbills and to solicit employees on Scholle property.

POSITION OF THE UNION

The union argued that because of the inaccessibility of the Scholle employees, reasonable attempts by nonemployees to communicate with them through the usual channels were ineffective.

Since the relatively small work force of Scholle employees was diffused through the City of Chicago and the various suburbs surrounding Northlake, Illinois, communication with them through media channels such as newspapers and radio was rendered unavailable in a practical sense. Because attempts at acquiring a mailing list from Scholle had proved unsuccessful and because the mailing list ultimately utilized was not known to be current or accurate, communication through the mails or by way of home visits was also impractical. Handbilling at the intersection of North and Railroad Avenues was clearly ineffective because of the problems of heavy traffic and of identification of Scholle employees.

In these circumstances, according to the union, the only practical way by which Scholle employees could be contacted by nonemployee organizers was for the union to be granted access to Scholle's parking lots for distribution of union literature. If the employees' rights under Section 7 of the Labor Management Relations Act were to be preserved under the circumstances of this case, the property rights of the company should be modified in a reasonable manner to accommodate the union organizing process. The union claimed that the distribution of union literature on the company's parking lots was not an unreasonable intrusion on company property, and it was the only practical way for the union to contact Scholle employees in this situation. For the company to deny the union such access was, in the union's view, a violation of Section 7 and Section 8(a) (1) of the act. The union requested that the company be ordered to permit union organizers to distribute union literature and to solicit union membership at appropriately designated points within the Scholle company's parking lots.

POSITION OF THE COMPANY

The company claimed that it had followed a long-standing ban on any outside solicitations by nonemployee personnel on its property. This ban had been uniformly enforced by both the Scholle Company and by the Automatic Electric Company which owned the private road.

The company claimed that its private property rights gave it the sole right to determine whether or not to permit union organizers to distribute union literature on company parking lots. The company decided in this case to maintain its uniform ban against any solicitation by nonemployee persons on company property. This in no way interfered with the union organizational efforts, since the union was pursuing other means of contacting Scholle employees. Further, claimed the company, the union had not exhausted other communication possibilities. By filing unfair labor practice charges, the union was attempting to force the company to "assist" the union in its organizing efforts by giving the union the most convenient access to the employees. There is nothing in the Labor Management Relations Act which requires a company to do this.

In summary, the company claimed that it was well within its private property rights to deny nonemployee union organizers access to its parking lots. The unfair labor practice charges should be dismissed.

QUESTIONS

1. Was the company obligated under the act to provide a mailing list of all names and addresses of current hourly employees? Discuss.
2. Since the company had maintained a uniform policy against solicitation by any nonemployees on company property, was this a compelling argument that it was not interfering with union organizational efforts as prohibited by the act?

3. Which right should take priority in a case of this type: a company's property rights, or the employees' organizational rights under Section 7 of the act? Why is this a difficult dilemma to resolve?

4. Does the Labor Management Relations Act require a company to "assist" a union in its organizing efforts by giving the union convenient access to employees? Discuss.

2. SHOULD THE EDITORIAL WRITERS BE INCLUDED IN THE BARGAINING UNIT?

COMPANY: *Wichita Eagle & Beacon Publishing Company, Inc., Wichita, Kansas*

UNION: *Wichita Newspaper Guild, affiliated with the Newspaper Guild, AFL–CIO*

BACKGROUND

The company is engaged in the publishing, sale, and distribution of daily newspapers in Wichita, Kansas. In August 1970, the Wichita Newspaper Guild, affiliated with The Newspaper Guild, AFL-CIO, filed a petition with the NLRB seeking certification as the collective bargaining agent of the newspaper's news department employees. The regional office of the Board conducted a hearing on the petition and ordered an election to be held. In connection therewith, the Board found that two "editorial writers," Alice Sanford[1] and Hazel Jaeger, should be included in the proposed news department bargaining unit.

An election was conducted by the Board among the unit that it had determined was appropriate, and the union was certified as the collective bargaining agent for the unit. The newspaper filed an exception to the election under Sections 9(b) and 9(c) of the act, challenging the inclusion of Alice Sanford and Hazel Jaeger in the bargaining unit.

About the time of the election, the newspaper transferred Sanford to the Sunday magazine department from the editorial page department. The union claimed that this transfer was in reprisal for Sanford's part in helping organize the union, and the union filed unfair labor practice charges against the newspaper on her behalf. An Administrative Law Judge of the Board conducted a hearing on this matter and found that the newspaper had violated sections 8(a) (1) and (3) of the act by transferring Alice Sanford against her will

---

1 All names are disguised.

from the editorial page department to the Sunday magazine department "because of her union activities," and because she had been told by her employer that "consequences of her union membership and activity might be severe." The Administrative Law Judge recommended that she be reinstated in the editorial page department and that she be awarded any back pay she would have been entitled to, including increases in salary, but for her transfer. The newspaper filed an appeal to this decision, which was part of its continuing challenge to the original inclusion of both Sanford and Jaeger in the bargaining unit.

POSITION OF THE UNION

According to the union, Sanford's position prior to her transfer to the Sunday magazine department was that of an editorial writer. The editorial page department of the newspaper consisted of three people. Arthur Jackson, editor of the editorial page, was the supervisor of the two employees in the editorial page department, Sanford and Jaeger. Jackson was not included in the collective bargaining unit. Martin G. Patrick, editor and publisher of the newspaper, was also part of the editorial page department, but more in an "ex-officio" capacity.

According to testimony presented at the hearing, normal day-to-day procedure in the editorial page department included a midmorning conference, with Patrick, Jackson, Sanford, and Jaeger participating. At these conferences, each person in turn would be asked what he or she had in mind for an editorial. Sanford, for instance, when thus asked, might say that she had in mind writing a piece on ecology. Patrick or Jackson might say, "We had an editorial on air and water pollution last week, so we will not go on ecology again at this time." That would dispose of Sanford's proposal. Or, for instance, Patrick might have responded to Sanford's proposal in the following vein: "What particular aspect of ecology do you have in mind?" Sanford would respond with some details and elaboration; the matter would then be discussed by those present. Patrick might then say to Sanford, "All right, give it a try." On some other subject thus raised, Patrick might make it clear that there were certain specific things that he wished to be stated in the particular proposed editorial, e.g., "The theme of the editorial should be that, on balance, after weighing the arguments pro and con, the government should proceed with the development of the supersonic transport plane because of the need to maintain leadership in the field of air transportation and because of the need to maintain a viable aerospace industry and the tens of thousands of jobs involved in that and in satellite industries." The editorial writer would follow such a directive.

Following the foregoing type of daily conference with Patrick, the other three would return to their offices. They would then get together in Jackson's office and discuss at greater length topics that had received tentative approval at the conference with Patrick. Views and possibly conflicting contentions would be exchanged and argued. In most instances it would be at this tripartite conference that definite editorial topics would be assigned by Jackson to Sanford and Jaeger.

After a writer drafted or wrote an editorial, it was then submitted to Jackson. He might approve it, disapprove it, or prescribe changes or revisions. If the editorial cleared Jackson, it would then go to Patrick. Again, the editorial might be approved, rejected, or rejected subject to some particular revision being made.

The union claimed that the editorials of the newspaper functioned as the voice of the newspaper's ownership and management. What appeared in an editorial was the subjective viewpoint of management, that is, of Jackson and Patrick. In the union's view, neither Sanford nor Jaeger could exercise much independent judgment in their work as editorial writers. Nor were they responsible for the supervision of any other employees, and they had no part in determining wages, hours, and working conditions for other employees.

The union claimed, therefore, that both Sanford and Jaeger were employees within the meaning of Section 2(3) of the Labor Management Relations Act, and they should properly be included in the newspaper's bargaining unit. Consequently, the finding of unfair labor practices against the newspaper for transferring Sanford because of her union activities should not be dismissed on grounds that she was not covered by provisions of the act.

POSITION OF THE NEWSPAPER

The newspaper contended that editorial writers have the essential characteristics of managerial and confidential employees, and therefore the two editorial writers in question, Sanford and Jaeger, were improperly included in the collective bargaining unit. Therefore, the newspaper's action in transferring Sanford was not properly subject to the act's coverage.

Although the term *managerial employee* is not used in the Labor Management Relations Act, nor is provision made in the act for the inclusion or exclusion of such employees in bargaining units, the newspaper pointed out that the NLRB has long followed the practice of excluding employees designated as "managerial" from bargaining units in representation elections. It does so on the premise that certain nonsupervisory employees are so closely allied with management that they should be excluded from employment bargaining units.

In this case, according to the newspaper, Sanford and Jaeger were directly responsible to the editorial page editor, Jackson, and in turn to the editor and publisher of the newspaper, Patrick, concerning the content and direction of the newspaper's editorials. Both were active participants in "formulating, determining and effectuating" the newspaper's journalistic policies. The daily conferences between Patrick, Jackson, Sanford, and Jaeger attested to this relationship. Although subject to supervision in writing by the editorial page editor and the editor and publisher, both Sanford and Jaeger could and did propose topics for editorials, and they offered their own viewpoints in an effort to influence editorial policy on various subjects. They were "integral participants in the newspaper's subjective voice, its editorials." Whether termed a managerial employee, a confidential employee, or whatever, the relationship of Sanford and Jaeger to the newspaper and its staff placed them in a position where they were directly involved in "formulating, determining, and effectuating" the policies of the paper.

In the newspaper's view, for the NLRB to hold that a person who was involved in the formulation of editorial content of a newspaper is not aligned with the newspaper's management would come "perilously close to infringing upon the newspaper's First Amendment guarantee of freedom of the press."

In summary, the newspaper argued that Sanford and Jaeger should not have been classified as employees within the meaning of Section 2(3) of the act. In line with long-standing Board policy, editorial writers such as Sanford and Jaeger should be excluded from the newspaper's news department bargaining unit, since their duties were essentially managerial and confidential in nature. The unfair labor practice charges against the newspaper in connection with its transfer of Sanford correspondingly should be dismissed, since she was not covered by provisions of the act.

QUESTIONS

1. Evaluate the argument of the union and management concerning the managerial and confidential nature of the work of the editorial writers.

2. What is the difference between an editorial writer who is involved in "formulating, determining and effectuating" the policies of the newspaper as compared to simply writing material at the direction of the owner of the newspaper? Why is this a gray area on which the determination of this case depends?

3. Evaluate the newspaper's argument that to include the editorial writers in a bargaining unit would possibly infringe upon constitutional guarantees of freedom of the press.

4. If a person does not supervise any other employees and has no part in determining wages, hours, and working conditions for other employees, does this mean that the NLRB must classify such a person as a nonmanagerial employee eligible for inclusion in a bargaining unit? Discuss.

3. WHO IS ELIGIBLE TO VOTE IN A CERTIFICATION ELECTION?

COMPANY: *Lock Joint Tube Company, South Bend, Indiana*

UNION: *International Union of Electrical, Radio, and Machine Workers, AFL–CIO*

PRINCIPAL ISSUES OF THE CASE

There were three principal issues involved in this case. As a result of a series of incidents related to its organization attempts, the union filed several charges with the NLRB. The union claimed that company management had violated the Labor Management Relations Act by:

(a) Discriminating in violation of Section 8 (a) (3). This charge resulted from three layoff and separation actions, totaling 40 employees.

(b) Interference in violation of Section 8 (a) (1). This issue was brought about by activities of the company after the union filed an election petition. In addition, both the company and the union challenged the eligibility of a number of discharged employees and newly hired replacements to vote in the certification election as appropriate under Section 9(c) of the act.

BACKGROUND

Lock Joint Tube Company is an Indiana corporation having its office and place of business in South Bend, Indiana. The company is engaged in the manufacturing and finishing of electrically welded steel and butted tubing. About 40 persons were employed in production by the company in 1958.

The major issues in this case stemmed from organizational efforts begun by Lock Joint's employees in September 1958. The company had been in operation for many years, but employees previously had never been represented by a recognized bargaining agent.

Joseph Smith,[1] the president of the company, had shown previous opposition towards union organizational attempts. In 1956, when a different union tried to organize the company, Smith sent a letter addressed to each "employee and spouse" in which he said, among other things, "Remember, under protection of the National Labor Board, a union organizer or leader does not have to tell the truth."

Events Leading up to the First Layoff

In 1958, plant employee Jerry Friday assumed leadership in obtaining signatures upon union authorization cards furnished him by Al Keane, a field representative of the International Union of Electrical Workers. Between September 16 and 19, 18 employees signed these cards, and on the latter date Keane notified Smith by letter that he was filing a petition with the National Labor Relations Board seeking a certification election.

In his written response dated September 22, Smith said:

In reply to your letter of September 19, 1958, I do not consent to any agreement with your affiliation for any of our employees.

I do not believe that your union represents the majority of our employees and we will request a hearing by the National Relations Board [sic] in the event the matter is brought to our attention by that Board.

Smith then spent a good part of the same day in calling plant employees to his office, individually or in small groups, where he questioned them as to whether or not they had signed union cards. To a number of them he said that they did not have to tell him because he would find out anyway. If a hearing were held, he explained, the union would have to show him the cards. To several he termed the IUE as "Communist"; he further told several employees that "a union like that he would never accept." Two employees were told that he would eliminate another mill if necessary, and Smith warned them that if the employees went on strike they would be "walking out there a long, long time." Smith asked one group of three employees to reveal the names of anyone who had approached them asking them to sign cards.

On the evening of October 6, IUE representative Keane met with all the employees on the night shift, either at the company gate or off company property. Among those present were Jerry Friday and Lead-

---

1 All names are disguised.

man William Jubel. The next morning Jubel informed Production Manager Joseph Metzler of this meeting.

Later that day (October 7) Chief Engineer Stibor and Mr. Smith decided to discontinue the plant's double-shift operation.

The Layoff of October 10

With no previous warning, all employees at the plant were notified two days later, on October 9, with the following bulletin signed by Mr. Smith:

TO ALL EMPLOYEES   OCTOBER 9, 1958

Certain business developments and change of conditions beyond the control of the Company require the discontinuance of the night shift effective at the close of such shift Friday night, October 10, 1958.

At such time it will be necessary to lay off the following employees for lack of work:

[11 employees listed by name]

The Company regrets the necessity for taking this action, but within the foreseeable future can see no opportunity of it being able to provide work for this group.

All other night shift employees will report for work on the day shift beginning at 8 a.m. Monday, October 13, 1958.

At least 9 of the 11 employees laid off had indicated their IUE affiliation by wearing union buttons on October 7 or earlier.

Events Leading to the Second Layoff and the Walkout

On October 16, about a week after the layoff, the NLRB regional office conducted a hearing on the petition for a certification election filed by the IUE. At this hearing, IUE representative Keane placed on a table before Smith and his counsel signed union cards, offering them for inspection. Smith's counsel told Keane that the company would not consider recognizing the IUE as the collective bargaining agency for the employees.

On October 23, Smith posted a notice announcing the layoff of seven more employees—all of whom were known by management to be IUE adherents, since they had openly been wearing union buttons. The notice listed the layoff at the close of the work shift the next day, October 24.

Among other things the notice said:

The Company regrets the necessity for taking the following action, but within the foreseeable future, can see no opportunity of it being able to provide work for this group.

That night, 22 employees gathered at Keane's home and voted unanimously to strike the next day in protest against the layoffs.

The Strike

About 9:30 a.m. on October 24, 23 workers walked out—only 7 production employees remaining—and proceeded to picket the plant carrying signs bearing legends protesting, among other things, against the "unfair layoffs."

Shortly after the strike began, Smith made the following statement to union representative Keane in a manner such that the strikers would be able to hear, "Thanks a lot, Keane, for letting me hire a new work force." He also made a statement to his leadman, "Them guys out there are all fired," and "Prepare to break in new help."

However, on November 25, the NLRB issued an order directing that a union certification election be held. The order stated that the critical date for eligibility to vote should be the payroll date immediately preceding issuance of the order, which was November 21. The same order contained the phrase: "ineligible to vote are employees who have, since that period, quit or been discharged for cause and have not been rehired or reinstated before the election date and employees who strike who are not entitled to reinstatement." After receipt of this direction, Smith sent 22 striking employees letters of discharge on December 4 and omitted their names from the eligibility list.

Each letter of discharge stated that the reason for termination was "misconduct in connection with current strike activities." All letters were of the same text; none cited any specific item of misconduct claimed for individual persons.

The Challenged Ballots

At the election on December 11, 1958 the company challenged the ballots of 27 voters on the ground that they had been strikers in an economic strike and had been replaced. As additional grounds for its challenge of 22 of this number, the company claimed that they had been discharged on December 4 for misconduct.

The company also challenged the ballots of two "former" employees on the ground that sometime after November 24 they notified the company that they had quit and obtained employment elsewhere. These two individuals were among the 11 laid off on October 10.

At the same election, the IUE challenged the ballots of 12 employees, all of whom had been first hired by the company on November 4 or thereafter. The union claimed that if the company had not illegally created job vacancies, none of these 12 new employees would have been hired.

POSITION OF THE UNION

In substance, the following arguments outline the position of the union in regard to each of the principal issues stated at the outset of this case.

The Discrimination Charge

1.   The company had rejected overtures toward union recognition and collective bargaining.
2.   Dismissal of 11 employees on October 10 was done as a result of their union organization activities.
3.   Layoff of seven more employees on October 24 was again the result of company hostility toward the union's organizing efforts.
4.   Discharge of 22 strikers for misconduct was unjustified because:
     a)   No specific item of misconduct was charged in the individual letters to the employees.
     b)   Employer was engaged in a deliberate campaign to stop union activity among its employees.
     c)   All of the above constituted illegal discrimination.

The Interference Charge

1.   The company interrogated employees as to whether they had signed union cards.
2.   The company requested from employees names of their fellow employees who solicited union cards.
3.   The company had stated to employees that it would not accept the union and if they attempted to organize they would be locked out. All of the above constituted illegal interference.

The Election Issue

1. Discharged unfair labor practice strikers and discriminatorily laid-off employees should have been eligible to vote in the representation election.

2. Two discriminatorily laid-off employees who were permanently employed elsewhere should still be eligible to vote, since they were illegally forced into a position of obtaining other employment.

3. Twelve replacements for employees who had been improperly discharged or laid off should not be allowed to vote in the election.

POSITION OF THE COMPANY

Chief Engineer Stibor, who claimed that he "suggested" the lay-offs to Smith, testified while holding in his hands certain documents which he called "master production schedules": "Had we continued to operate two shifts, mill No. 1 would have been out of the schedule of work on the 17th of the same month, October 1958." He went on to state that the same records showed that for mill No. 2 there were no orders beyond October 15, none for mill No. 3 beyond October 20, and none for mill No. 4 beyond October 15. He further said that such records showed this to be the state of affairs on October 7, 1958.

When asked as to his reasons for deciding to lay off the night shift, Smith stated, "We had a further reduction in orders." Smith also claimed that his "financial situation" necessitated the layoffs. Further, Smith advanced his financial situation as a reason for interviewing employees on September 22, and claimed that just before this he had received from his accountants a report showing that for the first six months of the year he had had a loss of "approximately $20,000."

In support of its discharging of 22 striking employees for misconduct, management representatives testified as to a series of incidents which had occurred during October and November 1958. These were as follows:

October 24. Fourteen strikers blocked a driveway at the plant, not permitting a local employer named William Wiese to pass until police arrived.

October 24. A nonstriking employee was told by a striking employee "not to try to come in to work Monday or he would be sorry." This occurred as the nonstriker was driving through the gate.

October 27. Three nonstrikers were stopped by picketing employees for periods of up to 15 minutes as they tried to enter the plant to work.

October 28.   Smith was delayed some 10 minutes by pickets circling the gate to the plant before he could drive through.

November 3.   In three separate instances, nonstrikers were delayed by striking employees for periods of 10 to 15 minutes as they tried to enter the plant. One nonstriker, being subjected to profane language, drove home as a result.

November 5.   A car window of a newly hired employee was broken as he attempted to enter the plant. Some 100 people were gathered near the gate, including at least 8 strikers.

November 7.   Late in the afternoon, when a number of nonstrikers were leaving the plant, a large mob of unidentified people and many police were gathered outside the gate. The mob was unruly and disorderly, and the exit of the cars was impeded for about one half hour. The back window of one car was broken. Among the mass of several hundred people—according to management witnesses—were some nine strikers near the gate. The owner of the car was a newly hired employee, who testified that he saw a striking employee break the car window. [*Note:* The crowds of unidentified people present on both November 5 and November 7 included many people who had appeared at the plant as a result of the company's newspaper advertisement for new employees.]

November 13.   As Stibor was leaving the plant with a number of nonstriking employees in his car, some 13 pickets whom he identified were circling in front of the exit gate. Police were there, opened the way, and Stibor went through.

November 28.   On this occasion, IUE representative Keane put a hand on the arm of one newly hired employee and told him not to go in. This same employee decided not to go in and accepted Keane's invitation to ride back into town with him. Later that afternoon, as nonstrikers left the plant, they were called names.

In light of all of these incidents, management witnesses claimed that their discharges of the 22 striking employees for misconduct on December 4 were justified. Therefore, these employees were not eligible to participate in a representational election, and the unfair labor practice charges against the company should be dismissed.

The company further challenged the ballots of seven other employees who had originally been laid off on October 10. On November 24 the company had offered reinstatement to nine of the laid-off employees in view of a "better economic position of the company." Five of these individuals failed to respond to the company's offer of reinstatement; therefore, management claimed, they had refused employment with the company. Also, two "former" employees who tried to vote in the December 11 election had notified the company in November that they had found employment elsewhere and did not wish reinstatement. Therefore, they, too, no longer were employees of Lock Joint Tube Company and had forfeited their voting eligibility. In support of this position, the company cited the NLRB order of November 25, which specifically stated that employees who had quit or who had been discharged for cause were ineligible to vote in the IUE representational election.

QUESTIONS

1. Did the company violate Section 8 (a) (3) of LMRA in laying off the 11 night shift employees? in discharging the 22 unfair labor practice strikers? in the layoff of 7 additional employees during the second reduction in force?

2. What evidence must an employer develop if an economic reduction in labor force is to be legal within the provisions of the Labor Management Relations Act?

3. Did the company violate Section 8 (a) (1) of the act? If so, how and why?

4. Which of the discharged unfair labor practice strikers and laid-off employees, if any, should be ruled eligible to vote in the representation election? Why?

5. What, if any, remedial action should be taken in this case?

4. CAN UNFAIR LABOR PRACTICES BE COMMITTED IN A LOCAL CEMETERY?

COMPANY: Inglewood Park Cemetery Association, Inglewood Park, California

UNION: Miscellaneous Warehousemen, Drivers, and Helpers, Local 986, International Brotherhood of Teamsters, Chauffeurs, Warehousemen, and Helpers of America

BACKGROUND

Inglewood Park Cemetery Association is a California corporation engaged in the operation of a cemetery located in Inglewood, California. From July 1, 1962 through June 30, 1963 the association received revenue in excess of $500,000 from the sale to the public of services, burial lots, crypt spaces, and related items. In addition, it had purchased goods directly from outside the state of California totaling $3,086.

Miscellaneous Warehousemen, Drivers, and Helpers, Local 986, International Brotherhood of Teamsters, Chauffeurs, Warehousemen, and Helpers of America is the labor organization which filed unfair labor practice charges against the cemetery association on behalf of four employees of the association, John Lavan, Sam Doyle, Hector Lopez, and Willie Zobo.[1]

On June 26, 1963, Lavan, Doyle, and Lopez, after having completed their work for the day, went to the office of the business representative for the union. They made inquiries concerning how Inglewood Park Cemetery employees might obtain membership in that organization. The union business representative explained the procedures to be followed and gave them a number of authorization cards. On the following day, before and after working hours and during the lunch period, the three employees distributed a number of these cards to their fellow workers.

---

[1] All names are disguised.

78

During the afternoon of June 27, the foreman of the cemetery association ground crews approached Lavan, and asked him if he had passed out union cards. Lavan asked the foreman who had given him such information. The foreman replied that another employee had told him. Lavan requested that he be confronted with the foreman's informant. The foreman did not comply with Lavan's request, but told Lavan that if the superintendent of the cemetery association ever found out that employees were passing out union authorization cards, he would discharge them immediately.

On June 28, all employees were assembled in the cemetery chapel to hear the superintendent, A. H. Ponder. Ponder stated that he had heard that employees were trying to form a union, and that he would fight against it. He told them that workers at a nearby cemetery had joined a union and were receiving an hourly wage less than that paid by Inglewood Park. He reminded them that Inglewood Park also gave its employees uniforms and a Christmas basket. Finally, he stated that unionized employees at the other cemetery were dissatisfied with their union, and were waiting for the year to expire so that they could get out of the union.

When the meeting was over, each of the three employee organizers, Lavan, Doyle, and Lopez, plus a fellow worker, Willie Zobo, were summoned to Mr. Ponder's office. The four were ushered into the superintendent's office separately. Each was told that he was discharged and was given his final paycheck. Lavan and Doyle were informed that their discharges were for insufficient productivity and wasting time on the job. Lopez and Zobo, who worked together as marker trimmers, were told that as a team they had done nothing but "fool around" for three years, and therefore they were being discharged.

Subsequently, the union filed unfair labor practice charges against Inglewood Park Cemetery Association alleging violations of Section 8 (a) (1) and Section 8 (a) (3) of the Labor Management Relations Act.

POSITION OF THE UNION

The union charged that the management of the cemetery association had engaged in unfair labor practices when: (a) the foreman approached Lavan inquiring about his union organizational activities; (b) when Superintendent Ponder made coercive statements to the group; and (c) when the same superintendent discharged the four em-

ployees, not for poor work records, but for union activities of an organizational nature.

The union presented evidence which indicated that each of the
four employees had received periodic wage increases during their
terms of service, which ranged from 4 to 11 years. Prior to the date
of their discharges, the employees claimed that they had never received any warnings to the effect that their work was unsatisfactory,
or that they were wasting excessive time. The union claimed their
discharges were therefore based upon their union activity—including
Zobo's discharge, since management felt that both Lopez and Zobo
were closely related by the nature of their work.

The union claimed that since the association had received revenues
of over $500,000 annually, and since a cemetery could be considered
as a retail enterprise, the association was subject to the requirements
and provisions of LMRA.[2]

The union argued that the cemetery association should be required
to restore each employee to his former job, including all back wages
and seniority rights; and further, that all discriminatory antiunion
activity by management should be prohibited.

POSITION OF THE COMPANY

Inglewood Park Cemetery Association admitted the foregoing facts
of the case with respect to the four employees, but management denied
that these facts constituted unfair labor practices. Management contended that Inglewood Park Cemetery Association was not engaged in
interstate commerce; consequently, the association and its employees
were not subject to the Labor Management Relations Act. In support
of this, management contended that its dollar purchases of only
$3,000 worth of goods outside of California were not sufficient for the
NLRB to classify the association as being engaged in interstate
commerce.

Management further claimed that the discharges of the four men
were "coincidental" with their union activities. The work of the men
had been unsatisfactory for a long period of time, and their union
activities were the culmination of management's dissatisfaction with
the men as employees.

Management's primary argument, however, rested upon the asser-

---

2 *Note:* Under Section 6 of the act, the NLRB is authorized to set standards for
asserting jurisdiction over various enterprises. See page 7 for jurisdictional standards
used by the NLRB.

tion that a local cemetery was an *intrastate* business and, therefore, Inglewood Park Cemetery Association was not subject to federal labor law within the meaning and definitions under Sections 2 (6) and 2 (7) of LMRA. The association requested that the unfair labor practice charges should be dismissed.

QUESTIONS

1. What is the central issue upon which the decision in this case rests?
2. Did the association violate Section 8(a) (3) and Section 8 (a) (1) of the Labor Management Relations Act? Why?
3. Does the NLRB have jurisdiction in this case? Why? Are the standards used by the NLRB in asserting jurisdiction in this type of situation clear and reasonable?
4. Are remedial actions justified in this case? If so, what remedy should be taken?

5. THE CHALLENGED ELECTION RESULTS DUE TO ALLEGED EMPLOYER MISCONDUCT

COMPANY: The Singer Company, Albuquerque, New Mexico

UNION: International Association of Machinists and Aerospace Workers (IAM), AFL–CIO

BACKGROUND

The Singer Company had operated a calculating machine production plant at San Leandro, California, where the International Association of Machinists and Aerospace Workers had represented the employees of the plant for the preceding 25 years. In an effort to attain lower labor costs and thereby to compete more favorably with foreign-produced calculating machines which Singer believed had caused a drastic decline in its share of the domestic market, Singer in 1969 established a new manufacturing facility at a temporary location in Albuquerque, New Mexico. The new plant was moved to its permanent facility in August 1970.

In June 1970, the IAM union began a campaign to organize and represent the employees of the new plant. The campaign was characterized by the distribution of extensive literature and numerous general meetings with the employees by both Singer and IAM. On September 11, 1970 the union notified Singer of its campaign activities, and on October 22, 1970 the union requested recognition on the basis of a card check. Singer refused and insisted on an NLRB election, which was held on December 10, 1970. The election resulted in the union's being rejected by a 63–44 margin. The union filed objections with the NLRB to certain preelection conduct by Singer and requested that the election results be set aside because of alleged violations by the company of Sections 8(a)(1) and 8(a)(3) of the Labor Management Relations Act.

POSITION OF THE UNION

The IAM union's objections were based primarily upon three charges of preelection misconduct on the part of the company.

The first alleged misconduct involved an incident on September 17, 1970 when seven employees reported to work wearing shirts colored in a manner and with insignia displayed to identify them as union shirts. The men were told by an officer of Singer that they would not be permitted to work in the plant while wearing the shirts. Under protest, the men removed the shirts. According to the union, the right to wear union insignia on an employer's premises during working hours is guaranteed by Section 7 of the act, as long as such wearing of union insignia does not interfere with the normal duties of employees and their efficient and safe work performance. In this case, the shirts in no way interfered with the employees' plant duties, or anything else. The company's prohibition of the employees' rights to wear union insignia was primarily designed to interfere with the union election campaign in the plant.

The second allegation of misconduct was that George Vasquez,[1] a plant supervisor, held "coercive interrogations" of employees concerning the union sympathies of employees under him. This took place in a series of interviews held by Mr. Vasquez during September 1970, in which Mr. Vasquez tried to get employees to indicate their feelings and their estimates of the union's supporters in the plant.

Closely related was a third allegation that Singer had "exerted coercive pressure" on its employees through statements made by it during its preelection campaign. These statements were made verbally by company representatives and also in company literature distributed to employees. According to the union, the dominant theme of Singer's antiunion campaign was that the IAM union would bring strikes, a loss of jobs, and possible closure of the plant itself. The company's literature attributed the loss of 14,000 jobs to unionization at various plants, and it was illustrated by specific examples of other plants which had, after voting for union representation, been closed with an attendant loss of jobs to the work force. In the union's view, these types of statements were clearly threats aimed at the possible consequences of unionization at the Albuquerque facility.

Because of these alleged violations of Sections 8(a) (1) and 8(a) (3) of the act, the union argued that the results of the election should be set

---

[1] The names of all individuals have been disguised.

aside by the NLRB. The union argued that the Board should order the union to be certified to represent the plant employees; or at the very least, that another representational election should be held under Section 9(c) of the act; and that the company should be required to cease and desist in its unfair labor practices accordingly.

POSITION OF THE COMPANY

The company argued that all the union's allegations of unfair labor practices committed by the company were unfounded and should be dismissed for the following reasons:

1. The company's prohibition against the employees' wearing union insignia in the plant was necessary in view of interfactional hostilities between union supporters and nonunion advocates at the plant, and the possibility of further disruption if the shirts were permitted in the plant. As proof, Singer pointed to a drop in production on the particular day (September 17, 1970) in question. The company had the right to maintain discipline in the plant, which it sought to do in this matter.

2. The interviews which supervisor George Vasquez had with various employees were "nothing more than casual conversations." Vasquez did not make any coercive statements. He was simply "curious" about the union's strength among plant employees. Regardless, these interviews had no influence on the outcome of the representational election.

3. The company contended that various statements made by company representatives and included in its literature during the election campaign were merely "an attempt to disclose the economic facts as they existed and to indicate possible eventualities if the economic situation changed unfavorably for Singer." An employer's statements which are not coercive are protected under Section 8(c) of the act, and cannot form the basis for a Section 8(a)(1) violation.

The company emphasized that it made no statements to the effect that the Albuquerque plant would be closed as a consequence of unionization.

In summary, the company claimed that its activities and statements during the union representational campaign were both permissible and legal under LMRA. The union's unfair labor practice charges should be dismissed, and the results of the election should be certified by the NLRB.

QUESTIONS

1. Did the union proponents have the right to wear union insignia under the circumstances of this case? Compare this case situation with the situation in the "Offensive Sweatshirts" case [Case No. 20]. Was there a significant difference in these two case situations?

2. Were the interviews of the plant supervisor permissible under the Act, even if they were nothing more than casual conversations?

3. Were the company's statements concerning the economic consequences of unionization protected as free speech under Section 8(c) of the act, or were they threats aimed at discouraging unionization? Discuss.

4. Were the employer's actions in this case either singly or collectively of sufficient magnitude to justify an NLRB order not to certify the results of the representation election? Why, or why not?

6. DISCRIMINATION CHARGES DURING A UNION ORGANIZING CAMPAIGN

COMPANY: Northwest Propane Co., Inc., Farmington, Michigan

UNION: Local 614, International Brotherhood of Teamsters, Chauffeurs, Warehousemen and Helpers of America

BACKGROUND

During a union organizing campaign at the Northwest Propane Co. of Farmington, Michigan, a series of events occurred which brought unfair labor practice charges filed by the Teamsters Union against the company. Each of these incidents will be described separately, although they did not necessarily occur sequentially as presented in this case.

The Discharge of Employee Don Meyers[1]

Northwest Propane Company sells propane gas and related products at Farmington, Michigan. Its business is seasonal, and its peak season occurs between November and March. During the slack season, the company usually reduces its work force.

Company offices and the main plant are situated along a main highway known as Northwestern Highway. The office building is approached by a large driveway which leads from the highway and passes along the front of the office. Offices of the company president and other executives are in the front of the office building, directly overlooking the driveway and also the highway.

Around May 12, 1971 Rollie Johnson, one of the company's employees, phoned an organizer of the union. The organizer advised Johnson that he would go to the company's premises the following day to handbill and to solicit authorization card signatures.

---

1 All names are disguised.

At around 4 p.m. the next day, the organizer went to the company's premises and stayed there for about an hour and forty minutes. During the time that he was handbilling, he wore a bright blue jacket on the back of which was written the word "Teamsters" in gold letters. He stationed himself at the driveway entrance leading into the company's property. While he was there the company president, Ken Schader, drove into the property, parked his car on the driveway, looked in the organizer's direction, and then went into the main office building. Sometime later, Schader and office manager Anton Gibson repeatedly looked out the window of the office building to observe the union organizer.

While the organizer was handbilling the employees, employee Rollie Johnson, employee Jack Tobin and a third employee, Don Meyers, left the company premises in Meyers' Mustang car. After driving south on Northwestern Highway, they reversed direction and crossed the highway stopping on a crossover area approximately 150 feet from the company office. Johnson, who initially had contacted the organizer, waved his hand and called to the organizer; Johnson was seated on the passenger side of the front seat of the car. Tobin, who was seated on the right hand passenger seat in the back of the car, also called and waved to the organizer. At this moment, both Tobin and Meyers observed President Schader standing in his office window.

After the union organizer had left the company premises, he met with a group of employees at a local restaurant. All the employees present signed authorization cards. These employees included Tobin, Johnson and Meyers.

The following afternoon, company President Ken Schader terminated Meyers. Schader told Meyers he had been terminated because business had slowed down, and the employer could not use Meyers' services. Meyers was employed as a truck driver, and he had a weak, defective left hand which made it difficult for him to load and unload gas cylinders. Schader reminded Meyers that he had been told previously in April that his employment would not be continued during the upcoming slack season.

The Discharge of Employee Jack Tobin

Employee Jack Tobin heated his home with propane gas and also owned a rental property heated by propane gas. Tobin purchased the gas for his two properties from Northwest Propane Company.

In early May, Tobin received a call from the owner of the property adjacent to his rental property. The owner asked Tobin to remove three propane gas cylinders which were lying near the rear of Tobin's rental property. These cylinders had been ordered by Tobin for use at his rental property. However, the rental property was vacant, and the cylinders had not been hooked up but were lying unattended on the ground for several months. That same day Tobin loaded the cylinders in his car and brought them to his residence.

On the Monday after Tobin took the three propane gas cylinders home, he told office manager Gibson that he had the cylinders at his home. Subsequently, pursuant to instructions by Gibson, Tobin brought two of the cylinders back to the company storage area, but the third cylinder remained at his home.

A few days later, because Tobin had not received his own bulk delivery of propane gas from the company, Tobin told the office manager that if he did not receive his bulk delivery, he would probably have to hook up the remaining cylinder to maintain heat and hot water in his home. Gibson replied that he could do so. Subsequently, Tobin hooked up the remaining cylinder to the heating system in his home.

On May 25, President Schader discharged Tobin for "stealing" this gas cylinder.

The Discharge of Employee Joyce Dees

In late May, the office manager, Anton Gibson, told the bookkeeper and another employee that, "If the union gets in, the employer will close the business!" The bookkeeper, Joyce Dees, was one of the union's supporters. On June 7, she went to President Schader and complained that during the preceding several weeks, office manager Gibson had followed her whenever she went to the restroom or got a drink of water. In response to Schader's inquiry, Dees stated that the office manager had been following her because she was talking to her fellow employees about the union.

Later the same day, Dees was informed by Schader and Gibson that she was being discharged effective immediately. They told her that she was discharged because she had various work deficiencies, including failure to finish her bookkeeping work on time, rudeness to customers, and general disruption of the office by talking to other employees about the union on company time.

The union filed unfair labor practice charges on behalf of each of these employees and also a general complaint against the company alleging an overall pattern of antiunion activity.

POSITION OF THE UNION

In the case of the employee Don Meyers, the union claimed that Meyers had been illegally discharged in violation of Section 8(a) (3) of the Labor Management Relations Act because of his union activities. The union claimed that Meyers was discharged because he was observed as the owner and driver of a car whose passengers waved to the union organizer, and because Meyers had signed a union authorization card. The union claimed that this discharge action was part of the company's total pattern of activities designed to interfere with and discriminate against the union organizing campaign. The union requested that Meyers be reinstated and be given full back pay for employment that he had missed.

In the case of employee Jack Tobin, the union argued that Tobin similarly was discharged because of his union activities, thus violating Section 8(a) (3). The union claimed that Tobin did not steal any propane gas cylinders. Tobin had been a good employee for four years, and his discharge did not occur until after the company had learned that Tobin was involved in the union campaign and a request for a representational election had been filed. Concerning the alleged stealing of the gas cylinder, the union claimed that this was strictly a fabricated charge and pointed out that Tobin actually had received permission from the office manager to hook up the one cylinder to his heating system in his home. The union requested that Tobin be reinstated with full back pay for any period of employment missed.

In the case of employee Joyce Dees, the union again claimed that the company had violated Section 8(a) (3) by discharging Dees for her union sympathies and activities, not the alleged work deficiencies which company management had stated. Dees had been a satisfactory employee for over five years. The union argued that she could have been discharged at any time previously in the five years for work deficiencies. The union also pointed out that office manager Gibson had told Dees that her talking about the union with fellow employees on company time was part of the company's reasons for taking disciplinary action against her. The union requested that Dees be reinstated to the position of bookkeeper, and that she be granted full pay for wages missed during the time of her termination.

The union also filed a general complaint which claimed that the company had violated Section 8(a) (1) of the act by continued surveillance of its employees' union activities and by threatening employees with closing of the business if a union was successful in the organizing drive. The discharge actions against the three employees cited previously were part of a concerted total management effort to defeat the union. The union requested that the company be ordered to cease and desist from discouraging union membership and, in any other ways, from interfering with the process of having a fair representation election held at the company premises.

POSITION OF THE COMPANY

The company denied that it had embarked on a systematic effort to spy on employees involved in union activity. The company claimed that its actions taken against the three employees in this case were reasonable and fair under the circumstances and only coincidental with the union organizing campaign.

In the case of employee Don Meyers, the company pointed out that he had been told that his employment would not be continued during the slack season. Meyers was not physically capable of performing as much work or of performing his work as satisfactorily as other employees because of his defective left hand. The fact that Meyers was observed riding in a car with two other employees who waved to a union organizer was not related to the termination of Meyers. The company claimed that Meyers' termination was strictly due to economic reasons, plus the fact that Meyers was not physically capable of carrying out the required job duties.

In the case of employee Jack Tobin, the company claimed that this discharge action was strictly for the attempted theft of the gas cylinder involved in the case. The company claimed that it was clearly against company policy for any employee to have unauthorized private possession of company-owned gas cylinders for private use. There was a communications misunderstanding between Tobin and the office manager concerning the hooking up of the cylinder to his private premises. All of the three cylinders in question should have been returned to the company premises, since they were not being utilized at Tobin's rental property where they had been delivered. Tobin knew that he had no right to hook up the cylinder at his home, but he did so anyway. Consequently, claimed the company, Tobin was discharged for his actions which the company considered to be as "stealing the cylinder," and the discharge was not due to his union activities.

Concerning employee Joyce Dees, the company again claimed that she was discharged for work deficiencies, and not for union activities. Dees had been wasting considerable time talking to employees about the union on company time; she knew she was not permitted to do this. Her discharge was the culmination of various types of poor job performance which had existed over a long period of time. The fact that her discharge came partly as a result of her talking to other employees about the union was because this was "the straw which broke the camel's back." The company further claimed that its statement to Dees regarding closing the business was meant not as a threat, but rather it was a reflection of the fact that increased operating costs associated with a union in its situation might cause the company to go out of business.

The company claimed that it had not violated the Labor Management Relations Act by its various actions and that all of the unfair labor practice charges against it should be dismissed.

QUESTIONS

1. Evaluate the union charges of unfair labor practices concerning each of the three employees. What remedies, if any, should be effected?
2. What is meant by the union's charge of the company's "total pattern of activities" designed to interfere with and discriminate against the union organizing compaign?
3. How can the NLRB determine whether the incidents were isolated or part of a systematic management effort in violation of the law? Discuss.
4. Why must the burden of proof in this case rest upon company management to demonstrate that its actions were for reasons that clearly did not have an antiunion origin?

7. THE PREELECTION POLL CONTEST

COMPANY: *Glamorise Foundations, Inc., Williamsport, Pennsylvania*

UNION: *International Ladies' Garment Workers Union, AFL–CIO*

BACKGROUND

A representational election was to be held among employees at the Williamsport plant of Glamorise Foundations, Inc. The election was scheduled to be held during the last week of July 1971. On June 30, 1971 about a month before the scheduled election, company management sent a notice to the employees announcing a contest. This contest was one in which employees were invited to guess the number of "no" votes which would be cast in the forthcoming union representational election. Supervisory personnel helped distribute flyers to employees captioned in large letters as follows: "IT IS IMPORTANT TO VOTE. HERE'S A CONTEST TO INTEREST YOU TO VOTE ON ELECTION." Among other things, the flyer also stated, "We all know that the employees will reject the International Ladies' Garment Workers Union. But who can give us the score?" The winning entry was to be identified by a numbered receipt which the employee was to retain, and employees were told that it was not necessary for them to sign their names. The employees were given until the close of the following day to deposit their entries in a box placed near the plant's timeclocks. After the end of the next day, the box was sealed and it was not to be opened until after the election results were known. A $50 U.S. savings bond and a $25 bond were to be given to the two employees who came closest to guessing the total of "no" votes cast in the election.

Upon announcement of this contest, the union immediately protested the contest as being illegally interfering with and trying to influence the outcome of the election.

Subsequently, the company decided not to open the sealed box in which the contest entries were placed because a union representative stated at the conclusion of the union representation voting in late July that he was filing objections to the election outcome because of the company-sponsored contest. Management decided to keep the contest entries sealed pending a ruling by the National Labor Relations Board. The union did lose the election and immediately filed unfair labor practice charges against the company relating to the preelection contest.

POSITION OF THE UNION

The union filed exceptions to the outcome of the election under Section 9(c) of the Labor Management Relations Act, claiming that the company contest was illegal interference in violation of Section 8 (a) (1) of the act. The union claimed that the company contest essentially was a poll of employee sentiment concerning the outcome of the election. This type of poll, in the union's opinion, was a type of "straw ballot" which was aimed at influencing employees in their decision concerning union representation. Further, the union claimed that the poll was designed to help the company obtain information concerning union sentiments, since employees would talk about the various votes that would be taken, and a general discussion of estimates was sure to come to the attention of the company. The union argued that the poll was a very significant factor in the result of the election, and it requested that the results of the election be set aside and that a new election be held free of any illegal employer interference.

POSITION OF THE COMPANY

The company contended that the contest which it sponsored was not a private poll of employee sentiment. The company claimed that it was merely a type of "raffle" intended to stimulate interest in the election, and therefore the election should be permitted to stand on its merits. No employee was coerced to participate in the poll, and safeguards were included to guard the identity of any employee until after the actual representational election was held. There was no intent on the part of the company to interfere illegally with the free choice of the employees concerning the matter of union representation. The company claimed that the union was simply using this issue as a means to obtain another election. The company requested that the unfair labor practice charges be dismissed, and that the election results be certified.

QUESTIONS

1. Was the company poll a type of "straw ballot" aimed at influencing employees in their decision concerning union representation? Why, or why not?

2. Evaluate the union charge that such a poll might help the company obtain information concerning union sentiments, even though the poll itself was secret and results would not be available until after the election.

3. Evaluate the company's argument that the poll was merely a type of "raffle," and that the union was simply using the issue as a device to obtain another election.

4. Is there a difference in the legal right of a union to try to measure employee sentiments concerning union representation prior to an election as compared to management's right in this regard? Discuss.

5. If the Board should rule that the company preelection poll was illegal interference, was the interference of sufficient magnitude to justify a new election? Why, or why not?

8. RESTRICTIVE USE OF THE PLANT'S PUBLIC ADDRESS SYSTEM

COMPANY: *The Heath Co., a wholly owned subsidiary of Schlumberger Technology Corp., St. Joseph, Michigan*

UNION: *United Steelworkers of America, AFL–CIO*

BACKGROUND

A union representation election was scheduled for October 27, 1970 to be held in the Heath Company plant. The proposed bargaining unit consisted of about 700 production and maintenance employees. A few weeks before the election, the company personnel director prepared a list of about 25 to 35 supervisors and nonbargaining unit employees. An administrator in the personnel department subsequently contacted these individuals for the purpose of tape recording antiunion speeches for broadcast by the company over its public address system. About a dozen of those individuals contacted agreed to make such speeches for the company. No management representative was present during the 12 separate taping sessions. Although the antiunion talks were monitored before being broadcast by company management, there was no attempt by management to write or otherwise influence the content of the speeches.

Six of the 12 taped speeches were played over the company's plant public address system on October 22 and 23. They consisted of noncoercive but otherwise favorable testimonials on the company's behalf and against unionization.

All but one of the speechmakers were supervisors within the meaning of Section 2 (11) of the Labor Management Relations Act. The exception was Maria Hoover,[1] a nonbargaining unit employee.

After listening during work time to the broadcast of the antiunion speeches over the public address system in the plant, several employees asked an official of the personnel department whether they could use

---

[1] Name is disguised.

95

the system to reply to those testimonials. They were denied access to
the system on the ground that only management was entitled to use it.
In any event, they were told, other means were available for contacting prounion employees. The employees who asked to use the public
address system were given permission to use the cafeteria during lunch
to present the union's case to their fellow employees.

On October 27, the representation election was held. Of the 692
eligible voters in a unit of all production and maintenance workers in
the plant, 293 cast valid ballots for, and 355 cast valid ballots against,
the union. There were five challenged ballots and two were void.

Subsequently the union filed unfair labor practice charges, contending that the company had illegally interfered in the election
process.

POSITION OF THE UNION

The union contended that the actions of the company constituted
interference in violation of Section 8 (a) (1) of LMRA. Specifically,
the union held that it should not have been denied access to the
public address system to reply to the six antiunion testimonials given
over the system by procompany employees. These testimonials, given
only several days prior to the election, were, in the union's opinion,
very influential in the outcome of the election, which was very close.

The union claimed that the use of the public address system by the
company to present "antiunion propaganda" during work hours to
all employees was an unfair advantage. The public address system
should have been made equally available to the union, but the company prohibited such access in violation of the union's rights.

The union also objected to the company's actions in soliciting
supervisors and nonbargaining unit employees to deliver the speeches.
The union particularly claimed that the company had coerced a nonsupervisory employee, Maria Hoover, to deliver an antiunion speech.
This, too, claimed the union, violated Section 8 (a) (1) of the act. For
these reasons, the union argued that the results of the representation
election should be set aside, that a new representation election should
be held, and that the company should be ordered to stop its illegal
interference during the period prior to the next election.

POSITION OF THE COMPANY

The company held that it did not engage in illegal preelection conduct in soliciting its supervisors to tape record and broadcast state-

ments over the public address system. These statements, by the union's admission, were not coercive and did not include any threats or promises of benefit to workers dependent upon the outcome of the union representation election.

The company claimed that it did not exert pressure on Maria Hoover to make the statement, which she agreed to do. Further, her statement was only about a minute in duration, and it could hardly have had any major impact on the outcome of the representation election.

But, primarily, the company claimed that the union had no inherent right to utilize the company's public address system on an equal basis to reply to the six statements which the union considered to be antiunion. Although it was not required to do so, the company did permit union supporters to use the cafeteria during lunch time to present their views. This afforded reasonable opportunity to union supporters to explain their positions to employees.

The company requested that the unfair labor practice charges be dismissed, and that the results of the representation election be upheld.

QUESTIONS

1. Should the union have been given equal access to the company public address system to reply to the antiunion statements made by the company supervisory personnel? Why, or why not?

2. Evaluate the union's arguments that the alleged antiunion statements by supervisors were "very influential in the outcome of the election" and constituted an "unfair advantage" to the company side.

3. Was the company guilty of an unfair labor practice in soliciting supervisors and nonbargaining unit employees to deliver the so-called antiunion speeches? Why, or why not?

4. Was the company obligated to permit union supporters to use the cafeteria during the lunchtime to present their prounion views? Did this provide a reasonable balance for the speeches made over the company public address system by the supervisory and nonbargaining unit personnel?

5. If the NLRB rules that unfair labor practice charge or charges should be upheld, were the violations of sufficient magnitude to justify a new election? Discuss.

9. THE DISCHARGE OF THE NEWLY HIRED EMPLOYEE

COMPANY: *L. J. Folkins Company, A Standard Oil Company Distributor, Spokane, Washington*

UNION: *International Brotherhood of Teamsters, Chauffeurs, Warehousemen & Helpers of America*

BACKGROUND

The company distributes petroleum products in Spokane, Washington, under contract with Standard Oil of California. On Sunday, February 11, 1973 Al Benton,[1] a delivery route driver who had just quit his job with the company, told his friend Bob Bruckner that there might be a job for the latter if he appeared at the employer's facility the following morning. Bruckner did so, and he was hired.

On the morning of February 12, Bruckner began riding with one of the company's other drivers, Bill Evers. However, shortly after, Evers' truck broke down, and the company manager, Gene Calhoun, told Bruckner to ride with another driver, Alvin Commons. Bruckner spent the balance of the day with this driver, who mentioned a meeting to be held at the union hall that evening.

That evening, Bruckner and three others went to the union hall. The union obtained signed authorization cards from Bruckner and two others. The following day, two union representatives visited company manager Calhoun in his office. They requested recognition of the union as bargaining agent for a unit consisting of five truck drivers employed by the company. They furnished Calhoun with copies of three authorization cards that the union had obtained from among the five truck drivers employed by the company. Company manager Calhoun later asked each employee whose signature appeared on a card if his signature was genuine. Each said that it was.

Bob Bruckner was riding with another driver on February 13. At about noon, Mr. Calhoun met Bruckner and told him that he "could

---

[1] All names are disguised.

see no opening." He explained that it appeared, from information received that morning, that he had just lost a package lubrication contract with the City of Spokane. Further, the "energy crisis" and an attendant limitation of production availability would cause reduced business for the company. Additionally, the truck that had broken down the day before would be "down" for a considerable period. Bruckner was terminated effective at 5:00 p.m.

Subsequently, the union filed unfair labor practice charges against the company claiming that Bob Bruckner had been discharged for signing a union authorization card. The company's action allegedly was in violation of Sections 8 (a) (3) and 8 (a) (1) of the Labor Management Relations Act.[2]

POSITION OF THE COMPANY

The company argued that its reasons for terminating Bob Bruckner on February 13, 1973 were motivated solely by economic reasons, not because of Bruckner's union status. According to the company, Bruckner was hired as a temporary, not a permanent employee replacement.

Company manager Calhoun claimed that he had agreed to give the newly hired employee a job in anticipation of a warehouse audit to be conducted by Standard Oil of California on February 14. However, a combination of circumstances came to the company's attention on February 12, which necessitated the termination of Bruckner's employment. The company was informed by Standard Oil that the warehouse audit was postponed. Therefore, Bruckner's services in the warehouse would not be needed. The company also learned that day of the loss of a package lubrication contract with the City of Spokane, which was a loss of some 8% of the company's anticipated business. The breakdown of one of its trucks made it economically impossible to keep Bruckner on the payroll in any capacity. The overall uncertainty of the energy crisis at this juncture contributed to management's decision to terminate Bruckner, a newly hired employee with only two days of service with the company.

The company argued that the unfair labor practice charges against it should be dismissed, since its motives in this matter were economically justified.

---

2 *Note:* The union did not file charges at this time concerning the question of whether the company should be required to recognize the union for purposes of collective bargaining. A representational election subsequent to this incident was later conducted by the NLRB.

POSITION OF THE UNION

The union argued that the company had violated Section 8 (a) (3), and therefore also Section 8 (a) (1) of the act, by discharging Bob Bruckner. The union claimed that Bruckner had been hired for a permanent position, not as a temporary employee as claimed by the company. Regardless, Bruckner's discharge occurred on the same day that the union demanded recognition and the employer had learned that Bruckner had signed a union card. Since the union had received signed authorization cards from three employees in a proposed five-employee unit, the discharge of one card-signer would destroy the union's majority. Bruckner, as the most recently hired employee, was chosen by the company for discharge.

The union argued that the company's reasons alleging that Bruckner was hired on a temporary basis were not persuasive. Bruckner was hired immediately after another driver had quit. Bruckner never worked in the warehouse, but spent all his time accompanying other drivers.

Further, the union claimed that the loss of the city package lubrication contract amounted to a loss of perhaps 1 percent of the employer's business, not the 8 percent indicated by the employer. Regardless, the company knew on February 12, and perhaps earlier, that the loss of this contract was likely.

With respect to the unavailability of the broken-down truck for several days, the union said that a standby truck was ready for use. The postponement of a warehouse audit was irrelevant to the hiring or retention of a truck driver, and the company knew of the "energy crisis" weeks before the new employee was hired.

For all of these reasons, the union claimed that Bob Bruckner really had been discharged because of signing a union authorization card. This discharge was in clear violation of the act. The union asked that Mr. Bruckner be restored to his position with full back pay for the time off that he was illegally discharged.

QUESTIONS

1. Were the company's arguments of economic justification for terminating the new employee persuasive?
2. Why is the timing of the discharge of the new employee of critical significance in determining the company's motives and actions in this dispute? Discuss.

3. Are temporary employees protected by the provisions of the Labor Management Relations Act? Why, or why not?

4. Although the union apparently did not contest the action, was the company's query of each employee concerning the signatures on the union's organization cards in violation of the Labor Management Relations Act? Why, or why not?

10. THE EMPLOYER'S PREDICTIONS AND THE REPRESENTATION ELECTION

COMPANY: Lenkurt Electric Co., San Carlos, California

UNION: San Francisco & Vicinity Printing Pressmen, Offset Workers and Assistants' Union No. 24, International Printing Pressmen's & Assistants' Union of North America, AFL–CIO

BACKGROUND

The Lenkurt Electric Company is engaged in the design and manufacture of communications equipment for sale in interstate commerce. It maintains a manufacturing plant at San Carlos, California. At the time of this case, the company employed approximately 3,500 employees of whom some 2,800 were represented by various unions. The remaining personnel were primarily supervisory and administrative personnel, engineers and other professional employees, and the employees in department 83, the publications service department. The employees in department 83 prepare and publish the printed material which the company ships with the products it sells.

On August 29, 1966 the union filed a representation petition with the NLRB seeking an election for certification as the bargaining representative of 14 unrepresented employees in the Publications Production division of department 83. These employees operated certain printing equipment used in the production and duplication of printed matter. After a representation hearing, the regional director for the Board ordered that an election be held on October 14, 1966.

About two weeks before the election, the manager of the department, Mr. Theo Herald,[1] held a series of informal meetings with various employees to discuss the unionization issue.

---

[1] Name is disguised.

In his conversations with the printing department employees, Mr. Herald suggested that if the employees were to unionize, it was possible that a more strict regimentation of working hours would be implemented. He explained that under the present working conditions, company policy with respect to coffee breaks, lunch hours and conversations while working had been fairly casual in the printing department, while employees were strictly controlled as to coffee breaks, lunch hours and general attention to their labors in the unionized departments of the plant. Mr. Herald further explained that if the printing department employees were unionized, the basis of their compensation would likely be changed from monthly salary to that of an hourly rate, which was the basis for compensation of other union employees in the plant. Also, employees should anticipate that there would be a more strict observance of time worked, rest periods, late arrivals and similar matters. These comments were based largely on his own personal observations of other employees in the plant who were unionized and had gone to an hourly basis of compensation.

Mr. Herald further suggested that working conditions might be made more difficult as a result of unionization, because the company might seek to reduce operating costs by using less expensive paper stock in the printing department. He explained that, while the employees usually worked with "premium stock" paper, if it were necessary to reduce costs he would probably introduce lower quality stock, which might cause more problems for the operators of the various machines.

In the course of these meetings, Mr. Herald also stated that sick leave and other fringe benefits, particularly the company's policy of providing working smocks and laundry service to the employees, might be changed by unionization. With respect to sick leave, Mr. Herald explained that it was his understanding that employees with the International Brotherhood of Electrical Workers Union, which represented most of the employees in the plant, did not get paid if they did not come to work. The possibility of discontinuing the laundry service and working smocks was described as potentially necessary to reduce costs and to "remain competitive."

Subsequently, the representational election was held as scheduled. The election resulted in a rejection of the union by a vote of seven to five, with two ballots being challenged. The union thereafter filed an unfair labor practice charge and objections to certain conduct of the company which allegedly affected the outcome of the election.

POSITION OF THE UNION

The union contended that manager Theo Herald's remarks to employees in the two weeks prior to the representation election violated Section 8(a) (1) of the Labor Management Relations Act. Thus, the union held that Mr. Herald's remarks "restrained and coerced these employees in the free exercise of their rights under Section 7."

The union argued that the preelection statements made by Mr. Herald, considered in the context in which they were made, constituted an implied threat that the company would deprive its employees of certain benefits and employment and would impose more rigid working conditions if the union were elected as the employees' bargaining representative.

The union argued that the company should be found guilty of an unfair labor practice, and that the results of the representational election should be set aside. As a remedy, the union argued that the company should be required to recognize the union as the bargaining agent for the Publications Production division employees, or at the very least, a new representational election should be held free of employer interference.

POSITION OF THE COMPANY

The company contended that Manager Theo Herald's statements simply were "fair comment and permissible predictions of the consequences of unionization." The company held that such statements were protected under Section 8 (c) of the Labor Management Relations Act which states:

The expressing of any views, argument or opinion, or the dissemination thereof, whether in written, printed, graphic, or visual form, shall not constitute or be evidence of an unfair labor practice under any of the provisions of this Act, if such expression contains no threat of reprisal or force or promise of benefit.

The company argued that Mr. Herald's statements did not constitute either an expressed or implied threat of retaliation should the union gain bargaining rights at Lenkurt Electric Co. His statements merely were predictions of possible disadvantages which might arise from economic necessity or because of union demands or policies, and all of these predictions had factual basis. The company requested that the unfair labor practice charges should be dismissed.

QUESTIONS

1. Did Mr. Herald have the legal right to discuss the question of unionization with his employees? Why, or why not?

2. Were the statements made by Mr. Herald in the course of his meetings
   with employees within the permissible limits under Section (8) (c) of
   the Labor Management Relations Act, or were they implied threats
   that were illegal under the act? Discuss.

3. Why is it difficult for the NLRB to draw a clear dividing line between
   the provisions of Section 8(c) as compared to the requirements of
   Section 8 (a) (1)?

4. Evaluate the company argument that Mr. Herald's statements were
   "predictions of possible disadvantages which might arise from economic necessity or because of union demands or policies, and all of
   these predictions had factual basis."

11. WERE THE FIVE "SUPERVISORS" A COLLECTIVE BARGAINING UNIT?

COMPANY: *Crimptex Incorporated, San German, Puerto Rico*

"BARGAINING UNIT": *Rafael Vega, Ramon M. Cuevas, Luis A. Nazario, Angel Cruz, Angel Gonzalez; and International Ladies' Garment Workers Union, AFL–CIO**

BACKGROUND

Although the offices of the president of Crimptex, Inc. are head-quartered in the state of Rhode Island, Crimptex is a Puerto Rican corporation with its principal office and plant at San German, Puerto Rico. Since 1958, the company has been engaged in the manufacture of yarn at the San German location.

In 1962, when operating during normal production periods, 25 machine operators were employed at San German to run 11 machine units used to produce Canlon, Crimptex's major product. Normally, three eight-hour shifts were scheduled, with starting times of 8 a.m., 4 p.m., and midnight; eight to ten machine operators were employed on a rotating basis on each shift. During the day shift, two maintenance mechanics were employed in the machine shop. A single maintenance mechanic was on duty during the other two shifts.

Rafael Vega, Ramon M. Cuevas, Luis A. Nazario, Angel Cruz, and Angel Gonzalez were assigned on a rotating basis to duties as maintenance mechanics on the three operating shifts. The company gave these men the job classification title of "supervisor," which was accepted by them as appropriate.

In 1958, Vega, Gonzalez, and Cruz attended a course in the United States where they were trained in the maintenance and operation of the machinery used in the San German plant. Upon their return, they were made responsible for assisting in the training of production

---

* The names of all individuals have been disguised.

106

employees. In addition, they repaired, adjusted, maintained, and serviced production machinery. Also, daily during the operators' relief and half-hour lunch periods, they performed production tasks, substituting for the operators.

On weekdays, during the hours from approximately 8 a.m. to 5 or 6 p.m., the plant manager, Henry Pelletier and/or his assistant Henry Enriquez were on duty in the plant. The "supervisors" on duty took their directions and instructions directly from either Pelletier or Enriquez when they were at the plant.

However, after 5 or 6 p.m. and on the weekends or holidays, neither the plant manager nor his assistant was normally at the plant except for unscheduled appearances. Occasionally, Pelletier would come to the plant at these times because of a telephone request from the maintenance mechanic "supervisor" on duty. It was during nighttime hours, weekends, and holidays that the maintenance mechanics as "supervisors" were technically responsible for the plant's performance.

The Certified Bargaining Unit

In June 1959, Crimptex, Inc. and the International Ladies' Garment Workers Union, AFL–CIO, executed an agreement for a consent election to be conducted in a unit described as:

> All production and maintenance employees employed by the Company at its plant at San German, Puerto Rico, excluding all professional and clerical employees, guards, and supervisors as defined in the Act.

The question of whether to include Rafael Vega et al. in this unit was brought up and discussed by the company, the union, and an NLRB agent. It was agreed, by the union and management, that the names of Rafael Vega, Ramon Cuevas, Luis Nazario, Angel Cruz, and Angel Gonzalez would not appear on the representation eligibility list. Vega and Cruz asked Pelletier if they could vote in the election; they were told that they could not because they were "supervisors."

The election was held on July 2, 1959 and the employees voted to be represented by the International Ladies' Garment Workers Union. The names of Vega et al. did not appear on the eligibility list used in conjunction with this election. The five "supervisors" continued to perform their duties as before and were not made part of the ILGW Union.

Circumstances Leading to Layoffs

During the month of July 1962, Crimptex's operations entered a seasonal lull, and production was scheduled on the basis of a two- or three-day work week. In August, all operations were halted completely, and all personnel were laid off, including the five "supervisors."

On August 19, 1962 the five "supervisors" sent a jointly signed letter to Henry Pelletier, the plant manager, demanding a management clarification of their authority and responsibilities as "supervisors." They also demanded on their behalf the following: increased salaries, improved vacations and sick leave benefits, and assurances against periodic layoffs. Pelletier responded to this letter on August 21, 1962, by informing the "supervisors" that their letter had been referred to the president of the company; he assured them that he (Pelletier) would contact them as soon as he received instructions.

After Pelletier received instructions by telephone, he arranged for a meeting and met with Vega and the others at his office on September 7, 8, and 10.

At their first meeting on September 7, Pelletier discussed with the five "supervisors" their demands. Pelletier offered them 2 weeks' vacation as compared to their present $1\frac{1}{2}$ weeks, 15 days' sick pay, and 3 or 4 days' guaranteed pay during slack periods. Also, he requested that they return to work, since production orders had increased and their services were needed.

The five men responded by saying that they accepted the wage, vacation, and sick benefits offer; but they demanded, as a condition of their return to work, a guarantee of a five-day work week during slack periods, and that the benefits orally promised should be put in writing. Pelletier refused to accept these demands, and after an hour's discussion the meeting ended with the parties in disagreement only on the latter point—that the agreement be put in writing.

The second and third meetings ended much like the first, with both sides unable to agree that the terms be reduced to writing. However, before the third meeting on September 10, the "supervisors" sent a letter to the president of the company stating that they intended to "stay out of work" until they received a formal and satisfactory answer to their letter of August 19, 1962.

Upon being shown a copy of the letter, Pelletier said, "That is the best thing you can do; let's wait, then, for an answer to that letter." He suggested that they resume work on the basis of the benefits orally granted. The employees refused to work unless their demands had been agreed to in writing by the president of the company.

On the following day, September 11, Pelletier sent a telegram to Rafael Vega which read as follows:

> This is to confirm personal notice given you yesterday to report to your job in Crimptex on the 8 a.m. shift tomorrow Wednesday.

Each of the other "supervisors" received identical telegrams except for the reporting time. During the day, Pelletier and Enriquez talked individually with Gonzalez and Cruz, and with Nazario and Cruz together, telling them "to forget about the rest and go back to work."

That evening, the five men went to the plant and spoke with Pelletier. They again stated their demand that the terms agreed to orally should be put in writing. Pelletier refused to agree to their demand.

On September 13, Pelletier sent the following letter (which is reproduced in part) to each of the five "supervisors."

> Since the day of September 13 has gone by without you having reported to work, notwithstanding the notices given to you, nor your having informed of any impossibility to do so, I understand your not having reported to work demonstrates that you are not interested in continuing working for this company.

On September 18, the group of five men went to the San Juan office of the International Ladies' Garment Workers Union and there spoke with two union officials. Each of the men signed a union authorization card. The following day the five met with Pelletier and unconditionally offered their services, withdrawing their previous demand of a written agreement. Pelletier told them that he had already hired replacements.[1]

Again on September 27, the five men went as a group and offered to return to work unconditionally. Pelletier answered that he had no work for them, since they had been replaced. At this time, however, the men did not inform Pelletier that they had signed ILGWU authorization cards, nor did they request him to recognize and bargain with them as a collective bargaining unit.

Subsequently, in separate charges filed with the NLRB on October

---

[1] Testimony revealed that four men were hired to replace the five "supervisors." One was hired on September 18, another on September 19, and two on September 23. At the time of the case hearing, a permanent replacement for Gonzalez had not yet been hired.

2, 1962 by Rafael Vega, Ramon Cuevas, and Luis Nazario, and separate charges filed on November 8, 1962 by Angel Cruz and Angel
Gonzalez, the five former "supervisors" brought unfair labor practice
charges against Crimptex, Inc. Specifically they claimed that:

1. Rafael Vega et al. constituted a labor organization within the
meaning of Section 2 (5) of the LMRA, since as a group the five men
had negotiated with management concerning wages, hours, and conditions of work.

2. Management had discriminated in regard to the tenure of their
employment, thereby discouraging membership in a labor organization of its employees. Therefore, the company had engaged in unfair
labor practices within the meaning of Sections 8 (a) (1) and 8 (a) (3)
of the act.

POSITION OF THE FIVE "SUPERVISORS"

In their individual charges, the five "supervisors" contended that
they were a group of unrepresented employees who were not included in the original agreement between Crimptex, Inc., and the
International Ladies Garment Workers Union. They claimed that
they were really only maintenance mechanic "leadmen," and not
"supervisors" as defined by the act. However, by their unified efforts
to present their collective and individual interests to Crimptex for
the purpose of discussing economic demands, working conditions,
and grievances, they constituted a bona fide labor organization within the meaning of the act.

Since Crimptex, Inc., and specifically Mr. Pelletier, did recognize
and deal with these five employees collectively with regard to their
wages, hours, and working conditions, the subsequent discharging of
the five employees because of their refusal to return to work, i.e.,
their declaration of a strike against Crimptex, Inc., was in violation
of the act. The company refused to reinstate the employees, although they made an unconditional request that they be given back
their old jobs. Because of these actions, the group's position was that
the company had violated Section 8 (a) (1) and Section 8 (a) (3)
of the Labor Management Relations Act.

The group requested that the company be ordered to return them
to their job positions, and that they be made whole for all lost income
and benefits. Further, the group requested that the company be required to recognize them as a labor organization and to bargain with
them collectively as required by the act.

POSITION OF THE COMPANY

Crimptex, Inc., did not deny any of the basic facts of the case. However, its position was that: (*a*) Rafael Vega, Ramon Cuevas, Luis Nazario, Angel Cruz, and Angel Gonzalez were indeed supervisors as defined by Section 2(11) of the act and therefore not entitled to the protection of provisions of the act; (*b*) they did not constitute a group of "employees" within the precedents set by the NLRB; (*c*) the mere fact that they acted in a united way when they presented common demands did not constitute a recognized labor organization; and (*d*) the discharge of the "supervisors" was for their failure to respond to the employment available and offered to them at the end of the seasonal layoff. The company requested that the unfair labor practice charges should be dismissed.

Testimony at the cases's hearings focused primarily upon the nature and duties of the five "supervisors" at Crimptex. This was relevant to the company's contention that the five men were supervisors within the meaning of Section 2 (11) of the Labor Management Relations Act and thus employees not entitled to the protection of the act.

It was determined that the five men as "supervisors" signed time charts which showed the hour when a machine was started, when it was shut down, and how much yarn was produced. Both the "supervisor" and the operator were required to initial the entries.

If an operator did not report for work in the evening or if one became ill while at work, the "supervisor" would report this by telephone to Pelletier, who either obtained a replacement or ordered adjustments to be made, with instructions to the "supervisor" as how to accomplish the adjustments. If the "supervisor" was not particularly busy that evening, he would occasionally substitute for the missing operator and not call Pelletier at all.

The "supervisors" had the responsibility of seeing to it that the operators were at their work stations and finding out why they were not. But they lacked authority to independently discipline such employees; they were expected to report any violations, absences, indolence, etc., to Pelletier through the use of written reports.

Crimptex displayed rules on the employee bulletin board for a number of years that required all employees to secure permission from their "supervisor" when absent or late, to abide by his instructions, and to receive permission from their "supervisor" when in doubt about job standards.

The "supervisors" also made recommendations concerning the discharge of employees. In one instance, Gonzalez sent an employee home before his shift was over because the employee had "incurred an act of discipline" and "was very undisciplined" to Gonzalez. On another occasion another employee was discharged because he assaulted Vega after the midnight shift was over. Vega had called this employee's attention to the fact that he was spending an excessive amount of time in the washroom. Pelletier testified that both employee discharges resulted from the recommendations of the "supervisors" involved.

The company claimed that unless the men classified by the company as "supervisors" actually possessed supervisory powers, some eight to ten employees would have been working two night shifts and weekends without responsible supervisory direction.

QUESTIONS

1. What is the key issue upon which this entire situation rests? What are the precedent-setting implications of this case?
2. What is the meaning of the term "supervisor" as defined under the Labor Management Relations Act? Why were supervisors excluded from the protection of the act?
3. How might a company avoid situations such as this in establishing which employees are supervisors and which are not supervisors?
4. What constitutes a collective bargaining unit? Discuss.

12. A QUESTION OF "ROLL-BACK" RIGHTS

COMPANY: *E. I. duPont De Nemours, Florence, South Carolina*

UNION: *Local No. 382, International Brotherhood of Electrical Workers, AFL–CIO*

BACKGROUND

In 1959, the company opened its plant in Florence, South Carolina. The entire plant was nonunion and remained so until the fall of 1971. From the beginning, the company advanced its employees through a seniority and progression system. The plant was divided into various work unit groups, and employees were placed in job levels, for promotion and pay purposes, ranging from I (lowest) to VIII (highest). The employees would acquire plantwide seniority from the time they were hired and work group seniority from the time they were placed in a certain work group. By using both types of seniority, an employee could advance not only within his or her own work group but could bid for transfers to other work groups within the plant. In the event of a layoff within a work group, an employee's work group seniority controlled who left the group. Although an employee may have lacked sufficient seniority to retain employment in a work group, the employee was permitted to "bump back" or "roll back" to a plantwide labor pool; and by exercising plantwide seniority, one could displace employees within the pool having less plantwide seniority.

Promotion practices differed slightly in two of the work unit groups —the general mechanical group and the control equipment (or control mechanics) group. In those groups, employees who sought to advance up the pay scale were required to undergo a series of tests. A trainee who failed his or her first progression test was rolled back into the plant labor pool where the employee might exercise plant seniority to enter another work group.

In early 1971, the control mechanics group numbered about 28

113

employees out of a total plant employment of some 420 workers. At this time, the control mechanics sought to be designated as a separate bargaining unit within the plant and to be represented by Local No. 382 of the IBEW union. The company opposed this move. On August 27, 1971 the NLRB decided that the control mechanics were entitled to a representation election as a separate bargaining unit. The election was scheduled for September 23, 1971.

On September 21, 1971 two days before the election, the control mechanics were required to attend a company-called meeting in the plant conference room. During the meeting, they were addressed by the plant manager, Arnold Soll.[1] Among other things, Soll told the control mechanics that the union was not needed, and that if it came in, "all present benefits, including roll-back rights, would have to be negotiated from the bottom up." Soll also said, in effect, that if the union came in, the company would "hire and fire from the gate" with respect to their work group, and that if one of them failed a progression test, he would have no right to be rolled back.

The representation election was held on September 23, 1971 and the union won. On October 1, 1971 the union was certified to represent the control mechanics.

On October 25, 1971 Elmer Kenny, a control mechanic trainee, failed a progression test. Kenny was a member of the bargaining unit, but he was not a member of the union. Under the prior established policy, Kenny would have been rolled back to his prior work group or to the plant labor pool. However, because the control mechanics were now represented by a union, the company took the position that roll-back rights were negotiable matters to which control mechanics were no longer entitled. The company then discussed Kenny's situation with the union. No agreement was reached, and Kenny was discharged on November 26, 1971.

The union filed unfair labor practice charges against the company claiming that the company had violated Sections 8(a) (1) and 8(a) (3) of the Labor Management Relations Act.

POSITION OF THE UNION

The union claimed that the statements of plant manager Arnold Soll in the meeting of September 21, 1971 were "coercive" in nature,

---

[1] The names of all individuals have been disguised.

designed to threaten employees and to influence them to vote against union representation. Even though the union won the representation election, Soll's statements were in direct violation of Section 8(a) (1) of the act. The company's subsequent decision in the situation of Elmer Kenny supported the conclusion that Soll's statements had an antiunion motive.

The union further claimed that company had violated Section 8(a) (3) of the act when it discharged Elmer Kenny, a control mechanic trainee, after he failed a progression test. When the company discussed Kenny's position with the union, the union contended that the previous policy in effect before the control mechanics became unionized should prevail. Under this policy, Kenny would have been "rolled back" or "bumped back" to his prior work group or to a plant labor pool. In the union's view, roll-back rights constituted a term or condition of employment, inasmuch as they had existed since 1959 and had been granted to all employees. The union claimed that the company discriminated against Kenny, since at the time he was discharged (a) he was the only employee who had lost his roll-back rights, and (b) the company acted before it had determined roll-back rights of the entire bargaining unit by bargaining with the union.

The union claimed that the company's motives in this case were antiunion in nature, designed to discourage other employees in the plant from seeking a union to represent them. Further, this was clearly a case of discrimination against a bargaining unit person, since Kenny was the only worker in the entire plant who ever had been denied roll-back rights.

The union argued that the company should be required to return Kenny to his former position in the plant with full restoration of pay, seniority and other rights. The union also requested that as required by Section 8(d) of the act, the company should be ordered to bargain collectively in good faith with the union over the matter of roll-back rights for bargaining unit personnel.

POSITION OF THE COMPANY

The company claimed that the statements of its plant manager Arnold Soll were not threatening or coercive in nature. Section 8(c) of the Labor Management Relations Act permits an employer to communicate to employees his general views about unionism, "if such expression contains no threat of reprisal or force or promise of benefit." Soll's statements were based on his objective analysis of the effect which unionization would have on certain plant policies and practices, including employee roll-back rights.

In the situation involving Elmer Kenny, the company discussed the matter with the union. However, no agreement was reached, and the general problem of how employees from a bargaining unit could be rolled back, if at all, to nonbargaining unit positions was not determined. The company had no choice in the matter but to discharge Kenny, since no position was available within the control mechanics' bargaining unit to which Kenny might be rolled-back. Since there was no agreement with the union to the contrary, the company had the managerial right to discharge Kenny in this situation. The company's discharge action was not antiunion in motivation, but it was a necessary consequence of a broader problem situation which needed eventually to be settled by negotiation.

The company argued that the unfair labor practice charges should be dismissed.

QUESTIONS

1. Were the statements of the plant manager coercive in violation of the act, or merely an objective analysis of the effect which unionization might have on company policies and practices? Discuss.

2. When a union gains representation rights for a group of workers, does this mean that all past and present policies and practices are no longer valid but must be negotiated?

3. Evaluate the union's argument that the company was discriminating against a bargaining unit person, even though the employee in this case was not a member of the union.

4. Discuss the company's argument that it had the managerial right to discharge the bargaining unit employee, since there was no agreement with the union concerning how a bargaining unit person could be rolled back to a nonbargaining unit position.

13. WAS A PREARRANGED AGREEMENT TO RECOGNIZE THREE UNIONS LEGAL?

COMPANY: *Wickes Corporation, Wickes Manufactured Housing Division, Lansing, Michigan*

UNION: *International Union, United Automobile, Aerospace and Agricultural Implement Workers of America (UAW)*

BACKGROUND

Wickes Manufactured Housing, a division of Wickes Corporation, manufactures single-family residential units. Around March 1, 1971 the company opened a plant in Mason, Michigan. Shortly thereafter, management contacted Carpenters Local 1191, Plumbers Local 388, and Electrical Workers (IBEW) Local 655 (collectively referred to as Tri-Trades), and asked for a meeting "to discuss Tri-Trades' labor agreements as they related to modular homes." In early April, the company and Tri-Trades discussed the possibility of recognizing Tri-Trades as the bargaining representative of the employees. The company and Tri-Trades entered into a series of bargaining sessions. On June 15, they reached agreement on the terms of a collective bargaining contract subject to Tri-Trades securing signed authorizations cards from a majority of the employees.

After the contract was agreed upon, Tri-Trades arranged for a union meeting to be held in Holt, Michigan, some 15 miles away from the company's facility. On June 16, the day of the scheduled meeting, a secretary in the company office gave a janitor about 200 Tri-Trades authorization cards and instructed him to attach the cards to the employee's timecards. A foreman also posted a notice informing the employees of a Tri-Trades union meeting scheduled for that evening. At the request of a Tri-Trades representative, the plant manager announced the meeting over the plant address system of the plant.

At the union meeting that evening, Tri-Trades representatives informed employees of the previous negotiations and contract agreement. When a number of employees expressed opposition to certain features of the contract, one of the Tri-Trades representatives stated that, "We had two weeks to ratify a contract . . . or else there would be no union at all at the . . . plant."

Ultimately, a secret ballot "yes" or "no" vote was taken. The voting resulted in a predominantly "yes" vote, 74 to 9. Thereafter, most of the employees present signed and turned in the authorizations cards that had been appended to their timecards.

On the following day, Tri-Trades submitted the signed cards to the company and requested formal recognition. By a letter dated June 22, the company granted recognition, and on June 23, it executed the previously agreed-upon contract.

In the meantime, on the day after the Tri-Trades meeting, (i.e., June 17) one of the employees, Bill Brock,[1] contacted the United Automobile Workers Union (UAW). He was given several UAW authorization cards, and before the start of his shift the following day, he began soliciting card signatures at the plant gate. After Brock had obtained a few signatures, Plant Superintendent Gil Smith approached him. In response to the superintendent's inquiry, Brock stated that he was employed by Wickes Corporation. Superintendent Smith then went through the gate.

Shortly before the start of his shift, Brock stopped soliciting card signatures and went through the gate. However, he was stopped by Smith who told Brock that he had been discharged.

On June 22, Brock returned to the plant to pick up his paycheck. He was met by his foreman, Bob Tora, and Superintendent Smith who told Brock of his "shortcomings as a worker." The next day, however, Brock was offered his job back. Brock accepted the offer, and after he was reinstated Brock was paid for the time he had missed because of his discharge.

Brock was not reinstated to his former job which included layout work. Instead, he was assigned to a sanding operation which was described by Brock as being "the worst job in the plant." Within a few days, however, Brock was reassigned to his previous layout work. But on his first day back on layout work, Brock was given a written reprimand which asserted that an error he had made resulted in "delaying the job three man-hours."

---

1 All names are disguised.

Around July 1, a foreman told another employee to take off a UAW button he was wearing or "he'd be fired."

On July 8, while Brock was talking to another employee concerning some materials that he needed in connection with his work, foreman Tora approached him and told Brock to stop talking about union business on company time. Although Brock denied the foreman's charge, later that day he was given a disciplinary note signed by the foreman and the superintendent. This note stated that Brock had been repeatedly observed by Tora "promoting UAW on company time."

Later, while Brock was punching out, he individually notified other employees who also were punching out that a UAW meeting was going to be held. Two days after the UAW meeting, Wickes Corp. posted a rule which stated that "no solicitation for any reason will be permitted on company property during working time." At the time the rule was posted, one copy of the rule was personally handed to Brock by Tora with the statement, "This is especially for you."

Shortly thereafter the UAW filed unfair labor practice charges against the company, claiming that Wickes Corporation had violated various sections of the Labor Management Relations Act and requesting remedial actions accordingly.

POSITION OF THE UNION

The union maintained that the Wickes Corporation had violated Section 8 (a) (2) of the Labor Management Relations Act by recognizing three unions as representatives of the employees and agreeing to a collective bargaining contract with these unions before a majority of the employees had designated these unions as their bargaining representatives. The union argued that many of the employees did not understand the vote taken on the evening of June 16, 1971 as a vote for ratification or rejection of the contract that had been prearranged between the company and the Tri-Trades unions. The UAW union claimed that the company had no legal right to assume that Tri-Trades had obtained a majority status for employee representation purposes. This prearranged system of recognition and the contract were in clear violation of the obligation of an employer not to interfere with the rights of workers to freely choose which union or unions they wanted to represent them.

The union further argued that the company had violated Section 8 (a) (3) of the act when it discharged a known union adherent (Brock) and reprimanded him twice after reinstating him, since the company's actions were due to Brock's activities on behalf of the UAW. The pattern of activities which company representatives displayed clearly were discriminatory toward Brock and his sympathies with the UAW.

The union also claimed that the company violated Section 8 (a) (1) of the act by posting a "no solicitation" rule, since the purpose of this posting was to curtail union organizing activity on behalf of the UAW. The union noted that, at the time the "no solicitation" rule was posted, Brock was told that the rule was especially for him. Further, the union claimed that, despite the rule, the company continued to permit the holding of football and other "pools," and also permitted Tri-Trades' representatives to solicit dues checkoff authorizations during working time.

The union further claimed that the company violated the act by threatening another employee with discharge if he did not remove the UAW union button that he was wearing.

The union requested that the company be required to withdraw its recognition of Tri-Trades as the bargaining agent for the employees and that its contract with Tri-Trades be declared illegal. The union requested that the company be ordered to cease its discriminatory activities on behalf of Tri-Trades and against employees sympathetic to the UAW. The union further argued that a representation election should be held in the future to establish the true representation rights for employees in the plant.

POSITION OF THE COMPANY

The company claimed that the Tri-Trades unions were the free choice of the employees in their plant. Despite the fact that a general meeting had been held between company management and Tri-Trades, there was a free and open election in which the employees overwhelmingly voted for the Tri-Trades unions to represent them and to ratify the agreement that had been developed between company and Tri-Trades' representatives.

The company claimed that employee Brock had been reprimanded for his failure to perform his job duties and for soliciting employees on behalf of a union on company time. The company claimed that disciplinary actions against Brock had been rescinded, except for those actions which clearly were related to Brock's inability to perform his job properly. The company had the right to prohibit Brock from soliciting employees on company time. The company claimed that it did not object to Brock advocating the UAW union, but that his union solicitation activities had to be conducted off of company premises.

The company requested that the agreement with Tri-Trades be recognized as a valid agreement, and that the unfair labor practices against the company be dismissed.

QUESTIONS

1. Why did the United Automobile Workers Union file unfair practices charges against the company when such charges might just as logically also have been filed against the Tri-Trades unions?
2. Why would the company enter into an agreement of this nature with the Tri-Trades unions prior to an official authorization election from the employees involved?
3. Was the election in which the employees voted for the Tri-Trades unions to represent them and to ratify the prearranged agreement sufficient evidence of their choice to have Tri-Trades as the legal bargaining agent for the employees? Discuss.
4. What decision should the NLRB reach in this case? What remedial actions, if any, should be taken?

14. A REFUSAL TO BARGAIN CONCERNING SELECTION OF AN INSURANCE CARRIER

COMPANY: The Connecticut Light and Power Company

UNION: System Council U–24, International Brotherhood of Electrical Workers, AFL–CIO, comprised of Local Unions 420, 753, 1045, 1175, 1226, 1317 and 1817

BACKGROUND

Connecticut Light and Power Company is a public utility engaged in the production, distribution and sale of electricity and gas. System Council U–24, International Brotherhood of Electrical Workers, AFL–CIO, and its Local Unions 420, 753, 1045, 1175, 1226, 1317 and 1817, together serve as the exclusive representative for all the company's employees within the relevant bargaining unit. For many years, the company and union have had a collective bargaining relationship.

The company had long provided its employees with a noncontributory, company-paid medical-surgical insurance plan. Since 1967 the carrier of this insurance plan, which included major medical coverage, had been the Aetna Life Insurance Company (Aetna). Prior to 1967, the company had contracted with Blue Cross–Connecticut Medical Service (Blue Cross) for the basic medical-surgical insurance, and with the Hartford Accident and Indemnity Company for major medical insurance.

In 1969, the union informed the company of its dissatisfaction with Aetna's administration of the insurance plan. As a result, the company negotiated and secured various changes from Aetna. Nevertheless, during the 1971 collective bargaining negotiations, the union again expressed its dissatisfaction with Aetna and sought to include in those negotiations the reinstatement of Blue Cross as the carrier for the employee insurance plan. The company did bargain during the

1971 negotiations with respect to coverage, benefits and administration of the plan. But the company steadfastly refused to bargain about the selection of the carrier, maintaining that the company had the right unilaterally to choose the carrier.

On May 14, 1971 the union filed unfair labor charges with the NLRB alleging a refusal by the company to bargain in violation of Section 8(a) (1) and (5) of the act. The union claimed that the selection of an insurance carrier under the circumstances was a mandatory subject for bargaining within the meaning of Section 8(d) of the act.

POSITION OF THE UNION

The union argued that Section 8(a) (5) and Section 8(d) of the Labor Management Relations Act require an employer to bargain with a union concerning "wages, hours, and other terms and conditions of employment." It is well established that included within that language are such "nonwage" benefits as the group health insurance here involved.

The NLRB has held repeatedly that the term *wages* must be construed to include certain employee benefits, like pension and insurance benefits, which may accrue to employees out of their employment relationship. These benefits become an integral part of the entire wage structure.

In this case, the company refused to bargain with the union concerning which insurance company should be the carrier for the employees' medical-surgical insurance plan. This was despite the fact that the union had raised objections and expressed general dissatisfaction with the Aetna Company's administration of that insurance plan. It is impossible to separate the insurance benefits available to employees from the insurance carrier which administers an insurance plan. Certainly, the choice of the insurance carrier has a major impact on the nature of the benefits made available to the employees in the bargaining unit. Therefore, the company should be obligated to bargain over the question of the insurance carrier, just as it is obligated to bargain with the union concerning the insurance benefits themselves.

The union requested that the Board find the company in violation of the act, and that the company should be ordered: (*a*) to cease and desist from refusing to bargain collectively as to the selection of an insurance carrier; (*b*) to bargain in good faith on that subject upon request of the union; and (c) to take necessary other affirmative actions to comply with this requirement.

POSITION OF THE COMPANY

The company pointed out that in its 1971 negotiations with the union, there had been no specific allegations made by the union concerning any desired changes in coverage, levels, or administration of the plan. All the union had alleged was general "dissatisfaction" with Aetna as the insurance carrier. Previously, the company had responded to several specific complaints with good faith negotiation, and the company was able to obtain several modifications from Aetna in its plan.

In the company's view, this was all that it was obligated to do under the mandatory bargaining requirements of the Act. The company pointed to several previous rulings of the NLRB and federal courts, which have held as follows:

Since practically every managerial decision has some impact on wages, hours, or other conditions of employment, the determination of which decisions are mandatory bargaining subjects must depend upon whether a given subject has a *significant or material relationship* to wages, hours, or other conditions of employment.[1]

The company agreed that the benefits, coverage, and administration of its insurance plan were proper bargaining subjects. However, since the company had negotiated about those matters, it was free to choose any carrier that would satisfy the company's agreement with the union.

In summary, the company claimed that it had at no time refused to negotiate with the union concerning any subject that "vitally affected the terms and conditions of employment." The company, therefore, requested that the unfair labor practice charges should be dismissed.

QUESTIONS

1. Evaluate the union's argument that it was not possible to separate the insurance benefits available to employees from the. insurance carrier which administers an insurance plan.
2. Evaluate the company's arguments that it was only obligated to bargain

---

[1] *Westinghouse Electric Corp.* v. *NLRB* 66LRRM 2634.

over benefits, coverage, and administration of the insurance plan, and not the specific insurance carrier.

3. What criteria should the NLRB and courts use in determining whether a given bargaining subject has a significant or material relationship to wages, hours, or other conditions of employment?

4. Even if the company should choose to bargain concerning the selection of an insurance carrier, would the company still have the right to select an insurance carrier to which the union might still object? Discuss.

15. WAS THE EMPOYEES' REFUSAL TO WORK OVERTIME PROTECTED BY LABOR LAW?

COMPANY: *Polytech, Incorporated, Overland, Missouri*

EMPLOYEE GROUP: *Philip Bergt, Jack Shepley, Thomas Hall, Ernest Dowling, George Lesseg**

BACKGROUND

The company manufactures transparent plastic sheets and related products at its plant in Overland, Missouri. At the time of this case, the company employed some 12 to 15 employees divided into fabrication and casting departments.

The casting work required the lifting of heavy molds and was performed under hot and uncomfortable conditions. The casting of 73 transparent plastic sheets was scheduled for each working day. At this time there were seven casting employees, including one woman. Casting usually was completed within the regular working day, but sometimes it required overtime of an hour or so for completion of the scheduled 73 sheets. Production occasionally was scheduled for a Saturday to gain a workday, and clean-up work was also regularly scheduled as overtime work.

The seven casting employees had worked seven hours on Saturday, March 13, 1971 and eight hours on Saturday, March 20. They also worked overtime two or three days in each of the following two weeks. Company President Dan Gehrmann had told the employees toward the end of March that he expected them to cast the scheduled 73 plastic sheets each day.

On April 5, 1971 one employee, Del Reinke, was absent. Another employee, Jack Shepley, was inexperienced. Production fell behind schedule, and it was apparent that there would be overtime required that night to complete the scheduled 73 sheets. After the morning

---

* All names are disguised.

break, Thomas Hall told leadman Philip Bergt that he was not going to work that night. Bergt said that that "sounded fine" to him. At lunch, Bergt and Hall spoke to Jack Shepley, Ernest Dowling, and George Lesseg about not working that night. The five men agreed at the afternoon break around 2 p.m. that they would not work that night. The one female employee in the casting department, Minnie Gersting, was not told about the plan to refuse to work any overtime.

The normal quitting hour was 4 p.m. At 3:40 p.m., George Lesseg started to close down the glass washer, and the other men worked to complete the work in process. The Company Vice-President, Nancy Gehrmann, entered the casting room about this time and asked Lesseg why he was shutting down the glass washer, saying, "We are not done yet; we have more to come." Lesseg answered that the men were "tired of staying late almost every night," that they were tired that day, and they had decided not to work that night. Nancy Gehrmann told Meyer to run the washer until 4 o'clock. Meyer turned the washer back on and Gehrmann walked out. She returned a few minutes later with Dan Gehrmann. She asked the five men if they were going to work that night. As each man answered "no," she said, "Well, we don't have any work for you, then, for the next two days." She asked the men what they were trying to prove. They replied that they were not trying to prove anything, but that they were tired that day and did not want to work. The five men left the plant at 4 o'clock and returned to work on April 8 after completing a two-day suspension without pay.

Although the five employees were not represented by a labor union, shortly thereafter employee Philip Bergt on behalf of the entire group filed unfair labor practice charges which claimed that the company's suspension of the employees was in violation of rights guaranteed to groups to act on a concerted basis even though they are not represented by a labor union.

POSITION OF THE EMPLOYEE GROUP

Counsel for the employee group argued that the employees' refusal to work overtime on April 5 was a single strike of limited duration to protest against working conditions and the assignment of what the men considered to be excessive overtime. Counsel argued that several cases decided by the National Labor Relations Board and the courts indicated that when a group of unrepresented employees chose to take united action because of unsatisfactory working conditions or to protest employer practices, this type of concerted action could be entitled to the protection of the Labor Management Relations Act as guaranteed in Section 7. In particular, a case involving the First National Bank of Omaha was cited, where a group of unrepresented employees refused to work overtime because of dissatisfaction with the employer's overtime policy. In this case the NLRB held that such employee action was protected under Section 7, since the refusal to work overtime was limited in duration and was not part of a total pattern of employee activities designed to dictate policies to the employer in the future.[1]

Employee Thomas Hall testified that, at the meeting of April 5, the employee group discussed only to refuse working overtime on that evening; they did not discuss future problems or actions that they might take. Counsel for the employee group argued that this was a single concerted action by a group of unrepresented employees —similar to the Omaha case—designed to protest what they considered to be undesirable working conditions and excessive overtime. Counsel argued that this was the only practical alternative open to this group of employees under the circumstances, since they were not represented by a union with an enforceable grievance procedure. By suspending the employees for two days, argued counsel for the employee group, the company had illegally interfered with the rights of employees guaranteed under Section 7 of the act and thus was guilty of an unfair labor practice under Section 8 (a) (1) of the Labor Management Relations Act. The employee group requested that they be compensated for the earnings that they lost during the two days of their suspension, and that the company be ordered to cease and desist from this and other such unfair labor practice actions.

POSITION OF THE COMPANY

Company representatives argued that the refusal of the employee group to work overtime in this case was tantamount to a rebellion against carrying out a legitimate work order. According to the company, the work on April 5 was not unusual. The employees had completed the casting of heavy sheets during regular hours, and they had comparatively light work to perform during the overtime period. The statement of the employees that they would not work overtime because they had been working "almost every night and were tired"

---

[1] 171 NLRB 152.

was calculated to put the company on notice that the men might walk out again whenever they felt they had been working too much overtime. The company argued that management was within its rights to issue a two-day suspension, since the company could not tolerate such rebellious conduct. Management was not trying to discourage the men from registering a legitimate protest against working overtime. In fact, Nancy Gehrmann had asked the men to tell her what the walkout was all about. The employee group refused to do so and simply stated that they were tired and did not want to work any more overtime. Without some management response to this situation, there could be a complete breakdown in employee discipline throughout the plant. In summary, the company argued that the employees' refusal to work overtime constituted an attempt by the employee group to work overtime on their own terms and to dictate policy to the company. This required imposition of a management disciplinary response which, in this case, was reasonable and not excessively punitive. The company argued that the unfair labor practice charge was without merit and should be dismissed.

QUESTIONS

1. Was the employees' refusal to work overtime "concerted action" which was entitled to the protection under the Labor Management Relations Act, Section 7? Why, or why not?

2. Evaluate the employee group argument that "this was the only practical alternative open to this group of employees under the circumstances, since they were not represented by a union with an enforceable grievance procedure."

3. Why did company management consider the refusal of the group to work overtime as being tantamount to a rebellion against carrying out a legitimate work order?

4. Was management's disciplinary action in this situation justified? Reasonable? Was it legal under the law?

5. On what fundamental issue does a decision in this case ultimately rest?

16. COULD THE EMPLOYEES REFUSE TO CROSS ANOTHER UNION'S PICKET LINES?

COMPANY: Diamond National Corporation, Superior, Montana

UNION: Union No. 3–249, International Woodworkers of America, AFL–CIO

BACKGROUND

Diamond National Corporation has plants at Superior, Montana, Albeni Falls, Idaho, and Coeur D'Alene, Idaho. Employees at all three plants are represented by local affiliates of International Woodworkers of America (IWA), AFL-CIO.

At the time of this case, the collective bargaining agreement which covered employees of these three plants contained the following relevant provisions:

Article 14—Strikes and Lockouts
Section 1. At no time shall employees be required to act as strikebreakers or go through picket lines or armed guards. . . .
Section 2. If the Plant is affected by any labor dispute, both parties agree to do all that is feasible to bring about a prompt and fair settlement. . . .
Section 3. Irrespective of all other provisions of this Agreement, it is understood and agreed that the Union will notify the Company in writing not less than ten (10) consecutive calendar days in advance of the date and time that any strike action is to be commenced. Under no circumstances shall such notice be given until after: first—a meeting has been held between top Western States Regional Council of IWA . . . and the Union being dissatisfied with the results of that meeting; second—the Union requests the intervention of the Federal Mediation and Conciliation Service, and either that Service has advised both parties in writing that it refuses to assert jurisdiction, or that Service has had the opportunity of holding at least one meeting of the parties in an effort to resolve the dispute involved.

Article 18—Grievance Procedure

Section 1.   In the event there be any dispute as to the interpretation of any provision of this Agreement, or any grievance arising out of the operation of this Agreement, the matter shall be referred to the Shop Committee immediately.

Section 3.   It is agreed that during the period of this Agreement there shall be no strikes, cessation of work, picketing, or lockouts, until the procedures specified in this Article have been exhausted.

In August 1969 Diamond National Corporation let a contract for remodeling work at the Superior plant to a nonunion contractor. The company set up a reserved gate for the contractor's employees. A local of the Carpenters union began to picket both the main and the reserved gates protesting the use of nonunion employees for this remodeling work. Diamond National employees who were represented by the Woodworkers union refused to cross the picket line.

At a meeting with the union representatives, the company took the position that the employees were on strike in violation of Section 3 of Article 18 of the collective bargaining agreement. The union representatives, on the other hand, asserted that the employees were exercising their right not to cross a picket line as guaranteed in Section 1, Article 14 of the contract. Following the meeting, the company sent the union a letter, with copies to all employees. The letter outlined possible legal remedies for an alleged breach of the no-strike clause, but urged the employees to return to work promptly and promised no reprisals if the employees did so. The picket line was removed the following day, and the employees returned to work. There were no reprisals.

Somewhat similar incidents took place at the Albeni Falls plant on September 11 and at the Coeur d'Alene plant on September 15. The same sequence of events occurred: unidentified pickets appeared at these plants and the company employees refused to cross the picket lines. The company wrote letters to the union and the employees; these letters outlined possible legal steps to remedy the alleged breach of the no-strike clause; pickets did not appear on the following day; and the employees then returned to work. However, at the Coeur d'Alene plant the company took a firmer stance. In the letter to employees of that plant, it threatened to discharge all employees who did not report for work. It also imposed two-day disciplinary layoffs on three union stewards who were active in encouraging employees not to cross picket lines.

On September 14, Diamond National management received reports that the unidentified pickets who had earlier appeared at the Albeni Falls and Coeur d'Alene plants were going to picket the Superior plant. On September 15, Diamond National dispatched a letter to the union and the employees of the Superior plant reading as follows:

Gentlemen:

We have heard rumors that roving pickets, on strike from a Diamond National Plant at Marysville, California where a lumber and sawmill workers' union is involved, may establish a picket line at our Plant tomorrow. If such a picket line is established and our Superior employees choose to "honor" it, such action will constitute a most serious violation of our Working Agreement with your Union.

The Agreement makes it completely clear that you are not to strike our operation except under certain spelled out procedures. We believe that a strike under circumstances mentioned above would completely violate our Working Agreement, in which event our attorney has indicated that we might take any or all of the following courses: (1) sue your Union and its leadership for damages occasioned by the illegal strike; (2) seek an injunction to bar such strike action; (3) file unfair labor practice charges against your Union and its leadership, for taking such action without prior negotiations and following the steps required by our Working Agreement; (4) terminate all employees or just the leaders for engaging in conduct in violation of our Working Agreement; (5) terminate the Working Agreement because of its violation.

In the event our employees go on strike under the circumstances first above mentioned, they will have subjected the Union and themselves to possible legal action.

However, no pickets showed up to picket at the Superior plant. Employees reported to work as usual, and the company took no action against any employees. However, shortly thereafter, the union filed unfair labor practice charges with the National Labor Relations Board, contending that the company's letter had violated Section 8 (a) (1) of the Labor Management Relations Act.

POSITION OF THE UNION

The union argued that the company had violated Section 8 (a) (1) by sending its letter of September 15 to the Superior plant employees and the Woodworkers union. The union argued that Section 1 of Article 14 of the collective bargaining agreement guaranteed employees the right to refuse to cross another union's picket line, and that Section 3 of Article 14 and Section 3 of Article 18 of the agreement were applicable to disputes only between the Woodworkers union and the company regarding various provisions and benefits for Superior plant employees. The union said that the company was wrong in stating in its September 15 letter that employees who refused to cross unidentified picket lines at the Superior plant would thereby breach the existing collective bargaining contract and expose themselves to legal liability and disciplinary action. The union contended that, by its erroneous letter and other pressure tactics, the company had coerced, restrained, and interfered with the rights of employees guaranteed by Section 7 and Section 8 (a) (1) of the act.[1] The union argued that the company should be found guilty of an unfair labor practice, that it should be required to cease and desist from such activity, and that the company should be required to send a letter to the employees and the union rescinding the letter which it had sent to them on September 15, 1969.

POSITION OF THE COMPANY

The company contended that the articles in dispute in the contract were independent of one another. The company noted that introductory words of Section 3 of Article 14, "irrespective of all other provisions of this Agreement," emphasized that this provision was to have paramount status in the labor agreement, and that refusal to cross a "stranger" picket line would be a strike that first required following the detailed procedures set forth in Section 3 of Article 14. The company claimed that its letter of September 15 correctly stated that the strike or proposed strike would be a direct violation of Section 3 of Article 18 of the bargaining agreement and that the company was justified in describing the steps that it could take to remedy the situation. For these reasons, the company argued that the unfair labor practice charges should be dismissed.

QUESTIONS

1. Could this case conceivably have been heard by a arbitrator under a grievance procedure? Why, or why not?

---

[1] The union also had filed unfair labor practice charges regarding the earlier letters that were written concerning the incidents at the other plants and had filed unfair labor practice charges regarding the disciplinary layoffs of the union stewards at the Coeur d'Alene plant. The Regional Director of the NLRB had declined to issue complaints based upon these earlier charges.

2. Why are the provisions of Article 14 and Article 18 of the labor agreement somewhat contradictory and confusing? Why does intent and meaning of the agreement become a crucial point of contention?

3. Were the company's actions and letters in this case motivated from a desire to weaken or break the union strike action, or were they merely an attempt by management to force the union to observe the agreement as management interpreted it? Discuss.

4. In effect, the NLRB was asked to issue a decision interpreting the meaning of clauses in the collective bargaining agreement. Does the Board have the legal authority to do this? Are issues such as this better left to the parties themselves, or should they be handled through a grievance-arbitration procedure?

17. THE COMPANIES' LOCKOUT DURING NEGOTIATIONS

COMPANIES: *Inland Trucking Co., co-partner with Wesley Meilahn, doing business as Oshkosh Ready-Mix Co., Cook & Brown Lime Co., and Waupun Ready-Mix, Oshkosh, Wisconsin*

UNION: *General Teamsters, Warehouse and Dairy Employers, Local Union No. 126*

BACKGROUND

Oshkosh Ready-Mix (Oshkosh RM) and Waupun Ready-Mix are engaged in selling and delivering ready mixed concrete to the building and construction industry. Cook & Brown Lime Company is engaged in fabricating steel products and in selling and delivering ready mixed concrete, fuel oil, steel products, and other related products.

Cook & Brown had bargained with the union for over thirty years. Oshkosh RM had a labor agreement with the union since 1964. Waupun's ownership changed hands in 1965, after a previous agreement with the union had expired. In 1965, all three employers negotiated union contracts, which were to expire on May 1, 1968.

Cook & Brown and Oshkosh RM negotiated jointly with the union in the 1968 bargaining sessions. Prior to the start of these negotiations, one of Waupun's owners told the union that Waupun wanted to delay discussion of its contract until after the Oshkosh RM contract had been negotiated, since he wished to continue the prior agreement under which Waupun and Oshkosh RM had similar agreements except for a 25-cent wage differential.

The Waupun contract was discussed at some of the negotiations between the union and the other two employers. Whenever such discussions occurred, however, they were kept separate from the Oshkosh RM and Cook & Brown negotiations, and took place after the end of regular negotiations for the day. Moreover, Waupun consistently took the position that negotiations for Waupun were to be delayed until the Oshkosh RM negotiations were concluded. There was no agreement between the union and Waupun that the Oshkosh RM contract terms would control the Waupun agreement.

Six bargaining sessions were held between March 29 and April 30. On April 30, the union was told that there would be no further offer from the employers; if the current offer was not accepted, an employer attorney said, the companies would lock out their employees when the contracts expired.

On May 1, the union telegraphed each employer to advise that it had no intention of striking when the current contracts expired and that it would give the employers at least a week's notice before a work stoppage.

Upon receipt of this message on May 1, each of the three employers handed their employees notices stating that the "union's refusal to compromise its wage demands has created an unfortunate situation which forces us to engage in a lockout." The employees were instructed "not to report for work until further notice."

As of May 2, Cook & Brown had 29 employees on its payroll, including eight on seasonal layoff; Oshkosh RM had eight employees at work and two on layoff; and Waupun had four employees on its payroll, all at work. None of these employees were permitted to work during about a two-and-a-half-month period while negotiations continued intermittently between the companies and the union. Nevertheless, the companies continued to operate, using supervisors, management personnel, and new employees to do work normally done by the locked-out employees. The new employees were given to understand that their tenure might be only temporary.

It was not until July 19, 1969 that agreement on a new contract was reached, and the locked-out employees then were permitted to return to work.[1]

As a result of the employee lockout, the union filed unfair labor practice charges alleging that the companies had engaged in an action which discriminated against employees and which was in violation of employee rights guaranteed under the Labor Management Relations Act.

POSITION OF THE UNION

The union did not contend that the lockout was unlawful at its

---

[1] Not all of the locked-out employees returned to work. Some found permanent employment elsewhere.

inception, but it argued that the companies violated LMRA by maintaining the lockout while employing replacements for the locked-out employees and thus continuing operations during the negotiating period.

Specifically, the union held that the companies violated Sections 8 (a) (1) and 8 (a) (3) of the LMRA by engaging in conduct discriminatory to union membership and destructive of employee rights protected by the act.

The union argued that the real purpose of the lockout was to try to force a capitulation of the union to the companies' terms by depriving the employees of their livelihood for an indefinite period, thus penalizing them for their resistance to those terms and tending to weaken and divide their bargaining power.

Such conduct was in clear violation of the rights of employees guaranteed under Section 7 of the act to bargain collectively through their selected representatives and to engage in concerted activities for the purpose of collective bargaining or other mutual aid or protection.

The union asked that the companies be found in violation of the act, and that all employees affected by the lockout should be reimbursed for all wages and benefits of which they were deprived during the illegal lockout.

POSITION OF THE COMPANY

The companies defended their lockout actions as a reasonable and legal approach within the collective bargaining process. They argued, first of all, that they were justified in their actions by the fact that their contracts had expired and the union was free to strike. Since the contracts had expired, the companies were under no legal obligation to retain the employees on the payroll, even though negotiations were continuing with the union.

But the companies' main argument was based upon a previous NLRB case which had been carried to the Supreme Court of the United States.

In a case involving the American Ship Bldg. Corp., the Supreme Court held "that an employer violates neither Section 8 (a) (1) nor Section 8 (a) (3) of the LMRA when, after a bargaining impasse has been reached, he temporarily shuts down his plant and lays off his employees for the sole purpose of bringing economic pressure to bear in support of his legitimate bargaining position."

Footnote 8 to the opinion of the Court said: "We intimate no view whatever as to the consequences which would follow had the employer replaced its employees with permanent replacements or even temporary help."[2]

The companies contended, in effect, that the question left open in the American Ship case required an answer favorable to employers. Counsel for the companies argued as follows:

Stated another way, the Supreme Court has interpreted the Act as sanctioning the use of the lockout by employers as an economic tool to be utilized either offensively or defensively within the process and procedure of collective bargaining as well as sanctioning an employer's hiring and use of temporary employees during the defensive lockout. In view of this settled law, the companies are simply asking for the logical extension of this law to include the hiring and use of temporary employees during the period of an offensive lockout as a legitimate right of employers. The circumstances of this case present a rational and logical basis upon which to close the heretofore incomplete perimeter of employer's rights when they resort to the lockout device as an economic tool in the process and procedure of collective bargaining.

The companies requested that the unfair labor practice charges should be dismissed.

QUESTIONS

1. Evaluate the union argument that "the real purpose of the lockout was to try to force a capitulation of the union to the companies' terms by depriving the employees of their livelihood for an indefinite period, thus penalizing them for their resistance to those terms and tending to weaken and divide their bargaining power."
2. Was company management legally free to resort to a lockout because the contract with the union had expired? Why, or why not?
3. Evaluate the company's argument concerning its rationale for use of an offensive lockout and hiring temporary employees based upon the American Ship case.
4. Assuming that bargaining is carried on in good faith, must a company wait until a union actually strikes before it resorts to actions, such as hiring replacement workers, designed to bring economic pressure on the union? Discuss.

---

[2] *American Ship Bldg.* v. *Labor Board* (1965), 380 U.S. 300, 318, 58, LRRM 2672.

18. THE CHALLENGE TO THE ARBITRATOR'S AWARD

COMPANY:　Illinois Bell Telephone Company, Centralia, Illinois

UNION:　Local 339, International Brotherhood of Electrical Workers, AFL–CIO

BACKGROUND

The facts of the case were not in dispute. Elisha Morgan[1] had been employed by the company as a janitor since October 1964. Between 1967 and 1970, he was examined on three separate occasions by management officials with respect to stolen property, but it was never established that Morgan took the property in question and accordingly he was never disciplined.

On December 22, 1973 Morgan worked overtime between the hours of 3 a.m. and 5 a.m. cleaning a garage located across from a district office building of the company. Although he was not assigned to work in the district office that morning, he entered the building at approximately 4 a.m. in order to retrieve a daiquiri glass which he had given to another employee the previous night. In the course of looking for the glass, Morgan unsuccessfully attempted to pull open the desk drawer of his supervisor, Barney Trottman. He subsequently discovered the glass on the desk of the employee to whom he had offered the drink and began to exit the building.

The district office building alarm system, installed in late 1973 after a number of thefts had been reported, sounded in the local police station at the time Morgan was in the building. When Morgan exited, a waiting policeman informed him that the alarm had gone off. The officer told him that he was to wait until District Supervisor Helen Carter arrived. Upon Carter's arrival, she informed Morgan that a few things had been missing from the building. While two policemen searched the building, Morgan and Carter retraced Morgan's route

---

[1] The names of all individuals are disguised.

inside. When the search was completed, Carter permitted Morgan to finish his work in the garage. Carter subsequently asked Morgan to turn over his key to the district office building and told him that she would talk to him later about "the situation." Morgan responded that he would be on vacation the following week but told Carter how he could be reached.

On December 24, Morgan described the incident to his union steward, Alvin Gray, and told him that Carter wanted to talk to him about it. The steward then informed Morgan of his "rights," among which he related was entitlement to the presence of a union representative when he met with representatives of the company in regard to the incident.

On January 2, 1974 Morgan's supervisor, Barney Trottman, asked him to speak with the company's chief security representative, Steven Flasker. Morgan refused to speak with Flasker without a union representative also being present. Trottman demanded Morgan's cooperation and ordered him to speak to Flasker. Morgan was told that it was company practice for employees to be alone when they spoke to security personnel. When Morgan again refused, Trottman collected his keys and I.D. card and told him he was suspended until such time as he would speak to security department personnel.

By letter dated February 26, 1974, the company warned Morgan that unless he cooperated with the investigation he would be discharged. The letter, in part, said as follows:

On or about 4:30 a.m., Saturday, December 22, 1973, you were in our building at 100 E. McCord Street, Centralia, Illinois. You were under no call or authorization from the Company to be anywhere in that building at the time in question.

It is important to the Company to be fully satisfied as to your total activity while in that building without authorization. For that reason you have been requested to discuss this matter with a representative of our Security Department in accordance with Company practice. You have a duty to cooperate in our investigation of this matter. Nevertheless, you have refused to meet alone with the Company's Security representative who requested to interview you. As you were told, our Security Department does not allow third parties to be present when an employee is interviewed.

Because of the questionable circumstances of your presence and your continued refusal to cooperate in the investigation, you leave the Company with no alternative but to base their decision in this matter on all the facts at hand.

Therefore, since you have had ample time to consider your refusal, unless you comply with the Company's instructions by Friday, March 8, 1974, we will move to dismiss you.

On March 11, 1974 Supervisor Trottman told Morgan that he had been suspended because he "refused to meet with the company without a union representative." He warned him that if he did not return to work by March 13 and speak to the security department, he would be discharged. Because he did not comply with Trottman's directive, Morgan was terminated on that date.

Local 399, International Brotherhood of Electrical Workers, AFL–CIO, grieved his discharge which eventually went to arbitration. In the arbitration proceeding, the company contended that, given the absence of a specific contract provision, Morgan had no right under the collective bargaining agreement to union representation in a purely investigatory interview. The union, which had also filed unfair labor practice charges with the National Labor Relations Board on behalf of Elisha Morgan, contended in the arbitration hearing that in cases such as this the NLRB had interpreted Section 7 of the Labor Management Relations Act so as to afford a right to employees to have union representation in an investigatory hearing.

On October 15, 1974 while this case was pending with the NLRB, the arbitrator issued an "Opinion and Award" in which he found that Morgan "was discharged for just cause." Accordingly, he denied the grievance. During the course of his decision, the arbitrator expressly refused to consider or decide upon the LMRA statutory issue presented by the union. Instead, he concluded that, "What is relevant to a resolution of this grievance is the meaning and intent of applicable contract terms." In this regard, the arbitrator found that the only time the contract expressly permitted or required the presence of a union representative was after a grievance had been formally referred to the company by the union. He found no language in the contract which would obligate the company to permit a union representative to be present at an investigatory interview. Nor did he find any evidence of a company past practice of allowing such representation. On the contrary, he found that it had been company practice to refuse employee requests for union representation prior to formal submission of grievances.

In his decision, the arbitrator referred to several arbitration awards finding that an employee is entitled to be accompanied by a union representative when an interrogation is related to prospective discipline, or when the employee has reasonable grounds to expect to be disciplined. The arbitrator concluded however, that based upon the record presented, (1) Morgan's interrogation was not related to prospective discipline, and (2) Morgan had no reasonable grounds to expect to be disciplined.

The arbitrator's award became a major aspect of the union's unfair labor practice charges against the company, which alleged that the company had violated Section 8 (a) (1) of the act in interfering with Elisha Morgan's Section 7 rights.

POSITION OF THE UNION

The union claimed that Elisha Morgan should have been allowed to have union representation with him if he was to be interrogated by the company's security department, since he had "reasonable grounds" to believe that disciplinary action might be taken against him. The facts of the case included the following particulars:

1. Morgan had previously been accused by the company of stealing tools and equipment;
2. his entry into the district office building on December 22 was completely unauthorized;
3. he acknowledged having unsuccessfully tried to open the desk drawer of his supervisor;
4. he was the only employee on the premises when the alarm sounded;
5. he was immediately detained by a police officer;
6. Supervisor Carter told him that some things were missing, took him back into the building, and asked him to retrace his steps; and
7. subsequently Carter asked Morgan to turn over his key to the district office building and be available for further questioning about the situation.

All factors pointed towards Morgan being a theft suspect. In the union's view, to conclude in the face of this evidence that Morgan did not have reasonable grounds to fear disciplinary action would simply be to ignore the facts.

The union argued that the arbitrator's decision under the grievance procedure in the labor contract between the parties was not binding upon the NLRB in administering the Labor Management Relations Act. The union claimed that Section 7 of the act guarantees individual employees the right to engage in "concerted activities" for "mutual aid or protection." In this case, Elisha Morgan was denied this right by the company, which refused to allow him to have a union representative with him during a proposed interrogation by its security department. The union argued that: (*a*) the arbitrator's decision in this matter should be disregarded by the NLRB; (*b*) the company should be found in violation of Section 7 and Section 8 (a) (1) of the act; and (*c*) Elisha Morgan should be reinstated to his position and made whole for all lost wages and benefits.

POSITION OF THE COMPANY

The company claimed that it had not violated any provisions of the Labor Management Relations Act. Elisha Morgan was discharged for insubordination for refusing to be interrogated by the company's security personnel. Such interrogation was standard company practice in situations of this type. The purpose of the proposed interview was not to discipline Morgan, but to get at the facts of the case. Since Morgan refused to submit to an interrogation without a union representative being present—contrary to company policy and practice—the company was forced to discharge Morgan for insubordination.

The company pointed out that its position was upheld by the arbitrator who heard the case under the grievance-arbitration procedure. Nothing in the labor agreement required the company to permit a union representative to be present when its security department interviewed individuals concerning security matters.

In the company's view, the union simply was trying to salvage Elisha Morgan's job by filing unwarranted unfair labor practice charges after failing to accomplish its objective through the grievance-arbitration process. The NLRB should not overturn an arbitrator's award unless there is substantial evidence to the contrary that the arbitration award was unjust.

The company requested that the unfair labor practice charges should be dismissed.

QUESTIONS

1. Why would the company refuse to permit an employee to have his union representative present for an interview as part of the security department's investigation? Is such a policy sound? Discuss.

2. Evaluate the arbitrator's refusal to consider or decide upon the Labor Management Relations Act issue presented by the union. Why do

arbitrators normally refuse to rule on legal matters presented as part of arbitration disputes?

3. Although the NLRB and the courts generally prefer to support private arbitration of union-management disputes, are they bound to defer to an arbitrator's award in a case such as this? Why, or why not?

4. Evaluate the company argument that the union simply was trying to salvage the employee's job by filing unfair labor practice charges against the company after having lost in the arbitration decision.

19. WITHDRAWAL OF A TRADITIONAL CHRISTMAS BONUS

COMPANY: *Century Electric Motor Co., Gettysburg, Ohio*

UNION: *International Union of Electrical, Radio, and Machine Workers, AFL–CIO*

BACKGROUND

The plant in which this case occurred was located at Gettysburg, Ohio. Small electric motors were manufactured for use in water systems. Century Electric Motor Company had purchased the plant from Tait Manufacturing Company in June 1967. During Tait's ownership, from 1957 until the sale to Century, Tait had paid plant employees a bonus each year at Christmas time. Since 1959 bonuses had regularly consisted of $10 for an employee's first year of service, plus $5 for each additional year. The payments had been made, however, without any provision in the collective bargaining agreement.

When Century purchased the plant, Tait advised Century management that the bonuses at Christmas were discretionary, and that the practice was subject to modification or revocation at any time. Nevertheless, Century agreed with the union to continue the obligations and relationships existing under Tait's collective bargaining agreement. Although the agreement contained no provision for any Christmas bonus and although Century had owned the plant for only the last half of 1967, Century made payment of a bonus for that year similar to the bonuses Tait had made in the past.

This payment was made by decision of the plant officers and not by action of the company's board of directors. When the directors held their first meeting in 1968, they reviewed the affairs of the corporation and the actions of the plant officers. The chairman of the board thereupon told the officers that the company was operating at a loss, and that there would be no more payments of Christmas bonuses until the business was making a discernible profit.

145

On November 27, as the end of 1968 approached, the plant officers reviewed all accounting reports available through October 31, 1968. Based upon these reports, they decided that they would not be entitled under the instructions given them by the board to make payment of a Christmas bonus for that year. The plant officers called a meeting of the employees that same day and announced to them that, "this has been a poor year from a sales standpoint, and the income has been such that it was necessary for us to forego paying a Christmas bonus this year."

Contract Negotiations

The union and the company for some weeks had been engaged in negotiation sessions on a new collective bargaining agreement. The previous agreement, made by Tait and assumed by Century, had an expiration date of November 8, 1968. The parties had by November 22 reached an understanding, or accord, on almost every major issue involved between them. A final session was held on December 10 at which all remaining issues pertaining to such things as contract language, super-seniority for stewards, and shop classifications were agreed upon. On that date, the contract was written into final form and executed.

The new agreement, like the prior one, was without any provision relating to Christmas bonuses. Further, there was included in its closing article a "wrap-up" or "zipper" provision which stated as follows:

The parties acknowledge that during the negotiations which resulted in this agreement each side had the unlimited right and opportunity to make demands and proposals with respect to any subject or matter not removed by law from the area of collective bargaining, and that the understandings and agreements arrived at by the parties after the exercise of the right and opportunity are set forth in this Agreement. Therefore, the Company and the Union, for the life of this Agreement, each voluntarily and unqualifiedly waives the right, and each agrees that the other shall not be obligated, to bargain collectively with respect to any subject or matter not specifically referred to or covered in this Agreement, even though such subjects or matters may not have been within the knowledge or contemplation of either or both of the parties at the time they negotiated or signed this Agreement.

The Union Demand

The union waited until a week had gone by after the signing of the agreement and then served the company with a demand that it meet and negotiate on the question of a 1968 Christmas bonus. The company did meet with the union, but the company took the position that there was nothing to negotiate concerning a 1968 bonus. Company management asked the union why it had not indicated its disagreement by bringing the question up at the December 10 session before the new collective bargaining agreement was executed, if it felt that the company did not have a right to take the position it had taken in the November 27 announcement.

The union officials responded that the bonus was not mentioned in the December 10 meeting simply as "a deferential courtesy." Since the plant had paid a Christmas bonus for some ten years, the union claimed it had assumed that the subject of the Christmas bonus nevertheless would be discussed prior to a final decision. The company responded that the matter of the Christmas bonus was purely within its discretion, and that it would not bargain with the union concerning this matter. Shortly thereafter, the union filed an unfair labor practice charge which alleged that the company had violated Section 8(a) (5) of the Labor Management Relations Act by unilaterally eliminating the Christmas bonus and thereafter refusing to bargain about this matter with the union.

POSITION OF THE UNION

The union argued that the Christmas bonus had become such a traditional part of the company's total compensation package that, in effect, it had become a condition of employment. The company could not unilaterally withdraw this Christmas bonus from the employees without discussing the matter with the union as required under Section 8 (a) (5). There was nothing in the contract to indicate specifically that the union had given up and waived its right to bargain over the Christmas bonus. The contract was silent on this issue, and the so-called "zipper" clause in the contract did not negate the union's right to raise the Christmas bonus issue as a subject for bargaining. Under provisions of Section 8(d) of the act and well-established NLRB rulings, argued the union, the company must bargain over a mandatory subject unless the union has specifically agreed not to bargain over such an issue. The union never agreed specifically to the company's unilateral abolition of the Christmas bonus.

The union argued that the company should be found guilty of an unfair labor practice in violation of Section 8 (a) (5), that a Christmas bonus should be granted to the employees for 1968, and that the company should be ordered to bargain over the issue of a Christmas bonus for future years.

POSITION OF THE COMPANY

The company argued that the union had waived its right to bargain over the Christmas bonus by its acquiescence and by not mentioning the issue of the Christmas bonus during 1968 contract negotiations. Failure on the part of the union to discuss the question of the Christmas bonus until after the contract had been signed on December 10 indicated that the union had waived its right to bargain about the matter. Further, the contract "zipper" clause specifically negated the company's obligation to bargain during the contract period concerning any subject not mentioned in the contract. Therefore, argued the company, it was not obligated to bargain over the Christmas bonus issue. And even if the company would have chosen to bargain the issue with the union, Section 8(d) of the act does not require the company to agree with or concede anything to the union.

The company requested that the unfair labor practice charge be dismissed.

QUESTIONS

1. Evaluate the intent and meaning of the "wrap-up" or "zipper" provision in the agreement upon which much of the dispute in this case hinges.
2. Was the Christmas bonus a matter completely within company management discretion, or had the bonus become a subject of collective bargaining as argued by the union? Evaluate the union's statement that the Christmas bonus "had become such a traditional part of the Company's total compensation package that, in effect, it had become a condition of employment."
3. Did the union waive its right to bargain over the Christmas bonus by (a) not mentioning the issue of the Christmas bonus during the 1968 contract negotiations, and (b) by agreeing to the "zipper" clause in the contract? Why or why not?
4. Does the fact that company management changed over the period of time of the Christmas bonus have direct or indirect bearing on the issues involved? How?
5. If the company should be found guilty of an unfair labor practice, must the company: (a) pay a Christmas bonus for 1968, and/or (b) bargain over the issue of a Christmas bonus for forthcoming years?

20. THE OFFENSIVE SWEATSHIRTS

COMPANY: *Southwestern Bell Telephone Company, St. Louis, Missouri*

UNION: *Communications Workers of America, AFL–CIO*

BACKGROUND

Southwestern Bell is a wholly owned subsidiary of American Telephone and Telegraph Co. Its principal office is located in St. Louis, Missouri. Since 1947, the union has represented employees at various facilities in a five-state area, including three St. Louis area exchange facilities involved in this case, known as Mission, Parkview, and Bridgetown exchanges.

On June 22, 1971 the company and union commenced negotiations for a contract to replace that which was to expire on July 17. On June 23, 18 employees at the Mission exchange appeared at work wearing sweatshirts with the slogan, "Ma Bell Is a Cheap Mother." Later that day two employees at the Parkview exchange wore shirts bearing the same slogan. On July 21, after the company and union had signed a collective bargaining contract and a seven-day strike had ended, 3 employees at Bridgetown wore the "cheap mother" shirts.

Company managers told the employees who wore the shirts that they would have to leave the company premises if they did not remove the shirts or cover up the "cheap mother" inscription. All 23 employees exercised the option of leaving the plant. None of them was paid for the time which they took off work, and all of them returned the day after they left, no longer displaying the "cheap mother" slogan.

The union filed unfair labor practice charges with the National Labor Relations Board, contending that the company's actions had violated Sections 8 (a) (3) and 8 (a) (1) of the Labor Management Relations Act.

149

POSITION OF THE UNION

The union argued that the slogan on the sweatshirts worn by the employees was only a "skilled, artful, and humorous form of highlighting the differences between the company and union in the negotiations then pending." The slogan should be considered as part of privileged free speech by union employees. The 23 employees wore the sweatshirts to support the union's position in contract negotiations with the employer. The slogans displayed on the sweatshirts were not offensive, obscene, or obnoxious as to justify the company's requirement that the employees remove or cover them, or else leave the premises. On their jobs, these employees did not come into contact with the general public. Nor did the wearing of these sweatshirts in any way interfere with the work performance of any employees.

The union contended that by its actions, the company had illegally interfered with these employees' protected union activities in violation of both Sections 8 (a) (3) and 8 (a) (1) of the act. The union requested that the company be directed to cease and desist such actions, and that the 23 employees involved in this case be made whole for the loss of pay they suffered while being forced to be off work by the company.

POSITION OF THE COMPANY

The company argued that the phrase in question on the sweatshirts was capable of more than a single interpretation—one innocent and the other obscene. Several union witnesses had even admitted that the slogan on the shirt could convey an offensive connotation, and that they heard the word "mother" used in an obscene context in this situation. Four management officials testified that they considered the slogan on the sweatshirts as vulgar and profane, as directed at them and the company, and designed to taunt them and provoke incidents. In view of the controversial nature of the language used and its "admitted susceptibility to profane construction," the company felt that it could legitimately ban the use of the provocative slogan as a reasonable precaution against discord and bitterness between employees and management, as well as to assure decorum and discipline in the plant.

The company contended that its actions in this situation were not in any way reflective of antiunion sentiments or interference with the union employees' rights of free expression. The company's order to these employees to refrain from using such slogans during working hours or else leave company premises was a reasonable and protected management prerogative. None of the employees was discharged or disciplined, except to the extent that they were docked for wages lost for the hours they elected to absent themselves. The employees could, and without company objection did, use other insignia to publicize their bargaining demands.

The company requested that the unfair labor practice charges should be dismissed.

QUESTIONS

1. Since the employees did not come into contact with the general public and since their sweatshirts did not directly interfere in work operations, did the company have the right to issue the ultimatum to the employees?

2. What are the limits of protected free speech in union-management relations under the Labor Management Relations Act?

3. Evaluate the union's argument that the slogan was a humorous and skilled slogan as compared to the company's argument of a possible obscence interpretation. By what standards can such value judgments be ruled upon by the NLRB?

4. Was the company's action interference in protected bargaining unit activities, or an attempt by the company to maintain employee discipline?

21. A "THREAT" TO PICKET, OR "COOPERATION" WITH A NEUTRAL EMPLOYER?

COMPANY: *Johns-Manville Products Corporation, Waukegan, Illinois*

UNION: *Truck Drivers, Oil Drivers, Filling Station and Platform Workers, Local No. 705, of the International Brotherhood of Teamsters*

BACKGROUND

Employees of the Trumbull Asphalt Company, an asphalt supplier in Waukegan, Illinois, are represented by Teamsters Local 743. This local was engaged in a strike for a labor contract from June, 1972, until the time of the hearing of this case in late February 1973. A Johns-Manville Company plant in Waukegan produces roofing materials; in its business at this plant, Johns-Manville purchases materials from Trumbull which in 1972 exceeded $1.2 million. In December 1972 when the alleged unfair labor practice occurred, Johns-Manville was receiving three to four truckloads of Trumbull materials per day.

On December 14, 1972 Tony Presko,[1] Local 705's business representative, accompanied by two other union officials, met with Johns-Manville's regional purchasing manager and employee relations manager, respectively William Driscoll and Arthur Carr. During the course of the meeting, Mr. Presko told them that he had received instructions from Jerry Holmes, Local 705's secretary-treasurer, to handle the problem that had arisen. Mr. Presko told the Johns-Manville representatives that Local 743 was a local of "inside" workers who were on strike at Trumbull. The sister local, Local 705, had members working for Heaffey Motors, which normally hauled Trumbull's materials to Johns-Manville's plant. Local 705's members were honoring Local 743's picket line. Business Representative Presko further

---

[1] All names are disguised.

stated that Trumbull was hauling its material into Johns-Manville's plant by using drivers and vehicles which it had brought in from its plant in Texas. Mr. Presko stated that in view of the action of Local 705's members in honoring Local 743's picket line, Local 705 had been asked to help Local 743 get the strike resolved. Mr. Presko said that he was going to be contacting several customers of Trumbull in the hope that they would stop accepting material for delivery. He further said that Local 705's representatives were there for the purpose of seeing if Johns-Manville would stop accepting deliveries from Trumbull. The union representative then declared that if the deliveries continued, Local 705 might have to "throw up a picket line at Johns-Manville's main gate" in which case "nothing would get in or out of the plant." Mr. Driscoll and Mr. Carr neither acceded to nor refused the union's request.

Johns-Manville shut down its roofing operation (the operation which uses Trumbull products) for preventive maintenance between December 16, 1972 and January 3, 1973 during which period no shipments were scheduled to be received from any source. In the meanwhile, on December 19, 1972 Johns-Manville filed unfair labor practice charges against Local 705, protesting the union's alleged threat to picket its plant as a violation of the secondary boycott provisions of the Labor Management Relation Act.

Local 705 received the charge on December 21, 1972. On December 29, 1972 the union sent a telegram to the company and the NLRB stating that the purpose of the telegram was to "remove the misunderstanding that the union had threatened to picket the Johns-Manville plant." Also mentioned in the telegram was a statement that the union had no intention of picketing the plant in the event it continued to use the services of Trumbull, because the sole purpose of contacting the company was "to ask for its cooperation."

Johns-Manville was never picketed by the union, and its business proceeded at all times in a normal manner. Trumbull shipments were resumed a few days after the roofing operations started up again in early January 1973.

POSITION OF THE COMPANY

The company argued that the statements of union business representative Tony Presko to company managers William Driscoll and Arthur Carr on December 14, 1972 constituted a "threat" in violation of Section 8 (b) (4) (i) (ii) (B) of the act. In the company's view, Mr.

Presko was acting under instructions from an officer of Local 705. The intent of Local 705's threat to picket the Johns-Manville plant was to force the company as a neutral employer to cease doing business with another employer with which Local 705's sister local had a primary dispute. The union's threat of picketing posed a threat of quick and substantial economic damage to the company, which was a neutral employer in this dispute. The union's telegram withdrawing this threat was sent only after the company had filed unfair labor practice charges against the union. During most of the period after the union's threat, picketing would have been of limited use because of the company's maintenance shutdown. Nevertheless, the union's threat to picket the company's premises represented a substantial possibility of serious interference, since about 100 or more trucks would pass daily into the Waukegan facility when the plant resumed operating in January 1973.

The company requested that the union be found in violation of the above secondary boycott provisions of the act, and that the union be ordered to cease and desist from this and similar threats and activities.

POSITION OF THE UNION

The union claimed, first of all, that the remarks of union business representative Tony Presko were not meant to be a "threat" as construed by the company. Mr. Presko had been instructed by his superior, Jerry Holmes, the secretary-treasurer of Local 705, to meet with Johns-Manville officials to ask for their "cooperation." The union merely had sought the "cooperation" of Johns-Manville in this matter, which the company could either extend or withhold.

Regardless, Mr. Presko's alleged "threat" was a single remark which was of de minimus consequences. Upon receiving a copy of the company's complaint to the NLRB, Local 705 sent a telegram to the company and the Board, which retracted any alleged "threat" to picket the Johns-Manville plant and denied any attempt of the union to interfere with the company's dealings with the Trumbull Company. This telegram, which clarified the union's lawful intent, should have rendered the unfair labor practice charges against it as moot.

Finally, the union pointed out that no picketing whatsoever was conducted by the union. For the NLRB to issue a cease and desist order would merely forbid the union to engage in conduct already forbidden by the act, and which the union had repudiated by its telegram of December 29, 1972. The union requested that the unfair labor practice charges should be dismissed.

QUESTIONS

1. Were the statements of the business representative a "threat" to picket or merely a request for "cooperation" with a neutral employer? Why is it difficult to determine the intent of a conversation of the nature described in this case?
2. Since the union sent a telegram to the company and the NLRB withdrawing any intention of picketing, did this render the unfair labor practice charges against the union moot?
3. Why would the company press unfair labor practice charges against the union, even though the union had withdrawn whatever "threat" might have been given to the company earlier?
4. Evaluate the union's argument that if the NLRB would issue a cease and desist order, this would merely reiterate what already was specifically prohibited in the act and which the union formally had repudiated.

22. THE PICKET LINE AND THE EXPULSION OF THE UNION MEMBERS

COMPANY: B. D. Morgan & Co. and Mecco, Inc., Middletown, Ohio

UNION: Local No. 18, International Union of Operating Engineers, AFL–CIO

BACKGROUND

B. D. Morgan & Company (Morgan) and Mecco, Inc. (Mecco) are engaged in contract engineering in the Middletown, Ohio, area. Mecco also is engaged in the rental of heavy construction equipment and in supplying sand, gravel, and ready-mixed concrete. Individuals who are members of the same family serve as officers for both corporations.

From about 1960 until 1970, Mecco had a series of collective bargaining contracts with Local 18 of the Operating Engineers union. However, the union never was officially certified as the representative of Mecco's employees. After a strike in 1969 and the expiration of the parties' last contract in June, 1970, Mecco did not resume contractual relations with the union.

Work on a major construction project for the Hills Department Store was to begin in November 1971. The general contractor on the project entered into a contract with the Mecco Company to provide certain grading and footing work. A prejob conference was called by the general contractor to discuss plans with several subcontractors and various labor unions who would be working on this project. At this meeting, Scott Murphy,[1] a business representative for the Operating Engineers union, stated that Mecco was "unfair" because it was a non-union employer. On January 3, 1972 Mr. Murphy demanded that the general contractor remove Mecco from the job. Later that day, in the presence of a business agent for the Laborers union, Mr. Murphy

---

[1] All names are disguised.

warned the general contractor that the Hills Store project would be picketed if Mecco employees were not removed. Immediately thereafter, Mr. Murphy told employees of another subcontractor at the job site that Mecco was unfair, and that the site would be picketed if Mecco continued to work. The business agent repeated this warning to the subcontractor's superintendent.

On January 4, Local 18 union pickets stationed themselves at both entrances to the project. All employees except those of Mecco stayed off the job a number of days until Mecco had completed its phase of the work, at which time the pickets were withdrawn.

On January 7, Delmont Burgess, an executive of Morgan and Mecco, talked with Mr. Murphy. Mr. Murphy told Mr. Burgess, "The problem is that you're not signatory to our contract, and not paying into our fringe benefit program for the Operating Engineers." During the same conversation, the business agent criticized Mr. Burgess for not agreeing to the union's demands. Mr. Murphy said that the union would be "forced to keep a strike banner on the department-store construction project and to keep employees of other subcontractors away from work."

Subsequent to this incident, the union took disciplinary action against three of its members who were then employed by the Mecco Company. These three men, Bill Tobias, Sam Moody, and Carl Church, had retained their membership in the union and had continued to pay union dues after the expiration of the union's last contract with Mecco. On April 10, 1972 the union fined each of the three members $100.00 each and expelled them from union membership. The union informed them that they were expelled because: (a) they had worked for a nonunion employer; (b) they had received substandard wages and working conditions; (c) they had entered into private employment agreements with Mecco; and (d) they had crossed their union's picket line to continue working at Mecco in January 1972.

The company filed unfair labor practice charges against the union alleging violations of Sections 8 (b) (4) (i) (ii) (B) and 8 (b) (1) (A) of the Labor Management Relations Act.

POSITION OF THE COMPANY

The company claimed that the statements of union business representative Scott Murphy and the union's picket line at the Hill's department store construction project were clear violations of Section

8 (b) (4) (i) (ii) (B), the secondary boycott provisions of the act. The union, after warning the general contractor and various subcontractors that they would not work with Mecco, picketed the site with signs addressed only to Mecco. The picketing resulted in the stopping of work by all union men on the project, although the Mecco men continued to work.

In the company's view, the union's objectives were: (1) to cause the neutral general contractor and neutral subcontractors to cease doing business with each other and with Mecco, with whom the union had a dispute; and (2) to force Mecco to recognize the union and to bargain with it, although the union had not been certified as the representative of Mecco's employees.

As a remedy for these violations of Section 8 (b) (4) (i) (ii) (B), the company requested that the union be issued a permanent "cease and desist" order by the NLRB.

In regard to the three Mecco employees, the company claimed that the union had violated Section 8 (b) (1) (A) of the Labor Management Relations Act by threatening these members that charges would be filed against them for crossing a picket line, by filing such charges, and by fining and expelling them from union membership for having worked behind the picket line, even though such picketing violated secondary boycott provisions of the act.

The company pointed out that Bill Tobias, Sam Moody, and Carl Church were employed directly by Mecco. Even though they had retained their membership in the union, they were not represented for purposes of collective bargaining by the union. For the union to both expel and fine these men for their refusal to participate in a secondary boycott action was in violation of their protected rights as stated in Section 8 (b) (1) (A) of the act. The company requested that the union should be directed to rescind in total its disciplinary action against these men and to make them whole for any economic losses sustained as a result of the union's actions.

POSITION OF THE UNION

It was the union's claim that the statements of its business representative and the picketing at the construction project were entirely directed at the Mecco Company. Therefore, it was entirely primary in nature and, hence, lawful. If there was any "secondary fallout," this was incidental and did not detract from the legality of the primary picketing by the union aimed at Mecco. Such primary activities are protected by the proviso in paragraph B of Section 8 (b) (4) which states:

... nothing contained in this clause (B) shall be construed to make unlawful, where not otherwise unlawful, any primary strike or primary picketing.

Concerning the three union employees of Mecco, the union argued that all these employees worked nonunion against the union's request, and accepted and continued to work at Mecco under conditions which adversely affected union standards. The union contended that the construction project picketing was primary and was directed at Mecco. Yet, these men continued to work and crossed the union's picket line. Under these circumstances, the men properly received a union expulsion and fine.

The union further pointed out that Section 8 (b) (1) (A) of the act states:

(b) It shall be an unfair labor practice for a labor organization or its agents—
1) to restrain or coerce (A) employees in the exercise of the rights guaranteed in section 7: Provided, that this paragraph shall not impair the right of a labor organization to prescribe its own rules with respect to the acquisition or retention of membership therein.

According to the union, this provision does not put any limitation with respect to the internal affairs of unions. Unions may expel any members they wish to expel, and they may try any of their members. All that unions cannot do is that if they expel a member for some reason other than nonpayment of dues, they cannot make his employer discharge him from his job and throw him out of work. This is provided in Section 8 (b) (2) of the act.

In summary, the union argued that its actions in this matter were: (*a*) directed at the Mecco Company in a primary, not secondary, dispute; and (*b*) protected by provisions of the Labor Management Relations Act. The unfair labor practice charges should be dismissed.

QUESTIONS

1. Why would the three employees in this case work for a nonunion employer while at the same time retain membership in a labor union? Did this place them in an awkward position?
2. Were the statements of the union business representative and the

union's picket line in violation of the secondary boycott provisions of the act? Why, or why not?

3. Evaluate the union's arguments that its statements and picketing were primary in nature, and that there was only incidental and "secondary fallout" in the events which transpired.

4. Does the Labor Management Relations Act prohibit a union from disciplining union members if they refuse to participate in an illegal secondary boycott? Discuss.

23. THE CONTRACT AND THE MEDIATION SERVICES

COMPANY: *Cream Top Creamery, Incorporated, Louisville, Kentucky*

UNION: *Milk, Ice Cream Drivers, and Dairy Employees, Local 783, International Brotherhood of Teamsters, Chauffeurs, Warehousemen, and Helpers of America (IBTCW)*

THE UNFAIR LABOR PRACTICE CHARGES

On July 17, 1963 the company filed unfair labor practice charges against the union alleging that the union had violated Section 8 (b) (3) of the Labor Management Relations Act by its failure to comply with Sections 8 (d) (3) and 8 (d) (4) of the act.

Section 8 (d) of the act states the following:

. . . That where there is in effect a collective-bargaining contract covering employees in an industry affecting commerce, the duty to bargain collectively shall also mean that no party to such contract shall terminate or modify such contract, unless the party desiring such termination or modification—

(1) serves a written notice upon the other party to the contract of the proposed termination or modification sixty days prior to the expiration date thereof, or in the event such contract contains no expiration date, sixty days prior to the time it is proposed to make such termination or modification;

(2) offers to meet and confer with the other party for the purpose of negotiating a new contract or a contract containing the proposed modifications;

(3) notifies the Federal Mediation and Conciliation Service within thirty days after such notice of the existence of a dispute, and simultaneously therewith notifies any State or Territorial agency established to mediate and conciliate disputes within the State or Territory where the dispute occurred, provided no agreement has been reached by that time; and

(4) continues in full force and effect, without resorting to strike or lockout, all the terms and conditions of the existing contract for a period of

sixty days after such notice is given or until the expiration date of such contract, whichever occurs later.

BACKGROUND

The Cream Top Creamery, Inc., is a corporation with its office and principal place of business in Louisville, Kentucky. The company is engaged in the processing of milk and related milk products such as chocolate milk, orange drink, ice cream, etc., and their sale and distribution at wholesale and retail levels. Total company sales were about $900,000 for the fiscal year ending September 30, 1963.

IBTCW Local 783 is the collective bargaining agent for a unit of about 24 employees working for the company. The employees covered in the bargaining unit consist of retail and wholesale milk drivers, ice cream drivers, and plant employees; office clerical employees, guards, and supervisors are not in the bargaining unit. The contract between the company and the union at the time of this case was entered into on April 1, 1960. The last article, Article 36, of the contract made reference to the general termination dates of the contract and read as follows:

This contract shall be effective from and after the date hereof and shall continue through March 31, 1963, and continue from year to year thereafter, ending on March 31, of each year thereafter, but subject to the right of any party hereto to terminate same as of April 1, of any year following the year 1962, by giving not less than 60 days' written notice of its intention to do so.

Another article germane to this case—Article 34—concerned welfare and pension funds. Section 3 of Article 34 of the contract covered payments to be made by the company to the pension fund for each employee for each month of a calendar year beginning with 1958. The monthly payment for 1958 was $5. Section 3 of Article 34 provided for an increase of $1 per month for each calendar year beginning with 1959. This would make the monthly payments for the years, 1963, 1964, 1965 equal to $10, $11, and $12 respectively.

Section 34 also embodied a special provision, Section 6, which dealt with the termination date associated with the pension and welfare commitments. The Section 6 provision read as follows:

Notwithstanding that this contract and the contracts which may follow it may be terminated prior to April 1965, it is agreed that until April 1965, neither the union nor any of its representatives nor any employee covered by this agreement shall make any requests that the amount which each Employer is required by Section 3 of this Article to pay to said Pension Fund be changed and during said period the Employers shall not have any obligations to negotiate or bargain with the union with respect to such change.

This pension fund agreement was drawn up in joint negotiations with eight other dairy companies in the area. However, each company signed a separate contract with IBTCW Local 783.

On January 30, 1963 Local 783 notified Cream Top Creamery of its desire to terminate the contract. The union made similar notifications to the other eight dairy companies which previously had joint negotiations with the union.

In the first week of April 1963 the union and the company began negotiations for a new contract. However, the union had not notified the Federal Mediation Service or the Kentucky Department of Labor of its contract termination proposal or the existence of a contractual dispute. Prior to meeting, the union presented proposals to the company and the company presented counterproposals to the union. On April 20, the counterproposals of the company were rejected by the union. From that time on, negotiations dealt primarily with the union's proposals, and except for Item 3 of the union's proposals, the union and the company reached tentative agreement on all other issues during May 1963.

Item 3 of the union's proposals provided for increasing the company's payment to the pension and welfare fund from $10, $11, and $12 monthly for 1963, 1964, and 1965, respectively, to $5 weekly for the first 2 years of a contract and $6 per week thereafter. The company did not include any changes in the pension fund payments in its counterproposals; the company's position was that changes in the pension fund payments were not a subject for negotiations until April 1965. However, in response to a number of threats by the union of a strike starting June 1, 1963 if the company did not agree to the union's proposals for the increase in pension fund payments, the company did offer to make some increase in the payments. Since the other eight dairy companies which previously had jointly negotiated with the union had agreed to the changes in the pension fund payments as demanded by the union, the union rejected the company's offer concerning the pension fund payments. The company then requested an oportunity to make its offer directly to its employees who were members of the union. The union indicated that it had no objections to the company's calling a meeting of its employees and informing them of the increase the company was willing to make. Shortly thereafter, company representatives met with the employees, and discussed the proposed increase with them. The employees later informed the company through the union's senior business representative that they, too, had rejected the company's offer.

On June 1, 1963 employees of the union struck Cream Top Creamery in support of their union's demands for increases in the monthly pension payments to be made by the company.

On August 8, 1963 the union, by telegram, notified the Federal Mediation and Conciliation Service and the Department of Labor of the State of Kentucky, that the collective bargaining contract between it and the company would expire "in the near future." Mr. George Martin,[1] the company's secretary-treasurer, met with a representative of the Federal Mediation and Conciliation Service on two occasions following the notice given to the Service by the union, and he also had several telephone conversations with FMCS representatives.

On September 3, 1963 Commissioner Carl Abel of the Kentucky Department of Labor addressed a letter to the Cream Top Creamery in which he informed the company of the notice which his department had received from the union. He also included in his letter a paragraph which stated that, "This is a routine notice as required by law which enables this department to contact the company and the union, advising them that this Department is at your disposal to assist you in any way possible."[2] Upon receipt of this letter on September 5, Martin telephoned Abel, and they briefly discussed the dispute. Martin informed Commissioner Abel that a strike had been in progress since June 1, 1963 and stated to him that nothing could be gained at that point by an attempt by Abel to mediate the dispute; Commissioner Abel agreed.

Subsequently, neither the Federal Mediation and Conciliation Service nor the Kentucky Department of Labor arranged to have representatives of the union and the company meet with their representatives to explore the possibilities of settling the dispute. The strike was still in progress when the case was heard by an NLRB Administrative Law Judge on September 30, 1963.

---

[1] The names of all individuals are disguised.

[2] Included as an appendix to this case is information concerning Kentucky Revised Statutes Section 336.140, which empowers the commissioner of the state's Department of Labor to inquire into and mediate labor disputes.

POSITION OF THE COMPANY

The Cream Top Creamery, in its unfair labor practice charges of July 17, 1963 and in amendments to the charges filed July 31 and August 31, 1963 claimed as follows:

Changes in the pension fund payments were not a subject for negotiations until April 1965, or 60 days prior to that date upon a written notification by the union for modification or termination, as specified under Section 8 (d) (1) of LMRA. As of June 1, 1963 there was complete agreement on every other negotiable section of the contract, and any strike by the union thus would be in violation of Section 8 (d) (4) of LMRA.

Section 6 of Article 34 of the contract specified that April 1965, was the earliest expiration date of the contract insofar as it provided (in Section 3 of Article 34) for monthly pension fund payments to be made by the company. Under the contract, the company had no obligation in 1963 to negotiate or bargain with the union with respect to a change in pension fund payments.

The union's strike against the company since June 1, 1963 was to enforce its demand for increases in the monthly pension fund payments made by the company; the union did not strike to enforce any demands relating to the other matters covered in the contract. Thus, the union's strike violated Section 8 (d) (4) of LMRA.

Further, the company maintained that the union did not give notification to the Federal Mediation and Conciliation Service or to the Department of Labor of the State of Kentucky within the 30 days after the union's January 31, 1963 notice to the company that it wished to terminate the existing contract. Since no agreement had been reached by the end of the 30-day period, the union had violated Section 8 (d) (3) of the act.

Therefore, by its strike actions and by its failure to notify federal and state mediation boards, the union had refused to bargain collectively, as required by the provisions of Sections 8 (d) (3) and 8 (d) (4) of the act, and therefore the union was guilty of unfair labor practices in violation of Section 8 (b) (3) of the act. The company requested that the union be ordered to cease and desist in its strike activity and in its refusal to follow required collective bargaining procedures under the law.

POSITION OF THE UNION

The union had several affirmative defenses for its actions. They were as follows:

First of all, the alleged violation of Section 8 (d) (3) by the union was a mere technicality of little importance. A technical mistake for the union's failure to give the required statutory notice was without a remedy, since the union and the company had bargained for two months following March 31, 1963 before the union initiated a strike on June 1, 1963.

Further, a business representative of the union testified that he had negotiated contracts for the union for 12 years, but in that time he had never called the Kentucky Department of Labor or its commissioner to conciliate or mediate a dispute.

Secondly, the union claimed that actually the strike was caused by the counterproposal of the company. The nominal concession by the company to increase its pension fund payments constituted a voluntary agreement by the company to waive the April 1965 contract expiration date concerning these payments. On June 1, 1963 when the strike began, the contract date as it related to the pension fund payments actually was not in effect. Therefore, the union was not in violation of Section 8 (d) (4) of the act by striking, since the union had fulfilled its requirements to bargain collectively in relationship to the March 31, 1963 termination date of the contract.

Thirdly, since the strike was actually over the counterproposal of the company, the Section 8 (d) (3) notices to the FMCS and the Kentucky Department of Labor should have been given by the company, not the union.

Finally, neither the Kentucky Department of Labor nor the Federal Mediation and Conciliation Service had held any meetings between the parties following the notice which the union gave on August 8, 1963. Therefore, this notice as required by Section 8 (d) (3)—which the union claimed should have been given by the company—was really of little practical consequence to this dispute.

The union claimed that the unfair labor practice charges should be dismissed.

APPENDIX

The Kentucky Statute

Kentucky Revised Statutes Section 336.140 of Chapter 336, with the heading *Commissioner to Investigate and Mediate Labor Disputes,* empowers the commissioner of the state's Department of Labor to inquire into the causes of strikes, lockouts, and other disputes between employers and employees, to endeavor to effect an amicable settlement, and to create within the department boards to which disputes between employers and employees may be submitted on the request of the employer and the employees for mediation. Another section of the same chapter (336.150) provides that the commissioner may act as mediator and conciliator and appoint similar persons in labor disputes whenever such intervention is requested by either party, and may offer services as a conciliator and mediator if any emergency by reason of a labor dispute is found to exist at any time. Whenever the commissioner's services as conciliator and mediator are accepted by both parties to a labor dispute, the commissioner is requested promptly to investigate and undertake to conciliate and mediate the dispute without delay. There is a proviso that the authority of this section shall not apply where the authority of a federal agency has been invoked or a federal agency assumes jurisdiction. Moreover, if the commissioner has assumed the jurisdiction, and a federal agency thereafter assumes authority, the authority of the commissioner shall cease pending federal jurisdiction.

QUESTIONS

1. Was the union guilty of unfair labor practices in striking in order to have the pension fund payments increased? Did the concession by the company to increase pension funds payments in June 1963 constitute an agreement to waive the April 1965 expiration date in the contract? Is this a key decision point in this case?

2. Evaluate the union's argument that the technical notification to the state and federal mediation boards was of little consequence to this case situation.

3. Evaluate the union's claim that the strike was caused by the counterproposal of the company.

4. What remedial action can be prescribed in order to assure that a union or company follows the notification procedures outlined under the Labor Management Relations Act?

24. SECONDARY BOYCOTTING, OR FREE SPEECH AND ACTS OF CONSCIENCE?

COMPANY: *New York Telephone Company, New York, New York*

UNION: *Local Union No. 3, International Brotherhood of Electrical Workers, AFL–CIO*

BACKGROUND

New York Telephone Company (Telco) has for many years subcontracted to independent contractors the jobs of installing telephone wire and cables and fastening certain iron work and terminals in buildings under construction or major alteration. In early 1971, Telco contracted with L. K. Comstock and Co. (Comstock), Lord Electric Co. (Lord), and J. Livingston and Co. (Livingston) to do such work on a number of Manhattan jobsites. The employees of these contractors were represented by Local Union No. 3, IBEW. Under the usual procedure, the material used by the contractor was delivered to the jobsite by Telco employees, who unloaded it from the trucks. The Local No. 3 members then would transfer the materials to the point of use, and install it.

In July of 1971, Telco employees, represented by the Communications Workers of America (CWA), went out on strike. Consequently, Telco management personnel were assigned the delivery jobs outlined above. Until August 31, 1971 these deliveries were generally accepted by the contractors' employees and installed, but a few instances occurred where several union members refused to accept or place the materials.

On August 31, a luncheon meeting took place between George Carr,[1] IBEW union business manager, Walter Weinhold, a Telco legal representative, Paul Schaeffer, Comstock's telephone superintendent, and Harry Tolman, Lord's general superintendent who also

---

[1] All names are disguised.

168

was a vice president of Local Union No. 3. The instances of non-acceptance of Telco deliveries were discussed. Mr. Carr would not say whether union members had been instructed not to accept such deliveries, or whether he felt that such actions were individual acts of conscience on the part of Local 3 members. The meeting did not resolve the dispute.

However, in an effort to avoid such problems, Telco management subsequently decided to contract with several independent truckers to deliver the materials to the jobsites. A number of such deliveries were accepted by Local 3 employees. However, on September 7, a telephone conversation took place between Mr. Carr and Mr. Weinhold. Weinhold was told that Mr. Tolman and Mr. Schaeffer had met with Carr, who informed them that the new delivery arrangement "might also lead to difficulties." Carr would not state that union members had been instructed to refuse deliveries; he only emphasized that this was a "distinct possibility."

On September 9, Local No. 3 held its regular monthly membership meeting. In the course of his business report, Mr. Carr discussed the Telco situation, and told the membership that it was his view that "when Telco management or independent truckers delivered materials to jobsites, they were acting as strikebreakers." He further stated that, "If we were to be true to trade union principles, there would be no basis for our men working under these circumstances." Mr. Carr emphasized, however, that this was "his personal view," and that others would "have to make up their own minds." Mr. Carr also made these views known in a number of individual discussions with Local 3 members after the meeting in various locations.

On September 10, a meeting took place between Mr. Weinhold and Mr. Carr. Weinhold told Carr that Telco was taking a serious view of any refusals to accept deliveries, and might either bring court action or eliminate the subcontracting system entirely, leaving the installation work to be done by Telco employees. Mr. Carr replied that he "was sorry," but "we have taken a trade union stand that we could not be in a position of aiding or abetting strikebreakers." He considered the material deliveries to be "strikebreaking."

At about the same time, a number of interruptions began to occur on Manhattan projects. On September 9, employees of Comstock on a job at 94th and Park Avenue, and employees of Lord at a job on Madison Avenue, refused to install wire and cable. On September 10, a Livingston foreman, a member of Local No. 3, refused to do a job at One Liberty Plaza involving deliveries by management personnel. On the same day, Livingston employees at 1409 Broadway refused to accept deliveries from "strikebreakers." On September 17, Livingston electricians at 919 Third Avenue refused to install material delivered by an independent trucker.

On September 21, 1971 Telco filed unfair labor practice charges against the union claiming violations of Sections 8(b) (4) (i) (ii) (B) of the Labor Management Relations Act. Pursuant to Section 10(l) of the act, the NLRB's regional director sought a temporary restraining order against the union's work interruptions. Such an order was issued by the District Court for the Southern District of New York on October 20, 1971.

POSITION OF THE COMPANY

In its arguments in support of the unfair labor practice charges,[2] the company claimed that the union's actions were violations of the following Section 8(b) (4) secondary boycott provisions of LMRA which make it an unfair labor practice for a union:

(i) to engage in, or to induce or encourage any individual employed by any person engaged in commerce or in an industry affecting commerce to engage in, a strike or a refusal in the course of his employment to use manufacture, process, transport, or otherwise handle or work on any goods, articles, materials or commodities or to perform any services; or (ii) to threaten, coerce, or restrain any person engaged in commerce or in an industry affecting commerce, where in either case an object therof is—

*   *   *   *   *

(B) forcing or requiring any person to cease using, selling, handling, transporting, or otherwise dealing in the products of any other producer, processor, or manufacturer, or to cease doing business with any other person . . .

The company pointed out that the various meetings and statements of IBEW union business representative George Carr were all directed toward causing a work stoppage or a refusal to perform work by IBEW union members. Carr was the business manager of the union, solely responsible for results in the field. He had stated at an official union meeting to his membership that his interpretation of trade union principles required a refusal by union men to handle

---

[2] The company also subsequently petitioned through the NLRB that the District Court be asked to issue a permanent injunction against the union's activities.

Telco deliveries. Soon following, there were a number of such refusals. While it may have been theoretically possible for a union
member to view Carr's statements as solely personal, and not the
official position of Local 3 of the union, it is far more likely that
Carr's statements were taken to be either an order or strong encouragement or inducement by Local 3 members to refuse to accept or install
Telco deliveries while the CWA union was on strike against Telco.
Regardless, it is clear in at least four instances that Local 3 members
employed by neutral contractors refused to accept or install materials
delivered by Telco management personnel or by independent truckers. These were hardly acts of individual conscience, but rather a
concerted effort on the part of the union.

The company asked that the union be found in direct violation of
the above provisions of the act, and that the union be ordered to
permanently cease and desist in such activities.

POSITION OF THE UNION

The union contended primarily that Mr. Carr's statements at the
September 9 union meeting represented only his own personal views
and that union members were explicitly told that they had to make
up their own minds concerning what they individually would do.
Thus, no "inducement or encouragement" prohibited under Section
8(b) (4) could have taken place. The refusals by a number of union
members to accept delivery or install materials from those whom the
union considered to be "strikebreakers" were individual acts of conscience. Such individual acts are not prohibited in the act.

Regardless, the union argued that even if Mr. Carr's statements
were assumed to be "inducement or encouragement," a number of
factors precluded the finding of Section 8(b) (4) violations. First the
union contended that the statements fell within the scope of Section
8(c) of the act, which provides:

The expressing of any views, argument, or opinion, or the dissemination thereof, whether in written, printed, graphic, or visual form, shall
not constitute or be evidence of an unfair labor practice under any of the
provisions of this subchapter, if such expression contains no threat of
reprisal of force or promise of benefit.

According to the union, this section means that only inducements
or encouragements which involve a threat of reprisal or force or
promise of benefit would be prohibited by Section 8(b) (4). Since these

factors were absent in Mr. Carr's statements, there was no violation under the act.

The union made the following additional arguments in support of its position.

1. In view of the fact that the refusals by Local 3 members to accept deliveries were few in absolute number and did not totally halt work on any project, no 8(b) (4) (i) or (ii) (B) "cessation of business object" was shown.

2. Since the purpose of the secondary boycott provisions is to protect neutral employers from entanglement in labor disputes not their own, no 8(b) (4) violation could be found in this case where Telco, not the contractors, was the charging party.

3. A part of Subsection 8(b) (4) (D) contains the following provision:

Provided, That nothing contained in this subsection (b) shall be construed to make unlawful a refusal by any person to enter upon the premises of any employer (other than his own employer), if the employees of such employer are engaged in a strike ratified or approved by a representative of such employees whom such employer is required to recognize under the Act.

In the union view—under the circumstances of this case situation—the term "refusal to enter" could well be interpreted to mean "refusal to work" or "refusal to handle" by members of Local 3, and thus would be activity protected by the act.

In summary, the union's main contention was that Mr. Carr's statements to union members were personal opinions, not "inducement" or "encouragement" prohibited by Section 8(b) (4), and that the refusals to accept deliveries were acts of individual conscience on the part of union members. But even if the NLRB would hold that Mr. Carr's statements were "inducement" or "encouragement," the various other provisions of the act cited above would support the position that the union had not committed unfair labor practices in this matter. The charges against the union should be dismissed.

QUESTIONS

1. Were the statements of the union business manager personal opinions, or were they inducement and encouragement prohibited under Section 8(b) (4) of the act?
2. Were the refusals of the union members to accept deliveries or install

materials individual acts of conscience, or secondary boycotting? Why is this difficult to ascertain?

3. Evaluate the union's argument that Mr. Carr's statements were protected under the free speech provisions of Section 8(c) of the act. Is there any contradiction between the provisions of Section 8(c) and Section 8(b) (4) in regard to permissible statements of management or union representatives?

4. Evaluate each of the arguments of the union that various provisions of the act permitted the statements made by the union representative and the acts of the union workers in this matter.

5. Why would the company request a permanent injunction against the union and not sue for economic damages under the act?

25. THE EMPLOYEE WHO WORKED ON DR. MARTIN LUTHER KING'S BIRTHDAY

COMPANY: *Bechtel Corporation, Morgantown, Maryland*

UNION: *Laborers' International Union of America, Local 832, AFL–CIO*

BACKGROUND

Bechtel Corporation is a major company which engages in the business of constructing power plants throughout the country. At Morgantown, Maryland, the company was involved in a project to construct a major power plant. Bechtel employed as laborers members of Local 832 of the Laborers' International Union which was located in this area.

During the three years that the Morgantown project was in progress prior to this case, there had been a tacit agreement between the company and Local 832 which permitted members of the local to observe Dr. Martin Luther King's birthday as a holiday if they wished to do so. This was a voluntary policy; however, most of Local 832's members refrained from working on this particular day.

In 1971, the union's members were informed by the union on January 14th that there would be no work on Dr. King's birthday, January 15th. On January 15th, Dan Hasler,[1] a member of the union who had been employed on the project from its beginning, showed up at the Morgantown job site to obtain a set of knee pads which he intended to use for a personal project at home. Upon arriving at the job site, Hasler was asked by the project's general superintendent if he would like to work that day with the carpenters who already were at work. Carpenters were members of another union who were not observing Dr. King's birthday as a holiday. Hasler agreed to remain at

---

1 Name is disguised.

the job site and worked with the carpenters for a full eight hours. On the following day, January 16, all of the workers, including Hasler, returned to work.

Early that morning, the Local 832 shop steward learned that Hasler had worked on Dr. King's birthday while the remainder of the Laborers' union local had been at home. On January 18th the general labor foreman, who was a member of Local 832, delivered a safety lecture to a gathering of the union's members who were present for the lecture. This foreman made a statement concluding that violators of safety regulations would be subject to layoff by the company and the union. Following the safety lecture, the union's business agent held a meeting for all of the labor foremen who were working on the Morgantown project and who were members of the union.

After some discussion of the safety problems, the conversation turned to the matter of Hasler's having worked on Dr. King's birthday. Some of the labor foremen were very resentful of the fact that Hasler had worked. Others were rather indifferent to the whole matter.

Eventually, Hasler's foreman sent him to talk to the union business agent. After talking with Hasler, the agent told him that, at 2 p.m. that day, by vote of the union Executive Committee, he was to be laid off for an indefinite period for having worked on Dr. King's birthday in violation of the agreement that the union had with the company.

Due to a combination of circumstances, however, Hasler was not laid off until a month later. When he was laid off by the union,[2] Hasler immediately filed unfair labor practice charges against the union, claiming that his rights as a union member and employee had been violated. The company contacted the union, and Hasler shortly thereafter was reinstated to his former position on the job. Nevertheless, the unfair labor practice charges were pressed by the company on behalf of employee Hasler, and eventually they were heard by an NLRB Administrative Law Judge.

POSITION OF THE COMPANY

On behalf of employee Dan Hasler, the company held that the Laborers' union had violated Section 8 (b) (2) and Section 8 (a) (3) of the Labor Management Relations Act by discriminating against

---

[2] This "layoff" was accomplished through a union hiring hall arrangement which existed in cooperation with employers in the area served by the union local.

Hasler because of his violation of the union's policy of not working on the birthday of Dr. Martin Luther King. The company argued that Hasler had every right to work on Dr. King's birthday, since there was nothing other than an informal agreement that this would be a voluntary holiday. The company argued that Hasler was being discriminated against because of a matter which was outside the Labor Management Relations Act. According to the Labor Management Relations Act, a union or employer may only discriminate against a union member for a failure to pay or tender periodic dues uniformly levied by a union. However, Hasler had consistently paid his dues. The company requested that the union be found guilty of an unfair labor practice, that Hasler be made whole for any loss of earnings caused by the discriminatory layoff instigated by the union, and that the union should be directed to desist in this kind of activity against its own members.

POSITION OF THE UNION

The union did not deny that it had threatened employee Hasler with the loss of his job on January 18 due to his having worked on Dr. King's birthday. However, the union pointed out that the actual layoff of employee Hasler did not occur until about a month later. The union held that Hasler's layoff was because he repeatedly had violated certain safety regulations. Further, the union claimed that a general reduction of the work force had resulted in Hasler's being laid off from the Morgantown project about 30 days after the King birthday incident involved in this case. The union pointed out that other members as well as Hasler had been laid off by the union for various reasons, but primarily due to a reduction in the labor force. The union claimed that the company was using this incident as a way of embarrassing the union, and that the company was insensitive to the feelings of the membership regarding Dr. King's birthday. The union asked that the unfair labor practice charges be dismissed.

QUESTIONS

1. Did the union violate the Labor Management Relations Act by threatening and later not permitting employee Dan Hasler to work under the circumstances of this case? Why, or why not?
2. Evaluate the union's argument that the company was using this inci-

dent as a way of embarrassing the union, and that the company was insensitive to the feelings of the membership.

3. Section 8 (b) (2), as related to Section 8 (a) (3) of the act, focuses upon the question of discrimination which would encourage or discourage membership in a labor union. Were the union's actions in this case motivated in this context? Why, or why not?

4. Why would the company pursue such a case as this on behalf of one of its employees in what could essentially be considered as an intraunion issue?

26. THE TURNCOAT UNION MEMBERS

COMPANY: Boeing Company, Michoud, Louisiana

UNION: Booster Lodge No. 405, International Association of Machinists and Aerospace Workers, AFL–CIO

BACKGROUND

Booster Lodge No. 405, International Association of Machinists and Aerospace Workers, AFL–CIO, and the Boeing Company were parties to a collective bargaining agreement which was effective from May 16, 1963 through September 15, 1965. Upon the expiration of the contract, the union commenced a lawful strike against Boeing at its Michoud, Louisiana plant, as well as at various other locations. This work stoppage lasted 18 days. On October 2, 1965 a new bargaining agreement was signed, and the economic strikers returned to work the following day. Both the expired agreement and the newly executed contract contained maintenance-of-membership clauses, which required all new employees to notify both the union and the company within 40 days of their acceptance of employment if they elected not to become union members. It also required those who were union members to retain their membership during the contract term.

During the strike period, some 143 employees of the 1,900 production and maintenance employees represented by the union at the Michoud plant crossed the picket line and reported to work. All of these employees had been union members during the 1963–65 contract period. Twenty-four of the employees who worked during the strike made no attempt to resign from the union during the strike. The remaining 119 submitted voluntary resignations from the union, in writing, to both the union and the company. Sixty-one of these employees who resigned did so before they crossed the picket line and returned to work; the other 58 resigned during the course of the strike, but after they had crossed the picket line in order to work. All of these resignations were submitted after the expiration of

178

the 1963–1965 contract and before the execution of the new agreement. Union members had not been warned prior to the strike that disciplinary measures could, or would, be taken against those who crossed the picket line to work, nor had any such discipline been imposed on members of Booster Lodge 405 prior to this time.

The Union Takes Action

In late October of 1965 the union notified all the members and former members who had crossed the picket line to work during the strike that charges had been preferred against them under the International Union constitution, for "Improper Conduct of a Member" due to their having "accepted employment . . . in an establishment where a strike existed." They were advised of the dates of their union trials, which were to be held even in their absence if they did not appear. Also, they were notified of their right to be represented by any counsel who was a member of the International Association of Machinists and Aerospace Workers. The International Union constitution provision permitted the imposition of disciplinary measures, including "reprimand, fine, suspension, or expulsion from membership, or any lesser penalty or combination," where a member had been found guilty of misconduct after notice and a hearing.

Disciplinary actions accordingly were imposed on all individuals who had worked during the strike. No distinction was drawn between those persons who had resigned from the union during the course of the strike and those who had remained union members. Employees who did not appear for trial before the union trial committee and those who appeared and who were found "guilty" were fined $450 each, and they were barred from holding a union office for a period of five years. The fines of about 35 employees who appeared for trial, apologized, and pledged loyalty to the union were reduced to 50 percent of the earnings they received during the strike.[1] In some of these cases the time period during which these persons were prohibited from holding union office was decreased to a period based upon the number of days of strikebreaking activity each respective person had engaged in. None of the disciplined individuals processed intraunion appeals.

---

1 Employees who worked during the strike earned between $2.38 and $3.63 per hour, or between $95 and $145 per 40-hour week. In some instances, earnings during the strike period were supplemented by the inclusion of bonus or premium rates for weekend and overtime work.

Although none of the $450 fines had been paid at the time of the case hearing, reduced fines were paid in some instances. The union sent out written notices to all individuals who had not paid the fines that the matter was being referred to an attorney for collection, that suit would be filed if the fines remain unpaid, and that reduced fines would be reinstated to $450 in the event of nonpayment. The union actually filed suit against nine individual employees to collect the fines (plus attorney's fees and interest). None of those suits had yet been resolved at the time of the hearing.

POSITION OF THE COMPANY

On February 18, 1966 the company filed charges with the National Labor Relations Board, alleging that the union had violated Section 8 (b) (1) (A) of the Labor Management Relations Act, which states that it is unfair labor practice for a labor organization to "restrain or coerce employees in the exercise of rights guaranteed in Section 7." Included among those rights is the right to refrain from engaging in any of the protected concerted activities enumerated at the beginning of Section 7.

The company argued that the union was in violation of 8 (b) (1) (A) in four areas: (1) by fining those employees who had resigned from the union before they returned to work during the strike; (2) by disciplining those employees who had resigned after returning to work to the extent that the fines were imposed for their working during the strike after their resignation; (3) by fining members for crossing the picket line to work; and (4) by fining members of the union on whom discipline was imposed to an extent which was an unreasonable amount.

The company argued that the levy of any fine in this type of situation was calculated to force individuals to pay money to the union and engage in conduct which would be against their will, and this would be true regardless of the ultimate collectibility of the fine. The company argued that the threat of a fine and the imposition of a fine, even if it is not collected by the union, coerces employees to forego their Section 7 statutory rights not to honor the union's picket line, rather than to exercise their own free judgment in a labor-management dispute.

The company requested: that the union should be found guilty of unfair labor practices; that it be ordered to cease and desist from such activity in the future; that the fines levied on the various union members should be deemed uncollectible; and that the various disciplinary actions imposed by the union on its members be declared unenforceable.

POSITION OF THE UNION

The union argued that its actions in disciplining members and former members who had crossed the picket line during the strike were legal and appropriate under the law and under the union constitution. The union claimed that this was an internal matter which must be left to the handling of the union itself if it was to be effective. The union argued that the significance of its membership relationship was the union's established authority over its members. In joining a union the individual member becomes a party to a negotiated union contract and the union constitution. Without waiving protected Section 7 rights under the Labor Management Relations Act to refrain from concerted activities, a union member recognizes that, by joining a union, he consents to the possible imposition of union discipline upon his exercise of that right. Without some form of internal control of its members, a union could hardly engage in concerted activities for the overall good of the total membership.

The union argued that even when members resigned from the union in the middle of a strike, they were not relieved from the burden of union discipline with respect to postresignation activity. The union claimed that it had the same right to discipline those who had resigned in the middle of the strike and who had crossed the picket line, as it did those members who did not resign from the union. In both cases, this was an internal union matter, not subject to the Labor Management Relations Act. Further, the union argued that the amount of the fines it imposed was an internal matter over which the NLRB had no jurisdiction. The union requested that the unfair labor practice charges be dismissed.

QUESTIONS

1. Evaluate the company's argument that a "threat of a fine and the imposition of a fine by the union, even if not collected, coerces employees to forego their statutory rights not to honor the union's picket line."
2. Does a labor union have the right to control its members through

various forms of discipline, even where such discipline appears to force union members to give up certain of their freedoms in the workplace? Discuss.

3. Does it make any difference in this case whether an employee resigned from the union before crossing the picket line? Why, or why not?

4. Why does the union argue that once a strike begins, regardless of the subsequent behavior of various members, it retains disciplinary control over the members involved?

5. Does the NLRB have any jurisdiction to rule on the reasonableness of the union fines if such fines are considered legal under the law? Discuss.

27. DID THE UNION FAIL TO PROPERLY REPRESENT A MINORITY EMPLOYEE?

COMPANY: *King Soopers, Inc., Denver, Colorado*

UNION: *Retail Clerks Union Local No. 7*

EMPLOYEE: *Tony Cortez,* acting as an individual.*

BACKGROUND

The company operates a chain of grocery stores in the Denver, Colorado area. On July 3, 1972 Tony Cortez,[1] a young man of Hispanic American descent, began working on the night shift at one of these stores as an all-purpose clerk. In late April 1974 Arthur Gribbins, a co-worker, was promoted to night crew foreman, a position that Cortez felt should have been given him. A similar decision not to upgrade Cortez occurred in August. He protested these promotional bypasses to management in both instances, claiming that he was passed over because he was Hispanic American. The situation was never resolved to his satisfaction, and around mid-September he filed a complaint with the Colorado Civil Rights Commission (CCRC). On September 18, he also formally complained to the Equal Employment Opportunity Commission (EEOC).

On September 17, 1974 Cortez' wife informed Shirley Steinman, the service department manager who was Cortez' supervisor, that her husband was ill and would not be at work that evening. The following day, pursuant to the service department manager's request, Cortez obtained a medical certificate stating that he would not be able to work for three days. On September 19, Mrs. Cortez presented this certificate to Carl Danforth, the store manager. An altercation over whether Mrs. Cortez should be the one to report her husband's illness ensued, and the manager asked Mrs. Cortez to leave. Subsequently, Tony Cortez and his wife reported this incident to Dan Kennedy, business representative for Local 7 of the Retail Clerks Union. Cortez

---

* The names of all individuals are disguised.

expressed concern that there would be trouble when he reported for work the next evening. Kennedy promised to talk the next day to the store manager, Danforth.

When Cortez reported for work the following evening, the store manager Danforth summoned him and asked him in words to this effect, "What's this with you? Who do you think is discriminating against you? Who in the hell do you think you are that you should be treated specially?" Cortez replied that he would not talk unless his union representative was present. Consequently, Danforth refused to permit Cortez to work that day. Cortez reported for work during the next two days, but each time he refused to talk without his union representative. Therefore, the manager refused to let him work.

On September 23, Cortez went to the union office and presented a written statement of his grievance. This statement protested the employer's refusal to permit him to work September 20, 21, and 22, and alleged that the employer's failure to promote him "was discriminatory." However, Kennedy, the union representative, replied that the grievance "could not be put that way; it had to be in accordance with company procedures."

On September 24, at a step one grievance meeting, Cortez advised Danforth that he had filed charges with the EEOC and CCRC. Danforth accused Cortez of "going over his head," and he then told Cortez that he was "suspended indefinitely" until he "dropped the charges." Cortez turned to Kennedy, the union representative, and said that the manager's decision violated the no-discrimination clause of the collective bargaining contract. Kennedy replied that Cortez also had "gone over his head, too," and that the matter was "out of his hands." After the meeting, Cortez and his wife complained to Mary Dilling, the union's secretary-treasurer, about Kennedy's answer and conduct. Dilling, the secretary-treasurer, promised to talk with Kennedy about the matter.

At the next grievance meeting on October 14, Albert Eley, the company's employment supervisor, advised Cortez that the company had decided "not to give him anything back under the grievance procedure," and that he could either start over again at the same store or be transferred to another store. Cortez protested that he would lose his seniority and asked his union representative, Kennedy, "to do something about it." However, Kennedy replied that he agreed with the company position, because Cortez would not have been working anyway due to a strike by another labor organization that temporarily had closed the store where he worked. Cortez replied that he was going to file unfair labor practices with the NLRB against both the company and the union. He asked Kennedy to take his grievance to arbitration, but Kennedy replied that he would not. After the meeting, Cortez and his wife again complained to the union's secretary-treasurer, Dilling.

About a week later, Cortez asked the secretary-treasurer if the union was going to take his grievance to arbitration. Dilling told Cortez that she did not want to talk with him, because Cortez "had filed charges with the NLRB."

POSITION OF TONY CORTEZ

Tony Cortez filed unfair labor practice charges against both the company and the union in this matter.

Cortez claimed that the company had discharged him, a Hispanic American employee, for filing charges with the Colorado Civil Rights Commission (CCRC) and with the federal Equal Employment Opportunity Commission (EEOC). Cortez claimed that he had filed these charges because the company had discriminated against him in failing to promote him as he felt was deserved. He was trying to make the company live up to the no-discrimination clause included in the collective bargaining agreement. Since the company had refused to consider his complaint as a union employee and subsequently discharged him because he refused to capitulate to an unfair economic threat, Cortez claimed that the company had violated Section 8(a) (1) of the Labor Management Relations Act.

Concerning the union, Cortez claimed that the union had violated Section 8(b) (1) (A) by failing to properly represent him in his dispute with the company. Cortez argued that the union had refused to fully and fairly process his grievance, because: (1) he had filed unfair labor practice charges against the company and union; and (2) he had attempted to enforce the no-discrimination clause of the collective bargaining contract by filing charges with the state fair employment practices agency and the Equal Employment Opportunity Commission. Cortez pointed to the fact that at the first step of the grievance procedure, union representative Kennedy had agreed with the company that Cortez should be suspended indefinitely until he dropped his charges with the Colorado agency and EEOC. Cortez claimed that Kennedy had demonstrated continued hostility toward his pursuit of the discrimination aspects of his grievance. When he asked Dilling, the union's secretary-treasurer, if his grievance would be taken to arbitration, she refused to talk to him because he had filed charges with the NLRB.

For all of these reasons, Cortez argued that the union had failed to properly represent him. This "restraint and coercion" exercised against him by the union was in clear violation of Section 8(b) (1) (A) of the act.

Cortez requested that both the company and union be found guilty of unfair labor practices; that he be restored to his job position; and that he should be made whole by either the company, the union, or both, for all lost wages and benefits resulting from his suspension and discharge.

POSITION OF THE COMPANY AND THE UNION

The company claimed that it had suspended and later discharged Tony Cortez for what it considered to be conduct detrimental to the best interests of the firm. The company claimed that after its actions against Cortez were carried out, the union did not process Cortez' grievance to arbitration, since the union leadership, too, felt that Cortez had been discharged for just cause. It would have been improper for the company to deal with Cortez as an individual directly, since Cortez was part of the bargaining unit and the company was obligated to follow provisions of the established grievance procedure.

Even granting the possibility that Cortez was discriminated against as a minority (i.e., Hispanic American) person, the company argued that Cortez' proper statutory remedy was to follow procedures under Title VII of the Civil Rights Act of 1964. The company argued that it had not violated Section 8(a) (1) of LMRA, and that Cortez was just using these charges as a way of trying to salvage his job. The company claimed that the unfair labor practice charges against the company were without merit and should be dismissed.

The union position was analogous to that of the company. The union claimed that it had properly represented Cortez in this matter. The union felt that Cortez' grievance was not worthy of processing any further under the grievance procedure. Not every grievance filed by a member of a bargaining unit is meritorious. In this case, the union concurred with the company's decision to discharge Cortez, and therefore the union did not process his grievance to arbitration. The LMRA does not require the union to take an employee's grievance to arbitration, just because a union member thinks it should be done. If Cortez felt he was being discriminated against by the union as well as by the company, his proper course for seeking relief was through provisions of Title VII of the Civil Rights Act of 1964. The union claimed that it had properly represented Cortez, and the union requested that the unfair labor practice charges against the union be dismissed.

APPENDIX

Subsequent to the hearings of this case by an Administrative Law Judge and before the case was appealed to the full NLRB, a District Director of the Equal Employment Opportunity Commission ruled that there was "no reasonable cause to believe that Respondents (i.e., the company and union) had violated Title VII of the Civil Rights Act of 1964," based on charges filed by Tony Cortez.

QUESTIONS

1. Evaluate the claim of employee Cortez that the company had violated Section 8(a) (1) of the Labor Management Relations Act because the company had failed to consider his complaint that he was trying to make the company live up to the no-discrimination clause in the collective bargaining agreement.

2. Evaluate the company's claim that it would have been improper for the company to deal with Cortez as an individual, since Cortez was part of the bargaining unit and the company had to follow the established grievance procedure.

3. Did the union fail to properly represent Cortez in his dispute with the company? Must a union process a grievance to arbitration if a union member requests it in order to carry out its duties under the Labor Management Relations Act? Discuss.

4. Evaluate the argument of the company and the union that Cortez' proper remedy, if any, was through the Civil Rights Act.

5. To what degree, if any, should the ruling of the Equal Employment Opportunity Commission noted in the Appendix of the case influence any decision which the National Labor Relations Board might render?

28. WHO SHOULD INSTALL THE CONCRETE PLANKS?

COMPANY: Spancrete Northeast, Inc., Ulster, New York

UNIONS: Local Union No. 417, International Association of Bridge, Structural and Ornamental Iron Workers, AFL–CIO (to be referred to as the Ironworkers union)

Local Unions No. 17 and No. 190, Laborers International Union of North America, AFL–CIO (to be referred to as the Laborers union)

BACKGROUND

In early 1975, the Spancrete Company contracted with the Eberhardt Construction Company to manufacture and install precast, prestressed hollow core planks, known by the trade name "Spancrete," at the town office building in Ulster, New York. Spancrete's president, Amos Hagen,[1] described the work of installing the planks as follows:

Rigging and placing would commonly be defined as the work that's related to the physical and actual rigging or set up of the crane, the actual and physical work related to the rigging or securing of a choker of a lifting device or a belt to the item that's to be picked up by the crane. Placing would refer to the guiding and hand handling and signaling to direct that piece to its final location on the structural frame of the building and removal of said chockers or sling from the member permitting the crane boon then to swing back to its beginning position over the load. . . . Upon completion of the rigging and placing, the material would be aligned. That means it's aligned into its final half-inch of position by pry bars or some other method of moving it slightly; leveling it, so that it's level with the member that's adjacent to it; the grouting; the cutting of any structural chases; and further the caulking of the underside joints to enhance the

---

[1] The names of all individuals are disguised.

188

ultimate appearance; the application of latex concrete underlayment to properly smooth the top surface.[2]

On February 14, 1975 before 8 a.m., Spancrete shipped five truckloads of its Spancrete product to the Ulster jobsite and ordered a crane from the Kingston Crane Service Company to provide the power equipment necessary for rigging and placing the planks. At about the same time, Spancrete dispatched to the construction site an erection crew consisting of three of its permanent employees, all represented by Laborers Local 190, and two local area employees, both represented by Laborers Local 17. At about 8 a.m. Spancrete's erection superintendent, Andy Ibsen, observed Ironworkers union business agent, Harry Burgess, at the jobsite with two pickets carrying signs which read,

This contractor does not employ members of the Ironworkers Local 417 on this job. We wish to inform employees and the public that we do not ask anyone to refuse to cross our picket line, refuse to perform work, or refuse to patronize any service or product.

At this point, the crane operator and the oiler refused to work because of the picketing. A few minutes later, Burgess told Mr. Amos Hagen that the Ironworkers union was demanding the work of rigging and placing the planks and threatened to permanently picket the site if the Ironworkers did not get the work of rigging and placing the planks. Hagen did not agree to Burgess' demands, and the Ironworkers continued to picket the jobsite.

The company filed unfair labor practice charges against the Ironworkers union claiming a violation of Section 8(b) (4) (D) of the Labor Management Relations Act. Under Section 10(k) of the act, the NLRB requested the federal district court to issue an injunction against the picketing by the Ironworkers union. The court issued this injunction in early March of 1975.

POSITION OF THE UNION

The Ironworkers union claimed that the work in contention belonged to the Ironworkers, and that the Ironworkers Union was justified in its actions which were necessary to preserve its contractual rights.

---

2 This final phase of the erection process—namely, the aligning of the precast, prestressed concrete products—always was performed by employees represented by the Laborers union, and it was not here in dispute.

First of all, the union pointed out that the Ironworkers union and the Eberhardt Company were signatories to a labor agreement wherein jurisdiction over the "fabrication, production, erection, and construction of precast, prestressed, and poststressed concrete structures" specifically was assigned to the Ironworkers. Therefore, the union was within its rights to picket the Eberhardt construction site in order to force Eberhardt to live up to this agreement.

Second, the Ironworkers union pointed to a 1972 decision of the NLRB[3] in which the Board awarded a similar Spancrete construction job in New York City to the Ironworkers union. The 1972 case was basically identical to this situation and supported the Ironworkers' claim to the disputed work.

Third, the union in the person of Mr. Burgess testified that other area contractors, with the exception of Spancrete, used Ironworkers to perform work similar to the work here in dispute, and that masons or laborers were normally hired to perform the final portion of the installation process—namely, the aligning, leveling, grouting, etc. In support of its position, the Ironworkers union introduced into evidence letters from area contractors to the effect that they assigned installation of this type of work to Ironworkers. Documentary evidence showed several area projects where Ironworkers were employed to perform similar functions, as well as several Joint Board[4] awards from other areas in the United States awarding the type of work in dispute to the Ironworkers union.

Finally, the Ironworkers union pointed out that the Ironworkers conducted a three-year apprenticeship program which included on-the-job and classroom instructions covering all phases of the disputed work. In the Ironworkers' view, members of the Laborers union did not receive comparable training in the rigging and placing phase of the installation of prestressed concrete planks. Thus, to promote the

---

3 Local Union No. 40, International Association of Bridge, Structural and Ornamental Iron Workers, AFL–CIO (Spancrete Northeast, Inc.), 197 NLRB 822 (1972).

4 This refers to the Imparital Jurisdictional Disputes Board of the AFL–CIO. All labor organizations affiliated with the Building and Construction Trades Department of the AFL–CIO and various employer associations who employ their members have signed a stipulation to be bound by decisions of the Impartial Jurisdictonal Disputes Board. In essence, when there is a dispute or potential jurisdictional dispute following an assignment of work, either the contractor/s/ or labor union/s/ involved may refer the issue to the Impartial Jurisdictional Disputes Board for a decision. There is a rather detailed procedure for both filing complaints and appealing rulings of the Board. See *Procedural Rules and Regulations of the Impartial Jurisdictional Disputes Board and Appeals Procedures,* a pamphlet published by the AFL–CIO Building and Construction Trades Department (June, 1973).

interests of efficiency, economy, and safety, this work should be awarded to the Ironworkers.

In summary, the Ironworkers union argued that its picketing action was necessary to protect work rights which historically, contractually, and properly belonged to the Ironworkers. The unfair labor practice charges should be dismissed, and the work in question should be awarded by the NLRB to the Ironworkers union.

POSITION OF THE COMPANY

The company pointed out, first of all, that Laborers Locals 190 and 435 had been certified by the Board as collective-bargaining representatives of Spancrete's employees at its South Bethlehem and Rochester facilities respectively. Neither certification, however, made specific reference to the crews which Spancrete used to perform erection work such as the one here in dispute.

Since it commenced doing business in 1963, however, Spancrete had executed a national agreement with the International Laborers Union of North America, AFL-CIO, which specifically covered "all field construction . . . and all work performed by the Employer. . . ." Additionally, that agreement provided that the covered work jurisdiction was specified in Article III, Section 1(b) of the International Laborers union's constitution which, in turn, encompassed the work outlined in the International Laborers union "Manual of Jurisdiction." That manual included within the Laborers' jurisdiction the following work:

Where pre-stressed or pre-cast concrete slabs, walls, or sections are used, all loading, unloading, stockpiling, hooking, setting, and barring into place of such slabs, walls, or sections. All mixing, handling, conveying, placing, and spreading of grout for any purpose.

Spancrete had also executed separate agreements with various Laborers' locals representing employees at each of its facilities. These agreements covered the manufacture and installation of Spancrete's concrete products. In accordance with the above, the Spancrete Company pointed out that it had been its practice to assign the installation of its products to an erection crew typically consisting of three permanently based Spancrete employees represented by the Laborers union and two employees hired locally for the particular job. The local employees would be represented by the Laborers local with jurisdiction over the particular geographical area in which the job was located. This practice was consistent with the specific provisions of the national agreement mentioned above, and Spancrete was satisfied with this arrangement. In the instant case, as noted previously, the crew's permanent employees were represented by Laborers Local 190, while the two employees hired locally were represented by Laborers Local 17. The only exception to this practice occurred in the New York City situation cited by the Ironworkers union. In that case, the NLRB had awarded the disputed work to the Ironworkers, since Ironworkers historically had performed this type of work in New York City.

Spancrete did not dispute the evidence produced by the Ironworkers union. However, the company claimed that since it commenced doing business in 1963, 95 percent of the 20 million square feet of Spancrete which it had produced had been installed by crews of Laborers under the arrangement described above. Of that total, about 1,065,000 square feet were installed in Ulster County (the town of Ulster is located in Ulster County) and the three neighboring counties of Greene, Duchess, and Orange. Thus, although there was evidence of area and industry practice to support the Ironworkers claim, it was also clear that in the areas where Spancrete operated, it had been its general practice to assign the disputed work to employees represented by Laborers. This was true in all areas except New York City as mentioned previously.

The company claimed that it employed permanent installation crews of Laborers who were required to go through work orientation and safety sessions, as well as a six-month on-the-job training period in order to perform rigging and placing work efficiently and safely. For the Laborers hired locally to supplement the permanent crew, Spancrete tried whenever possible to hire local Laborers whom it had employed before. When, by necessity, inexperienced local men were hired, they were tutored about Spancrete's safety rules and assigned to perform the less dangerous facets of the installation work.

Finally, as to factors of efficiency and economy, Mr. Hagen testified that the degrees of work coordination and scheduling, as well as the speed of erection, would be augmented if the disputed work were awarded to Laborers. It was advantageous to Spancrete to use a permanent crew of specialized workmen who were accustomed to handling its products and familiar with the best tools and procedures to achieve the desired results. In contrast, Mr. Hagen stated that Ironworkers were less familiar with Spancrete's products, and that an award in favor of them would result in a less effective and more costly operation. In this respect, the company claimed that Ironworkers would utilize more manpower to perform the same amount of work.

For all of the above reasons, the company claimed that it had the right to assign the disputed work to workers represented by the Laborers union. The company requested that the NLRB find the Ironworkers in violation of Section 8(b) (4) (d) of the act which prohibits a union from:

... forcing or requiring any employer to assign particular work to employees in a particular labor organization or in a particular trade, craft, or class rather than to employees in another labor organization or in another trade, craft, or class, unless such employer is failing to conform to an order or certification of the Board determining the bargaining representative for employees performing such work.

The company asked the Board: (a) to direct the Ironworkers union to cease and desist in its unfair labor practices; (b) to award the disputed work to the Laborers union; and (c) to issue a broad work award on behalf of the Laborers union to be applicable throughout the area in which the Spancrete company operated so as to prevent similar jurisdictional disputes.

QUESTIONS

1. Evaluate the arguments of the Ironworkers union in claiming jurisdiction of the disputed work.
2. Evaluate the arguments of the company in claiming that it had the right to assign the disputed work to the employees belonging to the Laborers union.
3. Why would the company prefer to have the Laborers union rather than the Ironworkers Union be awarded the disputed work by the NLRB?
4. If the NLRB should uphold the company position concerning the work jurisdiction, was the company's remedial request appropriate? Discuss.

29. ELIGIBILITY OF ECONOMIC STRIKERS TO VOTE IN A DECERTIFICATION ELECTION

COMPANY: *Gulf States Paper Corporation, EZ Packaging Division, Nicholasville, Kentucky*

UNION: *Paperworkers Union, AFL–CIO*

BACKGROUND

The union was certified as the collective bargaining representative of production and maintenance plant employees on September 10, 1973. Thereafter, the union and company conducted a series of negotiating meetings, but were unable to reach agreement on a contract. The employees went on strike on February 27, 1974 to protest the subsequent breakdown in negotiations between the parties. On March 14, 1975 a group of employees in the bargaining unit filed a decertification petition under Section 9(c) of the Labor Management Relations Act, requesting that an election be held to determine whether or not the union should continue to represent the unit employees. The strike was still in effect at the time of the hearing conducted by an NLRB official in April 1975.

At the time the strike began, there were 134 employees in the bargaining unit. Eight of these employees never participated in the strike; 27 abandoned the strike and returned to work at the company plant; 11 voluntarily terminated their employment. Of the remaining 78 employees who continued to be on strike, 43 had had their positions filled by permanent replacements.

The only issue raised at the hearing was the eligibility of the 78 employees still on strike to vote in the decertification election to be conducted more than 12 months after the commencement of the strike.

POSITION OF THE COMPANY AND
PETITIONING EMPLOYEES

In support of contentions of the petitioning employees, the company argued that none of the 78 striking employees should be eligible to vote in the decertification election. The company pointed to Section 9(c) (3) of the Labor Management Relations Act which states:

Employees engaged in an economic strike who are not entitled to reinstatement shall be eligible to vote under such regulations as the Board shall find are consistent with the purposes and provisions of this Act in any election conducted within twelve months after the commencement of the strike.

The company cited a previous NLRB case decision,[1] in which the Board had ruled that permanently replaced economic strikers, who were not entitled to reinstatement do not retain their eligibility to vote in any representational election conducted more than twelve months after the commencement of a strike. This precedent ruling would clearly indicate that the 43 strikers who had been permanently replaced with new employees by the company should not be eligible to vote in the decertification election at the Nicholasville, Kentucky plant, since the strike had been in progress for over a year.

Concerning the other 35 strikers, the company claimed that because of depressed economic conditions, it was forced to lay off many employees. The company had been operating with approximately 75 production and maintenance employees, down from the usual complement of 130. There had been a decrease in the number of orders being placed with the company, and it was unlikely that any of the 35 strikers would be rehired in the near future. The company argued, therefore, that the 35 remaining strikers could hardly be considered as employees entitled for reinstatement. Therefore, by analogous reasoning, these so-called employees, too, should not be permitted to vote in a decertification election being conducted more than a year after an economic strike had commenced.

POSITION OF THE UNION

The union argued that all 78 striking employees should be allowed to vote in the decertification election. Alternatively, the union contended that at least the 35 strikers whose jobs had not been perma-

---

1 *Warl Clipper Corporation,* 195 NLRB 684, 79 LRRM 1433 (1972).

nently replaced should be eligible to vote, claiming that the *Wahl Clipper Corporation* NLRB case decision cited by the company did not disenfranchise economic strikers who had not been permanently replaced.

The union pointed out that Section 2(3) of the act defines an employee as including "... any individual whose work has ceased as a consequence of, or in connection with, any current labor dispute, or because of any unfair labor practice. ..." It has been long-established NLRB policy that economic strikers retain their status of employees during the course of a strike, unless some clear action has severed the employment relationship. Neither Section 2(3) nor Section 9(c) (3) of the act specifically limit the time period eligibility of economic strikers to retain their status as employees.

The union pointed to another NLRB decision[2] in which the Board ruled that economic strikers retained their status as employees, except if the following specific circumstances were evident prior to a proposed representational election:

(a) if the economic striker/s/ had obtained permanent employment elsewhere;

(b) if the employer had permanently eliminated the job/s/ for valid economic reasons;

(c) if the employer discharged or refused to reinstate the economic striker/s/ for misconduct rendering such person/s/ unsuitable for reemployment.

The union argued that there was no evidence in the present case that the strikers had found permanent employment elsewhere, that the jobs of the strikers had been permanently eliminated, or that the company had discharged or refused to reinstate any of the striking employees for misconduct.

Even though the company plant employment was lower than previous, this did not suffice to show that the jobs of the strikers had been permanently eliminated or abolished so as to terminate the strikers' employment status and render them ineligible to vote in the election.

The union argued, therefore, that all 78 economic strikers should be declared eligible to vote in the proposed decertification election; or at the very least, that the 35 economic strikers whose jobs had not been eliminated and who had not been permanently replaced by other employees should be so eligible.

---

[2] *W. Wilton Wood, Inc.*, 127 NLRB 1675, 46 LRRM 1240 (1960).

QUESTIONS

1. Evaluate the company's arguments that the 43 permanently replaced strikers should not be eligible to vote in the decertification election.

2. Evaluate the company's arguments that the 35 remaining strikers were not entitled for reinstatement and should not be permitted to vote in the decertification election.

3. Evaluate the union's arguments that all 78 striking employees should be allowed to vote in the decertification election, or that at the very least the 35 remaining strikers should be eligible.

4. Compare the situation in the instant case with the previous case rulings of the NLRB cited by both management and the union. Were there inconsistencies in these decisions?

5. Why do the company and union have a vital interest in the outcome of the question of eligibility of strikers to vote in this decertification election?

PART TWO

Problems in Union–Management Relations

CASES FROM LABOR ARBITRATION

Conflict Resolution, Grievance Procedures, and Arbitration

Index to Cases for Part II

THE CASES

CONFLICT RESOLUTION, GRIEVANCE PROCEDURES, AND ARBITRATION[1]

The potential for conflict exists within every organization. This is true of the family unit, business organizations, social groups, or government agencies. Conflicts may range from minor differences of opinion to open hostility resulting in physical violence. Yet, humane democratic institutions attempt to resolve intraorganizational and interpersonal conflicts in an orderly manner. While conflict can be destructive, and it often is, it need not be so. Differences of opinion when openly confronted and fully aired can and often do lead to new understandings and subsequent improved relationships on the part of those involved.

The avoidance of conflict is important; its resolution is critical to personal, group, and organizational viability. Conflict creates within both individuals and organizations tensions and diversions which hinder or prevent the attainment of goals. Furthermore, striving to attain goals in itself creates tension and conflict. It is imperative that these conflicts be resolved in such a manner that striving to attain the goals of the organization will not be thwarted. Hopefully, conflict will produce new understanding and harmony, which will propel the organization toward its goals at an increased pace.

While an organization is concerned with the attainment of its goals and objectives, individuals within the organization are also concerned about the attainment of their own goals and objectives. Hence, the potenital for conflict between an organization and the individuals within it arises. For example, an organization's need for productivity may come into conflict with an individual's need for security in advancing years. As a consequence, differences may develop over the relative importance of productivity and length of service in determining layoffs.

---

[1] This section provides a brief introductory overview of major considerations and issues inherent in the grievance-arbitration process. It does not include, however, a discussion of the sizeable body of law on labor arbitration which has developed on this subject. This topic usually is covered fully in major texts with which these cases are normally used. A selected bibliography is included at the end of this section.

Not all individuals within an organization share the same objectives. For example, young employees may attach less importance to length of service in determining promotions than older employees. Interpersonal and intergroup conflict within organizations arises from such differences.

Ours is a democratic society which places a high value upon justice and upon the protection of individual rights. The democratic ideal has stimulated the concept of participation in organizations. Values attached to protection of human rights have stimulated the development of various mechanisms which aim to promote the administration of laws, policies, rules, and procedures in a humane and equitable manner, giving full consideration to human dignity and welfare.[2]

APPROACHES TO RESOLUTION OF CONFLICT

Concern for human rights in our society has resulted in the development of various means whereby injured parties may appeal decisions made by those exercising power over them. In fact, almost every type of organization has developed one or more appeal procedures.

Most government agencies have developed appeal procedures which enable employees to seek redress from acts of agency administrators. Labor unions have developed internal procedures for the protection of members from harassment within their own ranks. For example, the International Union of United Automobile, Aerospace, and Agricultural Implement Workers of America has expended unusual effort to provide its members a fair opportunity for defense against union decisions concerning them, and has provided well-defined and speedy avenues of recourse in the event of unjust acts by officers and administrators. Religious institutions have developed appeal procedures which provide members with avenues of recourse against the clergy. For example, the Roman Catholic Church has developed elaborate procedures which members may employ to seek redress.

Business organizations also have developed appeal procedures. They exist in both union and nonunion companies. Many nonunion organizations have developed formalized problem solving or grievance procedures which guarantee employees the right to appeal decisions made concerning them by their supervisors. In most instances, recourse may be sought all the way up through the organization to

---

2 For an excellent discussion of this aspect of arbitration, see Walter E. Baer, *Discipline and Discharge under the Labor Agreement* (New York: American Management Association, 1972), pp. 25–43.

the president. Many nonunion employers are even providing opportunities for "juries" of employees to render final decisions in complaints which have gone through a number of steps without resolution.

Formalized appeal procedures seem to become more necessary as organizations become larger and more institutionalized. Further, the more demanding and more urgent the goals and objectives of the organization, and the more that they press upon individuals in the organization, the less freedom an individual is able to exercise. The hierarchical and authoritarian nature of some organizations tends to produce dependency of the subordinate on the superior. Dependency, in turn, tends to create frustration in the individual seeking freedom of self-expression on the job. Inability to exercise freedom of self-expression, in turn, tends to block the individual in a search for satisfaction through work.

Thus, grievance procedures provide an opportunity for individuals to exercise greater control over their environment and may expand the opportunities for them to achieve their life goals through work. But probably most significantly, such procedures give individuals a chance to contest those decisions or actions of management which employees feel unfair and which violate their rights and the obligations of the employer.

GRIEVANCE PROCEDURES

Appeal opportunities are generally formalized in unionized organizations in grievance procedures which are included in the collective agreement. These formalized procedures vary considerably from organization to organization. Typically, however, they provide that, at the first step, the employee takes his or her grievance to either the immediate supervisor or the union steward.[3] The supervisor, the steward, and the employee discuss the issue and hopefully arrive at an amicable settlement. Most grievances are settled on an informal basis at this first step. If the parties are unable to agree, either because the supervisor disagrees with the request of the employee or because the supervisor lacks authority to make a decision, the grievance is appealed to the second step of the grievance procedure. Typically, the

---

3 A distinction is customarily drawn in labor relations between a *complaint* and a *grievance*. A complaint refers to any feeling of injury or injustice, real or imagined, expressed or unexpressed. A grievance is a complaint which has been formally presented to the supervisor, union steward, or some other union official under the provisions of a grievance procedure, alleging a violation of the labor agreement.

grievance committee of the union and the plant superintendent or office manager attempt to negotiate a settlement. However, grievances which are not settled at the first step of the grievance procedure may not be settled at the second step either; they are then usually appealed to the third step of the grievance procedure. At this level, the handling of the grievance is quite formalized; the parties negotiating the settlement may include members of top management of the company and members of the international office of the union. An estimated 97 percent of all collective agreements provide that if the parties are unable to arrive at a decision at the third (or fourth) step of the grievance procedure, either party may petition for arbitration of the dispute by a third party. Mediation and conciliation, including the possible help of an outside party, is always possible at any stage prior to the rendering of a decision by the arbitrator.

The following is a quite typical grievance procedure which shows the various steps to be followed in processing a grievance to ultimate resolution.[4]

ARTICLE VIII—ADJUSTMENTS OF GRIEVANCES
Section 1.

The procedure under this Section is available to either the Company or the Union for the presentation and settlement of grievances arising hereunder.

Section 2.

Any employee who believes that he has a justifiable request or complaint shall discuss same with his foreman with or without his Union committeeman being present, as he may elect, in an attempt to settle his request or complaint. Any such request or complaint which involves a question of the interpretation or application of, or compliance with the terms of this Agreement, shall constitute a grievance within the meaning of this Article. A grievance shall be processed in the manner set forth below and the specified time limitations, which shall be exclusive of Saturdays, Sundays and holidays, shall be strictly observed. When the grievance is not processed to the next step of the grievance procedure within the time limitations specified herein, it shall be considered settled on the basis of the answer given in the step of the grievance procedure in which it was last discussed.

Step 1.   If, in the discussion with the foreman, the grievance is not satisfac-

---

[4] 1975 Agreement between Universal Atlas Cement Division of United States Steel Corporation, Hannibal, Mo. plant, and Local 205, United Cement, Lime, and Gypsum Workers International Union, AFL–CIO, pp. 38–41.

torily disposed of, the employee may have his grievance presented to his department superintendent by his grievance committeeman, with or without the employee being present, as the employee may elect. Any such grievance must be submitted in writing to the department superintendent within thirty (30) days from the date the cause of the grievance occurs, except as specified in Article XI. The department superintendent shall answer the grievance in writing, within three (3) days of the presentation to him of such written grievance. If such written answer is unsatisfactory, the grievance may be presented to the Union Committee.

Step 2. The Union Committee, if it determines to carry the grievance further, shall, within five (5) days of the department superintendent's written answer in Step 1, present the written grievance to the Plant Manager for discussion at the next regularly scheduled monthly committee meeting. If the grievance is not satisfactorily disposed of in such a meeting, the Plant Manager shall, within ten (10) days answer the grievance in writing, unless a longer period for such answer is mutually agreed upon.

Step 3. The grievance, if not satisfactorily disposed of in Step 2, shall, within ten (10) days of the Plant Manager's written answer, be referred by letter, jointly addressed, to an official of the International Union and the Director—Personnel Services of the Company. They, or their designees, shall meet in the Hannibal area, preferably at the Hannibal Plant of the Company, as promptly as possible after they have been officially notified that the grievance is to be carried to Step 3. The Local Union shall be represented by the Chairman of the Local Grievance Committee, or his designee, and the local Plant Management by the Plant Manager or his designee. At such meeting no others shall be present except those deemed necessary by the parties for the purpose of giving information relevant to the grievance.

Step 4. If no agreement is reached in Step 3, either party may request in writing that an impartial umpire be appointed to determine the issue. Such request shall be made within fifteen (15) days of the Step 3 meeting. The designation of an impartial umpire shall be by mutual agreement between the parties. The fees and incidental expenses incurred by the impartial umpire in the determination of the controversy shall be shared equally by the Company and the Union. The decision of the umpire shall be final and binding upon both parties. Grievances involving the provisions of the collective bargaining Agreement and occurring so as to be processed to arbitration at the same time will be at the request of either party arbitrated before the same arbitrator. However, it is agreed that not more than four (4) cases will be heard at one series of hearings.

Section 3.

An umpire whom any grievance is submitted in accordance with the above procedure, shall only have jurisdiction and authority to interpret and apply the provisions of this Agreement insofar as it shall be necessary to the determination of such grievance, but he shall not have jurisdiction or authority to add to, or detract from or alter in any way the provisions of this Agreement.

Although grievance procedures are used for numerous reasons, the following are among the most important purposes which grievance procedures provide. First, they serve to locate problems which exist in the relationship between the union and the company, and also to locate problems which exist within both organizations. Second, they tend to open the channels of communication between employees and management. They are especially helpful in stimulating communication upward from employees to management, often to the discomfiture of the managers! Third, the grievance procedure is the instrument which enables the parties to initiate action, to interpret provisions of the collective agreement, and to apply the contract to new and changing aspects of daily relations between the employees and management. Finally, it serves as a valuable source of data at contract negotiation periods.

ARBITRATION

Arbitration constitutes the final step in a grievance procedure for settling disputes. It begins where the other procedures leave off, since the parties are presumed to have explored every avenue of negotiation and compromise before resorting to an arbitrator. When the parties turn to arbitration, they voluntarily agree to refer their dispute to an impartial third person. The arbitrator's determination will be made on the basis of the evidence and arguments presented by the disputants, who agree in advance to accept the decision of the arbitrator as final and binding.

In the United States, grievance-arbitration is a private and voluntary system. The federal government does not require the parties to include an arbitration clause in their collective agreement. However, the federal courts normally will defer to private arbitration those disputes which occur during the life of a labor agreement. Thus, grievance-arbitration is considered as a voluntary process in the United States, since an arbitration clause is the result of the negotiation process between management and a labor union.

Arbitration is usually viewed as a judicial process. However, the parties do influence this process by the internal policies which each has adopted with respect to it. For example, either the company or the union may follow a policy of carefully screening disputes which are referred to arbitration. Their objectives may be to present to arbitration only those cases which have merit and which the appealing party believes it has a good chance of winning. On the other hand, one or both parties may operate on a "percentage" basis. If they adopt this approach to arbitration, they may elect to appeal doubtful cases on the theory that arbitrators will tend to compromise. According to this reasoning, they expect to win certain points that they might otherwise have conceded. Of course, this approach to arbitration can be shortsighted; the theory that arbitrators will "split" decisions is generally not valid, since most arbitrators try to judge each case on the specific issues involved in the case. Thus, while the arbitration process is essentially a judicial one, in certain respects it is an extension of collective bargaining.

Arbitration has become an important means for the resolution of conflict. First, it has prevented open conflict, which tends to be very costly in terms of income lost to workers and profits lost to companies. Second, arbitration creates a better climate for the resolution of conflict. The parties resolve, as a matter of principle, to settle their disputes amicably. It can promote a spirit of cooperation which tends to pervade the entire grievance-handling process. Third, the parties know in advance that if they do not settle a dispute between themselves, it will ultimately be settled by a third party. While this may, in a few instances, prevent the parties from behaving in a mature and responsible manner, as a general rule arbitration has helped to develop mature dispute settlements. Finally, no-strike and no-lockout provisions in a collective agreement are possible only if an alternative means for ultimate settlement exists. If a union gives up the right to strike and if a company gives up the right to lock out employees over a grievance during the life of the agreement, both must be assured that some other method for settlement of disputes is available.

Many years ago, Harry Shulman, former Dean of the Yale School of Law and a distinguished labor arbitrator, summarized the role of arbitration and of the arbitrator in a classic statement as follows:

The arbitration is an integral part of the system of self-government. And the system is designed to aid management in its quest for efficiency, to assist union leadership in its participation in the enterprise, and to secure justice for the employees. It is a means of making collective bargaining work and thus preserving private enterprise in a free government.

* * * * *

The important question is not whether the parties agree with the award but rather whether they accept it, not resentfully, but cordially and willingly. Again, it is not to be expected that each decision will be accepted within the same degree of cordiality. But general acceptance and satisfaction is an attainable ideal. Its attainment depends upon the parties' seriousness of purpose to make their system of self-government work, and their confidence in the arbitrator. That confidence will ensue if the arbitrator's work inspires the feeling that he has integrity, independence, and courage so that he is not susceptible to pressure, blandishment, or threat of economic loss; that he is intelligent enough to comprehend the parties' contentions and empathetic enough to understand their significance to them; that he is not easily hoodwinked by bluff or histrionics; that he makes earnest effort to inform himself fully and does not go off half-cocked; and that his final judgment is the product of deliberation and reason so applied on the basis of the standards and the authority which they entrusted to him.[5]

LIMITS AND OBJECTIONS TO ARBITRATION

Voluntary arbitration is a valuable device for settling disputes during the life of a contract, when the arbitrator's function is primarily that of interpreting the language or intent of the parties. Both management and unions generally reject arbitration as a method for determining the language of the contract. The contract is "law," since it represents critical areas of managerial and union decision making. Matters in dispute often are considered by the parties to involve issues of "principle," "rights," or "prerogatives." Neither management nor unions wish to permit an outside third party to resolve such important issues. Not only do they fear losing control over their destinies, but they also fear that a provision of an agreement determined by arbitration could never be changed. This is in contrast to their belief that if an arbitrator's ruling on a clause of an existing contract indicates to a party that the clause is unsatisfactory, that

---

[5] Harry Shulman, "Reason, Contract, and Law in Labor Relations," *Harvard Law Review*, 1955, Vol. 68, p. 999.

party can hope to change or eliminate that clause in the next contract negotiation.[6]

Arbitration is most useful when the parties resort to its use sparingly and only as a last resort. Constructive conflict can lead to new insights and understandings by the parties. Agreements reached after serious negotiation also tend to be more acceptable than those imposed from outside. Serious negotiation further helps to develop maturity and responsibility. If the parties turn to an arbitrator as a means to escape a serious confrontation or to "save face," they reduce their potential for developing their collective bargaining skills and the maturity essential for a satisfactory relationship. In fact, arbitrators often make comments about unsatisfactory grievance handling such as the following: "This case should never have gotten to arbitration," or "The parties should have been able to resolve this case themselves."

ARBITRATION PROCEDURES

Arbitration clauses in collective agreements must be individually tailored to meet the specific needs of each union-management relationship. The American Arbitration Association, however, has developed a broad standard arbitration clause which is commonly used and which provides a model which can be tailored to meet specific needs of a particular union-management situation:

Any dispute, claim or grievance arising out of or relating to the interpretation or the application of this agreement shall be submitted to arbitration under the Voluntary Labor Arbitration Rules of the American Arbitration Association. The parties further agree to accept the arbitrator's award as final and binding upon them.[7]

However, many collective agreements are much more restrictive than the American Arbitration Association clause. For example, the following clause limits both the issues subject to arbitration and the authority of the arbitrator:[8]

Step 4.

In the event any employee's grievance is not settled to the satisfaction

---

6 See Frank Elkouri and Edna Asper Elkouri, *How Arbitration Works—3rd Edition,* (Washington, D.C.: Bureau of National Affairs, Inc., 1973), pp. 44–67.

7 American Arbitration Association, *Labor Arbitration, Procedures and Techniques* (New York: the Association, 1960), p. 7.

8 Agreement between Whirlpool Corporation (Fort Smith Division) and International Union of Allied Industrial Workers, AFL-CIO, Local 370, September 1974, pp. 40–42.

of the Union in the previous steps, the Union shall, within the time herein set out, request the appointment of an arbitrator. The selection of the arbitrator shall be carried out by the parties in accordance with the rules of the American Arbitration Association or the Federal Mediation and Conciliation Service. The parties will jointly stipulate the question to the arbitrator, or if they are unable to agree to a stipulation, each party shall submit to the other its written statement of the question at least five day in advance of hearing thereof, and both statements shall be submitted to the arbitrator.

The arbitrator shall have authority to decided only matters involving grievances which were processed and handled in accordance with the Grievance Procedure and which involve a dispute as to the meaning of terms found in this Agreement, or as to the existence of facts which affect the manner in which the terms found in this Agreement are applied. He shall have no authority to rule on any of the matters excluded from the Grievance Procedure or from arbitration by this Agreement and shall have no authority to add to, subtract from, or modify any of the terms of this Agreement, nor to establish any conditions not contained in this Agreement.

All expenses and fees of the arbitrator shall be shared equally by the Employer and the Union. Expenses of witnesses and other expenses incurred by the parties shall be paid by the party incurring such expenses.

Any decision made in conformance with this arbitration procedure shall be accepted by both the Employer and the Union and shall be final and binding on both parties and shall be compiled with within five working days after the decision is rendered.

The Grievance Procedure and arbitration provided for herein shall constitute the sole and exclusive remedies to be utilized for the determination, decision, adjustment, or settlement of any and all grievances as herein defined.

The American Arbitration Association also has developed a standard set of rules and procedures which govern any arbitration which it administers.[9] If American Arbitration Association rules are not utilized by the parties, the arbitration section of the collective agreement usually will contain a statement of policy indicating that certain disputes shall be arbitrated and will outline other rules governing the conduct of arbitration proceedings. Issues which must be met in the arbitration clause or by agreement by the parties include:

1. What is arbitrable? The clause quoted above provides that any dispute arising out of or relating to the interpretation or application of the agreement may be submitted to arbitration. On the other hand,

---

[9] See Maurice S. Trotta, *Arbitration of Labor-Management Disputes* (New York: American Management Association, 1974), pp. 390–393.

the parties sometimes wish to exclude certain matters from arbitration, such as wage rates or determination of production or quality standards. Presumably, the parties prefer to decide what course of action they will take, including the possibility of strike or lockout, if they fail to reach an agreement at the last step of the grievance procedure at the time when the deadlock occurs.

2. How is the arbitrator appointed, including what procedures shall be followed if the parties are unable to agree upon an arbitrator? Shall the parties appoint a "permanent" arbitrator to hear all disputes, or should an "ad hoc" arbitrator be appointed for each dispute? Many arbitrators are certified and obtained through either the Federal Mediation and Conciliation Service or the American Arbitration Association.

3. What are the rules and procedures governing the conduct of an arbitration? This includes methods for initiating an arbitration, time and place of hearings, swearing of witnesses, representation by legal counsel, recording of the proceedings, filings of briefs, rules of evidence, time within which an award will be made, and to whom it shall be delivered. Most of these issues will be determined by the parties themselves, but sometimes the arbitrator will be asked to rule on such procedural matters.

4. Who bears the cost of an arbitration? Typically, but not always, the parties will agree to share equally in these costs.

Disputes are brought to arbitration by one of two routes, either by a "submission" from the parties or by a "demand for arbitration" filed by either party. A submission agreement is a statement signed by both parties indicating the specific nature of the issue under contention and the specific relief which the injured party is seeking. A demand for arbitration is a formal request made by either of the two parties to the other for arbitration of an issue in dispute.

Among the major types of evidence and testimony presented and considered by arbitrators are:

1. The language of provisions of the Agreement;
2. The intent of the parties in negotiating Agreement provisions;
3. Past practice or precedents in handling similar or parallel matters;
4. Practices at other plants in the same industry or in other industries;
5. Equity or fairness in certain matters; "just cause" in disciplinary cases;

6.   Arbitration rulings and precedents established by other arbitrators;

7.   Industrial relations practices accepted as desirable or undesirable.

The American Arbitration Association has identified ten common errors committed by parties in arbitration.[10]

1.   Using arbitration and arbitration costs as a harassing technique;
2.   Overemphasis of the grievance by the union or exaggeration of an employee's fault by management;
3.   Reliance on a minimum of facts and a maximum of arguments;
4.   Concealing essential facts; distorting the truth;
5.   Holding back books, records, and other supporting documents;
6.   Tying up proceedings with legal technicalities;
7.   Introducing witnesses who have not been properly instructed on demeanor and on the place of their testimony in the entire case;
8.   Withholding full cooperation from the arbitrator;
9.   Disregarding the ordinary rules of courtesy and decorum;
10.   Becoming involved in arguments with the other side. The time to try to convince the other party is before arbitration, during grievance processing. At the arbitration hearing, all efforts should be concentrated on convincing the arbitrator.

The parties to a dispute seek an award from the arbitrator. The purpose of the award is to arrive at a final and conclusive decision with respect to the controversy. The arbitrator must not exceed the authority given him or her under the terms of the collective agreement. Most agreements, for example, state in some way that the arbitrator may not add to, detract from, or otherwise modify any part of the collective agreement. Even where this is not specifically stated in a collective agreement, this restriction is generally implied in the submission of a dispute to the arbitrator. The award of the arbitrator is to be accepted by both parties, and it will be upheld in the courts unless: the arbitrator exceeds the authority granted him or her by the parties; fraud or some other breach of ethics is proved; or the result is contrary to law (e.g., an arbitrator enforces an illegal union security provision).

Expedited Arbitration. Expedited arbitration represents a new, experimental approach designed to simplify and speed up the arbitration process. A typical arbitration may require several months to complete and cost from several hundred to several thousand dollars, if costs of personnel, lost time and the arbitrator's fees and expenses

---

[10] American Arbitration Association, *op. cit.*, pp. 20–21.

are calculated. The arbitrator's fees and expenses are on the average in the $500–$700 range, although some arbitrator's fees are much higher. Some require even more time and cost much more. In 1971, ten of the country's largest steel companies and the United Steel-workers Union agreed to a three-year experiment which they named "expedited arbitration" or "mini-arb." The experiment was success-ful, and they subsequently incorporated this procedure into their collective agreements. Numerous companies and unions are currently experimenting with this new procedure.

The expedited arbitration system is not a substitute for regular arbitration. It is employed to settle certain types of disputes at the second or third step of the grievance procedure only after the parties fail to agree at the first step, and then only after a joint labor-manage-ment committee agrees to the abbreviated procedure.

This arbitration technique is marked by informality. The hearing is usually conducted in the office or shop, sometimes at the workplace rather than in a hotel room or other "neutral" site. The arbitrator may interview witnesses on the spot. The more legalistic rules of evi-dence often employed in arbitration proceedings are considerably relaxed. The arbitrator normally renders his or her decision within 24 hours of the hearing. Sometimes the arbitrator renders it the same day, on occasion within minutes after the conclusion of the hearing. This is called a "bench" decision.

The procedure is more applicable to some cases than others. It has been most useful in settling minor disciplinary cases, although it has also been employed to decide nondisciplinary issues, including com-pensation and employee rights questions. It is less useful in resolving issues involving interpretation of the meaning of a contract clause or questions of "principle." Some disputes involve issues so fundamental to the parties that one or both may refuse to submit them to an ex-pedited arbitration. For example, questions involving the meaning of the wording of a clause in the contract, subcontracting, or produc-tion standards, are more appropriately resolved by means of a more thorough arbitration procedure.[11]

THE CASES

The cases included in this section all resulted from actual disputes which were processed through grievance procedures in their respective

---

[11] For a brief, but balanced, view of this topic, see: Lawrence Stessin, "Expedited Arbitration: Less Grief over Grievances," *Harvard Business Review*, 1977, vol. 55, no. 1, pp. 128–134.

collective agreements, remained unsettled, and were subsequently submitted to arbitration. The cases provide, in a condensed form, all the information available to the arbitrator. By studying the issues in these cases, one has the oportunity of experiencing actual arbitration situations and of arriving at one's own decisions with respect to the disputes.

SELECTED BIBLIOGRAPHY

Abersold, John R., and Howard, Wayne E. *Cases in Labor Arbitration: An Arbitration Experience.* Englewood Cliffs, N.J.: Prentice-Hall, Inc., 1967.

Baer, Walter E. *Discipline and Discharge under the Labor Agreement.* New York: American Management Association, Inc., 1972.

Baer, Walter E. *Practice and Precedent in Labor Relations.* Lexington, Mass.: D.C. Heath, 1972.

Baumback, Clifford M. *Structural Wage Issues in Collective Bargaining.* Lexington, Mass.: D.C. Heath, 1971.

Beal, Edwin, Edward Wickersham, and Philip Kienast. *The Practice of Collective Bargaining,* 5th Ed. Homewood, Illinois: Richard D. Irwin, 1976.

Brandt, Floyd S., and Daugherty, Carroll R., *Cases in Labor–Management Behavior,* Homewood, Illinois: Richard D. Irwin, 1976.

Dennis, Barbara D., and Summers, Gerald G., eds. *Labor Arbitration at the Quarter-Century Mark. Proceedings of the Twenty-Fifth Annual Meeting of the National Academy of Arbitrators.* Washington, D.C.: Bureau of National Affairs, 1973.

Donnelly, Lawrence. "Toward an Alliance between Research and Practice in Collective Bargaining." *Personnel Journal,* May 1971, pp. 372–99.

Elkouri, Frank, and Elkouri, Edna A. *How Arbitration Works,* 3d ed. Washington, D.C.: Bureau of National Affairs, 1973.

Fairweather, Owen. *Practice and Procedure in Labor Arbitration.* Washington, D.C.: Bureau of National Affairs, Inc., 1973.

Feller, David E. "A General Theory of the Collective Bargaining Agreement." *California Law Review,* vol. 61, no. 3, May 1973.

Fleming, Robben W. *Labor Arbitration Process.* Champaign-Urbana: University of Illinois Press, 1965.

Friedman, Joel W. "Individual Rights in Grievance Arbitration," *Arbitration Journal,* vol. 27, no. 4, December 1972.

Hays, Paul R. *Labor Arbitration: A Dissenting View.* New Haven: Yale University Press, 1966.

Keller, Leonard A. *The Management Function: A Positive Approach to Labor Relations.* Washington, D.C.: Bureau of National Affairs, 1963.

McDermott, Thomas J., and Newhams, Thomas H. "Discharge-Reinstatement: What Happens Thereafter," *Industrial and Labor Relations Review,* vol. 24, no. 4, July 1971.

Peters, Edward, and Prasow, Paul. *Arbitration and Collective Bargaining: Conflict Resolution in Labor Relations.* New York: McGraw-Hill Book Company, 1970.

Pops, Gerald M. *Emergence of the Public Sector Arbitrator.* Lexington, Mass.: D. C. Heath, 1976.

Prasaw, Paul. "The Theory of Management Reserved Rights—Revisited," In *Proceedings of the Twenty-Sixth Annual Winter Meeting of the Industrial Relations Research Association.* Gerald G. Somers, ed. Madison: IRRA, 1973.

Serrin, William. *The Company and the Union,* New York: Vintage Books, 1974.

Smith, Russell A., Merrifield, Leroy S., and Rothschild, Donald P. *Collective Bargaining and Labor Arbitration.* Indianapolis: Bobbs-Merrill, 1970.

Sovern, Michael I. "When Should Arbitrators Follow Federal Law?" In *Arbitration and the Expanding Role of Neutrals,* Gerald G. Somers and Barbara D. Dennis, eds. *Proceedings of the Twenty-Third Annual Meeting of the National Academy of Arbitrators.* Washington, D.C.: Bureau of National Affairs, 1970.

Stagner, Ross, and Rosen, Hjalmar. *Psychology of Union-Management Relations,* Belmont, Calif.: Wadsworth, 1965.

Stone, Morris. *Labor Grievances and Decisions,* New York: American Arbitration Association, 1970.

Summers, Clyde W. "The Individual Employee's Rights under the Collective Agreement: What Constitutes Fair Representation." In *Arbitration—1974,* Barbara D. Dennis and Gerald G. Sommers, eds. *Proceedings of the Twenty-Seventh Annual Meeting of the National Academy of Arbitrators.* Washington, D.C.: Bureau of National Affairs, 1975.

Tracy, Estell R. *Arbitration Cases in Public Employment.* New York: American Arbitration Association, 1969.

Trotta, Maurice S. *Arbitration of Labor-Management Disputes.* New York: American Management Association, 1974.

Walton, Richard, and McKersie, Robert. *A Behavioral Theory of Labor Negotiations.* New York: McGraw-Hill Book Company, 1965.

Updegraff, Clarence M. *Arbitration and Labor Relations.* Washington, D.C.: The Bureau of National Affairs, 1970.

Index to Cases for Part Two

	Management Rights	Union Rights and Activities	Seniority and Employee Rights	Discipline	Work Assignments and Job Bidding	Work Performance	Technological Change/Past Practices	Wages and Benefits	Employee Health, Safety and Security
30. The Mistaken Overtime Assignment			X		X		X	X	
31. Funeral Leave during an Employee's Vacation								X	
32. The Hot-Headed Pharmacist				X		X			
33. The Disputed Memorial Day Holiday	X				X			X	
34. Leave for Religious Festival			X	X	X			X	
35. The Stock Market Drop and the Profit Sharing Payments		X						X	
36. Must the Machinists Purchase Their Own Tools?	X		X	X			X	X	
37. The "Busted Radiator"				X	X				
38. Sick Leave Pay during a Strike								X	X
39. Caught with Pot				X		X			
40. A Drink "To Cut the Dust"				X					X
41. The Bomb Threat			X		X			X	X
42. Must the Company Select a Female Credit Trainee?	X		X		X				
43. The Reluctant Retiree	X		X					X	X
44. Can the Company Eliminate the Quatropulper Helper's Job?	X		X		X		X		
45. The Chronically Depressed Absentee	X		X	X		X		X	X

No.	Case	1	2	3	4	5	6	7	8	9
46.	Caught in the Act?	X					X			
47.	Stolen Kisses	X					X		X	
48.	A Painted Mistake	X					X		X	X
49.	Impaired Performance	X				X	X		X	X
50.	One Wife Too Many	X					X	X		
51.	Infringement of Bargaining Unit Work	X			X	X		X	X	
52.	The Speedy Finisher	X				X	X		X	
53.	Disabled by Police Bullets				X		X		X	X
54.	A Request for Parental Leave				X				X	X
55.	Riding the Tiger	X					X		X	X
56.	No More Coffee or Bottled Water	X			X			X	X	
57.	The By-Passed Senior Clerk	X			X	X		X	X	
58.	Too Much Telephone Time?				X		X		X	
59.	The Reluctant Inspector	X			X	X	X		X	X
60.	The "No Spouse" Rule	X			X			X		
61.	The Disabled Blower Motor	X			X			X		
62.	The Subcontracted Heaters	X			X	X				
63.	A Lump on the Leg	X			X	X		X		X
64.	The Car Pool and the Overtime Refusal	X				X	X			
65.	The Disputed Holiday Pay				X		X	X	X	X

30. THE MISTAKEN OVERTIME ASSIGNMENT

COMPANY: Standard Packaging Corporation, St. Louis, Missouri

UNION: International Association of Machinists, District No. 9, AFL–CIO

BACKGROUND

Jerry Smith[1] reported for work at 11 p.m. on a Saturday night shift November 12, 1966 through an error on his part. He had not been scheduled to work and he had not been called in, although a small crew was scheduled to work this shift.

At about midnight, Smith's regular foreman, Donald Smelser, entered the plant on a trouble call and questioned him regarding his presence in the plant. After some discussion both realized that Smith had reported in error.

Smelser informed Smith that he could finish out the shift; Smith worked eight hours. This was Smith's seventh consecutive day of work, and by contract he was paid at the rate of double time.

Howard Bell filed a grievance because Smith worked on a seventh day although he was junior to Bell in seniority. Bell claimed equal pay for the time Smith worked (eight hours at double time). He maintained that in accordance with the well-established practice at the company, overtime must be offered to employees in accordance with their seniority and their ability to perform the work involved. The issue was taken to arbitration.

POSITION OF THE UNION

The union argued that if Smelser had sent Smith home after he found him working, no grievance would have been filed. However, since the company and the union both agreed that the past practice

---
[1] All names are disguised.

had been and still was to let the most senior employees work all overtime, the union should be upheld in this case and Bell should be paid for all time at the appropriate rate that the junior employee was paid.

POSITION OF THE COMPANY

The company contended that it should not be required to pay another employee for 16 hours. In consideration for the employee who reported by mistake, the company allowed Smith to work out the full shift instead of sending him home with one hour's pay. The claim of the union was unjust and inequitable. No union employee, neither Bell nor anyone else, suffered any loss of work or income because the company acted in a considerate manner. No one was scheduled to perform such work that evening. If Smith had not erroneously reported for work, no one would have worked in that job. The company's action in allowing him to continue to work after he was discovered should be commended and not condemned.

QUESTIONS

1. If Jerry Smith had worked the entire Saturday shift without having talked with his foreman, would Smith have been entitled to payment for the unscheduled work on his part? Why, or why not?
2. Is Howard Bell entitled to overtime pay under the practice for offering overtime to employees in accordance with their seniority and ability? Why, or why not?
3. Evaluate the company's argument that the claim of the union was unjust and inequitable. Evaluate its argument that no union employee, including Bell, "suffered any loss of work or income because the company acted in a considerate manner."

31. FUNERAL LEAVE DURING AN EMPLOYEE'S VACATION

COMPANY: *Food Employer's Council, Incorporated, Los Angeles, California*

UNION: *International Brotherhood of Teamsters, Chauffeurs, Warehousemen, and Helpers of America, Local Union No. 683*

BACKGROUND

This grievance arose under the agreement between the parties in effect for the period September 7, 1964 to September 7, 1967 inclusive. In this agreement, companies in the Food Employer's Council of Los Angeles agreed to grant three days' funeral leave, with pay, upon the death of certain defined members of an employee's family. Article XII, the Funeral Leave provision of the contract stated:

Employees shall be allowed three days' funeral leave with full pay for a death in the imediate family. Immediate family shall be defined as the employee's parents, spouse, children and siblings.

In March, 1965 Al Nerl,[1] a male employee, and his family were enjoying a paid vacation in Oklahoma when notice was received of the death of the employee's father in San Diego. The employee left his family in Oklahoma and flew to San Diego to attend the funeral. Thereafter, he returned to his family and completed his vacation.

Upon returning to work from his vacation, Nerl requested that the company grant him three days' funeral leave pay, or grant him a three-day extension of his vacation with pay. Management denied this request. The employee filed a grievance and, with the matter unresolved, the parties submitted the question to arbitration.

---

[1] Name is disguised.

POSITION OF THE UNION

The union argued that the language of Article XII was direct and unambiguous. It clearly stated the employer's obligation to grant three days of funeral leave with pay to employees who suffer the tragedy of a death in the immediate family.

Since the clause contained no exceptions to this obligation, the union claimed that funeral leave should be payable whether an employee was at work or on vacation.

POSITION OF THE COUNCIL

The Council claimed that it was not the intent of any of the companies to grant funeral leaves to employees who suffered a death in their family at a time when they were absent from work and already receiving pay during the period of absence. Article XII speaks of employees being "allowed" funeral leave; therefore, it denotes some degree of management prerogative in ascertaining an employee's eligibility for such a benefit.

In support of its position, management cited the sick-leave and vacation clause provisions of the current agreement. The sick-leave clause did not entitle employees to sick-leave benefits if they were on vacation. Under the vacation clause, an extra day's vacation was granted if a recognized holiday occurred during an employee's vacation; but no such provision existed in regard to funeral leave. Management claimed that these clauses supported—by consistent reasoning—the Council's position that funeral leave should not be granted to an employee who is on vacation. The grievance should be dismissed.

QUESTIONS

1. What is the meaning of the clause "shall be allowed" in Article XII of the contract? Is this clause open to interpretation?
2. Evaluate the union's argument that the Council was obligated to pay the funeral leave to the employee who was on vacation.
3. Evaluate the Council's reasoning that the employee was not entitled to funeral leave pay. What are the precedent implications of this case to both union and management interests?

32. THE HOT-HEADED PHARMACIST

COMPANY: *Bartell Drug Company, Inc., Seattle, Washington*

UNION: *Retail Clerks Union, Local 330*

BACKGROUND

Howard Eaton,[1] chief pharmacist of Store No. 16 located in downtown Seattle, was discharged after two years employment at the Bartell Drug Company. The company's reason for discharging Eaton was that he could not get along with either customers or his fellow employees.

The Bartell Drug Company operates several retail drug stores in the Seattle area. Howard Eaton had been a licensed pharmacist for 19 years. His duties with Bartell consisted of filling prescriptions and waiting on customers.

On March 4, 1971 eight days after Eaton's discharge, the union sent the company a letter which read in part as follows:

In accordance with the terms and provisions of the collective bargaining agreement in force and effect between Bartell Drug and Local 330, R.C.I.A., we hereby protest and submit as a grievance, that the discharge of Howard Eaton was not proper, just, or for reasonable cause, and judgment of management in reaching a decision to terminate Eaton was not fairly and reasonably exercised.

The case eventually went to arbitration, where the union requested that Eaton be reinstated to his former position with full back pay and with restoration of all rights and benefits.

POSITION OF THE COMPANY

The company pointed out that the retail drug industry was highly competitive. If it was to compete successfully, company employees must not only be highly qualified but also possess the ability and desire to get along with both customers and fellow employees.

---

[1] Name is disguised.

The company recognized that Eaton was a qualified and able pharmacist, a fact which he demonstrated by his accurate and rapid filling of prescriptions. However, by Eaton's own admission, he possessed a very quick temper and easily became angry. In fact, his quick temper caused him on several previous occasions to lose jobs with other companies.

The company stated that it was aware of Eaton's quick temper and previous discharges at the time it hired him about two years previously. At the time Eaton was hired, both the manager of store number 16 and the operations manager of the parent company spoke with Eaton about his past behavior and pointed out that he would have to change both his attitude and actions toward customers.

The manager of store number 16 testified that he received the first customer complaint about Eaton's behavior about two months after he had been hired. Thereafter, he received a major complaint almost every week, and minor complaints from both customers and other Bartell employees almost every day. The manager stated that the company counseled with Eaton and did not discharge him immediately in the hope that his behavior might change. Eaton possessed excellent technical skills, which enabled him to fill prescriptions both quickly and accurately.

The operations manager stated that the company conscientiously attempted to work with Eaton. He and the store manager attempted to smooth over the difficult situations with customers.

The company stated, in response to inquiries by the union, that it did not record the names and addresses of complaining customers, because it was not good for customer relations to check on the complaints of angry customers or to indicate to them that they might be called upon to testify against an offending employee. Two of Eaton's fellow employees working in the same department with him cited several instances of his rude behavior both toward customers and toward them. They testified that they had heard him make sarcastic remarks to customers, use offensive language toward them and argue with them. One of the employees testified that, in a fit of anger, Eaton had struck her on the head with a writing pad and had grasped and twisted her arm. Both employees were members of Local 330, to which Eaton belonged, and both testified under oath against him.

The company admitted that it decided to discharge Eaton early in February 1971, but delayed action for two or three weeks in order to find another pharmacist to replace him.

All four company witnesses testified that they believed that Eaton disliked older customers and people on welfare. Many of the customers with whom he had difficulties fell into these two categories.

The company held that it possessed the right to discharge Howard Eaton under Section 22.1 of the collective agreement which read as follows:

The employer shall be the judge as to the competency of his employees and continuity of employment shall be based upon the Employer's judgement of the merit and ability of the individual employee, provided that such judgement shall be fairly and reasonably exercised.

Further, management representatives stated that Eaton violated Section 2b of *Company Rules and Policies* which read as follows:

Never argue with a customer even though you may be entirely correct. The customer is our Boss and comes first.

The company stated that this policy statement was well-known to all employees. Eaton was reminded of it on many occasions. It was a reasonable policy, and it reflected the spirit and philosophy of Bartell Drug Company.

The company cited several prior arbitration cases in which arbitrators upheld discharges of employees who were guilty of emotional outbursts and the use of bad language within the hearing of customers. The company also cited a case in which an arbitrator held that an arbitrator should not substitute his personal judgment for that of the company, if the company has acted in good faith after a proper and fair investigation. In view of the precedents cited and the evidence presented, the company asked that Eaton's grievance protesting his discharge should be denied.

POSITION OF THE UNION

The union contended that Eaton's behavior was not as bad as the company had alleged, since the company had retained him in its employ for approximately two years. The union also argued that, during this time, Eaton was promoted to chief pharmacist of store number 16.

Eaton admitted that his temper did have "a short fuse," but he stated that there was usually a just and good reason for his anger. Consequently, under oath, he testified that many of the instances which the company cited did not actually occur. He also admitted that he had occasional arguments with customers, but he also contended that he cheerfully had helped many customers who needed it. Although some customers complained when the arguments occurred, Eaton believed that no customer had ever asked that the company discharge him. When complaints about his behavior were lodged, he did not know about them immediately nor did he realize that his job with the company was in jeopardy. Eaton emphatically denied the charge that he disliked old people or people who were on welfare. Eaton admitted that he grasped a fellow employee and twisted her arm, but only because she had refused to say "hello" to him. However, he quickly apologized to her, and he also apologized to customers when there was an appropriate reason or an opportunity to do so. Eaton insisted that he got along well with his co-workers, including those who testified against him.

The union pointed out that if this dismissal were upheld, Eaton probably would not be able to find another job in the retail drug industry.

The union further attested that there may have been another reason for Eaton's dismissal. Under Washington state law, certain drugs, called exempt drugs, could be purchased without a prescription, depending upon the judgment of the pharmacist. Eaton often had refused to sell exempt drugs to some people, and he felt that the manager of the store wanted him "to look the other way" when such a sale could be made. Three other pharmacists had been dismissed in the past by the company, and the union argued that they had felt at the time that their refusal to sell exempt drug items against their better judgment was the reason for their dismissal.

The union objected strenuously to the testimony of company witnesses that Eaton did not get along well with customers. The union requested that the company provide the names of the alleged complaining customers in order that they might be cross-examined. Since the company claimed that it was unable to furnish such a list, the union claimed that Eaton's alleged poor relations with customers were only rumors and not fact. The union argued that the company's refusal or inability to furnish such a list constituted an unfair labor practice under the Taft-Hartley Act. Further, the union claimed that the company's refusal to supply the names of complaining customers violated Section 17.4 of the collective bargaining agreement which stated:

The Employer and the Union agree to make available to the other such pertinent data as each may deem necessary for the examination of all circumstances surrounding a grievance. The arbitrator shall be empowered to effect compliance with this provision by requiring the production of documents and other evidence.

The union also contended that, before the hearing, the company did not include poor fellow employee relations as a reason for dismissing Eaton and to do so now was late and unfair. The company should not be allowed to rely on one set of reasons in the first three steps of the grievance procedure and then add another set when arguing its position before the arbitrator. Consequently, only poor customer relations should be considered by the arbitrator, and testimony concerning poor employee relations should be stricken from the record.

In support of its case, the union cited several NLRB cases. One case concerned the Metropolitan Life Insurance Company in which failure on the part of the company to provide the names of complaining policy holders indicated that there was no just cause for discharge of three of the company's agents. Also, the union contended that in cases where names of accusers are withheld, discharge is too severe a penalty for an alleged display of poor attitude on the part of the employee. Therefore, the union argued that much of the Bartell Drug Company's case was based on inadmissable and unsubstantiated evidence. The union claimed that Howard Eaton should be reinstated to his job with full back pay.

QUESTIONS

1. Was employee Howard Eaton's behavior serious enough to justify discharge under provisions of the collective agreement? Why, or why not?

2. Evaluate the company's position citing an arbitrator who held that, "an arbitrator should not substitute his personal judgment for that of the company, if the company has acted in good faith after a proper and fair investigation."

3. Evaluate the union's argument that the company should provide the names of alleged complaining customers in order to cross-examine them. Should the arbitrator rule upon this issue in relationship to the company's duty to bargain under the Labor Management Relations (Taft-Hartley) Act?

4. Is it permissible for the company to include "poor fellow employee relations" as a reason for dismissing Eaton if, as the union alleges, this was not originally a reason for dismissing Eaton during the first three steps of the grievance procedure? Discuss.

33. THE DISPUTED MEMORIAL DAY HOLIDAY

COMPANY: *Highway Products, Inc., Kent, Ohio*

UNION: *United Automobile, Aeroscape and Agricultural Implement Workers of America, Local 1137*

BACKGROUND

The company fabricates and produces camping trailers and other camping equipment and supplies. In 1970, Memorial Day (May 30) occurred on a Saturday. Ten days prior to Memorial Day, the company posted the following notice:

May 20, 1970

To: All Highway Products Employees
Subject: Memorial Day Weekend
Under the terms of our Labor-Management Agreement, Memorial Day Holiday will be Friday, May 29, 1970.

Pay for Friday May 29, will be made to all those who are eligible in accordance with the terms of this agreement.

The company will cease all operations at the conclusion of the second shift Thursday May 28, 1970, and resume operations Monday morning, June 1, 1970.

No productive operations are anticipated for this weekend. However, if the need should arise to schedule work, the employees affected will be notified by their respective supervisor.

The company extends its best wishes for a safe and pleasant Holiday weekend to all employees and their families.

One week later, on May 27, the company posted a notice that certain departments would have to work on Friday, May 29, 1970. The notice, in part was as follows:

NOTICE

The Company regrets the fact that we must schedule the Fabrication Dept. and Loft and Template Dept. for work on Friday, May 29, 1970. Our decision was based on the following:

227

1. Bus Line shortages of fabricated parts have just about shut down the line and have already caused some layoffs.
2. Cortez is also dependent on our fabricated parts supply and is also threatened with a severe production cut-back. We hope our efforts can correct this situation.

Work Schedule: The Fabrication Dept. #100 is scheduled to work two 8-hour shifts on Friday, May 29. The Loft and Template Dept. #840 is scheduled to work one 8-hour shift on Friday, May 29. All employees will be paid straight time for Friday's work. All employees entitled to Holiday Pay for Memorial Day will be given an additional day's pay.

Shortly thereafter, the union filed a grievance, which read as follows:

On May 20, 1970 the company posted a notice which states that the plant will observe Memorial Day holiday as Friday, May 29, 1970. On May 27 at approx. 5:00 P.M. the company posted a notice that some Departments would be scheduled to work two 8 hr. shifts on Fri. May 29. The Union requests that all employees who worked on Fri. May 29, 1970 be paid the 3 times their straight hourly rate, as provided in the Agreement Article XV, Section 3.[1]

The grievance ultimately was carried to arbitration.

POSITION OF THE UNION

The union submitted that the company had the right, under Article XV, Section 6, to designate May 29 as the official Memorial Day holiday. But after declaring May 29 as the Memorial Day holiday, the company never rescinded this nor posted any notice revoking the designation. Further, when some fifty employees were required to work in the Fabrication department and the Loft and Template department on May 29, they were working on Memorial Day as designated by the company. Therefore, under Section 3 of Article XV, any employee who works on a holiday should be paid at the rate of three times the straight-time hourly rate. Since these employees had to work on a holiday, they should be paid the triple rate. The grievance should be allowed.

POSITION OF THE COMPANY

Representatives of the company claimed that the company could not legally change an official holiday from May 30 to May 29. Since

---

[1] See Appendix for applicable contractual clauses.

Memorial Day in 1970 fell on a Saturday, the company had the right, under Section 6 of Article XV, to declare the preceding work day, May 29, as a "day to be observed as a holiday." This is all the company could do under the agreement. Memorial Day itself did not change by the May 20 notice of the company.

The company further testified that the notice posted on May 27 was necessitated by a shortage of parts referred to therein. Under the agreement, the company had the right to revoke, as it did by the notice of May 27, the designation of May 29 as a Memorial Day holiday for certain employees. The employees who worked on May 29 received their regular rate of pay and, in addition, the holiday pay. All other employees (who did not work on May 29) were paid for that date as provided for under the company's first notice.

The company stated that it did not try to deprive anyone of holiday pay for Saturday, May 30 to which they were entitled under Section 6 of Article XV. Some employees worked four days and others five days during that week, but all received holiday pay. No employees worked on Saturday, May 30, the only day legally defined Memorial Day.

Therefore, no employees were entitled to triple pay for working on May 29. The company claimed that the union was trying to take advantage of a unique situation which would be unfair to the large majority of about a hundred employees who did not work on May 29. The union grievance should be denied.

APPENDIX

Applicable Provisions from the Agreement

Provisions for holidays were under Article XV of the Agreement, the pertinent sections of which are as follows:

Section 1. For the purpose of this Article, New Year's Day, Memorial Day, July Fourth, Labor Day, Thanksgiving Day, Day after Thanksgiving, Day before Christmas and Christmas Day shall be considered as holidays. One additional floating Holiday beginning in 1968, notification to be given by the Company at ratification the first year and not later than January 31st, in the second and third years.

Section 3. Any employee who works on any of said holidays shall be paid at the rate of three (3) times his straight time hourly rate.

Section 6. If any of the above holidays fall on Saturday, the employees will, at the option of the Company, either be paid for the holiday or given the preceding work day or the next succeeding day as a holiday.

Management rights are set forth in Article XVII as follows:

Section 1.   Except as herein expressly qualified, the Company retains the exclusive right to manage its business, operations and affairs and to direct the working force. Prominent among such unqualified rights, although by no means a wholly inclusive list thereof, are the following: to introduce new or improved products, methods, equipment or facilities, and to alter or discontinue any operation or product; to select suppliers and to determine whether to "make or buy" to maintain order and efficiency in its plant and operation; to determine processes, production methods, quality standards, degree of workmanship required, the size of the working force.

Section 2.   The Company not exercising rights reserved to it or its exercising them in a particular way shall not be deemed a waiver of said rights or of its rights to exercise them in some other way not in conflict with the terms of this Agreement.

QUESTIONS

1.   Evaluate the conflicting arguments concerning whether May 29 was, as the union claimed, the "official Memorial Day holiday," or as management claimed, only a "day to be observed as a holiday." Why is this a crucial difference in the positions of the parties?

2.   Why did the company feel that the union was trying to take advantage of a unique situation which "would be unfair to the large majority of about a hundred employees who did not work on May 29"?

3. · What are the precedent implications of this case in relation to clauses such as Section 3 and Section 6 of the agreement in the case?

34. LEAVE FOR RELIGIOUS FESTIVAL .

COMPANY: Armstrong Rubber Company, Southern Division, Natchez, Mississippi

UNION: United Rubber Cork, Linoleum and Plastic Workers of America, Local 303

BACKGROUND

The Armstrong Rubber Company discharged William R. Mallone[1] on October 20, 1971 because he had "violated Plant Rule 29." This rule included the following grounds for discharge of an employee:

Being absent from work three consecutive working days and either (*a*) not reporting absence or advancing a reasonable excuse for not reporting absence; or (*b*) having no reasonable excuse for being absent; or (*c*) falsifying the reason for being absent or not reporting the absence. Penalty for first violation: discharge.

William Mallone was hired into the Natchez, Mississippi, plant of Armstrong Rubber Company in September 1968, as an assistant machine operator in the color mix department. He was an excellent employee, and one year later was promoted to machine operator.

In early 1970, Mallone became a member of the Worldwide Church of God. This religious organization teaches absolute adherence to certain "holy days" and requires each member to observe these days as well as to attend certain religious festival meetings. One such period of holy days extends for a span of one week and is designated as the "Feast of Tabernacles and Last Great Days." Mr. Mallone considered his presence at these religious meetings to be a commandment from God. In 1971, this period of holy days extended from October 4 to October 11. Mr. Mallone was absent from work without leave from October 4 through October 13, 1971 to attend the various religious festival meetings of his church. It was the first occasion on which Mr. Mallone had been absent without authorization during his three years with the company.

---

[1] All names are disguised.

Mallone previously had followed required procedures stated in Rule 29 in requesting a leave of absence. He made three requests for a leave of absence for this period. On the first occasion, September 24, Mallone asked his immediate supervisor, Joseph Lorne, for a two-week leave of absence for "personal reasons." Lorne denied this request, telling Mallone that due to a backlog of work he was needed on the job. On September 30, Mallone then took his request for a two-week leave "to attend an important religious festival" to the plant's Assistant Industrial Relations Manager, Robert Botts. Botts checked with Mallone's department and found that a heavy backlog of work had accumulated in that department. Mallone's request was again denied, but Botts told Mallone that a two-day leave perhaps could be arranged. Mallone informed Botts that he needed an eight-day leave and that his attendance at these religious meetings was "a must." Subsequently, on October 1, Mallone made one final request for this leave, which again was denied by Lorne who stated that he was needed on the job.

Mallone did not report for work from October 4 through October 13, and he could not be reached by telephone at his home during that time. After he returned to work, a conference including company and union officials as well as Mallone was arranged to discuss this situation. On October 20, Mallone was discharged by the company for violating Rule 29. On Mallone's behalf, the union subsequently filed a grievance which eventually was carried to arbitration.

POSITION OF THE UNION

The union contended that the company engaged in religious discrimination in refusing to grant Mallone a leave of absence to attend a required religious activity of his church. According to Mallone's testimony, he was required by his church to attend the church's October 4–11 celebration of the "Feast of Tabernacles and Last Great Days." In support of this contention, the union produced as evidence an affidavit by a church official that Mallone's denomination "teaches absolute adherence to the annual holy days, and that it is the duty of each member to observe these days in order to maintain his status in this church."

The union also argued that Mr. Mallone had made a request for leave as required by Rule 29. In fact, he made repeated requests for leave because he did not wish to place his church and job in conflict with each other.

Mr. Mallone's absence was for a good reason, as also required by Rule 29. The union pointed out that the company recognized required religious activities as constituting a valid reason for absence. For example, employees who requested so in advance were excused on Good Friday, and no one worked on Christmas Day.

Finally, the union argued that Mallone was an excellent employee. He had always been regular in his attendance, had never been late, and always had met or exceeded production standards. Consequently, the union requested that the grievant, Mallone, be reinstated to his job with all seniority and back pay.

POSITION OF THE COMPANY

The company maintained that it had the right to discharge William Mallone for being absent without leave from his job from October 4–13. The company pointed out that it properly denied Mallone's request for leave due to a heavy backlog of work, which required Mallone to be on the job. High production was important during the months of September, October and November when new lines and designs were being produced to stock distributors' warehouses. Although the color mix department was small, it was critical for continued operation of the plant. Inexperienced operators thus could not be assigned to the department.

The company denied that it engaged in religious discrimination and claimed that it always had granted religious leaves whenever possible. In this situation, however, Mr. Mallone's request came at a time when he could not be spared, especially for the long period requested. The company could not afford to excuse Mallone's absence from work without permission.

The company stressed that nothing in the contract required the company to grant Mallone a leave to attend a religious function. Therefore, the company was well within its rights to deny Mallone's request for leave. Since Mallone deliberately chose to be absent from work, the company was completely justified in discharging him as provided for in Plant Rule 29.

The company requested that the grievance be denied, and that Mallone's discharge for cause be upheld by the arbitrator.

QUESTIONS

1. Must the company recognize attendance at religious activities as constituting a valid reason for absence from work by an employee? Discuss.

2. Did employee William Mallone meet the requirements for requesting leave under Plant Rule 29?

3. Could the company properly deny Mallone's request for a leave due to a heavy backlog of work, since nothing in the contract specifically required the company to grant Mallone a leave to attend a religious function? Discuss.

4. Why does a case such as this pose a difficult problem to company management from the standpoints of both employee policy and public relations?

35. THE STOCK MARKET DROP AND THE PROFIT SHARING PAYMENTS

COMPANY: *ITT Canteen Corporation, St. Louis, Missouri*

UNION: *Teamsters' Local Union No. 688, Affiliated with International Brotherhood of Teamsters, Chauffeurs, Warehousemen, and Helpers of America*

THE ISSUE

The issue as stated by the union in its grievance dated October 26, 1970 was that the company was in "violation of Article XXXIV, Section 4[1] of its agreement" with ITT Canteen Corporation. This agreement was in effect from March 16, 1970 to March 15, 1973. The union complaint on the grievance form was signed in the name of Alphonse Garnatz,[2] chief shop steward in the maintenance department. However, the complaint was made on behalf of all Division A employees defined in the agreement as Exhibit A, page 37. The union settlement requested was that the company should pay termination payments from the company profit sharing plan on calculated figures to be based as of the end of March 1970. The grievance eventually was submitted to arbitration.

In their testimony, company representatives agreed to the union's basic statement of the issue, subject to the clarification that the company itself did not have direct control over disbursements of its profit sharing trust fund, since the company profit sharing trust fund is administered independently of the company itself. Counsel for the company stated his position that the sole issue rested upon the interpretation of Article XXXIV, Section 4 of the agreement. As a result of the hearing, the arbitrator ruled that the issue could be restated as follows: "Did the company violate the agreement when it arranged

---

1 See Appendix for all applicable contract provisions. At the time of this case, approximately 60 employees were classified as Division A employees.

2 All names are disguised.

to terminate membership in the ITT Canteen profit sharing plan for Division A employees effective May 2, 1970, with termination payments based upon an evaluation of employee member accounts as of the end of May, 1970?"

BACKGROUND

Although the prior agreement had expired on March 15, 1970, negotiations between the parties continued throughout March and April, and it was not until the weekend of May 1–3, 1970 that agreement on the new contract was reached. Negotiations had included a reverse type of ratification procedure in which a list of demands was presented to the company as part of a "package" which the union membership said it would accept. Included in the list of demands presented to the company was a change which would bring Division A employees under the Teamsters' negotiated pension plan during the third year of the contract. These employees had been covered under a company profit sharing plan which included both employee and company contributions.[3] The change, which also would require these employees to be removed from the company profit sharing plan, was acceptable to the company. However, a misunderstanding concerning this issue arose when the membership of the bargaining unit subsequently voted that it wanted to be covered under the Teamsters' pension plan for the entire period of the new three-year agreement. Negotiations continued between Mr. Arthur Rudolph, representing the company, and Mr. Daniel Bolle, representing the union, in order to resolve the pension plan issue. The parties found it necessary to reconsider different items within the total settlement, since the prior "package" offer had been based upon the premise that the Division A employees would not enter the Teamsters' pension plan until the third year of the agreement. In order to bring Division A employees into the Teamsters' pension plan for the entire three years of the agreement, a number of "fringe" items were bargained lower, and special terms for the company's contributions for Division A employees in the Teamsters' pension plan were negotiated. Mr. Bolle and Mr. Rudolph determined that in order for Division A members to be covered during the three years of the agreement, the company contribution would be reduced from the "normal" $2 per week per

---

[3] Employee contributions to the company profit sharing plan are made by payroll deduction; the company contribution is based upon a periodic evaluation of company earnings.

employee to $1 per week per employed member. This figure was included in Article XXXIV, Section 3 of the agreement as follows:

Effective May 4, 1970, the Employer shall contribute for and on behalf of its employees covered by this Agreement, except Mobile Catering and Vending Attendants, to said Pension Plan and shall pay to said Trustees and Trust Fund established in Exhibit "B," the sum of One ($1.00) Dollar per week for each said employee.

Both the company and the union have policies prohibiting "dual coverage," i.e., simultaneous participation of bargaining unit employees in both a company profit sharing and a union pension plan. But during negotiations, there was no real consideration given to the question of the effective date of termination of Division A employee accounts in the company profit sharing plan. Both union and company representatives testified that the question of an effective date of termination of employees from the company profit sharing plan never really was discussed specifically. The parties did agree that the company would begin its contributions to the Teamsters' pension plan effective May 4, 1970 at the rate of $1 per week per employee, which coincided approximately with the weekend when the negotiations concluded.

According to the union, the May 4 date was requested by the company in order to save a certain amount of money in contributions to the Teamsters' pension plan, and the union agreed to this in the bargaining sessions. Mr. Bolle testified that his implied understanding was that the effective date for the coverage of the Teamsters' pension plan and the termination of the profit sharing plan would be March 16, 1970 since all other items in the agreement were retroactive to that beginning date. According to testimony by Mr. Rudolph, however, the May 4 date was significant to insure that there would be no dual coverage of employees in both the company profit sharing and union pension plan. Mr. Rudolph stated that, "We agreed that when the pension plan would come in, the profit sharing would go out. Although we never really discussed a termination date, my feeling was that profit sharing termination could not be retroactive to the March 16 date, because we never knew for sure whether it would be part of the final settlement."

When final settlement was reached, Mr. Rudolph instructed a letter to be written to the national office of the ITT Canteen Corporation requesting that Division A employees should be removed from company profit sharing coverage. This letter, dated May 4, 1970 was written by Mr. Peter Chruden of the St. Louis office to Mr. Sherman Witney in the national office. Since employee contributions to the company profit sharing plan had continued automatically during the entire negotiating period, the letter directed that payroll deductions to the profit sharing plan should be stopped for Division A employees with the pay period ending Saturday, May 2, 1970 and that accounts for these employees should be processed accordingly. The union did not participate in formulating and sending this letter, and the union did not receive a copy of this letter.

This matter did not become an issue until about fall, 1970, when Division A employees began receiving checks as their payments for being withdrawn from the company profit sharing plan. The checks paid to these employees were considerably less than the employees had expected due to a significant drop in stock market evaluation of their accounts which had occurred during the period from March through May 1970.[4] The market value of investments held by the company profit sharing trust fund had dropped some 20 to 25 percent during the period March to May 1970, and this drop was reflected in the termination checks paid to Division A employees. At this point, the issue of the proper evaluation date for termination of employees' accounts from the company profit sharing plan was raised and formalized in the union complaint heard in arbitration. As testified by both parties, this was the first time that the termination date actually became a significant issue in the minds of either the company or union representatives.

POSITION OF THE UNION

In his testimony, Mr. Bolle stated that, although the date for termination of Division A employees in the company profit sharing plan had never really been considered directly, he had simply assumed that it was March 16, 1970 to maintain the continuity and retroactivity of all the benefits from the old to the new agreement. The union representatives pointed out that the exact wording of Article XXXIV, Section 4 of the agreement stated:

---

[4] These checks varied considerably depending upon each individual employee's share in the company plan. The union testified that the checks ranged in amounts from "under fifty dollars to several thousand dollars." The company profit sharing fund is administered by an independent board of trustees. All withdrawals or termination checks from the fund to individual employees are based upon an evaluation of the "fair market value" of an account at the end of the month during which the withdrawal or termination takes place.

Effective March 16, 1970, when the Teamsters Negotiated Pension Plan becomes effective for Employees in Division "A," the Canteen Profit Sharing Plan will cease for such employees.

The union pointed out that this clause clearly stated that March 16, 1970 was the effective date for the beginning of coverage in the Teamsters' plan and the termination of coverage in the company plan for Division A employees. The May 4 date in Section 3 of the agreement merely stated when the company was to begin its contributions to the Teamsters plan on behalf of Division A employees.

Based upon this clause, the union contended that the proper date for termination and evaluation of the employees' accounts should have been based upon a March 16, 1970 date of withdrawal from the company profit sharing plan. The union requested (*a*) that the company should be directed to request the administrators of its profit sharing plan to determine any appropriate additional termination compensation to be paid to Division A employees based upon the March 16, 1970 date; and (*b*) that these employees also should have refunded to them the amount of their contributions to the company plan which had been improperly deducted from payroll checks during the period March 16–May 2, 1970. The union assumed that such a request as awarded in arbitration would be honored accordingly by trustees of the profit sharing plan.

POSITION OF THE COMPANY

In his testimony, Mr. Rudolph stated that, in his mind, the May 4, 1970 date to begin the company contributions to the Teamsters' pension plan was correspondingly the end of the Division A employees' participation in the company profit sharing plan. Mr. Rudolph testified that he was instrumental in having Article XXXIV, Section 4 placed in the agreement to be certain that there would be no duplication in membership of employees in both the profit and pension sharing plans. Upon cross-examination by the arbitrator as to why different dates were included in Article XXXIV, Section 3 and Article XXXIV, Section 4, Mr. Rudolph replied that he "honestly did not know." But he declared there was no intention in his mind to have retroactivity extended back to the March 16 date. Mr. Rudolph stated that an exact date for termination in the company profit sharing plan never was discussed, and he explained this as follows: "We were primarily interested only in determining when the one plan would come in, the other plan would go out. It wasn't until members received their termination checks from the profit sharing plan that the exact withdrawal date came up in anybody's mind. The drop in the stock market during this period was just one of those unfortunate coincidental things."

Mr. Rudolph further testified that his "blanket" request for withdrawing Division A employees from the company profit sharing plan was made by him because of the negotiated change of the status of these employees, and that to his knowledge there were no individual requests to withdraw. Normally, employees make individual requests for withdrawal, or they are terminated if they leave the company. Under the provisions of the ITT Canteen Corporation profit sharing trust fund, the termination or withdrawal payout checks normally are based upon an evaluation of each individual's account at the "fair market value" of the account at the end of the month of withdrawal or termination. Because of this negotiated situation, the "blanket" request for withdrawal was made by the company unilaterally.

Finally, Mr. Rudolph testified concerning the apparent confusion surrounding the date included in Article XXXIV, Section 4 of the agreement. He stated, "Why the March 16 date is there, I don't know. I saw that date there when I signed the contract, but it didn't make any impression on me then. I do know, however, that our mutual intention was to avoid double coverage in both the company and union plans. The March 16 date mentioned in the agreement obviously should have been May 4."

In this context, counsel for the company argued that Article XXXIV, Section 4 should be interpreted to mean May 4 rather than March 16, because otherwise there would be a gap in coverage of employees under the Teamsters' pension plan during these dates. With this proper interpretation of the intention of the agreement, the May date used for terminating Division A employees from the company profit sharing plan was therefore appropriate, and the union grievance should be denied.

APPENDIX

Applicable Contract Provisions

Article XXXIV—Teamsters' Negotiated Pension Plan

The Employer agrees to participate in and to contribute to the Teamsters' Negotiated Pension Plan on the following terms and conditions:

1. Said Pension Plan shall be administered by a Board of Trustees under

the uses and trusts as set forth in that certain Trust Agreement[5] attached hereto as Exhibit "B" and whose terms and conditions are herein incorporated by reference.

2. The Employer does hereby agree to be bound by and does hereby assent to all of the terms of said Trust agreement, including the Trustees therein named; the Employer further agrees to execute such other and further documents and papers (including said Trust Agreement) as shall be necessary or appropriate to evidence that it assents and subscribes to the terms thereof and accepts the Trustees therein named.

3. Effective May 4th, 1970, the Employer shall contribute for and on behalf of its employees covered by this Agreement, except Mobile Catering and Vending Attendants, to said Pension Plan and shall pay to said Trustees and Trust Fund established in Exhibit "B," the sum of One ($1.00) Dollar per week for each said employee.

4. Acceptance of the Employer as a contributing Employer hereunder shall be in writing by the Board of Trustees referred to in said Exhibit "B."

The Canteen Profit Sharing Plan will remain in effect for all employees in Division "B."

Effective March 16th, 1970, when the Teamsters Negotiated Pension Plan becomes effective for Employees in Division "A," the Canteen Profit Sharing Plan will cease for such employees.

EXHIBIT "A" (pp. 37–38 of agreement)

DIVISION "A" EMPLOYEES	SCHEDULE OF NEGOTIATED HOURLY WAGE RATES		
	3/16/70	3/16/71	3/16/72
MAINTENANCE	$4.25	$4.55	$4.80
SERVICEMAN	4.20	4.50	4.75
STOCKROOM	3.70	4.00	4.25
GENERAL LABOR	3.25	3.55	3.80
DELIVERY	4.20	4.50	4.75
INSTALLATION	4.03	4.33	4.58
ASST. INSTALLATION	3.63	3.93	4.18
CASUAL	3.00	3.25	3.50

HIRING RATES FOR NEW EMPLOYEES LISTED ABOVE:

NEW HIRES	75¢ UNDER BASE RATE
AFTER SIXTY (60) DAYS	60¢ UNDER BASE RATE
AFTER SIX (6) MONTHS	45¢ UNDER BASE RATE
AFTER TWELVE (12) MONTHS	30¢ UNDER BASE RATE
AFTER EIGHTEEN (18) MONTHS	15¢ UNDER BASE RATE
BASE RATE AFTER TWO (2) YEARS	

---

[5] This refers to the trust agreement which governs the Teamsters Negotiated Pension Plan. This trust agreement was attached to the contract as Exhibit B.

MOBILE CATERING   *SALESMEN'S WAGES*

The Wage Scale for Route Salesmen shall be as follows:

EFFECTIVE 3/16/70 $91.50 on their first $300.00 sales, plus 11½%
                           commission on all sales they make on their
                           respective routes over $300.00.

EFFECTIVE 3/16/71 $95.50 on their first $300.00 sales, plus 11½%
                           commission on all sales they make on their
                           respective routes over $300.00.

EFFECTIVE 3/16/72 $95.50 on their first $300.00 sales, plus 11½%
                           commission on all sales they make on their
                           respective routes over $300.00.

DIVISION "B" *EMPLOYEES:*	*SCHEDULE OF NEGOTIATED* *HOURLY WAGE RATES*		
	3/16/70	*3/16/71*	*3/16/72*
VENDING ATTENDANTS	$2.30	$2.60	$2.85

HIRING RATES FOR NEW EMPLOYEES LISTED ABOVE.

NEW HIRE   40¢ UNDER BASE RATE
AFTER SIX (6) MONTHS   20¢ UNDER BASE RATE
BASE RATE AFTER ONE (1) YEAR

QUESTIONS

1. Why does the crucial issue in this case center upon the question of the date that the company profit sharing plan was to terminate and coverage under the Teamsters' pension plan was to begin for the Division A employees?

2. Is there any basic conflict in the dates included in Article XXXIV, Section 3, and Article XXXIV, Section 4?

3. Evaluate the company's argument that "Article XXXIV, Section 4 should be interpreted to mean May 4 rather than March 16, because otherwise there would be a gap in coverage of employees under the Teamsters' pension plan during these dates."

4. Is equity to the employees' interest at issue in this case? Discuss.

5. Would this issue have occurred if during the period March to May, 1970 the stock market would have risen substantially resulting in an increased termination payoff to Division A employees?

36. MUST THE MACHINISTS PURCHASE THEIR OWN TOOLS?

COMPANY: *Stoody Company, Los Angeles, California*

UNION: *Local 803, International Union Allied Industrial Workers*

BACKGROUND

The Stoody Company is a major supplier for the Department of Defense, United States Government. In the fall of 1970, the company was subject to a quality control inspection and report by a Naval Nuclear Quality Control team. The inspection team was composed of representatives of major manufacturers, with staff help from governmental employees. In a report dated October 8, 1970 the Department of Defense recommended procedures for strengthening the company's quality control system. One recommendation was to "establish a calibration system meeting the requirements of MIL-C-45662[1] for the calibration and control of measuring and testing equipment." In discussing this recommendation, the report noted that the calibration on a number of the tools was improperly accomplished and that "no system exists to insure that defective personal micrometers are removed from service."

However, the report contained no recommendation that individual machinists own or buy their own tools.

Company management became concerned over the October 8 report and began to fear that its Defense Department contracts were in jeopardy. Consequently, management initiated a series of meetings with union representatives to determine which tools should be required of all machinists. It also established procedures for testing all machinists' tools, whether company-owned or employee-owned.

Prior to this time, the company had assumed that all of its machinists possessed the required tools of the machinists' trade. It was

---

[1] This is a code identification number for a Department of Defense regulation pertaining to this area.

243

only after the inspection began that the company learned that a considerable number of its machinists didn't own a basic set of tools.

Growing out of these inspections and several meetings and discussions with union representatives, the company, on December 16, 1970 issued a bulletin to "all machinists, turret lathe operators, and engine lathe operators" stating that effective March 19, 1971 all of these employees would be required to "possess a prescribed basic set of tools" consisting of items costing $256. The memorandum stated that required tools, if repairable, would be repaired by the company at no charge; if a tool was damaged beyond reasonable repair costs, an individual employee would be responsible for "replacing that tool at his own expense."

In the December 16 bulletin, the company described this list of tools as only "a basic set of tools to meet precision standards in work in various departments as well as tools needed to make necessary adjustments on the machines." The company had taken into consideration the frequency with which particular instruments were required. Many of the company's more than 50 machinists had all the tools on the list; some had more. However, the company had in its "tool crib," prior to December, each tool on the list in varying quantities. The machinists had had full access to the use of the various tools in the company tool crib.

At this time, the company had in existence a tool purchase payroll deduction plan. Under the plan individual employees could purchase up to $100 in tools and have deducted from their weekly pay, $10. The plan was available to any machinist or machine tool operator holding his present classification for more than 90 days. Also in the December 16 bulletin, the company modified its tool purchase plan; effective December 17, 1970 the maximum purchase amount was increased to $200 and the minimum weekly payroll deduction reduced to $5.

The March deadline was extended at the union's request. Further meetings were held. On April 7, 1971 the company issued a second bulletin to the machinists, engine lathe operators, and turret lathe operators stating that company inspection of individual tool sets had been rescheduled for May and that certain tools designated as required in the December list had been removed from the required classification. The total cost of the required tools on the revised list was $226.50.

In a meeting with union representatives on May 13th, the company again brought up the subject of required tools and asked whether the union agreed to the list. The union president stated it was his position that the list represented a fair amount of tools, but he did not agree that the company had the right to require the tools be purchased prior to a union vote on the proposal.

A few days before a scheduled union meeting at which the issue was to be raised, the company presented the union president with a letter dated May 19, 1971 stating that "all concerned employees (machinists, engine lathe opreators, and turret lathe operators) must possess the required basic machine tool set as itemized on the attached list," effective May 21, 1971. The company asked the union president to indicate his approval on the letter. The union president said he agreed that the tools represented a fair amount of individually owned tools, but that it was not his intent to make this binding on the machinists generally. The union president did sign the letter. There was also a signature line on the May 19th letter for the chairman of the union's bargaining committee. Subsequently, the company proposal was rejected at a union membership meeting. The bargaining committee chairman did not sign the letter. He, too, informed the company that the union believed the company did not have a right to require employees to buy tools, but that the union membership did not say that the list was unjust. He personally felt the list was reasonable and had obtained his own tools in December.

The Employee Disciplinary Actions

Karl Ford[2] had been a machinist for 40 years; he had been with the company 12½ years. Ford had some of his own tools, but he had been relying on using tools from the company tool crib. When he was hired, Ford was asked whether he owned his own tools, including a micrometer up to two inches; the company did not specify that he should own any particular tools other than the micrometer. After working for Stoody, Ford had disposed of some of his tools, since the company had furnished them and he saw no need for his own. In May 1971 his supervisor asked to see his tools. Ford told him that he could look at his tools to see if he had something he should not have, but not to see whether or not he had all the tools on the list. Previously, in March 1971 one of Ford's own micrometers had been submitted for inspection, and he was given a memorandum declaring that

---

2 All names are disguised.

,e is worn out of tolerance" and that the repair costs would
/ percent of the value of a new tool. In May, Ford stated that
,aken his micrometers home, and he was using company-owned
,neters when their use was necessary.
,i June 2, 1971 the Company issued a notice to Ford that:

As per the notice of December 16, 1970, and succeeding notices, the
,ompany has requested that you make your tool set available for inspection. You have refused to do so.

You, of course, have been given substantial notice of the requirement
that you produce your tool set for inspection. Since you cannot properly
perform your responsibilities as an employee of the Company without tools
which meet Company inspection requirements, this will advise you that
effective June 7, 1971, you will be suspended, for cause, from your employment with the Company until you have submitted your tool set for Company inspection.

The Company reserves the right to terminate you, for cause, at any time
subsequent to 30 days from the date of this notice if you have not brought
yourself into compliance with Company policy with respect to your tools.

On the same date, the company issued notices to employees Virgil
Gibson and Wesley Busch that they did not have certain required
tools. They were advised that they would be suspended effective June
7, 1971 until they had submitted satisfactory evidence that they had
the designated tools. The company further reserved the right to terminate them for cause, if the tools were not purchased within 30 days
from the date of the notice.

Gibson, a turret lathe operator trainee, was suspended on June
15th, but he was reinstated four weeks later after he had purchased
the additional tools required by the company. Gibson claimed that at
the time he was hired on the trainee program, he owned no tools.
From December 1970 to April 1971 he had purchased some of the tools
needed for the job. Gibson acknowledged that he knew he would
need some tools, but he felt that as a trainee he did not need all the
tools on the company list.

Under protest, Wesley Busch bought the tools and was never
suspended. However, Karl Ford steadfastly refused to buy the tools
"as a matter of principle." Ford was kept on the job until June 16th,
when he was suspended. He was terminated on August 6, 1971.

The union filed a grievance protesting the disciplinary actions of
the company and the rule of the company which required the
machinists to purchase the list of tools. The grievance eventually was
carried to arbitration.

POSITION OF THE UNION

The union argued that the company had no right to adopt a new rule forcing employees to own their own tools "mid-term of the contract." Under Article XXII, Section I of the agreement[3] governing past practice, the company cannot unilaterally change a long-standing rule or practice as was done by the company in this case. Further, the employees acted reasonably; even if the company's right to change the rule concerning the ownership of tools would be upheld, the disciplinary measures against the employees were not warranted and should be rescinded.

The union stated that the company had offered no evidence to show that it had been forced by the government or by any company customers to adopt the rule compelling employees to furnish their own tools. On the contrary, inspection of the calibration of precision tools could better be accomplished by maintaining tools in the tool crib rather than in each employee's possession. The company had furnished tools for many years. Because of this, a number of the employees, including Ford, sold or otherwise disposed of their tools, which was a reasonable reliance on company practice. The company's furnishing of tools over a period of years rose to the "dignity of a past practice." This was especially true when the employees, relying on the past practice, had sold or otherwise disposed of personal tools.

In addition to a normal past practice, the company, by furnishing tools, gave employees an additional benefit which should not be changed mid-term of the contract, because it affected the economic advantages of the working force. In this connection, the union cited other arbitration awards allegedly holding that benefits which had become, in effect, a form of wages could not be changed or withdrawn during the period of the contract. The union cited Article I, Section 1 of the contract which recognized the union as the sole bargaining representative of the employees for the purpose of collective bargaining in respect to "conditions of employment." The company was therefore obligated to bargain with the union concerning the issue of the purchase of the tools.

Finally, the union argued that the company acted hastily in disciplining the grievants, who acted reasonably. Once the tools were purchased, they would have had no recourse against the company. Therefore, by refusing to purchase the tools, they reacted in the only

---

[3] See Appendix for applicable contract provisions.

possible way they could. Ford, as a matter of principle, refused to capitulate to the company's one-sided edict.

In this case, refusal by employees to purchase the tools caused no immediate problem, since tools were available in the tool crib. Work was not disrupted, nor was the efficiency of the employees affected by their refusal to purchase tools. Ford, in particular, was a valued employee of the company. Ford would have continued to be an excellent employee if it had not been for the company's unfair action requiring him to purchase tools.

In summary, the union asked: (a) that the arbitrator require the company to bargain with the union over the matter of personal ownership of the required tools; and (b) that the disciplinary actions against Ford and Gibson be rescinded and these employees be made whole for any loss of earnings during their periods of suspension and termination.

POSITION OF THE COMPANY

The company argued that it had the right under the arrangement to adopt the rule requiring purchase of the required list of machinists' tools, and that the company was justified in disciplining the employees who refused to comply with the rule.

The company offered testimony concerning practices of other area employers who required employees to own their own tools. One company witness testified that the list required by the company was less than is typically required by most major defense manufacturers in the Los Angeles area. Another company witness who interviewed prospective machinists testified that as a matter of practice he asked prospective employees which tools they personally owned.

The company always had had the right to require the machinists to own the basic tools of their craft. When the calibration problem arose and the company learned for the first time that a number of machinists did not own a basic set of tools, the company moved to correct this situation. The company claimed that even though enforcement of its policy requiring employees to own a basic set of tools was left earlier to the good faith of the parties, nevertheless the employees knew of the company's policy generally. When the company became subject to Department of Defense criticism concerning the calibration of tools, it had no choice but to require ownership and inspection of personal tools. The consequent establishment by the company of more formal rules and regulations, after consultation with the bargaining committee, was reasonable.

Further, Article XXII Section 1 supported the company's position. As outlined above, the company clearly had a long-standing policy that machinists own their own tools. Article XXII Section 1 only required that "due consideration be given to employees' interests before changes were made" in past practice. The company's attempts to negotiate with the union a satisfactory list met the requirements of Article XXII.

The company pointed out that its machinists had purchased their own tools for a number of years prior to the new requirements issued for 1971. For the year 1971, up to May 13th, 14 of the 54 machinists had purchased tools through the company plan costing a total of $2,011. These purchases ranged from a low of $23 for one employee to a high of approximately $190. The plan was used in 1970 by nine employees, who purchased $1,416 worth of tools, and in 1969 by 12 employees, who purchased approximately $2,200 worth of tools.

All but three of the 54 machinists obtained the required tools. The remaining three, though not bound if the company had violated the contract, nevertheless were, in effect, told by the great majority of their co-workers that they felt the company's position was proper under the contract. It is impossible to believe that the machinists would have used the plan over a period of at least three years unless they understood that the company had a policy requiring that they personally own certain tools.

Finally, the company felt it had no recourse other than to suspend the three employees who refused to comply with the new rule. Ford, because of his adamant refusal, in effect terminated himself from employment with Stoody Company.

The company urged that the grievance be denied.

APPENDIX

Relevant Contractual Provisions

1.   Article XVIII Section 1 provided that employees will not be discharged "without just and sufficient cause."

2.   Article XXII Section 1 provided in part:

Certain methods, customs and practices, through long usage, have tended to become standardized. It is the Company's right to make any changes which do not violate this Agreement. However, the Company affirms that its policy will continue to be to respect tradition and precedence and that due consideration will be given to employees' interests before changes are made.

3.   Article XXII Section 4 provided in part:

Both the Union and the Company recognize that all jobs provided by the Company are made possible only by selling the Company's products and that in order to sell its products, the Company must use such materials, processes and services as will result in costs low enough to be competitive.

The Company policy has been, and is, to constantly seek additional work which it is qualified to do and to increase both its facilities and its work force. Its intention is to continue diligent efforts to promote sound growth and expansion of all its activities, with continuous consideration being given to the preservation of existing jobs and the creation of new ones.

QUESTIONS

1.   Did the company have the right to require employees to purchase their own tools? Why, or why not?

2.   Was the company obligated under the agreement to bargain with the union concerning the issue of the purchase of the tools? Discuss. Could the union have filed unfair labor practice charges with the NLRB concerning the issue of the company's not bargaining about the tool purchases as a condition of employment under the Labor Management Relations Act? Discuss.

3.   Discuss the union's argument that furnishing of tools to employees over a period of years had risen to "the dignity of a past practice."

4.   Did the company's actions in this case fulfill the requirements of Article XXII, Section 1? Discuss.

5.   Should it have any bearing on the arbitrator's decision that all but three of the 54 machinists had acquired the required tools?

6.   Should the arbitrator be influenced by the fact that employee Ford was a long-term employee who in this case was resisting the company edict at least partially as a matter of principle? Discuss.

37. THE "BUSTED RADIATOR"

COMPANY: *Veteran's Administration Center, Martinsburg, W. Va.*

UNION: *Local R4–78, National Association of Government Employees (N.A.G.E.)*

BACKGROUND

On July 6, 1971 Mr. James B. Biggs,[1] a nursing assistant, was due to work the day shift at the Veteran's Administration Center. The day shift began at 7:30 a.m. Shortly after 7 a.m., Biggs telephoned the nursing supervisor's office and spoke to Ms. Rose Hamilton, the night supervisor. Biggs told Hamilton that his car had broken down between Harper's Ferry, where Biggs lived, and Charlestown, which is on the way to Martinsburg. Biggs requested that he be permitted to take the day off on an emergency basis, as part of his annual leave, and he told Hamilton that he could not come to work on account of a "busted radiator" in his car. However, Hamilton was reluctant to grant this request; she told Biggs "to come in as soon as he could."

Shortly before Biggs called, another nursing assistant, Mr. Tom Short, had called in sick and was granted sick leave. Both Biggs and Short worked in the same ward. As a result of the absence of these two nursing assistants, this ward was shorthanded. Another nursing assistant was shifted from another assignment to fill the void. The situation was further complicated because Biggs' ward was in a state of transition and was very crowded. Consequently, both Hamilton and Ms. Dorothy Garrison, the day shift supervisor, were very anxious to have Biggs at work on July 6.

However, Biggs never made it to work that day. There was no public transportation or taxi service between the point where Biggs' car broke down and the hospital. Further, very few VA Center employees lived in the Harper's Ferry area. After a fruitless attempt to continue toward Martinsburg by hitchhiking, Biggs returned to the

---

[1] All names have been disguised.

repair shop in the vicinity of Harper's Ferry, where he had left his car. Biggs' car was not repaired until 2 p.m. at which time he felt it was too late for him to drive 20 miles from Harper's Ferry to Martinsburg to work on a shift that ended at 4 p.m.

The VA Center is staffed continuously. July 6 was Bigg's scheduled day off, but because of the work load at the Center, Biggs had been assigned to work on that day. If he had not experienced difficulty with his car and had he worked on July 6, he would have received double time for hours worked on that day. However, after reviewing the facts, the hospital officials decided to suspend Biggs for ten days for failing to report to work.

The union filed a grievance on behalf of Biggs which was ultimately carried to arbitration.

POSITION OF THE UNION

The union's arguments consisted mainly of Biggs' testimony and the circumstances surrounding his absence on July 6.

Biggs testified that his car had broken down between Harper's Ferry and Martinsburg. Since there was no public transportation or taxi service between Harper's Ferry and Martinsburg, and since very few VA Center employees lived in the Harper's Ferry area, Biggs' lack of success at hitchhiking was understandable.

The union argued that two prior disciplinary actions against Biggs by the VA Center were not related to this instance. Biggs had been reprimanded on two earlier occasions during the previous year for being tardy. These incidents should have no bearing in this case because on July 6 Biggs made a genuine effort to get to work. The unon supplied receipts and affidavits from the garage owner indicating that he had towed Biggs' automobile to its premises, that the car was inoperable, and that while waiting for repairs Biggs made several attempts to get to work, including attempts to hitchhike a ride and to rent a car.

The facts revealed that if Biggs had gone to work that day, he would have received double his normal day's pay since this day was considered a "holiday" for him. Therefore, Biggs had considerable incentive to make every effort to report to work.

The union noted that records revealed that sick leave was readily granted to VA employees, as evidenced by the granting of sick leave to Biggs' fellow employee, Tom Short. Knowing this, Biggs easily could have called in sick instead of reporting honestly that his car had broken down. The union suggested that it could logically be concluded that Biggs' car indeed had broken down, and that he had no means of transportation to get to work.

In light of the above testimony and circumstances surrounding this case, the union requested that this grievance be sustained, and that Biggs be reimbursed for the wages he lost due to the ten-day disciplinary suspension.

POSITION OF THE VA CENTER HOSPITAL

VA management argued that Biggs had an absolute duty to report to work on July 6, and that his excuse about his car breaking down was not sufficient to warrant his absence from work. Biggs had been told by Hamilton to come to work as soon as possible. The center maintained that Biggs should have found another method of getting to work if his regular means had failed.

Management pointed to Article XIX of the contract which stated as follows:

Article XIX—Annual Leave

Section 1. Full and part-time employees shall earn annual leave in accordance with applicable statutes.

Section 2. Approval of an employee's request to take annual leave shall be granted when he has given his supervisor reasonable notice and can be spared. Approval of annual leave for emergency reasons will be considered on an individual case basis and generally granted when conditions warrant.

Management called special attention to the second sentence of Section 2 which specified that annual leave "for emergency reasons will be considered on an individual basis and generally granted when conditions warrant." Since Biggs' ward was in a state of transition and overcrowded as well as being short-handed, the center argued that it was within its rights not to grant Biggs' request.

Finally, center officials cited two previous disciplinary actions that preceded this suspension. The first occurred about a year earlier when Biggs received a warning for arriving to work late. Biggs claimed that on that occasion he was late as a result of a minor accident on a icy highway while driving to work. The second warning occurred about six months earlier when Biggs said he had overslept as a result of his being weak and tired after being ill with the flu. In management's opinion, these prior warnings should have impressed on Biggs that he was expected to report to work on time and as scheduled. As a result of these circumstances, the center requested that the arbitrator dismiss the grievance.

QUESTIONS

1. Did employee James Biggs have an "absolute duty to report to work" on July 6th, as argued by VA management? If so, was his excuse sufficient to warrant his absence from work? Discuss.
2. Was the VA Center within its rights not to grant employee Biggs a day of annual leave to compensate him for the day in dispute? Why, or why not?
3. Should the previous disciplinary actions involving employee Biggs have any bearing on this particular case? Why, or why not?

38. SICK LEAVE PAY DURING A STRIKE

COMPANY: *Reliance Universal, Inc., Louisville Plant, Louisville, Kentucky*

UNION: *Local 604, International Chemical Workers Union*

BACKGROUND

Employees Art Wilson and Marvin Hill[1] were quite ill with the flu and other related ailments, and they were unable to report to work on Thursday, December 4, 1969. On this same day, another union in the plant, the Teamsters, went out on a legal strike at the end of its contract period and set up a picket line around the plant.

Both Wilson and Hill medically were able to return to work on Monday, December 15, but because of the Teamsters' strike and picket line, they refused to do so. Both employees did not return to work until December 26, 1969 the date which coincided with the termination of the Teamsters' strike.

Upon return to work, Wilson and Hill turned in a claim for sick pay and insurance reimbursement for the seven working days of their illness, during the period December 4–15, as provided in Article XXIV[2] of the agreement.

The company rejected the claims of Wilson and Hill on grounds that because of the Teamsters' picket line and their reluctance to cross it, they would not have reported to work anyway on the days involved in their claim. The company's insurance carrier, Connecticut General, explained the rejection thus:

Our Cincinnati Claim Office has had an opportunity to review the disability claims of employees Wilson and Hill.

The Active Service requirement in your contract with Connecticut General precludes any consideration of this claim and future claims, if any, during the work stoppage at your plant. In other words, the employees

---

1 All names are disguised.

2 See Appendix for applicable contract provisions.

255

who have chosen to refuse to cross the picket line are not considered as active employees performing the customary duties of their employment.

The union filed a grievance on behalf of Wilson and Hill which eventually went to arbitration.

POSITION OF THE UNION

The union contended that Wilson and Hill met every single requirement of paragraph 24.7 of the agreement in that they were "regular employees" and had the requisite "earned credits" for the benefits. They were also on a "regularly scheduled work day," had "no duplication of earnings," and had supplied the requisite medical report of their illnesses. Both were, by stipulation, so ill that they could not have reported to work under any circumstances; each had carefully telephoned the plant on each of the seven claimed days to report their illness. Therefore, asserted the union, the only conceivable reason why their claims were being denied was because subsequent to their illnesses they refused to cross a picket line as was their right under the agreement, Article V.

The union urged that Wilson and Hill should be reimbursed for the appropriate amounts, which were rightfully theirs under the sick pay and sick insurance provisions of the agreement.

POSITION OF THE COMPANY

The company contended that the real reason that Wilson and Hill were absent was their refusal to cross the Teamsters' picket line. This was self-evident since they did not return to work following their illnesses. The purpose of disability and sickness insurance, said the company, was to replace lost income. Since it is plain that the grievants would not have worked anyway, the company claimed that they could not be reimbursed regardless of how ill they may have been (and the company did not dispute the fact of their illnesses). The company pointed out that its insurance carrier, Connecticut General, stated in its letter of December 24, 1970 that the grievants did not meet the "active service" requirement if they refused to cross the picket line, and therefore they could not be considered active employees performing the customary duties of their employment. In this context, the company pointed out that during the strike, the company had maintained its usual schedules including those of the grievants, and it sought in every way possible to encourage employees to report for duty.

In summary, the company claimed that regardless of whether or not they were ill, Wilson and Hill would not have worked during the period of December 4–15 because of the Teamsters' strike and picket line. Under these circumstances, reimbursement under the sick pay and insurance provisions was inappropriate. The grievance should be denied.

APPENDIX

Pertinent Contract Provisions

Article V—Strikes and Lockouts

Section 5.2. Picket Line. This Article shall in no way restrict the individual's right to cross or refuse to cross a legal picket line at premises, authorized by the recognized collective bargaining representative of employees at such premises in its capacity as such bargaining agent, nor shall refusal to cross such a picket line be cause for discharge or disciplinary action.

Article XXIV—Miscellaneous

Section 24.7. Sick Pay. (1) Regular employees shall accrue paid sick leave, not to exceed five (5) days of paid sick leave per calendar year, at the rate of one (1) day of paid sick leave upon completion of each (2) months of active full time employment during such calendar year.

(2) Sick pay benefits accruing during any calendar year shall become available as of January 1 of the succeeding calendar year, must be used within such succeeding calendar year, and will not accumulate from year to year. For absence because of illness on days when the employee would otherwise have been regularly scheduled to work, sick pay will be paid beginning with the first (1st) full day of such absence and may continue until accrued sick pay available to the employee has been exhausted. Sick pay for any such full day's absence shall be equal to eight (8) hours straight time pay at the employee's regular base rate, excluding shift differential or other premium.

Section 24.9. Insurance. During the term of this Agreement (provided such coverages continue to be available): . . .

Memorandum for Agreement

It is understood that the Sickness and Accident Insurance provided for in Section 24.9 will be payable first day of injury, third day of sickness, for a maximum of fifty-two (52) weeks, and the weekly benefit will be seventy percent (70%) of the employee's forty (40) hours straight time base rate, not to exceed Sixty-Five Dollars ($65.00).

QUESTIONS

1. Aside from the money involved, why would the company and its insurance carrier be reluctant to pay the medical benefits to employees Wilson and Hill in this case?

2. Discuss the argument of the company and its insurance carrier that the grievants "did not meet the active service requirement if they refused to cross the picket line, and therefore they could not be considered active employees performing the customary duties of their employment."

3. Why does the arbitrator's decision in this case hinge upon the question of whether the absences of the grievants were primarily a result of their sicknesses, or of the picket line placed around the plant? Discuss.

39. CAUGHT WITH POT

COMPANY: *Vulcan Materials Company, Geismar, Louisiana*

UNION: *Oil, Chemical and Atomic Workers International Union, Local 4–620*

BACKGROUND

In November 1968 the Vulcan Materials Company opened a new plant in Geismar, Louisiana. This was the newest plant in a group of eight chemical plants located in Geismar. The plant produces a group of chlorinated hydrocarbons. The continuous process involves the manufacture of several potentially hazardous chemicals; production employees work rotating shifts to provide continuous staffing. The plant is highly automated; at the time of this case, it was operated by 45 production workers, who were members of Local 4–620, plus a small managerial and technical staff. Most of the employees live in four small surrounding communities.

On May 12, 1969 the company hired Robert Mead,[1] 22 years old, as a process technician. However, an incident concerning the possession of marijuana caused the company to discharge him on November 13, 1970 as an "undesirable employee." Mead and the union filed a grievance protesting that there was no just cause for dismissing him. They asked that Mead be reinstated with full seniority rights, and that he be reimbursed with full back pay, and all benefits, including overtime, shift differentials, and holiday pay. The grievance was eventually submitted to arbitration.

The incident leading to Mead's discharge occurred in early October 1970 when approximately 30 persons were arrested in Ascension Parish, Louisiana, for possession of marijuana. One of those arrested, a friend of Robert Mead's, agreed to cooperate with the authorities in determining the source of the marijuana.

On October 9, 1970 Robert Mead, in order to help his friend, vol-

---

[1] All names are disguised.

untarily surrendered to Sheriff Pierre Boisseau and admitted that he was the one who had supplied the marijuana. The authorities possessed no evidence indicating that Mead had supplied the marijuana; nevertheless, Mead admitted his involvement. He stated, however, that he was not a "pusher" and that he was not in the business of peddling marijuana, or any other drug. Mead was arrested following his admission to Louisiana state authorities that "he had supplied marijuana to 38 persons in Ascension Parish, Louisiana." After his release, and prior to court trial, Mead returned to his job and reported his arrest to his foreman.

On Monday morning, November 9, 1970 Mead requested a two-day leave of absence from his shift supervisor, Matt Jacobson. Mead stated that it was necessary for him to appear in court the following day. Later, at approximately 10 a.m., Mead was summoned to a meeting with three supervisors, including Superintendent Jack Horton. In this meeting, Mead informed the three supervisors that he was planning to plead guilty to the charge of possession of marijuana, and that the state authorities were going to fine him $500 as well as place him on supervised probation for two years. Superintendent Horton informed Mead that if anything like this happened again, he would be dismissed or severely disciplined by the company. Superintendent Horton then asked Mead to sign a written statement confirming Mead's understanding of the company's action. Mead requested permission to consult his union steward, Harold Wellborn, who advised him not to sign such a statement. Mead signed anyway and was then granted his two-day leave of absence. Neither the union nor Mead received a copy of this signed statement.

On Friday, November 13, 1970 four days after the meeting, the company telephoned Mead at his home to summon him and union steward, Harold Wellborn, to a meeting in the office of the plant manager, Henry Billings. Among those present at the meeting was Director for Administration Paul Drummond. At this meeting, Billings asked Mead what had transpired in his appearance at court on November 10. Mead stated that he had pleaded guilty to the charge; that he was fined $500, which he had to earn himself; and that he was placed on supervised probation for two years. In addition, Mead and Wellborn informed Billings of the events on November 9 concerning his meeting with the three supervisors. The company officials requested that Mead and Wellborn leave the meeting while they discussed the matter among themselves. Mead and Wellborn were subsequently called back into the meeting. Mead was asked by the company to either resign or be discharged. Mead refused to resign, and therefore he was discharged on November 13, 1970 by the company as an "undesirable employee."

POSITION OF THE COMPANY

The company presented the following arguments and evidence in defense of discharging Robert Mead:

1. The company stated that it was essential for it to maintain close and harmonious relations with other companies of the area and with the people in the neighboring communities. Widespread publicity concerning Mead's conviction of possessing marijuana would prove detrimental to the image of the company as a good corporate citizen, if it did not discharge him.

2. The company had established high employment standards. It carefully screened applicants, including an investigation for possible conviction of serious crimes, before hiring in order to avoid hiring undesirables. The company expected that employees, as a condition of continued employment, would behave themselves both on and off the job. The conduct of employees should reflect favorably upon the company.

3. The company stated that it considered its relationship with its employees to be a very important part of its personnel management program. The continued employment of Mead would have a very adverse effect upon company-employee relations. Further, his continued employment would place him in a position to encourage other employees to use marijuana.

4. Process technicians are responsible for the operation of a very sophisticated and complex plant worth almost 30 million dollars. They must be alert and attentive to duty at all times in order to operate the plant safely and efficiently. Emergency situations occur frequently; marijuana slows reaction time and impairs judgment. The consequences could be serious to fellow employees if Mead, or some other employee, were under the influence of marijuana.

5. The company argued that its decision was not hasty, capricious, or arbitrary. It made a careful and extensive investigation following Mead's conviction and only then took formal action against him.

6. The company attested that any discipline short of discharge would have been inappropriate, for the possession of marijuana is such a serious offense that it flouts the principles of corrective dis-

cipline. In the interests of employee safety and welfare, and community relations, the company could not tolerate off-the-job conduct of this nature on the part of any employee.

7.   The statement which Mead signed on November 9 did not constitute a formal warning and had no bearing on any disciplinary action subsequently taken. It was intended only as a memorandum of consultation or counseling for Supervisor Jacobson's file, and it was never made a part of Mead's personnel record. The company pointed out that it did not pressure Mead to sign the statement, and that he did so in the presence of and over the objection of his union steward.

8.   Finally, the company maintained that Mead admitted his guilt, and he was tried and convicted of an admittedly serious crime involving moral turpitude. It could not continue Mead's employment "without courting disaster."

POSITION OF THE UNION

The union presented eight arguments to support its position that Mead should be restored to his job with full back pay, restoration of all seniority rights and privileges, and compensation for all other benefits and monies lost as a result of the company's action:

1.   The company did not show just cause for discharging Mead, since his behavior away from company premises affected neither his attendance nor his work performance. Article 16 of the agreement[2] specifically states that disciplinary action is to be used by the company for the sole "purpose of impressing the employee that it is necessary to correct some undesirable work related problem. ...." The company offered no evidence that Mead's offense was in any way work-related or that any subsequent work-related problems resulted from his activity or conviction. The company agreed that Mead's work performance was satisfactory both before and after his arrest and conviction.

2.   The company offered no evidence that the performance of any employee was in any way influenced by Mead's conduct, arrest or conviction. In fact, none of his associates at the plant knew of these activities until his arrest, at which time several of his associates, including his foreman, volunteered to serve as character witnesses.

---

[2] See Appendix for full text of this provision and other applicable contractual clauses and legal statutes.

3. Sheriff Boisseau, the arresting officer to whom Mead voluntarily surrendered, testified strongly in Mead's behalf to the effect that he was convinced that Mead was merely an experimenter and not a hard-core pusher or user.

4. The sheriff also testified on a major legal change enacted by the Louisiana Legislature in 1970 to the effect that a first offense for possession of marijuana is no longer a felony with a mandatory minimum sentence of five years in prison. The new "Uniform Controlled Dangerous Substances Law" (Act 457 of 1970)[3] distinguishes marijuana from "narcotic drugs" and changes a first offense for possession of marijuana to a misdemeanor.

5. Section 977.1 of the 1970 Louisiana law cited above allows the court considerable latitude in handling cases such as this. The court may, as it did in the case of Mead and all others convicted with him, fine the offender and place him under supervised probation. In this case, Mead and all others over the age of 21 were fined $500 and placed on probation under terms which closely regulated their conduct.

6. The new law allows the court, as it did in Mead's case, to hold in abeyance a finding of guilt on a first offense and specifies that it be erased upon satisfactory completion of probation. The intent of the provision for the erasure, after a satisfactory probation, of any record of the offense is clearly to avoid branding a first offender as a convicted criminal, which the company had erroneously chosen to do.

7. The union pointed out that the company had no firm policy for dismissing all men convicted of misdemeanors, even for drunken driving or battery. In this context, the union quoted the testimony of Director for Administration Paul Drummond. Drummond testified that it was not company policy to discharge employees automatically for any and all criminal convictions, and that a determination as to whether a conviction without a jail sentence would result in discharge would depend on the offense and surrounding circumstances. He also testified: (a) that if the company knew of off-premises possession of marijuana but that no court action resulted, it would "probably not" discharge the employee; (b) that the company would consider a conviction more serious if it remained on the record than if it were expunged after successful completion of a probationary period; (c) that he was not aware, at the time the company decided

[3] See Appendix.

to discharge Mead, that the offense would be removed from the record after completion of the probationary period and payment of the fine.

8.   Finally, the union claimed that the company violated the contractual requirement for progressive corrective discipline both in its discharge of Mead for this offense and in its placing him in double jeopardy by discharging him after having settled the issue through a written warning on November 9. The recollections of Mead and of steward Wellborn clearly established that this November 9 memorandum was really a written warning, in spite of the fact that the company did not provide the union with a copy as required by the agreement. The union alleged that the company had steadfastly refused to produce the written warning or to offer the testimony of any of the three supervisors who signed it. The union further contended that after Superintendent Horton had obtained all the facts on the nature of the court proceeding and the penalty which had been imposed, he informed Mead and steward Wellborn that this warning would be the extent of the disciplinary action. It was with this understanding that Mead signed it against the counsel of his steward.

APPENDIX

Relevant Articles and Laws

Article 5—Management

5.1 Except as explicitly limited by a specific provision of this agreement, the Company shall continue to have the exclusive right to take any action it deems appropriate to the management of its operations and direction of the work force in accordance with its judgment. All inherent and common-law management functions and rights which the Company has not expressly modified or restricted by a specific provision of this Agreement are retained and vested exclusively in the Company.

5.2 Examples of this right include, but are not limited to, responsibility and authority for the following . . . relieving employees from duty when necessary due to lack of work or other legitimate reasons; . . . and taking action required in promoting, transferring, suspending, demoting, granting leaves of absence, and disciplining employees, including but not limited to discharge for cause.

5.3 The Company's not exercising any function hereby reserved to it, or its exercising any such function in a particular way, shall not be deemed a waiver of its right to exercise such function or preclude the Company from exercising the same in some other way not in conflict with the express provisions of this Agreement.

Article 16—Discipline and Discharge

16.1 When it is necessary for the Company to take disciplinary action against any employee for the purpose of impressing the employee that it is necessary to correct some undesirable work related problem, the recognized principles of progressive corrective discipline will be followed. In the event discipline or discharge is necessary following an investigation and development of facts, an employee may elect to have his steward present at the time the action is taken. The employee involved and the Union will be furnished a copy of any record prepared relative to any disciplinary action taken against the employee.

16.2 The Company will not discharge or discipline an employee without just cause . . . .

16.3 When an employee is discharged for just cause, the Union will be advised as to the reasons for such discharge prior to the Company's taking such action. In the event a discharge is determined to be without just cause, the employee involved will be reinstated with full seniority.

Uniform Controlled Dangerous Substances Law Act 457 of 1970, State of Louisiana

Section 977.1—Conditional Discharge for Possession as First Offense. Whenever any person who has not previously been convicted of any offense under this subpart relating to the unlawful use, possession, production, manufacture, distribution or dispensation of any narcotic drugs, marijuana, or stimulant, depressant, or hallucinogenic drugs, pleads guilty to or is found guilty of possession of a controlled dangerous substance under Subsection 971 (c), the court may, without entering a judgment of guilt and with the consent of such person, defer further proceedings and place him on probation upon such reasonable terms and conditions as it may require. Upon violation of a term of any such conditions, the court may enter an adjudication of guilt and reimpose upon such person the sentence of the court as originally imposed. Upon fulfillment of the terms and conditions, the court shall discharge such person and dismiss the proceedings against him. Discharge and dismissal under this Section shall be without court adjudication of guilt and shall not be deemed a conviction for purposes of disqualifications or disabilities imposed by law upon conviction of a crime including the additional penalties imposed for second or subsequent convictions under Section 978 of this Title. Discharge and dismissal under this Section may occur only once with respect to any person.

QUESTIONS

1. Evaluate each of the company arguments in support of its discharge action of Robert Mead.
2. Evaluate each of the union arguments in support of its position that Mead's discharge should be rescinded.

3. Was Robert Mead discharged for just cause as required under the provisions of the agreement? Why is this difficult to determine when the issue involves conduct of an employee that occurred off the company premises and was not directly work related?

4. From a management standpoint, is it desirable for a company to develop policies for dealing with situations of this sort involving employee behavior off the job? Would it be desirable to negotiate clauses into the agreement to cover these types of situations? Discuss.

40. A DRINK "TO CUT THE DUST"

COMPANY: Packaging Corporation of America, Container Plant, St. Louis, Missouri

UNION: International Brotherhood of Pulp, Sulphite and Paper Mill Workers, Local 535

BACKGROUND

Philip D. Blendon[1] had worked since 1958 at the Packaging Corporation of America as a ZA Auto-Taper operator.[2] On March 26, 1969 the company hired Sally Rollins as a feeder. Both employees worked at the Saint Louis, Missouri, plant, which manufactures corrugated shipping containers.

On September 18, 1970 both Blendon and Rollins were assigned to work on a band saw on the first shift. On this same day, Production Manager Jerry Dillings handed out paychecks in the plant. At 9:20 a.m., Dillings walked toward the band saw and noticed that it was not running. Since the morning break for the first shift ended at 9:10 a.m., Dillings knew that the band saw should have been operating. As he approached the band saw, he noticed that there were three loads of material pushed around the machine. Dillings looked around the three loads and noticed that Blendon and Rollins were kneeling down. He observed that Blendon took a drink from a whisky bottle, then handed it over to Rollins who put the cap back on and placed the bottle of whiskey in her purse. At this time, Dillings approached them and said: "Come on. Let's go to the office." All three went to the office where Frank Harder, the plant manager, and Donald Crowell, the chief union steward, joined them. Blendon and Rollins admitted to what Dillings had observed. They were immediately discharged by the company for violating Rule 2 of the company's Rules of Conduct.

---

1 All names have been disguised.

2 The ZA Auto-Taper applies a paper or fabric tape to the side seam of corrugated paper cartons.

Both Rollins and Blendon filed grievances which protested their discharge. The company denied these grievances, and the case eventually was submitted to arbitration.

The union asserted that Blendon was a good worker, and that his work attendance had been good. Before this incident occurred, Blendon had been reprimanded previously on only one occasion by the company and that was for taking excessive smoking breaks. This reprimand was meted out by a plant foreman, and it subsequently was rescinded and removed from Blendon's file in the course of the grievance procedure. The union pointed out that Plant Manager Frank Harder did not remember Blendon ever having been disciplined during the five years he had been plant manager. Production Manager Dillings had admitted that, prior to this incident, he had found no cause whatsoever to discipline Blendon. Further, the union submitted that the company should have taken into account the fact that Blendon had taken only one drink, and that he had never done anything of this nature during his 12 years with the company.

Blendon argued that certain other extenuating circumstances should have been considered by the company. On the day of the incident in question, the ventilation around the band saw was very poor, and he had gone twice to the water fountain to obtain a drink of water. When he returned from the water fountain the second time, he made a remark to Sally Rollins about the dust; specifically he told her that he would like to have something stronger than water "to cut the dust." Rollins then replied that, just by chance, she had some whiskey in her purse. Rollins offered it to him, and he then took a single drink.

Blendon added that he was not intoxicated. His mental and physical faculties were not impaired, nor was his judgment affected by only one drink.

The union pointed out that Blendon had had an excellent work record during his 12 years of employment, and that his behavior, other than for this offense, had been outstanding.

Concerning Rollins, the union pointed out that she never had been disciplined previously by the company; to discharge her for a first offense would be too severe a penalty. The union conceded that Rollins was wrong in offering Blendon a drink of whiskey and the union did not object to a penalty for her. But the union argued that something less than discharge was justified.

Rollins testified that certain mitigating circumstances were relevant to her case. She testified that, on the night preceding her discharge, she was at a party. She took several friends home in her automobile. When they got out of her car, they left a small bottle containing about two inches of whiskey in the car. She noticed the bottle when she arrived home and placed it in her purse, since she did not want to leave it in the car. She stated that she was in a hurry the next morning (the day of her discharge) and forgot about the bottle until she took a tissue from her purse shortly after 9:00 a.m. She testified that when Blendon said he could use a drink (or words to that effect)—that only then did she offer him the bottle. The union claimed that Rollins brought the bottle into the plant without any intent to violate Rule 2, and that her violation of the rule occurred when she offered Blendon a drink.

POSITION OF THE COMPANY

The company maintained that Philip Blendon and Sally Rollins, by bringing and drinking alcoholic beverages in the plant, had violated long-established work rules placed in effect for the safety and convenience of all employees.[3] The company pointed out that eleven months before the discharge of Blendon and Rollins, two other employees, Sam Gieger and Ed Kirk, had been discharged for similar offenses concerning the possession and drinking of alcoholic beverages. The company stated that on October 7, 1969 Production Manager Dillings had found almost a full can of beer belonging to Gieger, and the company promptly discharged him. Also, on July 31, 1970 the company discharged employee Ed Kirk, because Dillings had observed that Kirk was in no condition to continue working after the company physician had confirmed that Kirk had been drinking alcoholic beverages. The company stressed that neither the two employees nor the union had filed a grievance concerning these two incidents.

Moreover, the company pointed out that on February 9, 1970 Dillings held a meeting with all employees to discuss this problem of drinking alcoholic beverages in the plant; Dillings had warned the employees that the company would take action if this drinking continued. The company pointed out that both Blendon and Rollins were at the meeting.

The company further maintained that it had been trying seriously to reduce accidents in the plant as well as to improve the plant safety

---

[3] See Appendix to this case.

record. Company efforts in this direction would be in vain if employees continued to bring intoxicating liquor into the plant.

Finally, the company emphasized that both Blendon and Rollins should have been working instead of drinking at the time they were caught, since the company's morning break period lasted only until 9:10 a.m.

For all of these reasons, the company concluded that Blendon and Rollins were properly discharged for cause. The company requested that the grievances be denied.

POSITION OF THE UNION

The union recognized that Philip Blendon and Sally Rollins violated Rule 2 and that they should be penalized. However, the penalty of discharge was too severe.

The union argued that the case differed in several respects from that of former employees Gieger and Kirk, both of whom had been discharged. Gieger had knowingly brought a can of beer into the plant, whereas Rollins unknowingly brought the bottle of whiskey on company property. Kirk was under the influence of alcohol at the time he was discharged, whereas Blendon had only a single drink and had full possession of all his faculties. Finally, neither Gieger nor Kirk had come to their union steward seeking to file a grievance. The fact that both Gieger and Kirk decided, for reasons known only to them, not to file a grievance should not influence the arbitrator's decision in this instance.

Both Blendon and Rollins admitted to their offense and stated that they regretted their behavior. They were asking to be given another chance. The union requested that the discharge actions of the company be rescinded, and that Blendon and Rollins be returned to their jobs.

APPENDIX

Pertinent Provisions of the Agreement

Article I—Management Rights

It is recognized and agreed that the management and operation of the plant and the direction of the work forces are the sole and exclusive rights of the Company and that in the fulfillment and accomplishment of these functions, the Company has and retains all of the rights, powers, and authorities it would have in the absence of this agreement; provided, however, that nothing herein shall supersede any other provisions of this Agreement. The subjects and matters contained in the various articles of this Agreement shall be subject to the grievance and arbitration procedure.

Pertinent Provisions of the Plant Rules and Safety Instructions

Rules of Conduct

The following list of offenses, practices and actions may subject an employee to disciplinary action including immediate suspension or final dismissal without notice: . . .

2. Introducing, possessing or using on the property of the Company intoxicating liquors . . . or reporting for duty under the influence of such liquors . . .

QUESTIONS

1. Did the company have the right under the agreement to discharge the two employees for taking a drink on company premises? Are there any limitations to the rights of management to enforce its rules in this situation?

2. Should the fact that employees Blendon and Rollins had relatively long and good employment records influence the arbitrator's decision? Why, or why not?

3. Evaluate the testimony of Rollins concerning the mitigating circumstances which contributed to her bringing the whiskey on plant premises.

4. What are the precedent implications involved in a case of this sort, particularly in reference to enforcement of plant rules and safety considerations?

41. THE BOMB THREAT

COMPANY: *Goodyear Tire and Rubber Company, Dallas, Texas*

UNION: *Dallas General Drivers, Warehousemen and Helpers, International Brotherhood of Teamsters, Local 745*

BACKGROUND

At about 12:45 p.m. on July 8, 1970 the telephone operator at the Dallas plant of Goodyear Tire and Rubber Company received a bomb threat from an anonymous caller. The police were notified immediately, and arrived at about 1:20 p.m.

After conferring with the police and executives at company headquarters, management decided to evacuate all personnel before 2:30 p.m., the same time the caller indicated that the bomb would detonate. Everyone was out of the plant by 2:00 p.m., and work was suspended for the day.

Subsequently, the company decided that the 50 warehouse employees who were covered by the contract with the union[1] should be paid for this day until 2:15 p.m. These employees had begun work at 8:00 a.m. and received pay for five and three fourths hours. Four warehouse employees who had started work at 10:00 a.m. were paid for three and three fourths hours. However, the 175 office employees who were not in the union were paid for the full day. The union filed a grievance alleging that the company had discriminated against the warehouse employees in paying them for only five and three fourths hours (and three and three fourths hours), rather than the full eight hours on that day. The union also alleged that the company had discriminated against the warehouse employees, because the office employees were notified and evacuated somewhat earlier (about 20 minutes) than the warehouse employees. The union requested that

---

[1] See Appendix for pertinent contract provisions.

the arbitrator require the company to pay the warehouse employees for the full eight hours on July 8.

POSITION OF THE UNION

The union stated that no one at the Dallas plant could ever remember having been sent home early without receiving pay for the full day. The union argued that since office workers were paid for the full day, the company was acting discriminatorily in not also paying warehouse workers for the full eight hours.

The union further argued that the warehouse employees were available and ready for work and that they were deprived of the opportunity to work through no fault of their own. The company voluntarily closed the plant. In fact, the union pointed out that the company had received a similar bomb threat a few days later but did not send the employees home. Finally, the union contended that the contract specifies "major mechanical breakdown, fire, flood, or similar conditions" as cause for nonpayment, but that it nowhere mentions voluntary closing of the plant by the company.

POSITION OF THE COMPANY

The company agreed that office personnel were evacuated from the plant somewhat sooner than warehouse personnel. However, the reason for this was not a result of dereliction or discrimination by the company, since supervisors of both groups began notifying their people at about the same time. Police and management agreed that it would be inadvisable to notify personnel by means of the public address system. It was feared that use of the public address system might create panic conditions and that it would probably fail to reach everyone, especially the warehouse workers. The office occupies about 10,000 square feet, while the warehouse occupies about 200,000 square feet. The delay in contacting some warehousemen was caused by the much greater physical space involved and the time required to contact everyone personally.

The company stated that the warehouseworkers were not paid eight hours pay for the day, because it followed the provisions of the contract which did not require them to do so. A telephone bomb threat by an anonymous caller is clearly a condition "beyond the control of the company"; hence it was not obliged to pay for the time not worked. Therefore, the grievance should be denied.

APPENDIX

Relevant portions of the agreement between the parties, signed April 4, 1969, are as follows:

Article IX, Section 2 (c).   Unless notified otherwise, an employee reporting for work on his regular scheduled shift will be given a minimum of four (4) hours pay at his regular rate except in cases of major mechanical breakdown, fire, flood, or similar conditions beyond the control of the Company....

Article XXII, Section 4.   It is mutually agreed that this contract supersedes and negates any previous agreements, either written or oral, established by negotiation, contracts, force of law, mediation, or arbitration or otherwise, including but not limited to precedence and past practices, and incorporates all conditions of employment applicable to employees covered by this Agreement.

QUESTIONS

1. Did the company act discriminatorially against the union warehouse workers by not paying them for the full eight hours? Why, or why not?
2. Evaluate the union argument that the "employees were available and ready to work and that they were deprived of the opportunity to work through no fault of their own."
3. Was a telephone bomb threat a condition "beyond the control of the company" as specified in Article IX of the agreement? If so, how can this be reconciled with the union argument that the company had "voluntarily closed the plant"?
4. Should blue-collar employees covered by a union agreement be treated any differently than white-collar personnel who are not represented by a labor union? Is there a difference between what a company is obligated to do under an agreement as compared to what it may wish to do from some other point of view? Discuss.

42. MUST THE COMPANY SELECT A FEMALE CREDIT TRAINEE?

COMPANY: *Phillips Petroleum Company, Kansas City*
          Sales Department

UNION: *Phillips Petroleum Company Employees Union*

BACKGROUND

Ms. Marian McPhee,[1] 24 years old, was hired by the Phillips Petroleum Company in its Kansas City office on January 17, 1967 as a "typist-transcriber," a salary grade-four position. She applied on six different occasions for higher grade jobs between that date and May 27, 1967. She was turned down the first five times because of lack of seniority; however, by May 27 she became the senior qualified bidder for the job of "steno-transcriber" in salary-grade five, and she was awarded the promotion.

Early in June, McPhee reenrolled on a part-time basis at the Metropolitan Junior College in Kansas City to continue her studies in a prebusiness curriculum.

On July 7, 1967 McPhee applied for an assignment to the training program in the position of "credit trainee." The company reviewed her application and denied her petition "for lack of qualifications." She again requested on August 14, 1967 that she be considered for assignment to the training position. The company again refused her request, and on August 24 she filed the following grievance.

August 24, 1967

When I had my appraisal interview with my Supervisor Mr. Kay, he told me that I would start in the Typing Section, but that I could go as far as I wanted with Phillips Petroleum Company. Taking this into consideration, I started back to college.

Early in July, I requested by letter to Personnel Director Morton consideration for the Credit Training Program, which is necessary to be a Collection Analyst. On July 12, 1967, I was called to Mr. Morton's office,

---

[1] All names have been disguised.

at which time I was informed I had been turned down for the following reasons:

1. I was on probation at Metropolitan Junior College and considered a sophomore at this time.

2. I was also told, by Mr. Morton, that I needed 60 hours and to raise my grade point average.

3. Mr. Morton went on to say that Phillips did not always hire men right off campus with only a "C" grade average.

4. Mr. Morton said that my low grades were all in business courses and not my art and science courses, which, I pointed out to him, was incorrect.

I explained to him that a "C" is known to be a decent grade from Metropolitan Junior College; it is often comparable to a "B" at other colleges. I thanked Mr. Morton for the interview and left. However, I decided I would like to have a written explanation of the reasons I was "turned down at this time," so I went back to Mr. Morton's office and requested one. I was advised by him that no one anywhere in the office receives such a letter.

After completing two hours credit this summer and receiving my grades on August 14, 1967, I once again requested permission to take this program.

On August 23, 1967, I was called to Mr. Terry Wilton's office (Mr. Wilton is doing Mr. Morton's work while he is on vacation), As I walked in I saw Mr. Bill Majill, who is directly over my immediate supervisor. Mr. Wilton told me again that I had been turned down because my grade points were too low and said that I was still on probation as far as Phillips was concerned. I showed him a letter from Mr. W. D. Hartley, Administrative Dean of Metropolitan Junior College, stating that I was not on probation. Then, finding that they could not disqualify me through college, Mr. Majill spoke up and said my production is low in Steno and I talk too much. He went on to say that my work is unsatisfactory and very poor. On several occasions I have been told that my production is low and that I talk too much, but so does everyone else. They want fifty letters a day and do not care about quality,—all they want is quantity. I am used to doing things right the first time they leave my desk. Mr. Majill said he wants only one thing, and this is fifty letters a day.

I feel that Phillips Petroleum Company is discriminating against me because of my sex, and they are using everything they can throw at me to keep me from qualifying for this training program.

Mr. Wilton on August 24, 1967 called me to his office. I asked the President of our Union, Mr. George Lang, to go with me, which he did. Mr. Wilton had a copy of our meeting between himself, Mr. Majill, and me, and wanted me to read it and initial it. Mr. Lang read it and asked Mr. Wilton if there was a copy of the first meeting betwen Mr. Morton and myself. He said there was and Mr. Lang requested to see it; but Mr. Wilton did not know where this copy was.

Mr. Lang advised me not to sign or initial this copy until I had read the first one. I also told Mr. Lang I did not like the way this copy was worded.

As you can see by the above paragraphs, I get one story from one person and another from the other person. I feel like they are playing "Merry-go-round" with me, because I am a girl. I am qualified for the Credit Trainee Program and am being discriminated against because of my sex and because I am at present an employee of the Phillips Petroleum Company.

I am filing this grievance because the employer refused to appoint me to the position of Credit Trainee.

Marian McPhee
First Floor Steno
Credit Card Division

The grievance eventually was carried to arbitration.

POSITION OF THE UNION

The union argued that since the company refused to appoint Marian McPhee to the position of credit trainee, even though she met the requirements for this position, the company had discriminated against her due to her sex and because she was at present an employee of the company.

The union pointed out that, in spring of 1967, the company posted a notice to the effect that employees who had completed at least two years (60 units) of college courses in a prebusiness program would be eligible for consideration for the position of credit trainee. McPhee had already satisfied this requirement by completing 61 unit hours for prebusiness study at Metropolitan Junior College in Kansas City. In fact, the company had encouraged her to complete this work by financing 75 per cent of her tuition costs. The 61 units had been completed prior to her filing the final application on August 14.

The union pointed out that McPhee had almost two years of successful work experience prior to her employment by Phillips. She had worked for ten months in the accounting section of a securities company; subsequently she was promoted from that position into the accounts receivable section of the securities firm where she worked for one year handling customer accounts and insurance claims.

The union objected to the introduction into the case by the company of two reports written by McPhee's immediate supervisor Kay. These appraisals claimed that her work performance was less than satisfactory; that she did not adapt well to the various duties assigned her; that she was a low volume producer; that she talked excessively; and that at least on one occasion she had used obscence language especially inappropriate for a woman in an office. The union pointed out that both reports had been written subject to McPhee's request for promotion on August 14. The union claimed that the appraisals were deliberately constructed and slanted to "build a case" against her appointment to the training program.

The union further alleged that since the company continually recruited candidates for the credit trainee program from universities, it was discriminating against McPhee because she was presently a Phillips employee and not a graduate of a four-year college or university.

The union charged that the company had shown a consistent pattern of sex discrimination by the fact that no woman had ever been appointed to the position of credit trainee in the Kansas City office since the program began there in 1961. This pattern of sexual discrimination directly was in violation of the Federal Civil Rights Act of 1964 and the Fair Employment Practices Act of the State of Missouri as well as being in direct violation of Article XIV, Paragraph 4 of the agreement.[2] The union cited testimony of Robert Mount, manager of the credit card division, who reported that 115 men—no women—had completed the credit trainee program since its inception. Of these 115, 45 occupied supervisory positions and 70 worked as credit card analysts, collection analysts, or assistants. The union argued that these latter positions were particularly suited for women employees and that there could be no reason to deny these positions to women other than that the company was reserving the position to train men for future higher level supervisory positions. The union asserted that the effect of the company's discriminatory practices was to place a barrier in the promotional path of women who wished to advance, since satisfactory completion of the credit trainee program was a prerequisite to any salary grade level beyond grade seven.

For all these reasons, the union urged that the arbitrator should order the company to offer the credit trainee position to Marian McPhee, and that the company should be ordered to cease its sexual discrimination against female employees in future selection from among credit trainee applicants.

---

2 See Appendix to case.

POSITION OF THE COMPANY

The company argued that McPhee did not meet the company's standards for the credit trainee position.

The company stated that the sole purpose of the credit trainee position was to groom employees who possess considerable potential for advancement to more responsible positions in the finance and credit departments of the company, both in the Kansas City office and in various locations throughout the country. The company argued that since the training program was such an important source of supervisory talent, it must retain exclusive control over the selection and appointment of persons to the program.

The company cited Article II, Management Functions, and Article X, Sections 2 and 7, to support its right to exercise exclusive control over appointment to the program. Article II, it contended, clearly states that all rights held by the company prior to the time that the union became the bargaining representative were retained by the company except in those matters expressly limited by the collective agreement. The company had never bargained away or restricted its right to assign whomever it wished to the position of credit trainee.

The company further claimed exclusive jurisdiction over the Credit Trainee program by referring to Article X, Section 7. It argued that the language is clear and to the point—that is, jobs specifically designed for training purposes, including credit trainee, are not regular full-time vacancies and shall be filled by assignment. The selection of candidates was left to the sole discretion of management.

The company also cited Article X, Section 2, to support its right to maintain unilateral control over the credit trainee position. This provision outlines the job-bidding procedure for positions, except for jobs specifically excluded in Section 7. Management claimed that the union here was attempting to gain through arbitration something it was unable to obtain through negotiation.

According to the company, the educational requirements indicated in the posted notice of spring 1967 were only the minimum acceptable educational requirements for acceptance into the credit trainee program. These minimum educational requirements could in no way be construed to mean that all persons who possess them automatically would be taken into a training position. These minimum requirements were posted to inform present employees that workers with less than a college degree would be considered for acceptance if they were qualified in other ways. However, the minimum requirements listed in the notice dealt only with education; they did not include the many other factors which are considered. In fact, the notice stated that these were "minimum requirements."

The company denied that it had acted discriminatorily towards McPhee or any other employee because of their sex or present employee status. In the past, women had been considered for the credit trainee position, but none of the female applicants was found acceptable. Management representatives pointed out that, in their opinion, many features of the job made it unattractive to women: extensive travel, frequent geographical relocations, long hours, and occasional abusive language from customers. As a consequence, few women applied for the position. If, however, a female with genuine interest in the position, and with qualifications to succeed in this and related higher-level jobs, should apply, she would be given an opportunity to enter the program. However, this decision must remain with management.

The company stressed that past experiences indicated that college graduates with a specialization in finance or accounting had been the most successful trainees. However, the company wanted to leave "the door open" to outstanding employees who, through personal development, experience, and desire, could substitute other qualities for the college degree.

The company responded to the union's charge that 70 graduates from the program were engaged essentially in clerical work especially suited to women by stating that not all graduates were promoted immediately to managerial positions. The jobs of assistant collection analyst, collection analyst, and credit analyst were excellent training positions for promotion into management jobs.

Finally, the company argued that McPhee was not appointed to the credit trainee position because she simply was not qualified. Mount testified that the areas considered by him in selecting credit trainees included education, past work performance, ability to work with peers and superiors, quality and quantity of output, maturity in accepting responsibility, ability to handle more responsible assignments, willingness to travel, and ability to meet people, including dealers, jobbers, and the public. In his opinion, McPhee was found lacking in certain respects in most of these areas.

For all of the above reasons, the company urged that the grievance be denied.

APPENDIX

Provisions of the Collective Agreement between the Phillips Petroleum Company and the Phillips Petroleum Company Employees Union

Article II—Management Functions

All the rights, power and authority had by the Company prior to the time the Union became the bargaining agent, are specifically retained hereunder by the Company except to the extent that they are expressly limited by specific provision of this Agreement.

Article X—Promotions, Demotions, Transfers, Layoffs, Terminations and Re-employment

Section 2. Promotions. Job vacancies, as determined by the Company, which are to be filled on a regular full-time basis by promotion, shall be posted for bids for three full working days. Employees desiring to bid on such jobs shall file a written request with the Personnel Office within said three-day period. Promotions will be based on seniority and qualifications, the senior employee that is qualified being given preference. Until a successful bidder is determined and assigned to such a job vacancy, it may be filled by assignment. Where there are no qualified eligible employees bidding on job vacancies, such job vacancies may be filled by hiring from the outside or from any other source. Regularity of attendance shall be a factor in determining qualifications. Where it is not known how long a temporary vacancy will exist, it may be filled temporarily up to sixty (60) calendar days. If the vacancy is still filled on a temporary basis at the expiration of sixty (60) days, it will be posted as specified above.

In the event of promotion as provided in this section, there will be a probationary period of thirty (30) days. If at any time during said period the employee shall be determined to be unsatisfactory, he will be notified accordingly and may be returned to his previous classification at any time during the probation period.

Section 7. It is understood and agreed that jobs specifically for training purposes and carrying the title of Credit Trainee, Graduate Business Trainee, and Division Office Trainee, are not regular full-time job vacancies and shall be filled by assignment. Any employee desiring to be considered for one of these training positions shall notify the Personnel Office in writing. The Company agrees to give every consideration to anyone who so applies. A notice stating that employees may apply for these positions and outlining how they can reply, will be permanently posted on bulletin boards.

Article XIV—Miscellaneous

Section 4. There shall be no discrimination because of race, sex, national origin, creed or color or because of membership or non-membership in the Union.

Relevant Sections of the Civil Rights Act of 1964

Section 703 (a) of the Civil Rights Act of 1964, 42 U.S.C. 2000e–2 (a) provides:

(a)   It shall be an unlawful employment practice for an employer—
(1)   to fail or refuse to hire or to discharge any individual or otherwise to discriminate against any individual with respect to his compensation, terms, conditions or privileges of employment, because of such individual's race, color, religion, sex, or national origin; or
(2)   to limit, segregate, or classify his employees in any way which would deprive or tend to deprive any individual of employment opportunities or otherwise adversely affect his status as an employee, because of such individual's race, color, religion, sex, or national origin.

Relevant Sections of the Missouri Revised Statutes, entitled the Missouri Fair Employment Practices Act, Sections 297.010–296.070

It shall be an unlawful employment practice:
(1)   For an employer, because of the race, creed, color, religion, national origin, sex, or ancestry of any individual:

*   *   *   *   *

(b)   To limit, segregate, or classify his employees in any way which would deprive or tend to deprive any individual of employment opportunities or otherwise adversely affect his status as an employee, because of such individual's race, creed, color, religion, national origin, sex, or ancestry.

QUESTIONS

1. Evaluate each of the arguments presented by the union on behalf of Marian McPhee. Could the employee and/or union have filed sexual discrimination charges against the company under the Equal Employment Opportunity Act? Discuss.

2.   Evaluate each of the company arguments in denying Marian McPhee's petition for the credit training program.

3.   Under the agreement, did the company have sole discretion to select candidates for the credit training position? Why, or why not?

4.   Under the affirmative action programs of the Equal Employment Opportunity Commission, how might the company be considered in violation of the Civil Rights Act in this type of situation even though an arbitrator might uphold management in this specific case? Discuss.

43. THE RELUCTANT RETIREE

COMPANY: *Honneggers & Company, Inc., Indianola, Iowa*

UNION: *International Brotherhood of Teamsters, Chauffeurs, Warehousemen and Helpers of America, Local 90*

BACKGROUND

The company raises, processes, and sells livestock and poultry, and retails livestock feed at its Indianola, Iowa plant. The production and maintenance employees and truck drivers were represented by the union since November, 1968.

Ralph Winkle[1] had been hired on March 31, 1960 as a truck driver, a position he held at the time of this case. Winkle reached his 65th birthday on June 17, 1970. At the end of May he was informed by the Operations Manager, Carl Souci, that the company had a policy of compulsory retirement at age 65 and that he would be retired as of June 30. However, Winkle did not wish to retire, and he filed a grievance, charging that his employment had been terminated without just cause. The union carried the grievance to arbitration. The union contended that there was no clause in the collective agreement requiring retirement at age 65, and it requested that Winkle be reinstated with full back pay and with full restoration of all rights and privileges, including seniority.

The history of the company's compulsory retirement policy dated back to 1958 when the company established its "Employees' Profit Sharing Plan," which was since amended on several occasions. This plan provided that a participant would retire upon attaining age 65, but could remain in active service beyond that age if requested to do so by the company. The company's employees were not unionized at the time the plan was established. At the time of unionization in

---

[1] All names have been disguised.

1968, the agreement signed by the parties in that year was silent on the question of compulsory retirement.

In 1965, the company had issued a revised edition of its "Employee Manual," which originally was issued in 1962. The 1965 edition stated that the normal retirement age was age 65, but it did not mention compulsory retirement. Late in 1968, the company requested that employees return the 1965 Employee Manual, because several policy matters outlined in it conflicted in part with various clauses of the new union negotiated agreement.

Ralph Winkle had participated in the Employees' Profit Sharing Plan, and upon his compulsory retirement he received a lump sum payment of $383.11 from the profit sharing trust. He received no further payments, since the company did not maintain a pension plan.

POSITION OF THE UNION

The union contended that Winkle was improperly terminated in violation of Articles V and XVI of the agreement.[2] The union claimed that at no time had anyone ever informed Winkle that there was a compulsory retirement age of 65 until shortly before he was terminated in June, 1970.

The union argued that Winkle had never received a copy of the original "Employee Manual" published in 1962. Winkle testified that he received only the revised 1965 version which referred only to a "normal" retirement at age 65 and which did not mention compulsory retirement. The union thus argued that Honneggers & Company did not have a formally established retirement policy which required employees to retire at age 65.

The union further pointed out that the collective bargaining agreement did not contain a "Management Rights Clause," and that Articles V and XVI referred only to "discharge for cause." The union argued that the company had made no claim that Winkle was either physically or mentally unfit to perform satisfactorily his duties as a truck driver. By forcing Winkle to retire even though Winkle was a healthy and capable employee, the company in effect had discharged him without sufficient cause. This violated the agreement.

Finally, the union contended that neither Winkle nor any other employee was aware that the company had a policy concerning a compulsory retirement age. At no time during the 1968 negotiations did

---

2 See Appendix to case.

the company inform the union that such a policy was in effect. In order to substantiate this point, John Coleman, the union president and business representative who represented the union in negotiating the agreement, testified that he had never seen the "Employees' Profit Sharing Plan" until it was submitted by the company as an exhibit at the arbitration hearing. Horace Troutman, who participated in the negotiations on behalf of the company, corroborated Coleman's testimony. Coleman also testified that the question of compulsory retirement at age 65 was not discussed during negotiations.

The union submitted in evidence an affidavit, dated August 17, 1970, and signed by 15 active or former bargaining unit employees and the former plant manager of the Indianola plant, in which they stated that they "were not aware of any company policy which required retirement at age 65 by employees."

In summary, the union argued that the company had no cause for terminating the employment of Mr. Winkle under the provisions of the agreement, and that the company presented insufficient evidence to support its contention that there existed a long-established company policy of compulsory retirement understood and agreed to by employees.

POSITION OF THE COMPANY

The company contended that, in the absence of any provision in the collective agreement to the contrary, it had the right to follow its normal compulsory retirement policy. The company emphasized that the collective agreement placed no restrictions upon the company, and that the profit sharing plan in which Winkle participated prescribed a compulsory retirement at the age of 65 unless an employee was specifically requested to defer his retirement and consented to such request.

The company argued that, although the collective bargaining agreement did not say anything about compulsory retirement, this did not mean that management did not have the right to exercise its normal policy of retiring employees at age 65. Further, the company pointed out that, during negotiations with the union, compulsory retirement was not even brought up for discussion by the union. Since the union did not submit compulsory retirement as an important issue for discussion, the company asserted that it retained the right to terminate Winkle when he reached his 65th birthday.

The company pointed out that many years before the employees became unionized, the company had always distributed employee manuals which included information concerning its normal retirement policy to the employees. To further substantiate the fact that the company was following a consistent policy, the company pointed out that another employee, Philip Moreland, was also retired by the company at the Indianola plant upon his reaching age 65.

In concluding, the company argued that since compulsory retirement was not brought up for discussion during negotiations with the union, plus the fact that the agreement was silent on the issue of compulsory retirement, the company was justified in retiring Ralph Winkle as part of its consistent policy of compulsorily retiring employees at age 65. The grievance should be dismissed.

APPENDIX

Pertinent Provisions of the Agreement

Article V—Seniority

In case of layoff, if employee does not return to work when called back by registered letter to his last known address within one (1) week after the letter has been received by him, or within one (1) week after the letter has been sent, he shall lose his seniority rights. Seniority rights shall be lost by discharge for cause, transferring out of the unit without an express leave of absence, or voluntary quit.

Article XVI—Discharge

The employer shall not discharge any employee, except new employees during the first thirty (30) working days trial period, without just cause, and shall give at least one (1) warning notice of any complaint against such employee to the employee, in writing, and a copy of same to the Union, except that no warning notice needs to be given to an employee before he is discharged if the cause of such discharge is dishonesty, drunkenness, including the drinking of alcoholic beverages on the job. . . .

QUESTIONS

1. Did the company have the right to force employee Ralph Winkle to retire at age 65? Discuss.
2. Evaluate the union's argument that the agreement provided only for discharge for cause, and that by forcing Winkle to retire the company in effect had discharged him without sufficient cause.

3. If the agreement is silent on the issue of compulsory retirement, does the company retain the right to exercise its own policy forcing employees to retire at a specified age level? Why is this a very controversial area which preferably should be covered in a collective agreement?

4. What are the precedent implications of this case which go beyond the immediate problem of employee Ralph Winkle?

44. CAN THE COMPANY ELIMINATE THE QUATROPULPER HELPER'S JOB?

COMPANY: *Ethyl Corporation, Oxford Paper Company Division, West Carrollton, Ohio*

UNION: *United Papermakers and Paperworkers, Local 19*

BACKGROUND

On August 5, 1970, the company notified the union that it was putting into effect a new "quatropulper operator" job description. In its notice to the union, the company expressed a desire "to continue our discussions regarding the job description," but the company also stated in its notice that meetings had been held on August 3 and August 4 without the parties making "any significant progress regarding the listing of duties for this job."

As a result of the company action, the various duties defined in the job description of the "quatropulper helper" were combined with that of the quatropulper operator, and the lesser job was eliminated. The two former job classifications appeared in a section on "Job Classifications & Rates" in the labor agreement. A comparison of these two job descriptions indicated that a new number 7 was added to the duties of the quatropulper operator: "Brings dry stock from storage room to Quatropulper by means of a hand or power truck as required by order specifications." This was item No. 1 in the description of the helper's duties, and his other requirements were mainly to "assist" the operator in each category of their overlapping duties.[1]

The union filed a grievance protesting management's action in eliminating the quatropulper helper's job. The grievance ultimately was carried to arbitration.

---

1 See Appendix for various descriptions.

POSITION OF THE UNION

The union contended that the jobs of the quatropulper operator and quatropulper helper had not changed to the degree that the company could load one man, the operator, with two jobs. The union insisted that during the last 13 years there had not been any significant changes in these jobs.

The union introduced two witnesses with respectively 24 years' seniority and 13 years' seniority working on the quatropulper.[2] These witnesses stated that no significant job changes had been made in the last 13 years, that there was no physical relocation of equipment, and no introduction of automation. The only change which they noted over the years was that currently production of some 600 feet per minute was achieved, whereas ten years ago it was 400 feet per minute.

It was the union's position that the company completely abolished a job of 13 years' duration solely on the basis of its view of the economics involved. Yet, under Article XI, Section A of the agreement,[3] the company could not unilaterally change or abolish a job unless there was a significant change in job content. This was not the case with the operator's and helper's jobs.

Further, according to the union, the requirements of Article XI offset Article VI, the Management Rights Clause, and negotiation was required before a job could be abolished. If the company could abolish this job of helper, said the union, it could nullify any job and any job description in the agreement. According to the union, this would have the effect of undermining all jobs.

In summary, the union claimed that the arbitrator should uphold the union grievance by ordering reinstatement of the quatropulper helper's job classification and ordering the company to negotiate any proposed changes with the union. The union emphasized that this was exactly what the contract required. However, counsel for the union also stated as follows: "If by any miracle the award goes to the company, the union wishes the arbitrator to retain jurisdiction for the determination of an equitable rate for the new combined job description of quatropulper operator."

---

[2] The quatropulper is a large machine which is used to make paper pulp. It contains a tile tank with dimensions of a 12 foot diameter and 15 foot depth; several impellers churn and beat sheets of pulpwood and chemical additives such as clay, alum and titanium. The quatropulper mixes these raw materials into a slush with a proper consistency which then is pumped to the machines which actually manufacture the paper.

[3] See Appendix for applicable provisions.

POSITION OF THE COMPANY

The company basically argued that it was justified under the agreement in eliminating the quatropulper's helper's job because of: (1) significant changes in job requirements, and (2) economic necessities.

Company witnesses insisted that "substantial" changes had been made in the job of quatropulper operator by the elimination of the necessity for putting shavings into the quatropulper, a reduction in bag size for ingredients from 100 to 50 pounds so that they could be handled easily by one man, and by the installation of a so-called probe which senses the approach of the pulp mixture to the full point so that it was not necessary any longer for the operator to maintain constant surveillance to avoid an overflow.

According to company testimony, the change followed a thorough job study of the two old jobs indicating that the "incumbents of each" spent approximately 85 percent "waiting time" and only 15 percent "actual physical activity." Job studies since the change indicated 70 percent "waiting time" and only 30 percent "physical activity" for the remaining operator. The combined job was in no way too much work for one man to handle.

The company introduced considerable testimony indicating that the change was necessary in the interest of the plant maintaining a "competitive position in the market." Company witnesses expressed concern that it might be necessary to close this plant in the manner that the company's very old operation, in Lawrence, Massachusetts, recently was shut down. According to the company, the Management Rights Clause (Article VI) and the Declaration of Principles Clause (Article I) vested in management the responsibility to make those decisions which were required by economic necessity to promote efficient operation.

In support of its position, the company cited a number of decisions by other arbitrators for their persuasive effect in stating the principles which the company said should govern the case here. In a case at Edition Book Binders of N.Y., Inc., the arbitrator found that there was no contract provision fixing the crew compliment of any machine; that, said the company, was the situation here. An arbitrator held in a Georgia-Pacific Corporation case that under a broad management rights clause, such as that which existed in this instance, the company had the right to eliminate lower rated jobs and to reassign them for reasons of economy and protection of its economic position. The company further cited the award of an arbitrator at International Salt

Company. The arbitrator held that, where there is no provision in the contract forbidding it, an employer may unilaterally eliminate employees or vary crew size, provided that it is not capricious or arbitrary but is based on legitimate operation requirements. Finally, the company cited a case at the Lone Star Brewing Co. where the arbitrator ruled to the effect that the reduction of a two-man crew did not result in an "unreasonable" increase in the burden of other employees' job duties and therefore the reduction was sustained.

The company argued that all of these cases and other similar rulings of arbitrators supported the company's position in this case. The company claimed that the union's grievance was therefore without merit, and it should be denied.

APPENDIX

Pertinent Job Descriptions

1. *Quatropulper Operator* (prior to August 5, 1970).

Duties

Under the supervision of the Beater Department Foreman, Night Superintendent and Colorman, is responsible for the operation of a Quatropulper, pumps, and auxiliary equipment in the preparation of furnish for making paper.

Specific Duties:
1. Mixes, beats and hydrates pulp, broke, and other ingredients in Quatropulper to prepare furnish.
2. Charges Quatropulper with pulp, broke, book stock, mill bleach, fillers, size, alum, special chemical, and other ingredients as may be required by order specifications.
3. Operates pumps, valves, etc., to insure proper hydration and stock consistency.
4. Pumps furnish to storage chests and regulates agitators to maintain consistency.
5. Keeps record of all material used in accordance with instructions.
6. Cleans Quatropulper and other operating equipment as needed.
7. Cooperates to promote good housekeeping and safety within the department.
8. Performs, when assigned by his foreman or by the superintendent under whose jurisdiction the department falls, such temporary duties that are related to the job covered by this description, and such other temporary duties that are necessary for orderly operation of the mill when such work results from an emergency or an unusual temporary situation.

2. *Quatropulper Helper* (prior to August 5, 1970).

Duties

Under the supervision of the Beater Department Foreman, Night Superintendent and Colorman, assists the Quatropulper Operator in the preparation of furnish for making paper.

Specific Duties:
1. Brings dry stock from storage room to Quatropulper by means of a hand or power truck as required by order specifications.
2. Assists in charging Quatropulper with stock and broke according to order specifications.
3. Assists Operator in handling bagged material from storage and into Quatropulper.
4. Assists Operator in washing up on shut downs.
5. Assists Operator in cleaning up Quatropulper and other operating equipment as needed.
6. Assists Operator in addition of mill bleach and book stock as necessary.
7. Cooperates to promote good housekeeping and safety within the department.
8. Performs, when assigned by his foreman or by the superintendent under whose jurisdiction the department falls, such temporary duties that are necessary for orderly operation of the mill when such work results from an emergency or an unusual temporary situation.

3. *Quatropulper Operator* (after August 5, 1970).

Duties

Under the supervision of the Beater Department Foreman, Night Superintendent and Colorman, is responsible for the operation of a Quatropulper, pumps, and auxiliary equipment in the preparation of furnish for making paper.

Specific Duties:
1. Mixes, beats and hydrates pulp, broke and other ingredients in Quatropulper to prepare furnish.
2. Charges Quatropulper with pulp, broke, book stock, mill bleach, fillers, size, alum, special chemicals and other ingredients as may be required by order specifications.
3. Operates pumps, valves, etc., to insure proper hydration and stock consistency.
4. Pumps furnish to storage chests and regulates agitators to maintain consistency.
5. Keeps record of all material in accordance with instructions.
6. Cleans Quatropulper and other operating equipment as needed.

7. Brings dry stock from storage room to Quatropulper by means of a hand or power truck as required by order specifications.
8. Cooperates to promote good housekeeping and safety within the department.
9. Performs, when assigned by his foreman or by the superintendent under whose jurisdiction the department falls, such temporary duties that are related to the job covered by this description, and such other temporary duties that are necessary for orderly operation of the mill when such work results from an emergency or an unusual temporary situation.

Pertinent Contract Provisions

Article I—Declaration of Principles

Section A. It is in the mutual interest of the employer and employee to provide for the operation of the Plant hereinafter mentioned, under methods which will further, to the fullest extent possible, the economic welfare of the Company and its employees, . . . economy of operation, quality and quantity of output, . . .

Section B. It is recognized by the Agreement to be the duty of the Company and the Union and the employees to cooperate fully for the advancement of said conditions.

Article VI—Management

Section A. The management of the work and the direction of the working forces including the right to hire, promote, suspend or discharge for proper cause, or transfer, and the rights to relieve employees from duty because of lack of work or for other legitimate reasons, is vested exclusively in the Company. . . .

Article XI—Wages

Section A. The Job Evaluation and Job Descriptions agreed upon in writing betwen the parties on August 27, 1953, and amended through October 4, 1970, shall remain the basis of Job Evaluations and Job Descriptions for all present and any new jobs in this Plant. It is understood and agreed that future claims of job inequalities will not be made unless there has been a permanent change in job content sufficient to warrant a re-evaluation of the job.

QUESTIONS

1. Based upon the information in the case, had there been significant changes in job content of such a type and magnitude which required bargaining with the union over this issue? Discuss.

2. Evaluate the argument of the union that if the company could abolish the job of helper, it could "nullify any job description in the agreement." Why is this a very sensitive issue to a labor union?

3. Does company management have the right to eliminate a job because of economic necessities under the provisions in this contract?

4. Why did the company cite a number of parallel decisions in support of its position? Is an arbitrator obligated to consider parallel cases in reaching a decision in this case? Discuss.

45. THE CHRONICALLY DEPRESSED ABSENTEE

COMPANY: *Husky Oil Company, Salt Lake City, Utah*

UNION: *Oil, Chemical, and Atomic Workers International Union, Local 2–578*

BACKGROUND

Walter Jackson[1] began working at the North Salt Lake Refinery as a chemical operator trainee on June 23, 1961 and was terminated on August 13, 1974 for excessive chronic absenteeism.

Jackson's sick leave record from 1968 to August 13, 1974 was as follows.[2]

Year	Days of Sick Leave
1968	10
1969	20
1970	6
1971	17
1972	16
1973	29
1974 (to August 13)	20

The management of Husky noted Jackson's sequence of frequent short-term absences late in 1969. His supervisor, William Fielding, discussed his attendance problem with him first on April 5, 1972. Management again noted Jackson's excessive absenteeism in January 1974. Fielding sent him three written warnings between January and May 1974.

---

[1] The names of all individuals have been disguised.

[2] Husky Oil Company purchased the North Salt Lake Refinery in 1968. None of Jackson's records are available from the previous owner.

Relevant portions of these letters follow:

Letter of January 7, 1974

Dear Walter:

I am very concerned about your physical condition in regard to your ability to perform your job. This concern results from the fact that you have taken more sick leave than any other employee in the refinery, with the exception of three men. These three men were on sick leave for specific ailments or injuries, whereas you have been off on sick leave as a result of minor ailments.

I am requesting that you take a physical examination at the company's expense to determine whether or not you are physically able to perform your job. The company has the right to require you to submit to a physical examination according to Article 25.02 of the Agreement. If the results of this examination reveal that you are incapable of performing the various tasks that are part of your job, then we will take appropriate action. Article 5.16 of the Agreement states that if an employee becomes incapable of performing the duties of his regular classification through illness or accident, such employee may be transferred to a classification which he is capable of performing. The company has discussed this situation with the Workman's Committee and they are in complete agreement with our actions.

Letter of March 15, 1974:

Dear Walter:

I have recently reviewed your personnel records and I'm very disturbed by your sick leave record with Husky Oil Company during the past three years. In an effort to determine whether or not your physical condition was the cause of this extensive amount of sick leave, the company requested that you take a physical examination at the company's expense. ... This examination clearly indicates that your physical condition is not a reason for your poor attendance record during the past three years. We have checked the sick leave records at the North Salt Lake Refinery, and the average sick leave taken per man for each of three years is significantly below the number of days of sick leave that you have taken.

You were hired as a full time employee and you are expected to work as such since we pay you on that basis. Your attendance record to date with the company is little more than that of a part time employee.

The company has discussed this matter with you on several occasions. This letter is to warn you that your absenteeism will no longer be tolerated. Unless your attendance record improves very significantly, we will replace you.

Letter of May 10, 1974:

Dear Walter:

I am writing to confirm our discussion that took place on May 9, 1974, concerning your recent absenteeism. The company is very concerned about your attendance during the past few years as was pointed out in my letter to you dated March 15, 1974. You have taken 11 days of sick leave since my letter dated March 15 was sent to you. The company is aware that the sick leave taken during this period was for a legitimate purpose; however, the company is very concerned about the fact that your attendance has not improved in this last two months.

You stated at this meeting on May 9 that your attendance would improve. I informed you at this time that if your attendance did not improve then the company would terminate your employment. The company is very hopeful that you will improve your attendance record and that no further action on the part of the company will be necessary in this matter.

If I can be of any further help or you have any other matters that you need to discuss with me concerning this situation, please contact me at your convenience.

Jackson's work record, aside from his absenteeism, was very good. He advanced from a trainee position to that of chemical operator and finally to alkylation operator. This latter position was highly skilled and the second highest job classification in plant operations, requiring several years of training to perform competently. The Husky management found Jackson's performance on the job very satisfactory.

Jackson underwent the physical examination required by the company on January 18, 1974. He was found to be in good physical health and fully capable of performing the work of an alkylation operator.

The report on his physical condition was made without a full medical history. Jackson exercised his right to refuse to answer three questions on the "Report of Medical Examination" pertaining to: (1) personal history; (2) whether he had been hospitalized or a patient in a clinic, hospital, or sanitarium for observation, operation, or treatment during the past 10 years; and, (3) family medical history. He steadfastly refused to discuss the reasons for his absence with his supervisor, other than to cite medical reasons.

Jackson was again absent on August 10 and 11, 1974. After he finished the night shift on August 12–13, Fielding informed him that he was being released from his employment as of that date because of excessive absenteeism.

On August 23, 1974, Jackson and the union filed a grievance in which he denied excessive use of sick leave. The union claimed that Jackson had been discharged without just cause, and that he should be reinstated without any loss in pay or benefits.

Shortly after filing the grievance, Jackson and his union steward told company management that Jackson had a chronic condition of recurring mental depression which accounted for his frequent absences of short duration. The company refused to reinstate Jackson.

POSITION OF THE UNION

The union supported its contention that Jackson was discharged without cause with the following arguments:

1. Jackson had not indulged in excessive absenteeism. The sick leave time taken by him in a period of about six years totaled a "little over three months." For a person with his type of illness, three months out of six years is not excessive.

2. Jackson had not abused his sick leave. He was absent for legitimate illnesses and was officially excused for such absences by the company. The company had not disputed that these absences were excused and authorized under the Agreement.

3. The employee had not applied for long-term leave under Articles 15.04 and 15.05,[3] because he was utilizing his sick leave benefits as provided in Article 15.02 and which provided full pay while ill, rather than one-half pay under the long-term disability plan. In only one year, 1973, did he exceed his 25 days sick leave allowance. Jackson was entitled to use his full sick leave entitlement, before applying for long-term disability benefits.

4. Jackson had been given a clean bill of health by company physicians on January 18, 1974. Jackson was understandably reluctant to discuss his mental illness with management and company physicians. Mental depression carries with it a social stigma; though unwarranted, it is very real to those who suffer from it. It would be especially difficult for someone subject to this illness to discuss it with others.

5. Even though the company had incomplete knowledge of Jackson's condition, it failed to exhaust all available procedures and facilities before moving to discharge him. He was entitled to exhaust all his sick leave and long-term disability benefits before becoming subject to discharge.

6. Although Jackson was reluctant to discuss his problem with the

---

[3] See Appendix for relevant contract provisions.

company, he was being honest, certainly as honest as he could be, considering the problem he had. On his own, he went to both doctors and the hospital to try to correct his problem. He even used part of his vacation for this purpose. He was not malingering, but rather making an honest attempt to resolve his difficulties as best he knew how.

7. The company's contention that Jackson's frequent short-term absences created problems and ill-will among other operators because they had to work overtime to fill in for him was without foundation. Workers expect to help out both the absent employee and the company by filling in. This procedure had evolved over several years of experimentation by both the company and the operators.

8. Jackson's absences did not create a safety hazard as the company insisted. Any operator who became fatigued could be replaced by calling in another operator who was on his day off.

9. Jackson's excused absences should not be counted in assessing excessive absenteeism. Absences which are authorized and excused cannot count in determining absentee percentages. Jackson's absences were both authorized and excused by the company.

10. Jackson, during the six months he had been off his job, had successfully undergone therapy. He no longer needed drugs for his illness; in fact, he had not used them for four months. Jackson was mentally and physically fully capable of returning to work as an alkylation operator for the company, and he was entitled to reinstatement accordingly.

POSITION OF THE COMPANY

The company contended that Walter Jackson was discharged for cause based on excessive absenteeism, and the union grievance should be denied for the following reasons:

1. The company terminated the employment of Jackson because of his extreme lack of dependability which resulted from his frequent absences from work. The essential facts concerning his employment and absenteeism were not in dispute.

2. Jackson's frequent short-term absences reduced the value of his services "to a nullity," and as a result, the company had no choice in fairness to other employees but to terminate his employment. Such termination was necessary, even though the cause of the absences was a series of illness.

3. Jackson was fully and formally warned of the possibility of discharge if the absences on sick leave continued. He was counseled in

April 1972 and formally warned three times by letter during the period January–May 1974. Jackson was fully aware through these warnings of the consequence of continued excessive short-term absences.

4. The physical examination of January 18, 1974 indicated no basis for Jackson's short-term absences and indicated that he was physically capable of performing his work.

5. Jackson's absences made it impossible for the company to depend upon him. Implicit in the contract of any full-time employee is his obligation to attend work with reasonable regularity. When he does not so attend, the contract is broken and the company no longer has a duty to maintain his employment.

6. Although Jackson's record showed a high level of sick leave during the past six years, his record became intolerable during the past two years with 29 sick days in 1973 and 20 in 1974 prior to his termination. Of these absences, 43 occurred on the first or last day of his work period which provided him with "long weekends" at the beginning or end of his work period. Moreover, most of the absences were a single day in duration, presenting to the company the most difficult scheduling and manning problems.

7. Jackson had the highest number of absences of any employee in the plant.

8. When Jackson was absent, employees on the two adjacent shifts each worked an extra four hours to cover for him. The company not only had to pay four hours overtime to each substitute employee, but also pay Jackson his straight-time sick pay.

9. Jackson's absences created a serious safety hazard. The alkylation operator was a skilled position, also considered to be one of the most hazardous in the refinery. To require other employees to work repeated overtime created a special hazard because of the fatigue factor.

10. Jackson's repeated absences created considerable inconvenience, and even hardship, to other operators. As a consequence, morale suffered and the company received many complaints.

11. It was evident from his record that his attendance habits would not improve. The recurrent short-term absences had been going on for several years and even continued after three warnings and his promise to correct the situation.

12. Jackson's "cavalier attitude" toward his employment was illustrated by the fact that after repeated warnings, and knowing that his job was in jeopardy because of absences, he requested an extra day of absence from work at the end of June 1974 to get a "head start" on his one-month vacation. Further, upon his return July 29, he reported

for the wrong shift, causing great inconvenience to other employees.

13. The company had the right to discharge an employee for excessive absenteeism even though that employee had not exhausted his sick leave allotment. Sick pay is not cumulative; employees do not receive payment or other credit for unused days. An employee cannot claim a vested interest in sick leave where his frequent absences of short duration disrupt the business of the company. Sick pay, unlike vacation pay, is not vested in the employee. It is a cushion to be used when needed, but it is not intended to set standards for attendance.

14. The union's contention that Jackson would be eligible and should have been carried on long-term disability leave was groundless under Sections 15.04 and 15.05. These sections deal with long-term leave and therefore are clearly inapplicable to Jackson's case, for he had been absent for short durations for minor ailments.

15. The company's action with respect to Jackson was made in good faith, upon fair examination and careful consideration of the situation. Even the union did not allege that the company had acted arbitrarily, capriciously or unfairly.

APPENDIX

Relevant Provisions of the Contract

Article 9.01   A grievance may be filed for the purpose of adjusting complaints, disputes, claims or unfair treatment, or alleged discharge without cause involving the terms of this Agreement or the interpretation thereof.

Article 15.01   An employee required to be absent from work because of non-occupational injury to himself or non-occupational illness of himself will be allowed sick leave with pay as follows:
After 10 years work—up to five (5) weeks leave with pay.

Article 15.02   Any person claiming sick pay must have notified his immediate Supervisor as follows: If sickness occurs while the employee is at work, he shall report to his immediate Supervisor and secure permission to stop work. If sickness or disability occurs at home or while the employee is off duty, his Supervisor must be notified as soon as possible, giving the details concerning his sickness or disability. The company must be notified at least three (3) hours beforehand of when the employee will return to work. . . . The purpose of this clause is to provide the company with adequate notice of an employee's inability to work so that a replacement may be located if required.

Article 15.03 If an employee is ill or disabled and away from work, a doctor's certificate verifying the illness may be required for payment of sick leave or disability payments under this Agreement. . . . Sick leave shall not be cumulative from year to year. False statements or misrepresentations will be deemed a form of dishonesty.

Article 15.04 An employee with one (1) year of work for the company, who is a member of the Group Insurance Plan and absent from work because of non-occupational illness of himself or non-occupational injury to himself, will receive one-half (½) his regular rate of pay (Long Term Disability), minus other income benefits from the company, after he has exhausted all his full sick pay and vacation entitlement.

Article 15.05 An employee will receive this one-half (½) pay, referred to above, as long as he is disabled from performing his regular job but not exceeding six (6) months from the date disability begins.

Article 22.01 Except as expressly limited by this Agreement, the management and direction of the company is the prerogative of the company. This includes but is not limited to, the right to hire and assign employees, apply discipline, demote or discharge employees for cause, and determine the size of the working force.

QUESTIONS

1. Why is this case a difficult one from the standpoint of both the union and the company involved?
2. Evaluate each of the arguments of the union as countered by the arguments of the company. Which arguments are most crucial to the positions of each party?
3. Was employee Walter Jackson obligated to answer all of the questions placed to him concerning the reasons for his absenteeism?
4. To what lengths must a company go to accommodate an employee who has physical or mental problems such as the employee in this case? Discuss.
5. If an employee discharged for absenteeism is reinstated by the arbitrator, how excessive must any future absenteeism become on the part of the reinstated employee before the company may reinstate disciplinary action?

46. CAUGHT IN THE ACT?

COMPANY: *Kast Metals Corporation, Keokuk, Iowa*

UNION: *International Molders Local Union No. 333*

BACKGROUND

John Doerr[1] had been an employee of the company for about seven years at the time of the incident in question. He had been a satisfactory employee throughout his employment, and he was serving as a utility man in the cleaning department at the time of his discharge.

About 10:45 p.m. on February 25, 1975 George Burns, a security guard at the company, noticed someone in the plant parking lot "bobbing up and down" four or five times. Burns proceeded to the fifth row of the lot, and where he had seen the movement, and discovered Doerr squatting near the right rear wheel of a car. Burns asked Doerr if the car was his, and he felt that Doerr responded affirmatively. However, upon examination of the window sticker, Burns determined that the car belonged to another employee of the plant. Upon further examination of the area, Burns found a styrofoam coffee cup sitting just in front of the right rear wheel. The cup was half to three-quarters full of what appeared to be wine. Burns carried it back into the plant where he gave it to Thomas Hardin, Doerr's supervisor. Hardin examined the cup and concluded it contained wine and strong liquor which were "reddish" in color. Upon questioning about his presence in the lot, Doerr told Hardin that he was taking a break.

Burns related to Hardin that he had seen Doerr "bobbing up and down" beside the car, that Doerr had said the car was his, and that he had found the cup of wine near where Doerr had been crouching. Burns also told Hardin that Doerr had not mentioned his being on break at any time in the lot.

A decision was made by company management about 12:30 a.m. on February 26, 1975 to discharge Doerr, and he was so informed. The company based its action on Doerr's violation of "Discharge Rules—

---

[1] The names of all individuals have been disguised.

Group II" (see Appendix), which prohibited possession or consumption of alcoholic beverages in the plant.

Doerr then filed a grievance on February 27, 1975 charging that the company did not have just cause for his dismissal as there was insufficient evidence of his violation of Discharge Rule—Group II.

POSITION OF THE UNION

The union maintained that there was insufficient evidence to warrant Doerr's discharge for violation of the "no alcohol" rule. No one saw Doerr in actual, physical possession of liquid of any kind, either alcoholic or otherwise. All witnesses agreed that Doerr did not appear to be under the influence of alcohol, nor could they smell it on his breath. Neither was there any bottle or flask on Doerr or near the car by which he was discovered, although there was no major effort undertaken to locate such an item. No analysis was ever conducted to determine the actual contents of the cup.

At the arbitration hearing, Doerr denied telling Burns that it was his car. He stated that at the time he spoke to Burns he had been on his way to the adjacent parking lot to move his truck nearer to the plant in order to leave more quickly at the end of the shift. He said that he had stopped beside the car in order to remove some slag from his shoe. He also testified that after having been taken to the office, he had offered to take a breath analysis test.

Since the company had failed to bear the burden of proof to show conclusively that Doerr either had consumed alcohol or had it in his possession, the discharge action was improper. The union asked that Doerr be returned to his job with full restoration of lost pay, benefits and seniority rights.

POSITION OF THE COMPANY

The company argued that there was sufficient evidence of Doerr's activities to warrant the conclusion that he had alcohol in his possession for purposes of consuming it; therefore his dismissal was justified.

At the hearing, Burns testified that Doerr had told him he was on his break when discovered near the car, and he related the other events and dialogue in the parking lot. Hardin stated that neither he nor any other witness could detect alcohol on Doerr's breath, but that Doerr was discharged on the basis of "the suspicions created by the circumstances as related by Burns' oral report." The company maintained that those circumstances and their implications were sufficient to constitute "just cause" for dismissal of Doerr for violation of Discharge Rules—Group II, and the company was within its rights as outlined in the contract under Article III. The company requested that its discharge action should be sustained.

APPENDIX

Relevant Provisions of the Agreement

ARTICLE III
FUNCTIONS OF MANAGEMENT

Nothing in this Agreement shall limit the Company in the exercise of its functions of management under which it shall have, among other things, the right to hire new employees and to direct the working force, to discipline, suspend or discharge for a just cause, transfer, or lay off employees because of lack of work; require employees to observe company rules and regulations not inconsistent with the provisions of this Agreement, to decide the number and locations of its plants and the products to be manufactured, the methods and schedules of production, including means and process of manufacturing, all matters relating to finance, sales, and pricing of the product, provided that the Company will not use these functions of management for the purpose of discrimination. It is agreed that the enumeration of these functions of management shall not be deemed to exclude other functions not enumerated.

DISCHARGE RULES—GROUP II

Any of the following will be sufficient grounds for immediate discharge:
Possession or consumption of alcoholic beverages within the plant or reporting for work under the influence of intoxicants in any degree whatsoever.

QUESTIONS

1. To what degree is circumstantial evidence sufficient or insufficient in this case to support the position of the company?

2. Was the explanation of the employee about the circumstances of this case believable, or was the employee's explanation primarily self-serving?

3. Many arbitrators in discharge cases require a company to show that the "preponderance of evidence" is sufficient to warrant upholding discharge action. Did the company demonstrate conclusive evidence to justify discharge action? A lesser penalty?

47. STOLEN KISSES

COMPANY: *Williams Brothers Markets, Santa Maria, California*

UNION: *Retail Clerks Union, Local 899*

At 11:00 a.m., October 5, 1974 Henry Hampton,[1] vice president of Williams Brothers Markets, discharged Joyce Stephens and George Folsom for "unbecoming conduct." In a letter of discharge addressed to them jointly, Mr. Hampton stated:

We believe that two adult married people are morally wrong when they kiss (on many occasions) at their place of employment. We believe that this is not socially acceptable and therefore is unbecoming conduct.

The company claimed that the employees' activities were in violation of Section A of Article III of the collective bargaining agreement which reads:

The Employer shall have the right to discharge an employee for good cause, such as dishonesty, insubordination, incompetency, intoxication, unbecoming conduct, failure to perform work as required, and excessive absenteeism.

Joyce Stephens immediately filed a grievance in which she asked for reinstatement to her former position, payment for lost wages, and restoration of all rights and benefits.

BACKGROUND

Joyce Stephens was a checker at Store No. 3 in Arroyo Grande, California, a position she had held since February 1974. At this same time George Folsom was employed as a produce manager in the same market. On September 17, 1974 Folsom confided to Arnold Singleton, produce merchandiser, that he was in love with Stephens. Singleton told him that the company could not tolerate "two married people

---

[1] The names of all individuals have been disguised.

playing around on the job." He also advised Folsom to terminate the relationship. Singleton immediately reported his "confidential" conversation to Store Manager Daniel Vandenberg, who indicated that he had already been aware that Folsom had a "greater than average attraction to Stephens."

On September 23, Willis Goode, an auditor for the company, was at the store investigating a money shortage problem. He noted that both Stephens and Folsom had gone into the produce processing room, and that Folsom acted "very excited." Goode followed them into the room where he observed them kissing.

Goode, Vandenberg, and Hampton agreed that if any disciplinary action was to be taken, they should catch Stephens and Folsom in the act of kissing. They set up a "blind" in the produce processing room, and on October 5 confronted them in the act of embracing and kissing. It was at this point that Hampton discharged them "on the spot."

POSITION OF THE UNION

The union contended that Stephens had been observed kissing on only two occasions, neither of which were while she was on duty. No customer or employee had observed the kissing or embracing; nor had any customer or employee complained. On the two days in question, Stephens had not "clocked in." In other words, she had not started work. It was customary for her to arrive about 15 to 20 minutes early to check the produce department for recent price changes and to check for new price changes and specials throughout the store. It was her practice to check the price lists and then go into the produce processing room to have a cup of coffee before starting work.

The union also contended that Stephens did not encourage Folsom's "amorous antics." She admitted that he was kissing her when they were discovered. She claimed, however, that she was not returning the kiss, and that in fact, she was attempting to discourage his advances. She said that they were good friends, they had a number of acquaintances in common, that they had a mutual approach to problems, and that on their breaks they spent time discussing matters of mutual interest.

The union also pointed out that Stephens was a good employee. Her performance appraisals described her as a "good checker," "better than average," and "competent." She had never received any warnings or complaints, either written or verbal, regarding her work. While both Singleton and Vandenberg had warned Folsom about having an "amorous relationship" with another employee, no such warnings had ever been given Stephens.

The union added that the company had never adopted any standards defining unbecoming conduct. It was not until October 5 after this incident that a policy had been decided upon. The company had acted arbitrarily in discharging the employee without warning and without prior notice of what constitutes unbecoming conduct.

The union requested that Joyce Stephens be returned with no loss of seniority to her position as checker, and that she be made whole for all loss of pay and benefits while she was off work due to her improper discharge.

POSITION OF THE COMPANY

The company contended that the conduct of Stephens and Folsom was detrimental to the conduct of business. In the company's view, the public is sensitive to the behavior of employees in retail organizations. Customers who disapprove of amorous behavior between married adults will trade elsewhere if the company condoned such behavior on the part of its employees.

The company also argued that it is commonly accepted that an employer cannot tolerate married employees kissing and embracing others than their spouses at their place of employment. It is not necessary to spell out this type of behavior as specifically constituting unbecoming conduct.

The agreement specifically gives the company the right to discharge employees for unbecoming conduct. The company exercised this right appropriately in this matter, and the grievance should be dismissed.

QUESTIONS

1. Was the behavior of the female employee in relationship to the produce manager "unbecoming conduct?" Was it conduct of sufficient gravity to justify discharge in this case? Discuss.

2. Did management under the agreement have the right to determine standards for defining "unbecoming conduct"? Why, or why not?

3. Should conduct of employees in a retail supermarket be of a higher standard than in a factory situation where employees do not come into regular contact with the public?

4. If the arbitrator should return employee Joyce Stephens to her position, would the company be obligated also to return the produce manager back to his position? Why, or why not?

48. A PAINTED MISTAKE

COMPANY: *W. C. Richards Company, Blue Island,*
Illinois

UNION: *United Steelworkers of America, Local 4775*

BACKGROUND

Stephen Fox[1] began employment at the W. C. Richards mill operation on August 26, 1971.

On several occasions, Fox was involved in safety offenses. After his second safety violation, management issued a written warning to Fox which read:

October 3, 1973

Subject: Warning Notice

On September 21st, you were observed jumping from the roof down to the platform over mills 4, 5 and 6. Monday, the 24th, Don Habich called this incident to your attention and instructed you not to do this any longer.

On September 28th, you were again observed on the roof by Rudy Hartman and he told you to stay off the roof because of the danger involved. He also told you that you are endangering your life, and that it was company policy to walk around and not jump off the roof when working on outside mills.

You evidently are not aware of the dangers involved in this type of conduct. There is approximately an area of 3 feet between the building and the platform thru which you could fall in the process of jumping, if you slipped. You could also lose your balance after you jump and fall into one of the mills. This type of conduct also may encourage other people to try the same thing, or similar type dangerous conduct.

We cannot tolerate this blatant disregard for common sense safety rules. Since this is the second incident, and because of the serious nature of this incident, we are compelled to warn you that any future infraction of this nature will result in disciplinary suspension or dismissal.

Two days later, Fox received the following disciplinary layoff notice:

---

[1] The names of all individuals have been disguised.

Today, Friday, the 5th of October 1973, your foreman, Wilson Parker, found you urinating against the inside wall of Building #2.

For this breach of conduct, you are hereby suspended for three days without pay.

Fox did not protest this layoff, as he admitted he had been wrong.

On Friday, October 5, 1974 Fox returned to work from a sick leave occasioned by injuries sustained in a fall from one of the mills. As he was working on Mill #5, he failed to lock-out the switch system. Because of this oversight, approximately four or five thousand gallons of industrial paint and hundreds of metal balls were dumped onto the ground. The value of these materials was approximately $330.

Following this incident, management discharged Fox and, in a letter dated October 17, 1974 stated as its reasons:

Stephen Fox was discharged for just cause: that is, because of his violation of company safety rules in the context of his prior violations of such rules and/or misconduct.

Fox then filed the following grievance:

The Company is in violation of the Collective Bargaining Agreement, agreed upon by the parties on January 22nd, 1974 by unjustly and discriminatorily discharging the aggrieved.

The Union demands that the Company reinstate the aggrieved employee immediately with all loss of earnings and his full seniority rights as per agreement.

(Agreement Violation) Article V—No Discrimination and any and all other related articles.

Failing to reach accord, the company and union agreed to submit the issue of whether Fox was discharged for "just cause" to arbitration.

POSITION OF THE UNION

The union maintained that the company was guilty of severe discrimination against Fox related in part to his union activity as departmental shop steward. The union claimed that other employees in the past had also spilled the contents and materials of the mills, and yet no disciplinary action had been taken against them.

In relation to the accident of October 5, 1974 Fox testified that he had been in a hurry on the day of the accident. When he came to Mill #5 and noticed the lock was not on, he had thought it was Mill #6 and that there would be no problem. The union conceded that Fox had made a mistake, but maintained that his discharge was not for "just cause." The union claimed that an employee should not be discharged for making an honest mistake, particularly when other employees had made even more serious errors and they were not disciplined.

POSITION OF THE COMPANY

The company maintained that it had a duty to provide safe working conditions for all of its employees, and that Fox's repeated safety violations jeopardized the safety of other employees and frustrated the company in attempts to insure safe conditions. Company management cited the fact that other workers could have been in the area of Mill #5 on October 5, 1974 and could have sustained serious injuries.

The company also contended that lesser disciplinary actions imposed on Fox on previous occasions had failed to improve his conduct. This indicated a total disregard by Fox for the authority of the company and the welfare of himself or his fellow employees.

Concerning other employees' job records on the mills, the company testified that one employee had worked on the mills in Fox's job for ten years and never spilled a load. It also presented evidence that, of the two employees who had spilled loads and had not been disciplined, one had been on his second day of a temporary assignment to that job when the spill occurred; the other had been an elderly employee greasing the mill who had no instructions as to safety procedures on this mill. Neither of these employees had any prior safety violations.

At the arbitration hearing subsequent to Fox's discharge, the company also raised the question of his falsification of facts on his employment application form. According to the company, Fox told the employment interviewer that his 4–F military draft status was due to poor eyesight, rather than because of a perforated ulcer as he had written on the form.

In the company's view, Fox's discharge was for proper and just cause, and the grievance should be denied.

APPENDIX

Relevant Provisions of the Agreement

ARTICLE V—MANAGEMENT

(a) Subject to the provisions of the Agreement, the management of the plant and the direction of the working forces, including the right to plan, direct, and control plant operations; to hire and instruct; to attain maximum operating efficiency; to introduce new, improved or altered production methods or facilities; to promote, demote, transfer, lay off, discipline, and to suspend or discharge for proper cause, is vested exclusively in the Company.

QUESTIONS

1. Was the mistake of employee Stephen Fox of sufficient gravity to justify his discharge by the company?
2. Does it appear that the company was consistent in its disciplinary actions involving spilling of materials by different employees?
3. Was the matter of the falsification of the employment application form of any relevance or germane to the issue of discharge? Why, or why not?
4. Does it make any difference in this case that this was not the first offense in which the discharged employee had been involved? Discuss.

49. IMPAIRED PERFORMANCE

COMPANY: *Public Service Electric and Gas Company, Burlington, New Jersey*

UNION: *Public Utility Construction and Gas Appliance Workers, Local 274*

Having satisfied the job requirement of typing 50 words per minute and meeting the other application prerequisites, Nancy Bell[1] was hired as a General Clerk, Second Class by the company on December 22, 1969. She began work in the Burlington District Office, and in December 1971, she was promoted to General Clerk, First Class, a job which principally required strong typing skills. She was regarded as an excellent worker; periodic management appraisal reviews noted her good typing ability, quickness to learn, and rated her as an above average to excellent performer.

On December 6, 1972 Nancy Bell suffered serious head injuries in a three-car accident. She remained comatose for two weeks, and then began to slowly recover from a spastic left hemiplegia. In mid-January 1973, she began receiving occupational therapy at Thomas Jefferson Hospital and was eventually released from the hospital on January 28, 1973. Following her hospitalization, Bell remained under close medical supervision until August 29, 1973. She was then discharged from full-care, and she returned to her job on September 4, 1973 with her doctor's approval that she was physically capable of such work.

Bell still had difficulty walking, as her left-side coordination was weak. Following an examination on September 26, her physician at Thomas Jefferson Hospital reported that "she still has evidence of a very mild organic brain syndrome with periods of emotional liability." However, he, too, concluded that she was capable of returning to work.

From the beginning, Bell's work did not match her former level of performance, either in quality or quantity. Her typing output was

---

[1] The names of all individuals have been disguised.

slow and often contained many errors. Initially management chose to overlook her poor performance, attributing it to her long absence and physical problems. However, on January 31, 1974 she was advised that her work performance had been very poor, and that if she did not improve within three months, she would face "more severe disciplinary action." Bell's typing, nevertheless, remained below the minimum requirement of 50 words per minute, and she continued to perform her other tasks at an unsatisfactory level. On February 25, 1974 her supervisor again reviewed her poor performance with Bell, and informed her that if her work did not improve to a level satisfactory to the company by April 30, 1974 the company would consider her discharge.

Recognizing her difficulty, Nancy Bell enrolled in an evening typing course at a local high school in an attempt to improve her speed and accuracy. She reported that she had increased her productivity from 37 words per minute with five errors to 55 words per minute with no errors by the end of May. Management, however, did not notice any significant improvement in her performance on the job. Subsequently, in June 1974 management reassigned her to the Dispatch Office as a General Clerk, Second Class, although she continued to be paid as a General Clerk, First Class. In this position, Bell was primarily responsible for receiving emergency telephone calls, logging information, and preparing service orders, a job to which most persons adapted within a few days. Nevertheless, Bell's work over the next few months continued to be rated "unsatisfactory" by her supervisor, principally because of her slowness, and in early October 1974 she was transferred back to the District Office.

Again, her work did not show any improvement, and on October 24, 1974 the division superintendent requested that the company physician examine her to determine if she was "capable of improving her work output to acceptable levels." She was examined by Dr. Charles Wallace on November 14, 1974. He concluded that Bell had suffered a "cerebral contusion with post-traumatic cerebral edema and partial left hemiparesis." He went on to conclude in his report:

In my opinion, this young woman has reached a point of recovery which will not progress any more. I also feel that her recovery has been nothing short of remarkable considering the severity of her accident. She has lost some mental facility because of the prolonged coma secondary to the cerebral edema and brain damage. It is my feeling that this facility will never be regained. Without specific psychological testing, it is impossible to precisely pinpoint her main areas of deficiency. However, one gets the impression that her ability to think automatically and relate one thing to another is somewhat impaired. She must study everything, make a decision and then go ahead. Apparently, when she does this, she performs adequately but obviously this process is quite slow. It is my medical opinion that she can do the type of job she is now assigned to, but management must accept the fact that her work will be slow and her output less than that of someone who has not had a severe brain injury.

Several weeks after receiving Dr. Wallace's report the company decided to terminate Bell. She was placed on a six-month disability leave beginning December 10, 1974 and was then terminated.

The union filed a grievance on Bell's behalf alleging that the company lacked "just cause" (See Appendix for Article II of the agreement) for its discharge of Bell and seeking her reinstatement to active service with the firm.

UNION POSITION

The union contended that the company had not done all within its power to determine whether Nancy Bell's work could be further improved. The union maintained that she was fully capable of performing at an acceptable level, based upon Bell's assertion that she could perform "adequately." She argued that she was, at the time of arbitration, capable of performing at a level close to what she was doing before the accident, and she felt she would continue to improve. For these and for humanitarian considerations, the union requested full reinstatement of Bell to her former or to an equivalent position.

COMPANY POSITION

The company maintained that it had given Nancy Bell ample opportunity to achieve an "acceptable" level of productivity. Management maintained that it regretted her inability to perform adequately, and pointed out that it had allowed her an extensive period of readaptation to her work routine. However, it contended that Bell had demonstrated that she was unable to achieve acceptable levels of performance, and management was well within its rights to discontinue her from its service. The discharge action should be sustained.

APPENDIX

Relevant Provisions of the Agreement

ARTICLE II

UNION-EMPLOYER RELATIONSHIP

It is specifically agreed that the management of the plant, and the direction of the working forces shall be vested exclusively in the Employer. This right shall include but not be limited to, the right to hire and discharge (for just cause), the right to suspend from duty (for just cause), and the right to transfer personnel from one position to another (for just cause), provided, however, that the foregoing shall not impair any of the rights of the Union or the employees granted by other provisions of the Agreement.

QUESTIONS

1. Did the company give the employee reasonable time and opportunity to achieve an acceptable level of performance following her accident? Discuss.

2. Is a company obligated to assist an employee in a rehabilitation program following a serious physical and mental injury?

3. Evaluate the union's argument that humanitarian considerations should be considered in asking for reinstatement of employee Nancy Bell.

4. Why is a case of this sort difficult for all parties involved, including the arbitrator who is asked to decide the issue?

50. ONE WIFE TOO MANY

COMPANY: *Pennsylvania Power Company, Philadelphia, Pennsylvania*

UNION: *Utility Workers Union of America, Local 140*

On February 26, 1975 Lawrence J. Groves,[1] Manager of Personnel Relations of the Pennsylvania Power Company received an anonymous telephone call from a woman who claimed to be "a friend of Mrs. Lieber." The caller stated that one of the company's employees had a woman falsely registered at the Northside Youngstown Hospital as his wife. Groves telephoned the hospital which, after some investigation, reported that a Laura Robertson was, in fact, registered there as Mrs. John Lieber.

After a thorough investigation of the case, Groves sent Lieber the following letter:

On Monday, March 10, 1975, you were suspended until further notice. Effective Tuesday, March 18, 1975, your employment with Pennsylvania Power Company has been terminated.

This action is taken as a result of claims you submitted for hospitalization and doctor services for a person other than an eligible family member.

All benefits are cancelled including your Group Life Insurance Plan and Hospitalization and Surgical-Medical Insurance Plan. Your anniversary date is March 17, 1959 which entitles you to three weeks or fifteen working days' vacation. Payment for this accrued vacation will be included in your final pay check.

On March 20, Lieber's personal attorney wrote a joint letter to the company and to the president of Local Union 140, making the following observations:

We represent Mr. John Lieber who on March 18, 1975, was given notification of his discharge as an employee of Pennsylvania Power Company.

Under all the facts of this case, the discharge of Lieber was unwarranted

---

[1] The names of all individuals have been disguised.

and unjust and accordingly, we have been authorized by Lieber to give you notice of his objection thereto.

Please consider this letter as the filing of a complaint to discharge as required under the provisions of Article 5, Paragraph (C) of the agreement dated November 6, 1974 between Pennsylvania Power Company and Utility Workers Union of America, Local Union 140. [See Appendix]

The company and the union agreed to submit the case to arbitration. They stipulated that the issue was:

Did the Company violate the agreement on or about March 18, 1975 when they discharged the grievant, John Lieber, for a claim submitted for hospitalization and doctor services for a person other than an eligible family member?

BACKGROUND

When Lawrence Groves, the manager of personnel relations, first called John Lieber into his office on February 28, 1975, Lieber refused to answer questions about the woman registered at the hospital as his wife. The following day, Lieber returned to Groves' office and said, "She is my wife." Groves told Lieber that he knew that the woman was not his wife. Lieber then asked Groves not to notify the Prudential Insurance Company until he had an opportunity to talk with his attorney. Groves agreed to this.

The company then undertook a complete review of its records. It discovered that between 1971 and 1974 (exclusive of the current 1975 incident responsible for Lieber's discharge), Prudential had paid out over $3,600 in claims for a woman purporting to be Nora Lieber, the wife of John Lieber. The company paid the entire cost of premiums for hospitalization and medical insurance.

During the investigation, Lieber stated that he was long separated from his wife and "there's no divorce possible." He had been living with Laura Robertson since 1970. When she became ill, her doctor diagnosed her illness as ulcerated colitis. The prescribed medication did little good. She received further treatment, including X-rays and additional medicine. By this time she had lost her job as a nurse. When her physician had her hospitalized, Lieber told her "to use my wife's name to get an appointment there." He said, "I felt Prudential would cover it." She returned home after one week, but the condition returned about nine months later. She returned to the hospital as Mrs. Lieber. About six months later she was returned to the hospital for further treatment, and she entered a fourth time on

August 28, 1974 for an operation; she was discharged on September 9, 1974. Her fifth and final hospitalization occurred on February 19, 1975; she was still in the hospital on March 18 when Lieber was dismissed.

Lieber was hired in 1959. At the time of discharge he was a Lineman "A," a position he had held for the previous nine years. He had made good progress on his job. The quality and quantity of his work was good. He had been cited once for excessive absenteeism and once for insubordination during his 16 years of employment.

POSITION OF THE UNION

The union argued first that the "punishment does not fit the crime." Lieber was in the process of making restitution of money to Prudential. The $3,600 in claims paid by Prudential during the period 1971–1974 was small compared with the $2,088,000 which had been paid by the company to Prudential during this same period. The union agreed that Lieber's actions were dishonest, and that he should repay the $3,600. On the other hand, this sum was trivial in comparison to the size of the premiums paid, and the size of both the insuror and the company.

The union further argued that Lieber was being discharged for the entire amount of which the company had been defrauded indirectly, rather than for $1,305.50 in hospital charges incurred in 1975. The previous charges should not be considered because the company did not know of them at the time of discharge.

The union also contended that Lieber had not intended to defraud either his employer or Prudential. He had never sought medical benefits for both Laura Robertson and his legal wife. He had claimed only one person, Laura Robertson, as a dependent. She was, in his view, his "wife."

The union also pointed out that life styles have changed during the past quarter century. Many men and women have maintained a loving relationship without going through the formality of a wedding ceremony. In fact, Lieber had demonstrated that his relationship with Laura Robertson was a stable and loving one, enduring over many years both in sickness and in health.

Finally, the union contended that Lieber did not intend to defraud the company. His actions, although not to be condoned, were understandable, considering the circumstances. He acted impulsively to protect a person whom he loved and whom he perceived to be desperately ill. Furthermore, he did not feel that he had done anything wrong with respect to Pennsylvania Power Company, since he had made claims against the Prudential Insurance Company.

The union requested that John Lieber be reinstated with full back pay and that all rights and privileges be restored to him.

POSITION OF THE COMPANY

The company stated that the discharge was based on the "fraudulent use of the hospitalization plan using a claimant other than what is described in the union contract"—that is, a wife and children.

The company argued that Lieber's intent was to defraud the company and the insuror. Even in 1971 when he first registered Laura Robertson as his wife, his salary was over $12,000 per year. In addition, he owned a bar-restaurant and had sizable savings with which he could have paid her medical and hospitalization expenses. Furthermore, his fraudulent behavior continued over a period of years, negating any possible claim that he had acted impulsively.

Lieber's behavior was directed toward defrauding the company, since the company paid the premiums and premiums are based upon the claim experience of the company.

The company argued that it was justified in arriving at its decision to terminate John Lieber, and the grievance of the union in this matter should be denied.

APPENDIX

Relevant Provisions of the Contract

Article V. (C) When an employee is summarily discharged, an officer of the Local Union shall be notified as soon as practicable. Any employee who feels that he has been unjustly discharged, shall file a complaint in writing with the company and the union within three (3) normal work days of twenty-four (24) hours each after discharge. Unless the complaint is filed within such time, it shall be deemed waived. It is recognized by both the company and the union that such a complaint should be settled at the earliest possible time and should take precedence over complaints or grievances of a different nature and that settlement should be reached within five (5) days if possible.

If a settlement cannot be reached in that time, the Committee appointed by the Executive Board of the union and the representatives of the company shall continue to meet on days to be mutually agreed upon until the matter is disposed of, and if it is found that such employee has been unjustly discharged, he shall be reinstated with all rights and privileges enjoyed before said discharge and shall be compensated for all normal time lost at his regular rate of pay.

If settlement cannot be reached by the procedure set forth above, the matter shall be submitted to arbitration as set forth in Article 4.

QUESTIONS

1. Was the action of employee Groves in this matter fraudulent, or was it an impulsive action based upon an emotional involvement? Discuss.
2. Does the fact that the employee had sixteen years of service and a good employment record mitigate against sustaining a discharge action? Why, or why not?
3. Should the fact that the employee was making restitution be considered by the arbitrator as a significant factor in support of the union position?
4. Evaluate the union argument concerning the comparison in claims paid by the insurance agent as compared to the company premium payments to that insurance agency. Why would the union introduce an argument of this type?
5. With life styles and society mores changing, should companies become more flexible in their benefit plans to accommodate situations of this type? Discuss.

51. INFRINGEMENT OF BARGAINING UNIT WORK

COMPANY: *Lammerts Furniture Company, St. Louis, Missouri*

UNION: *Furniture Warehousemen, Teamsters Local Union No. 688, St. Louis, Missouri*

On Saturday, August 9, 1973 Ronald Cunningham[1] and Joseph Foley, the manager and assistant manager, respectively, of Lammerts' St. Louis Hills store, spent the day moving and rearranging stock in the store. The St. Louis Hills store was scheduled to be closed and vacated by October 1, 1973 and Cunningham and Foley were shifting the store's inventory in order to display and sell as much stock as possible by the closing date. Their work primarily involved moving furniture from the smaller second floor to the larger display areas on the first floor and basement levels, and rearranging various major displays on the lower levels to accommodate the additional furniture moved from the second floor.

On Monday, August 11, 1976 Henry Walton, a receiving clerk at the St. Louis Hills store and a member of Teamsters Local 688, reported to work at the store. Upon noticing the changes which had been made over the weekend in the arrangement of displays and stock, Walton telephoned David Roberts, the union shop steward, who worked at Lammerts' Clayton store. Walton explained the changes effected at the St. Louis Hills store, and noted that all of the moving had been performed by nonunion employees over the weekend. Roberts visited the St. Louis Hills store on Tuesday, August 12, where Walton showed him the empty second floor and pointed out various display alterations on the lower levels. Walton estimated that about 20 recliners and ten dinette sets had been moved from the second floor to the lower two levels and noted that numerous other items had been rearranged throughout the store. Roberts estimated

---

[1] The names of all individuals have been disguised.

that to carry out the changes alleged by Walton would have required at least eight hours work by two employees.

Because no union personnel had been involved in the movement of the furniture on Saturday, August 9, Walton and Roberts felt that the warehousemen's contractual rights had been violated, and filed the following complaint on August 13, 1975, alleging:

Violation of Article XIII and any other Articles that may apply. Sales people and employees other than bargaining unit employees have been performing bargaining unit work.

Settlement requested: Eight hours pay to the affected employees on layoff for every day work was performed. Time and one-half for Saturday work; fringes to be paid accordingly.

On August 18 the company sent the following reply to the union:

Grievance denied. On this grievance and others of a similar nature, the company has always maintained that it has the right to move furniture for display purposes, regardless of distance, once it had been placed on the display floor by a warehouseman.

John Mann, Vice President
J. P. Payne, General Manager, Operations

The company cited Article II, Management Rights, and Article XIII, Work Assignments, to substantiate its position.[2]

The parties failed to resolve their dispute in the grievance procedure and finally submitted the following issue to the arbitrator for resolution:

Did the Company violate the Agreement when it had non-bargaining unit personnel move furniture in its St. Louis Hills store on August 9, 1975?

POSITION OF THE UNION

In the arbitration proceedings, the union first presented the testimony of David Roberts. Roberts stated that he had been with the company for 14 years and had been the shop steward for one year. He then related the incident of Walton's call on August 11, 1975 and his visit to the St. Louis Hills store the following day. He testified that he had not been at the St. Louis Hills store within two weeks prior to August 12, and thus was relying on Walton's statements concerning the rearrangement of displays and merchandise.

---

2 See Appendix.

Roberts stated that warehousemen typically brought furniture onto the floor of the stores where the managers decided on arrangement of the pieces. The arrangement was then typically performed by salesmen with or without the assistance of warehousemen. Roberts tesified that such adjusting usually involved moving an item from one display area to another or rearranging displays to show pieces more effectively. Normally, however, movement or alteration of a total display area was performed by warehousemen. He stated that, to his knowledge, union personnel had always moved furniture from one floor of a store to another floor. He said the union had never objected to the occasional rearranging of display pieces for decorating or sales purposes, but that in the instant case the union was objecting to the large-scale movement of furniture by nonbargaining unit personnel, a task properly reserved to union personnel.

Stephen Murdock, business representative for Local 688, then testified concerning two previous similar incidents which involved use of nonunion personnel to move furniture. Both occurred within the previous 12 months. One such incident occurred at the company's South County store where Murdock received numerous complaints from union members. Murdock stated that in a closed union meeting concerning the problem, the warehousemen voted to "go along with the company" in order to allow management flexibility in rearranging furniture. However, he noted that the men had also voted that this was not to be considered a final and binding precedent for any future incidents.

A second similar incident occurred at the company's Clayton store where employees had filed a grievance protesting the major movement of furniture by nonbargaining unit personnel during a remodeling project. In this instance, too, the union personnel unanimously agreed to drop the grievance because the situation at the Clayton store was a temporary one.

The union acknowledged that Article XIII of the agreement provided for some flexibility in moving furniture by union and nonbargaining unit personnel. The union noted evidence of this principle of flexibility in the first part of Article XIII which allowed nonunion performance of bargaining unit work "where agreed by the union to cover special contingencies." However, the union noted that the primary effect of Article XIII is to limit company assignment of bargaining unit work, in order to protect work "regularly performed by members of the bargaining unit."

The union contended that the August 9 incident constituted a violation by the company of Article XIII "beyond a degree of reasonable flexibility" intended by that article. It alleged that bargaining unit personnel customarily moved furniture from one floor to another, and also customarily moved entire display areas within the store as appropriate. The union did not object to nonbargaining unit personnel moving furniture within a display area, or single movements of furniture involving replacements and minor rearrangements. But the union did object to the wholesale movement of furniture between floors, one floor to another, and across floors. This was definitely bargaining unit work.

Finally, the union pointed out that during periods of economic recession, this type of issue becomes more sensitive to union members. Union members had been reasonable in interpreting the agreement. Failure to press this issue in the past did not constitute the waiving of their right to do so now. In this case the union felt that "the line had to be drawn," and abuses of the intent of the agreement had to be brought to a halt.

The union asked the arbitrator to uphold the grievance which the union was limiting to this grievance alone. It also requested an award to Henry Walton of eight hours pay at the appropriate overtime rate, plus all associated fringe benefits for the work he could have performed on August 9, 1975.

POSITION OF THE COMPANY

The company presented the testimony of John Mann, vice president of Lammerts, who stated that the arrangement of display layouts was the responsibility of the individual store managers, buyers, and the president of the company. He noted that changes in layouts were made from time to time to improve sales impact. Normally, there was minimal movement between floors, but considerable shifting of pieces on the same level. Mann stated that, in his judgment, bargaining unit work consisted of receiving furniture in the warehouse, moving it into the store display areas, and removing it for sales, transfer, and loading. Historically, movement of furniture in the stores had been done by the store managers, assistant managers, buyers, the company president, and warehousemen when they were available.

Regarding the instant grievance, Maan noted that the St. Louis Hills store was scheduled to be closed October 1, 1975 and the manager moved the furniture down from the second floor in order to promote sales of the remaining stock. He stated, "This was a degree of movement; it was a bit unusual, but the difference was only one of degree."

Mann also cited the two incidents noted by Murdock in which management personnel were involved in large movements of furniture in the South County and Clayton Stores. Mann stated that the problem at the South County store arose when the store was being readied for opening. Over a period of about a month, large quantities of furniture were moved by the entire management group, sales personnel, and two warehousemen from Local 688. He said, "We moved furniture all over in order to get the store ready on time." Mann pointed out that the situation at the Clayton store was also a temporary one occurring during a major remodeling project when management and sales personnel, as well as men from Local 688, were all involved in major movements of merchandise.

He further stated that while the union protested the movement of furniture on both occasions at these stores, the issues were resolved without serious difficulty.

Phillip Schneider, manager of Lammerts' South County store, also testified for the company. Noting that he had advanced from salesman to manager over a period of 21 years with the company, Schneider testified that in stores in which he had worked, warehousemen had placed furniture in the stores, but anyone involved in sales or displaying the furniture could move it within the store. He attested that for movements within the store, he would "use warehousemen when they were available." He noted, however, that nonunion personnel had previously moved furniture between store floors without union objection, although he was aware of the two incidents referred to by Murdock in which the union had objected to such activity.

In its closing arguments, the company asserted that the primary question involved in the grievance was that of interpretation of the respective rights of the company and the union as stipulated by Article XIII of the agreement. Since the parties had never arrived at a specific understanding of the provisions of Article XIII, the arbitrator must limit his interpretation to the words of that provision. The company pointed out that Article XIII only restricted management from doing bargaining unit work which was "regularly performed by members of the bargaining unit." The company interpreted regular work of warehousemen to be limited to bringing furniture into the stores and onto the floors. Union personnel would be utilized for intrastore rearranging of furniture if they were available, but the company maintained that such work was "irregular" for bargaining unit personnel and subject to the prerogative of management under the agreement.

The company asserted that the interpretation of the scope of Article XIII of the agreement was a matter which needed to be resolved through negotiation between management and the union. However, it contended that the arbitrator was not empowered to restrict management's rights under the provision.

The company maintained that it had not violated any of the agreement provisions on August 9, 1975 and requested that the grievance be denied.

APPENDIX

Relevant Provisions of the Agreement

ARTICLE II
Management Rights

The management of the company and the direction of the working forces, including the right to plan, direct, change and control company operations, working practices, and work tasks will be vested exclusively in the Employer, not inconsistent with other provisions of this Agreement.

ARTICLE XIII
Work Assignments

Except where agreed by the Union to cover special contingencies, employees other than those in the Bargaining Unit may not perform the work regularly performed by members of the Bargaining Unit, provided that one (1) employee not of this Bargaining Unit may assist a customer in removing his or her merchandise if a warehouseman is not present, provided it is not a scheduled will-call. On all scheduled will-calls at least one (1) member of this Bargaining Unit shall be present.

QUESTIONS

1. Evaluate the union argument that the incident of August 9, 1973 was a violation by the company of the agreement "beyond a degree of reasonable flexibility."
2. Since both parties agreed that union personnel and non-bargaining unit personnel had moved furniture within the store, how can either party claim jurisdiction over the contested work? Discuss.

3. Were the previous occurrences cited by the union and management relevant to the instant case situation, or were they unrelated incidents which should not influence the arbitrator's decision?

4. Evaluate the company's argument that an arbitrator is not empowered to restrict management's rights under Article XIII of the agreement.

5. What is meant by the provision within Article XIII restricting management from doing bargaining unit work which is "regularly performed by members of the bargaining unit"? Why is this type of provision often the focal point of dispute between management and a union?

52.   THE SPEEDY FINISHER

COMPANY: Olin Corporation, East Alton, Illinois

UNION: International Association of Machinists and Aerospace Workers, Victory Lodge 609

At 4:00 p.m. on November 16, 1973 Roy Walker,[1] a stock repairman in the Finishing and Repair Department of Arms Operations, received the following disciplinary action notice from Dan Robinson, his department foreman:

On November 16, 1973, you informed another employee that her production was too high and that she should adjust such production to a limited fixed amount of 100 pieces to be consistent with the "pegged" output of the group.

Inasmuch as this violates the no strike provision of the Labor Agreement you are suspended from 11–16–73 up and including 11–20–73, and you are further warned any further occurrence will result in your discharge.

On the following day, Walker filed a grievance claiming that the five-day suspension levied against him violated Article 23 (See Appendix) of the collective agreement.

BACKGROUND

On November 15, 1973 Mary McCarthy, a subassembler in the Shaping and Sanding Department, was temporarily transferred because of a lack of work in her department to the Finishing and Repair Department to work on gun stock repair. Supervisor Dan Robinson assigned her to repairing gun stocks rejected by the Quality Control Department for a condition called "open grain." This task involved rubbing the stocks with steel wool to eliminate rough and uneven spots left after final sanding. He also instructed McCarthy to set aside stocks with obvious defects, such as cracks and dents, and to work only

---
[1] The names of all individuals have been disguised.

on those which could be made right by rubbing with steel wool.[2] Mary McCarthy processed 580 units that day.

The following day, November 16, McCarthy was again assigned to the Finishing and Repair Department to perform the same work she had done on the preceding day. At about 11:00 a.m., in a distressed condition, she appeared at Robinson's office located about 50 feet from her work area. She reported that one of the employees told her she "was doing too much work and that she should do only 100 pieces per day." Robinson asked her to remain in his office while he went to the work area to ascertain which employee had made the statement.

Robinson first met Henry Allen who worked next to McCarthy. Allen told Robinson that he thought that Roy Walker had said something to her. When Robinson asked Walker about speaking to McCarthy, Walker at first denied it, but then admitted saying, "You are a better worker than I am." Robinson then returned to his office and, after arranging to transfer McCarthy back to her regular department, reported the incident to Ralph Harkens, general foreman. Harkens in turn phoned Peter Dawkins, labor relations administrator. Harkens and Dawkins agreed that an investigatory hearing should be convened immediately.

At the investigatory hearing, Walker denied that he had made any remark directly to McCarthy regarding her output. He testified that he had remarked aloud, within the hearing of others, that she was a better worker than he was. Dawkins, however, claimed at the hearing that Walker had previously told him that he had told McCarthy that "she had done many racks and that she was a better worker than he was." Walker also denied that he had engaged in a slowdown, or that the stock repairmen had restricted their production.

The company decided to suspend Walker for five days based on information produced during the hearing.

Immediately following this decision, Dawkins told McCarthy that Walker had been disciplined on the basis of her statements and asked her to sign a statement for the record. She signed the following statement:

On November 16, 1973, I was working as a Stock Rubber when Walker approached me and said, "What are you doing?"

---

[2] Many of the gun stocks rejected by Quality Control have cracks and dents requiring the use of various hand and power tools to make needed repairs. On occasion, the repairmen are instructed to set aside defective stocks requiring substantial time to repair, and to work on the refinishing of those stocks requiring the steel wool treatment.

Mary: "I'm rubbing stock."

Walker: "How many did you do yesterday?"

Mary: "Almost 600."

Walker: "You're a damn fool. You're just making it hard for the rest of us. I'll be goddamned if I'll do that many a day. We only do 100 a day."

Mary: "I don't care how many you do. That's my business how many I do and it's your business how many you do a day. I'll work the way I feel like it."

Walker: "Well you're a damn fool."

POSITION OF THE UNION

The union argued that the evidence did not establish that Walker made statements directly to McCarthy regarding her output. Mc-Carthy did not testify at the investigative hearing and at no time, either at the hearing or subsequent to it, did the accused have the opportunity to confront his accuser. The accuracy of McCarthy's statements must be questioned. The union claimed that her emotional state at the time of the alleged statements by Walker reflected nothing more than "a greater-than-normal sensitivity to criticism." Nothing that Walker said, even in McCarthy's signed statement, could be construed as a threat. As a matter of fact, he did not even expressly request her to reduce her output. There was no objective basis for her strong reaction.

The union also rejected the company's contention that Walker limited his output, or that the employees in the Finishing and Repair Department conspired to limit their output. Production records of stock repairmen (a group of five to seven employees) for the period June–November 1973 showed an average daily output of 87 units. One employee, however, averaged about 140 units, another achieved 260 units one day, and Walker on two occasions produced 150 units. This data proved that employees did not limit daily output to 100 units. Regardless, the company had never indicated any dissatisfaction with employee performance prior to this incident.

Finally, the company had not shown that Walker had violated Article 35 (see Appendix), the no-strike clause of the agreement, as alleged in the company disciplinary notice to Walker. Even if there was a violation in spirit, the company itself violated the clause by failing to comply with the requirement that written notice of such violation be sent to the union.

Since the company had not shown that Walker's suspension was for sufficient cause, the union requested that the disciplinary suspension be rescinded, and that Roy Walker be made whole for the five days' earnings which had been unjustly denied him.

POSITION OF THE COMPANY

The company argued that since the termination of an incentive wage plan in 1969, it had observed a "tendency by employees to peg production." Walker's statements to McCarthy constituted direct evidence that employees in the Finish and Repair Department had arbitrarily limited production. They owed the company a fair day's work and had a duty not to discourage others from doing the same.

Mary McCarthy was highly upset by Walker's remarks to her on the morning of November 16. She did not testify in person later that day because of her emotional condition. However, she prepared and signed a written statement of her conversation with Walker. She was unavailable for direct testimony, because she left the employ of the company since the incident occurred.

The company also contended that Walker did not deny that he was the person accused by McCarthy. Furthermore, McCarthy appeared at Robinson's office in a distressed state growing out of an attempt to intimidate her because she exceeded, by a very large margin, the customary output in the department.

The threats of Walker were a direct challenge to the company's rights to manage the business efficiently. Further, such threats were in violation of Article 35, in which the union pledges not to restrict work or strike. The company had ample cause to discipline Walker, and its five-day suspension action was not excessive. The grievance should be denied.

APPENDIX

Relevant Contract Clauses

ARTICLE 23
DISCIPLINE AND DISCHARGE

An employee shall not be disciplined or discharged without good and sufficient cause.

ARTICLE 35
NO STRIKE OR LOCKOUT

35.1 No strike or lockout
a. There shall be no lockout on the part of the Company.

b. The Union shall not authorize any strike as defined in the Labor Management Relations Act, 1947, as amended, nor authorize any refusal by any employee to enter upon the premises of the Company and to perform work hereunder because of any strike or picket line.

35.2 Union Responsibility

a. In the event of the occurrence of any such unauthorized refusal to enter upon the premises of the Company and to perform work hereunder, the Union shall immediately upon receiving notice thereof, which will be confirmed in writing, inform the employees that such action is not authorized by the Union and deliver to the Company a letter advising that such action is not authorized by the Union and move to prevent loss to the Company and bring about an immediate cessation of such strike or refusal to enter upon the premises of the Company and to perform work hereunder.

b. All employees who participate in or are responsible for any unauthorized strike or refusal to enter upon the premises of the Company and to perform work hereunder shall be subject to disciplinary action, including discharge by the Company.

c. It is understood and agreed that the Union shall have no financial liability for the acts of its members which are not authorized by the Union.

d. It is understood and agreed that the Union's responsibilities under Section 35.2 of this Article shall not be applicable in the event the Company fails within ten (10) days to comply with an arbitration award, unless the Company, during the ten (10) day period, notifies the Union of the Company's intent to seek clarification of the award or to have the award set aside.

QUESTIONS

1. Evaluate the statement of employee Mary McCarthy concerning the conversation which she had in the plant with employee Walker. Were Walker's statements threats or attempts at intimidating McCarthy to restrict output?

2. How does one explain the production of McCarthy compared to the production record of most of the other employees? Does this suggest that employees deliberately were "pegging" production? Discuss.

3. Evaluate the company argument that Walker's statements were in violation of the no-strike clause of the agreement.

4. Must an employee who signs a written statement of charges against another employee be present at an arbitration hearing in order to be cross-examined by the person whom the employee has accused? Does this depend on the situation?

53. DISABLED BY POLICE BULLETS

COMPANY: *United States Steel Corporation, Eastern Steel Division, Lorain-Cuyahoga Works, Cleveland, Ohio*

UNION: *United Steelworkers of America, Local 1298*

BACKGROUND

A. In the spring of 1973, Robert Denny,[1] an employee at U.S. Steel's Lorain-Cuyahoga Works, was sought by the Cleveland, Ohio police department for alleged involvement in a statutory rape. In the process of taking him into custody, Denny was shot in the leg by a police officer. He was immediately taken to a hospital for treatment, but it was found necessary to amputate the right leg above the knee, resulting in a permanent disability.

Denny was indicted for his alleged role in the rape, convicted and sentenced to three years on probation. In the trial process, the police report of the incident involving Denny's capture and injury was presented. This police record, written by one of the officers involved in the incident, identified Denny as Subject #4 and recorded the details of the shooting as follows:

Received a R/R to Pasadena & Second. A rape in progress upon our arrival we were met by a Louis Peoples, Jr., Police Tow Trk. Driver who pointed out 4 M/W's running across second toward the rear of 92 Pasadena. 1 obs. subj. #1 who was wearing what appeared to be a blue jean jacket and dk. pants. Subj. #2 was wearing dk. pants and a light colored print shirt. Subj. #3 was wearing dk. pants, light shirt. Subj. #4 was wearing a white shirt with light blue stripes, dk. pants. I ordered subjects to halt. I also identified myself. Subj. continued to run. At this time I obs. "subjects 1, 2 & 4 attempt to run into rear of 92 Pasadena. I drew my service revolver and fired 2 shots at subj. #4. My partner fired 1 shot. I obs. subject #4 fall into the house. At this time other cars arrived at the scene surrounding the house. As I approached the rear of 92 Pasadena subj. #3 stood

---

1 The names of all individuals have been disguised.

335

up and stated "I give up." Subj. #3 was arrested at the rear of 92 Pasadena. At this time Sgt. Allen came to the rear with Ptr. Kemper. I informed both men that 3 more subj. ran into the house. Ptr. Rothman arrived at the scene I turned the prisoner over to him. I entered the house with Ptr. Kemper and Sgt. Allen. I obs. blood on the floor leading to the bedroom located on the west side of the house. Investigation revealed Subj. #4 lying on the floor bleeding from both legs from apparent gunshot wound. Subj. #4 was arrested in the bedroom. Subj. 1 & 2 were arrested in the dining room. All 4 subj. were arrested on above charge and were advised of their constitutional rights.

Following his injury, Denny filed a claim with the company under Paragraph 2.0 of Section 2 of the Program of Insurance Benefits (see Appendix). He alleged that he had satisfied the requirements of the paragraph in that he was totally disabled as a result of the accident, and that he had been under the care of a licensed physician during this period and was thus entitled to benefits under the insurance program. The company conceded that Denny had been totally disabled and that he had been under the care of a licensed physician. However, it denied his claim on the grounds that the employee had been engaged in the commission of an illegal act at the time he sustained his disabling injury, and consequently the incapacitating event did not qualify as an "accident" within the meaning of the Program of Insurance Benefits (PIB).

Denny filed a grievance concerning the rejection of his claim on May 15, 1974, which stated:

I, Robert Denny—charge management with violation of Aug. 1, 1971 Basic Labor Agreement of Section 1 and 19, and the Aug. 1, 1971 PIB Program of Insurance Benefits Sec. 2; Pr. 2.0.

Management refuses to pay me sickness and accident benefits under the PIB. I was under the care of a licensed physician during my Tem. Total Disability.

To be paid all monies due to me under this program.

B. In the Summer of 1973, Joseph Moss, another employee at U.S. Steel's Lorain-Cuyahoga operation, was also involved in a shooting encounter with police. According to police reports, Moss was attending a party during which he fired a shot close to a fellow guest in order to scare the other visitor. Moss then called the man a "punk" and told him to get away. The guest fled from the party, and Moss also left the house. As he entered his car, the police arrived and ordered him out of the car. Moss was shot by police as he stepped out, sustaining an injury which left him totally disabled for the period from August 24 through October 8, 1973. Moss was convicted in criminal proceedings of shooting and sentenced to three years on probation.

Moss also filed a claim for benefits under Paragraph 2.0 of Section 2 of the Program of Insurance Benefits, alleging that he had satisfied the provisionary requirements, and seeking compensation under the insurance program. As with Denny, the company conceded that the claimant was totally disabled as a result of a physical injury, and that he had been under the care of a licensed physician during the period of his disability. However, the company also rejected Moss's claim on the grounds that he was engaged in the commission of a criminal activity at the time of his injury, and therefore the disabling event did not qualify as an "accident" within the meaning of the PIB.

On August 17, 1974, Moss filed a grievance against the company which read:

I, Joseph Moss was denied Sickness and Accident Benefits in violation of the PIB agreement Section 2 PR 2.0.

I was disabled totally by gun shot wounds received by me in a misunderstanding with the Cleveland Police. I was under the care of a licensed physician while recovering from my injuries.

That I be paid S & A Benefits for the time I was off and under Doctors care.

Although the grievances of Denny and Moss were filed separately, meetings between the company and the union in regard to both complaints were held concurrently because of the common questions and similarity of circumstances. When no accord could be reached between the union and the company, both grievances were submitted to arbitration with the principal issue being whether the injuries sustained by Denny and Moss were "accidents" within the meaning of Paragraph 2.0 of the Program of Insurance Benefits.

POSITION OF THE UNION

At the arbitration hearings, Denny testified that he had been convicted in a jury trial of statutory rape, and sentenced to three years probation. In questioning at the hearing, Denny stated the incidents surrounding his shooting as follows:

Q: What happened after that point? After all you guys had reconvened in your uncle's home, you had a farewell, goodbye and left, or what happened?

A: We was standing there at the dinner table and my cousin's mother was in the living room and there was a tow truck across the street. I thought it was a tow truck. I didn't know for sure.

Q: Could you identify why you thought it was a tow truck; why weren't you sure about it?

A: Because it was backed up to the car. It had lights up here (indicating) and lights on the back of it.

Q: You mean the flashers were going?

A: Right.

Q: Then what happened?

A: When Chester come in—that was the boy that was with me—he said the girls had left. I asked him, "Why did they leave? I thought they was going to ride with me until I dropped them off." And he said that he didn't know. I was sitting at the table and his mother said there was somebody around the house.

Q: Whose mother?

A: Neil's, my cousin's.

Q: Okay, then what happened?

A: She started through the house and I was sitting at the table, sitting like that (indicating). I was sitting on this side (indicating) and she come and I stepped up and got to the door and it hit me.

Q: What hit you?

A: The bullet.

Q: The bullet hit you?

A: Yes, sir.

Q: Who fired the bullet, who shot you?

A: I didn't know at that time.

Q: Then after being shot, when, as you recall, when did the police actually arrive in the scene?

A: When I turned around and walked back in the house and laid on the bed.

Q: Then the police came into your uncle's home?

A: Yes, sir.

Q: Can you recall, were you conscious as to what was going on, can you recall what happened at that point?

A: Yes, sir. I was laying on the bed and my cousin's daughter—she's married and she lives upstairs—she was downstairs and she got a wet towel and put it around me. Then they come in—the law—the police come into the house.

Q: I assume you were confined in a hospital? Did they take you to the hospital then?

A: Yes, sir.

Denny denied any involvement in the crime for which he was convicted. He maintained that he was not attempting to flee the scene of the crime at the time of his shooting. The union argued that Denny's testimony and denial at the hearing served to prove that he was not involved in the group assault with which the girls charged him. The union claimed that the shooting was either a mistake or over-reaction by a police officer, and thus an "accident."

The union further contended that even though Denny was convicted of a crime which he was judged to have committed earlier in the day, his disabling injury was not sustained as part of the crime. The union again maintained that the shooting was the result of over-reaction by a policeman, and the injury was not a foreseeable consequence of criminal activity. Thus, the shooting should be found to have been an "accident" within the coverage of the Program of Insurance Benefits. Since the company had conceded that the total disability had been sustained as the result of physical injury, and the grievant had been under the care of a licensed physician, the union maintained that the benefits were properly due to him.

In regard to Moss's claim, the union presented Moss's recounting of the events leading to his shooting in support of its contention that he was not injured while involved in the actual commission of a crime. Moss testified that he had attended a party during which he took a shot close to another guest in order to scare him, had called the man a "punk," and had told him to get out. The other man then left, and he, too, departed. Moss testified that after he had entered his car, the police arrived and ordered him to "get out" and that he was shot as he did so. Upon questioning, Moss stated:

A: As much as I can remember, they said for me to get out of the car.

Q: Did you get out of the car?

A: Yes.

Q: Then what happened?

A: The next thing I know, is that I started getting shot.

Q: Then what happened—do you recall what happened thereafter?

A: I don't know; I fell down, passed out.

Q: The police claim you shot in the direction of them. Did you shoot at the police?

A: No, I didn't.

Q: Did you have to go to court?

A: Yes, I did.

Q: Did you plead guilty to shooting at the police?

A: No, I pled guilty to shooting, because they told me after I got well, they told me that I had shot the gun as I was falling. That is what they told me.

Q: You do admit your gun had been fired that day, am I correct?

A: Yes.

Q: But you don't claim to have been in a gun battle with the police?

A: No, no, no.

Moss further testified that he had been convicted of shooting and sentenced to three years on probation.

Again, the union maintained that the injury leading to Moss' disability—as in Denny's case—was related neither to criminal activity nor to the foreseeable consequences of criminal activity. Thus, the union reasoned, the injuries were properly classified as "accidents" under the insurance benefit program. Because the company had conceded Moss' total disability and compliance with the eligibility requirements of Paragraph 2.0 of Section 2 of the PIB, the union maintained that Moss, too, was properly entitled to benefits of the insurance program.

The union further maintained that even if the benefit claims were rejected by the insurer, Paragraph 9 of the Insurance Agreement provided that the company was primarily liable for the payment of benefits. In the event the insurer failed to provide such benefits awarded to an employee in grievance proceedings, the company must provide such benefits.

POSITION OF THE COMPANY

The company denied eligibility for either Denny or Moss on the grounds that the disabilities sustained by both grievants were not the result of "accidents" as the term is commonly understood and as it had been interpreted in administration of its sickness and accident program. Two witnesses, Dale Evans, Manager of Insurance for U.S. Steel, and Edward Holt, Regional Benefits Manager of Equitable Life Insurance Society—the insurer who administered the program jointly with U.S. Steel—were presented by the company. They testified that the "Sickness and Accident Plan" at U.S. Steel had been in operation since 1950. They also stated that since 1950, numerous claims had been rejected because the disability was incurred as the result of criminal or illegal activity, although they cited no specific examples. Holt indicated that judgments concerning claims were made on an individual, case-by-case, method, stating as a standard that:

The judgment really revolves around whether the man could reasonably have expected to incur some bodily harm by the performance of such an act.

He further testified that benefits would not be denied to a claimant who had sustained injuries as the result of a traffic violation, even if foreseeable, but that serious crimes, the commission of which had a causal relation to the injury, generally led to denial of claims.

Coinciding with Holt's stated standard of "reasonable expectation of bodily harm," the company argued that the disabilities sustained by Denny and Moss were foreseeable consequences brought about by their own deliberate illegal actions. The company contended that it would be inconsistent with public policy and the intent of the parties to interpret Section 2.0 of the Program of Insurance Benefits as requiring the company to pay benefits to an employee who was disabled in the course of committing a serious crime.

The company noted that the Basic Labor Agreement of 1965 contained the first provision allowing employees to process complaints related to the Program of Insurance Benefits as grievances in the normal grievance procedure. Prior to this, an employee's only recourse for denial of benefits had been to bring a civil action against the insurer. However, the company maintained that this alteration in procedure did not serve to change the terms or interpretation of terms in the PIB any way.

The company also explained that in administering the insurance program, the company paid routine claims which met the standards of Equitable without prior approval of the insurer. If claims did not meet such standards, they were referred to Equitable for determination. Decisions by either the company or the insurer in administration of the sickness and accident program were made in compliance with the Insurance Agreement between the company and union, the PIB booklet, and administration rules and regulations of Equitable, though not expressly stated in the PIB booklet, were incorporated by reference in the negotiated language of the Foreword (see Appendix). The company argued that its refusal to recognize the disabling wounds as "accidents" was supported by these rules and regulations of Equitable. Thus, the decision was properly made and served to ban the instant claims.

The company requested that both grievances be denied.

APPENDIX

Relevant Provisions of the Program of Insurance Benefits Booklet

Foreword

Details relating to the operation of the Program will be included in reasonable rules, regulations and arrangements with insurance carriers. . . . The Company has elected to have the Life Insurance and Sickness and Accident Benefits provided through a group insurance policy issued to the Company by The Equitable Life Assurance Society of the United States. . . . The Insurance Agreement and the rules, regulations and arrangements referred to above form the basis on which the Program is administered, but if there is any inconsistency, the Insurance Agreement governs.

Section 2, Paragraph 2.0

If you become totally disabled as a result of sickness or accident so as to be prevented from performing the duties of your employment and a licensed physician certifies thereto, you will be eligible to receive weekly sickness and accident benefits. Benefits will not be payable for any period during which you are not under the care of a licensed physician. In order for you to be eligible for benefits the Company must receive written notice of your claim within 21 days after your disability commences, but this requirement will be waived upon showing of good and sufficient reason that you were unable to furnish such notice or have it furnished by someone else on your behalf.

Relevant Provisions of the Insurance Agreement of August 1, 1971

Administration of the Program

7. The Program shall be administered by the Company or through arrangements provided by it. . . . Sickness and accident benefits and life insurance shall be provided by such method and through such carriers, if any, as the Company in its sole discretion shall determine. Any contracts entered into by the Company with respect to the benefits of the Program shall be consistent with this Agreement and shall provide benefits and conditions conforming to those set forth in the booklets.

(b) "Program" means the program of insurance benefits established by this Agreement and described in the booklets adopted by the parties, each booklet being applicable to the Employees referred to in its title, such booklets constituting a part of this Agreement as though incorporated herein; . . .

QUESTIONS

1. Were the injuries suffered by the grievants in this case accidents within the meaning of the company insurance plan?
2. Does it make any difference whether an accident occurs in a situation over which an individual may have a certain amount of control? Discuss.
3. Should a company have established guidelines for judging claims of this sort, rather than examining claims on an individual case-by-case method such as used by the company? Discuss.
4. Are the company's and the insurance carrier's arguments of past practice persuasive in application to this case situation? Why, or why not?

54. A REQUEST FOR PARENTAL LEAVE

COMPANY: *South Bend Community School Corporation, South Bend, Indiana*

UNION[1]: *National Educational Association, South Bend, Indiana*

BACKGROUND

In the fall of 1972 it was brought to the attention of the South Bend Community School Corporation that the maternity sick leave provisions of the 1972–73 teaching contracts might be inconsistent with the requirements of the Equal Employment Opportunity Commission. The school then entered into discussion with the South Bend chapter of the National Education Association in order to draft a new provision. The union proposed contract language which would have provided for parental leave following pregnancies for both males and females. The school corporation resisted such provisions, because it felt that these provisions were not required by the Equal Employment Opportunity Commission guidelines. The union's parental leave proposals were rejected, and a new maternity sick leave directive was issued by the corporation in January, 1973, which did not contain such language. Similar arguments by the union were rejected in contract negotiations for the 1973–74 and 1974–75 school year agreements.

Having signed a teaching contract for the 1974–75 school year in the spring of 1974, Mrs. Carol Franklin[2] notified the school corporation on May 22, 1974 of her pregnancy and expected delivery date of June 28, 1974. She also enclosed a physician's confirmation of her pregnancy, and informed the corporation of her intention to take sick leave for maternity purposes commencing August 26, 1974. The corporation's assistant superintendent of personnel, John Woodson, dis-

---

[1] The arbitrator in this case refers to the National Education Association as a "union." The authors have employed his terminology although some chapters of the NEA consider themselves to be professional associations, rather than labor unions.

[2] The names of all individuals are disguised.

344

cussed the subject with a union official, but no notice of approval or rejection was ever sent to Franklin.

Following the birth of the baby on June 24, Franklin sent another note to Woodson dated July 8, 1974 confirming her earlier correspondence, informing him of the baby's birth, and again indicating her request for sick leave with pay commencing on August 26. At this time, she had accumulated 33½ days of paid sick leave and wanted to take all of this beginning August 26. She also informed the corporation that she did not wish to teach any classes during the 1974–75 school year, but intended to return to full-time teaching in August 1975. Her requests were not based on any alleged illness suffered at that time, but on a desire to take time off following her pregnancy.

In a telephone conversation in early August 1974, Woodson told Mrs. Franklin that according to the Aritcle X "Sick Leave" provisions of the contract (see Appendix), a medical statement certifying a present illness was necessary to grant the sick leave. This was because the maternity sick leave provision of the contract, Article XIII, Section 1, did not provide for paid sick leaves in periods during which sick leave was not required because of pregnancy or recovery [e.g., summer months, Christmas holiday vacation].

Franklin did not submit any such medical certification. Nevertheless, in a letter dated August 23, 1974 Woodson approved her requested leave of absence for the 1974–75 school year, but reiterated the requirement of a physician's statement of "present illness" necessary for her to obtain paid sick leave.

Mrs. Franklin contended that Section I of Article XIII of the contract entitled her to receive 33½ days of paid sick leave for the period beginning August 26, subsequent to the birth of her child.

The contract provided for ten paid sick leave days plus two paid personal leave days each contract year beginning on August 1. Mrs. Franklin claimed that she was entitled to accumulate and receive those 12 paid sick leave days, in addition to the 33½ previously accumulated sick leave days, during the 1974–75 year she was to be on leave of absence. The corporation denied that she was entitled to any of the 45½ sick leave days for which she claimed payment.

The parties stipulated that the issue to be submitted to the arbitrator should read as follows:

Under the applicable collective bargaining contract, and applicable policies or practices, if any, was Carol Franklin entitled to sick leave for maternity purposes for any period after August 26, 1974? If so, for what period was she entitled to such sick leave?

POSITION OF THE UNION

The union maintained that Section I of Article XIII allowed a teacher who was absent from teaching on a maternity sick leave to receive her salary, if desired, to the extent of her normal accumulated sick leave. The union argued that this provision was intended to allow the teacher to receive paid sick leave during the period of absence due to pregnancy, regardless of whether she was ill or not. The union further argued that because there was no requirement of present illness, there was similarly no need to submit a physician's statement of such illness in order to obtain accumulated paid sick leave. The union sought from the Corporation Franklin's accumulated paid sick leave beginning August 26, 1974 plus an additional 12 days based on her contract for the 1974–75 school year.

POSITION OF THE CORPORATION

The school corporation claimed that maternity sick leave was the same as any sick leave, and, as such, required medical evidence of present illness if the corporation requested it. The corporation noted that, historically, postmaternity sick leave had not exceeded 24 days, and only during that part of the year when the teacher would normally be expected to be at work. The corporation also maintained that in light of the language of the contract and its surrounding negotiations, the sick leave provisions were designed to grant leave only to those who were presently ill, sick, or disabled, and to extend coverage beyond those limits would be contrary to the purpose of the provisions.

The school affirmed its willingness to rehire Mrs. Franklin for the 1975–76 school year without loss of her accumulated 33½ days of sick leave, but contended that such leave should not be granted for the period beginning August 26, 1974 as sought by Mrs. Franklin.

APPENDIX

Relevant Provisions of the Contract

ARTICLE X—SICK LEAVE

Sick pay is a benefit provided by the school district to permanent employees to insure against loss of income due to short-term personal illness. Sick pay is not to be used for any reason other than illness and is given only for illness-caused absence on scheduled work days.

I. Eligibility

Although sick pay benefits accrue from the date of hire, a teacher may receive sick pay only after having completed six months of continuous service.

A teacher will not be given sick pay unless having given proper notification of illness to her supervisor. That is, prior to her scheduled work time, she must contact her supervisor to inform him that she will be unable to report for work. If the absence is longer than one day, the teacher must keep her supervisor notified of her condition on a daily basis or some other basis that is satisfactory with her supervisor.

In order to establish eligibility for sick pay for any absence due to illness, lasting five work days or less, a teacher, at her supervisor's discretion, may be required to submit a physician's statement. For any illness which causes a teacher to miss more than five work days, she is expected to submit to her supervisor a physician's statement of the nature and length of her illness and that she is able to return to work and to resume her normal duties without restriction.

II. Use of Sick Days

Sick days will be deducted from a teacher's reserve of sick days at the rate of one day for each day of illness.

If a teacher is a permanent employee and has more than ten sick days accumulated at the outset of her illness and is not ready to return to work when her total number of paid sick days expires, she must go on a leave of absence at that time if eligible or be terminated.

If a teacher is a permanent employee and has ten or less sick days accumulated at the outset of her illness and is not ready to return to work when her total number of paid sick days expires, she will be allowed up to a total of ten days off before being required to go on a leave of absence.

ARTICLE XIII—MATERNITY LEAVE

I. Sick Leave for Maternity Purposes

Section 1. A teacher who is pregnant shall be entitled upon request to sick leave. The teacher's absence shall begin at a time mutually agreed upon between the teacher, the Assistant Superintendent of Personnel and the teacher's physician. Said teacher shall notify the Assistant Superintendent of Personnel, in writing, at least 30 days prior to the date on which she desires to begin her sick leave and shall include in her communication a statement from her physician certifying her pregnancy.

A teacher who is pregnant may continue in active employment as late into her pregnancy as best determined after consultation with her physician, the Assistant Superintendent in charge of Personnel and herself.

A teacher who is absent on sick leave for maternity purposes may receive salary, if she desires, for days lost to the extent of her accumulated sick leave.

Section 2.   A teacher who is granted sick leave for maternity purposes shall comply with the following rules.

It shall be the responsibility of the teacher to notify the Assistant Superintendent of Personnel the date upon which she desires to return to active employment. The notification shall be made within a 30 day period, in writing, following the termination of pregnancy.

During the period of sick leave for maternity purposes, the teacher's position will be filled by a substitute teacher. Upon the receipt of notification to return, the Assistant Superintendent of Personnel and the teacher shall determine the exact date upon which she will resume her previous assignment. Prior to the resumption of her teaching duties, the teacher shall provide the Assistant Superintendent of Personnel with a statement of her good health from her physician. Failure by the teacher to notify the Assistant Superintendent of Personnel within the aforesaid 30 day period after the termination of pregnancy of her desire to resume teaching shall relieve the School Corporation of any responsibility for holding the teacher's position beyond the 30 day period.

QUESTIONS

1. What is meant by the term *sick leave* as normally utilized in union-management agreements? Does an individual have to be physically or mentally ill to be eligible for sick leave benefits?

2. Is maternity a sickness? Discuss.

3. Should an employee be entitled to accumulated sick leave benefit payments at any time when an employee would like to receive such payments? Discuss.

4. A 1976 U.S. Supreme Court decision ruled that under the Civil Rights Act, an employer is not required to provide disability benefits to female employees who are absent from work due to pregnancy. Several state courts have reached different decisions from that of the Supreme Court. Why is this apt to be a continuing area of debate from both a legal and societal point of view?

55. RIDING THE TIGER

COMPANY: *Randle-Eastern Ambulance Service, Inc., Miami, Florida*

UNION: *Transport Workers Union, Local 500*

BACKGROUND

James Kellerman[1] was hired by the Randle-Eastern Ambulance Service in May 1974 as an ambulance attendant. He performed his job well, receiving a commendation for service during a major disaster. Further, Kellerman had a generally good record of attendance and behavior, and he was promoted to ambulance driver within a few months.

On November 11, 1974 while driving an ambulance, Kellerman was struck by another vehicle and suffered a cracked vertebra in his back. He was then placed on compensatory sick leave by the firm to allow for his recovery. On March 13, 1975 Kellerman was examined by a physician and the following report was submitted to the firm.

TO WHOM IT MAY CONCERN:

On March 13th, 1975, the above patient was seen in my office for his fractured vertebra.

At that time, x-ray showed that there was still not enough solidity to allow him to do heavy work, such as lifting stretchers and putting any great stress on his back. However, the back was comfortable on motion. He had a good range of motion and percussion did not produce any pain.

At that time, we felt that it was safe for him to drive an ambulance but he should not be doing any lifting. We suggested that he not do any strenuous activities with his back for another four weeks. At that time, we told him he could swim but we told him he was to do no diving, no running around, no horsing around in the pool, simply to go in and float around and swim gently to exercise the back muscles.

Respectfully,
Anthony Bomarito, M.D.

---

[1] The names of all individuals have been disguised.

Following his examination on March 13, and while still on sick leave from Randle-Eastern, Kellerman contacted Frances Anderson, the Assistant Information Director at Gulfstream Race Track, a local horse track. Prior to his employment at Randle-Eastern, Kellerman had been a jockey working principally at Gulfstream. For several previous years, Kellerman had participated in a novelty animal race staged as part of the festivities on Florida Derby Day. This had involved his riding such animals as ostriches, brahma bulls, camels, and buffaloes. Kellerman contacted Anderson inquiring about the possibility of again participating in the 1975 race. Anderson affirmed that there was still an "empty saddle" and hired Kellerman to ride a Bengal tiger in the race. He agreed to pay Kellerman $100, with the understanding that he could withdraw from the event at any time if he considered the assignment to be dangerous.

On March 29, 1975 while still on sick leave from the ambulance firm, Kellerman finished second in the Florida Derby Day race. The tigers used in the race were domesticated, trained animals which were rather lethargic and had to be led through the race by their trainers who claimed the animals were completely harmless. (Kellerman blamed his loss on his mount's lack of competitive spirit.)

Upon learning of Kellerman's participation in the race, company officials called him into the office and charged him with a violation of Section E, Paragraph 7 of the company Operating Manual, which stated:

An employee desiring other employment while off duty from the Company is responsible for obtaining written Company permission to assure that the other employment would not be detrimental to the best interests of the Company or the employee.

The company discussed the incident with Kellerman and his union representative, then informed him that he was discharged from the firm. In dismissing him, the company based its action on the potential risk involved in such activity, and the possible detrimental effect upon Kellerman's health.

On April 10, 1975 subsequent to his discharge, Kellerman received another physical examination. A portion of the report from this examination stated:

On April 10th, 1975, this patient was seen to have a full range of motion and no pain. His x-rays showed that he had sufficient solidification for me to discharge him and allow him unrestricted activities. Because of his deformed vertebrae, a 5% permanent partial disability of the body as a whole was assigned to the patient. At no time did I give this patient permission to ride a bengal tiger.

Signed: Anthony Bomarito, M.D.

Kellerman filed a grievance, which eventually was submitted to arbitration. In the arbitration proceedings, the issue agreed upon by both parties was whether Kellerman violated Section E, Paragraph 7 of the Operating Manual and thus provided the company with "cause" for discharge by his participation in an exhibition in which he allegedly rode a tiger at Gulfstream Race Track.

POSITION OF THE UNION

The union presented a series of arguments in support of its position that the company did not have "cause" to discharge Kellerman.

1. The union challenged the company's claim of broad authority in its exercise of Article 18, the Disciplinary Provision, of the contract.[2]

2. The union denied the company's assertion that management had the unlimited right to establish rules to govern employee conduct. The union acknowledged the company's right to establish operating rules, but maintained that the union reserved the right to challenge any such rule or attempted enforcement.

3. The union contended that there were 36 pages of rules contained in the Operating Manual, and Kellerman was unaware of the restrictive provisions of Section E, Paragraph 7 and their application to his job at the race track. He could not be expected to be familiar with every implication of all of the rules.

4. The union maintained that because of the large amount of rules contained in the Operating Manual, the company was under an obligation to explain the application of the rule concerning outside employment to its employees. There was no evidence that the company had made any effort to do so, and the union argued that Kellerman should not be held to such strict compliance as the company attempted to impose.

5. The company had misinterpreted its own rule by construing the words "off duty employment" too broadly. The union contended that the terms of a rule should be construed as the "proverbial reasonable man" would understand them, and that in this case a reasonable interpretation of the rule would be that it referred only to "full time

---

[2] See Appendix for relevant contract provisions.

employment" and not to occasional work. The work schedule for company employees consisted of shifts of 24 hours on and 24 hours off, a system which would seemingly readily present the option to an employee for working another job. This might become a potential source of conflict if an ambulance attendant's performance or availability for extra work suffered because of fatigue due to the second job. Thus the rule had some reasonable basis, but the union asserted that it was not intended to apply to one-time or occasional jobs.

6. The union argued that the company failed to take into consideration all of the circumstances of Kellerman's activity on March 29, 1975 and erroneously characterized it as "employment." The company contended that its dismissal action was based on the potential risk involved in the race; yet the union asserted that the race was merely a staged entertainment. Kellerman was experienced and had the option of backing out at any time, and there was no foreseeable risk of injury to Kellerman, nor could the activity be seen as potentially detrimental to the company.

Based upon these arguments, the union sought reinstatement of Kellerman to his employed status with the firm with no loss of applicable pay or benefits.

POSITION OF THE COMPANY

The company's arguments supporting the propriety of the discharge rested on several points:

1. The company claimed broad discretionary authority described in the agreement and a limited right of the union to challenge that authority. It maintained that the company was only required to show that it had "cause" to penalize the employee, not that the particular penalty was appropriate.

2. The company contended that the labor agreement recognized management's unlimited right to make rules to govern employee conduct and to discipline employees for violation of such rules.

3. The Operating Manual contained rules to govern employee conduct. These rules were known by both the employee and the union. Kellerman, in spite of everything the company had done, violated Section E, Paragraph 7 by accepting employment at Gulfstream Race Track.

4. Any activity in the nature of work for another, particularly when there is compensation, as in this instance, comes within a normal definition of "employment" and makes the application of Section E,

Paragraph 7 appropriate. In support of this argument, the company referred to an earlier arbitration award which dealt with the issue.

The award cited by the company was *Armstrong Rubber Company* v. *Rubber Workers* (57 LA 1267), in which the arbitrator upheld a company discharge action. The arbitrator ruled that:

Under a contract providing for termination of employee's seniority whenever he works on another job while on leave of absence, the employer properly discharged the employee, who, while on sick leave worked for another employer on commission basis. The employer is entitled to enforce prohibition against work at another job, since prohibition serves to speed an employee's return to full-time duty. The fact that the employer stopped sending sickness and accident checks to the employee does not justify the employee's violation of agreement.

The company claimed that in view of its broad, discretionary authority in such matters as the case in question, plus the fact that the employee should have been aware of the rules, the discharge should be upheld.

APPENDIX

Relevant Provisions of the Contract

Article 3—Management Rights

Management retains the sole and exclusive right to, and responsibility of, without being subject to the grievance or arbitration provisions herein, any and all functions and rights which it enjoyed prior to the selection of the union as bargaining agent, except to the precise extent such functions and rights are explicitly, clearly, and unequivocally, taken away from management by the express terms of this Agreement.

In addition, the company being a quasi-public agency, must, without qualification, except to the precise extent such qualifications are explicitly, clearly and unequivocally made by the express terms of this Agreement, continue to implement its policies and practices, particularly relating to safety, security, discipline and control, as done in the past and as deemed desirable in the future.

The management of the company and the direction of its employees; including the establishment of working conditions, the hiring, promoting, demoting, transferring, subcontracting, changes in operations or mode of operations, rehiring of employees, determination of qualifications of employees, and the layoff and recall to work of employees in connection with any reduction or increase in the work force, are the exclusive and sole functions and responsibility of management to the extent that any such matters are not otherwise explicitly, clearly and unequivocally covered or provided for in this agreement; and provided that in the exercise of such functions, the company shall not discriminate against any employee because of his membership in, or lawful activity on behalf of the union.

Article 6—Sick Leave

(d) Any employee who by reason of bona fide illness as defined in Article 6 will be granted appropriate leave of absence. Only union seniority will continue to accrue during such leaves. In no event will seniority accrue for more than one (1) year. An employee accepting gainful employment while on leave of absence except as approved in writing by the company automatically terminates his employment with the company.

Time spent on medical leave of absence shall not count for any other purposes.

A medical certificate will be required upon return to duty stating the employee's ability to perform his regular duties.

During such leave of absence an employee may continue his hospitalization and life insurance at his expense subject to the insurance carrier's approval. (e) These sick leave provisions do not apply to sickness, injury or disability within the purview of Workmen's Compensation.

Article 7—Workmen's Compensation

Any employee who has been determined by the company's Workmen's Compensation carrier to have been injured on the job, will be paid the difference between the Workmen's Compensation Insurance benefits and the employee's pay for eight hours regular pay for each consecutive calendar day's absence occasioned by a said on-the-job injury beginning with the eighth calendar day's absence and ending with the twentieth calendar day's absence, not to exceed a total of said difference as applied to forty hours.

Article 11—Grievance and Arbitration

An employee who believes that he has been unjustly dealt with or that any applicable provision of this agreement has not been properly applied or interpreted may present a grievance and/or arbitration as follows:

Arbitration

1. . . . It is expressly understood that the only matters which are subject to arbitration under this Article are grievances which were processed and handled strictly in accordance with the foregoing grievance procedure and which were made subject to the grievance and arbitration provisions of this Agreement.

3. The arbitrator shall have no power to alter, amend, change, add to or subtract from any of the terms of this Agreement, but shall determine only

whether or not there has been a violation of this Agreement in the respect alleged in the grievance, in accord with the test of coverage set out in subparagraph 1 above. The rights of Management enumerated in Article 3 are hereby incorporated by reference herein, and those rights and all other rights of management not clearly, specifically and unequivocally limited by the clear and explicit language of a clause of this Agreement, and the provisions of the Article prohibiting strikes or work stoppage during the life of this Agreement are specifically excluded from arbitration under the provisions of this Article. The decision of the arbitrator shall be fair and equitable and be based solely upon the evidence and arguments presented to him by the respective parties in the presence of each other.

4. This Agreement constitutes a contract between the parties which shall be interpreted and applied by the parties and by the Arbitrators in the same manner as any other contract under the laws of the State of Florida. The function and purpose of the arbitrator is to determine disputed interpretation of terms actually found in the Agreement, or to determine disputed facts upon which the application of the Agreement depends. The arbitrator shall therefore not have authority, nor shall he consider it his function to include, the decision of any issue not submitted or to so interpret or apply the Agreement as to change what can fairly be said to have been the intent of the parties as determined by generally accepted rules of contract construction. The arbitrator shall not give any decision which in practical or actual effect modifies, revises, detracts from or adds to any of the terms or provisions of this Agreement. Past practice of the parties in interpreting or applying terms of the Agreement can be relevant evidence, but may not be used so as to justify, or result in, what is in effect a modification (whether by addition or detraction) of the written terms of this Agreement. The arbitrator shall not render any decision or award solely because in his opinion such decision or award is fair or equitable. The ordinary rules of evidence shall prevail in any hearing.

6. Any dispute not specifically brought under this article by the terms of this Agreement is not subject to this article, but is to be settled exclusively by management.

7. Specifically, the standards relating to safety or security are not arbitrable, and they are not in any manner subject to evaluation, question, qualification, interpretation or judgment by the arbitrator.

Article 18—Discipline

(*a*) The company shall have the right to discharge or discipline any employee for "cause," as defined solely by the company. The term "cause" shall include, but not be limited to, the following: failure to perform assigned duties, failure to perform duties efficiently, failure to meet required standards of work performance, negligence in the performance of duties likely to cause personal injuries or property damage, dishonesty, insubordination, the use or being under the influence of drugs or alcoholic beverages during working hours, performance of duties in such a manner as to reflect unfavorably upon company, lack of neatness, courtesy, cleanliness, or inability to maintain proper decorum with the using public, excessive tardiness or absences, improper attitude toward the job, the company, fellow employees, customers and customer employees, improper conduct or attitude relating to Government or hospital physicians, employees and representatives, failure to comply with or pass company security or safety of applicable Federal, State, County or Municipal laws, rules or regulations, violation of this Agreement or failure to comply with company rules. Any grievance or arbitration with respect to the exercise of this right to discharge or discipline shall be limited to the question of whether or not one of the above listed offenses, or other "cause," occurred and shall not include whether or not the type of discipline selected was appropriate.

(*b*) The right to maintain and the manner of maintaining discipline and efficiency of employees is vested exclusively in the company, provided, solely however, that no employee shall be discharged or discriminated against for exercising his rights as set forth in Section 7 of the National Labor Relations Act, as amended.

Article 21—General

(*f*) The company will publish an operating manual stating company policies and defining areas of responsibility of all employees. This manual will be updated from time to time and copies will be distributed to each employee. A copy will be provided to the union.

(*g*) Employees will abide by the company's rules and regulations as contained in the company manual or in bulletins or notices which may be posted from time to time. A copy will be provided to the union.

QUESTIONS

1. Must an employee be aware of a company operating rule before discipline may be imposed on that employee? Discuss.
2. When an employee is on a sick leave, does this mean that the employee has no right to work for pay for another employer either on a temporary or full-time basis? Discuss.
3. What standards should an arbitrator use to apply the "reasonable man" concept advocated by the union?
4. Evaluate the last sentence of Article 18, the disciplinary provision of the agreement. How does this provision limit the arbitrator?

56. NO MORE COFFEE OR BOTTLED WATER

COMPANY: *Ametek California Spring Company, Pico Rivera, California*

UNION: *United Automobile, Aerospace and Agricultural Implement Workers of America, Local 509*

On April 7, 1975 a directive was issued by the company plant manager informing employees that (1) coffee was no longer to be prepared during company working hours, and (2) the bottled water stations scattered throughout the plant had been replaced by water fountains as a result of a new plumbing installation. Martin Adams,[1] an employee of the company for over 20 years, immediately questioned his supervisor, John Willis, concerning the memorandum. He reminded Willis that he had been preparing a 36-cup pot of coffee in his department every working day for the previous 19 years. He noted that the practice had been initiated at the request of a foreman who was no longer with the firm, and that it only took five minutes of his time each morning unless a second pot was required later in the day. The coffee was available to anyone in the plant during their break periods, and the only limitation was that each person pay ten cents for each cup in order to pay for supplies. Adams further noted that the company had acknowledged and supported the practice several years before by installing a water outlet in the first aid room. This enabled Frances Miller to obtain water for the coffee when Adams was on vacation, since he normally obtained water from the faucet in the men's room. Willis listened to Adams' protest, but informed him that the order came from the plant manager and it had to be enforced.

The union then filed a grievance protesting the company's unilateral action in terminating the coffee-making privilege and removing six bottled-water stations in the plant. The union maintained that

---

1 The names of all individuals have been disguised.

the company had violated past practice and Section 3 of Article XIII of the Agreement which stated:

The Company shall not take away any privileges that are now enjoyed by the employees.

The question eventually reached the arbitration level, where the parties agreed that the issue to be resolved by the arbitrator should be:

Did the Company violate Article XIII by removing the bottled water and refusing to allow employees to make coffee on Company time?

POSITION OF THE UNION

At the hearing, Martin Adams related the background and procedure of his daily coffee brewing, just as he had commented to Willis on the day of the directive. He particularly noted the long duration of the practice and the apparent company acquiescence in allowing it to continue and even promoting the brewing by installing the water faucet in the first aid room. The union acknowledged that several times in the previous three or four years management had mentioned discontinuation of the practice, but that no serious effort had been made prior to April 17, 1975 actually to effectuate that policy.

The union maintained that both the coffee brewing and bottled-water stations, which had been located in the plant for approximately ten years, were established past practices which could not be unilaterally discontinued by management. It argued that the company had acquiesced to the coffee brewing for over 19 years and had provided bottled water since the plant facility's inception. The union cited Section 3 of Article XIII of the agreement and alleged the company had violated those provisions.

The union requested the arbitrator to order the company to restore the coffee-making privilege and the bottled-water stations in the plant.

POSITION OF THE COMPANY

Alfred Perry, general manager of the plant, testified that after joining the company in his present position in 1969, he had become aware of the practice of coffee being made on company time. Mr. Perry stated that over a period of three or four years he had instructed supervisors approximately a dozen times to stop the practice, and each time he was informed that the directive had been enforced.

Management representatives further argued that the preparation and drinking of coffee on company time wasted a considerable amount of time and interfered with efficiency. Management claimed that it had the right to abolish the coffee-making under Section 1 of Article II of the contract which reads:

It is the responsibility of the management of the company to maintain discipline and efficiency in its plant.

Perry and the plant manager, Jerome Epps, also testified concerning the bottled water. They affirmed that the company had provided bottled drinking water in the plant over the years. They maintained that this was due to the fact that in the past the company had had inadequate facilities for drinking fountains. However, the remodeling completed in the spring of 1975 provided plumbing facilities so that water fountains could be installed at various points in the plant. The company argued that the need for bottled water no longer existed, and that it had acted legitimately in terminating the bottled-water system.

Finally, management contended that the installation of drinking fountains constituted an improvement in working conditions, as well as being more efficient.

The company urged that in the interests of maintaining efficiency in the plant, its position in prohibiting the preparation of coffee on company time and the installation of drinking fountains be upheld.

QUESTIONS

1. Was the coffee drinking privilege a well-established practice in the plant? Was the providing of bottled water stations a well-established past practice? Evaluate.

2. To what degree are Section 3 of Article XIII and Section 1 of Article XI of the agreement somewhat contradictory? Which of these provisions is "superior" in the circumstances of this case?

3. What standards should an arbitrator utilize to determine whether something is a well-established past practice, or whether something is within the province of management rights to handle as appropriate to efficient operation? Discuss.

57. THE BYPASSED SENIOR CLERK

COMPANY: *Marion Food Towne, Incorporated, Marion, Illinois*

UNION: *Retail Clerks International Association, Local Union 896*

BACKGROUND

In June 1975, Raymond White,[1] co-owner of Marion Food Towne, Charles Ridgeway, manager of the store, and Frank Costilli, assistant manager, unanimously concluded that because of increased business it was necessary to hire an additional full-time clerk at the store. At that time, seven part-time clerks were employed at the store, and the managers decided to first consider the three part-time clerks with highest seniority for the new position.

Robert Sharp, who was in his early 50s, had worked several years in a part-time position and held highest seniority among the part-time clerks. He had been passed over several times during those years by management in hiring full-time clerks, because he was considered to be too slow in carrying out his duties. In spite of this, however, the managers considered him valuable for stocking in the evening when he normally worked. James Moran, 20, having been hired on April 29, 1974 was second in seniority among the part-time stock clerks. John Anthony, having been hired on June 17, 1974 also 20, was third on the seniority list. He worked on essentially the same jobs as Moran.

The managers again decided in this instance that Sharp was too slow to be promoted, although he requested the job. They then evaluated the work performance of Moran and Anthony in an attempt to determine the best man for the position. Although they considered seniority in arriving at their decision, White, Ridgeway, and Costilli were primarily concerned with hiring into the full-time position the person with the best performance record who gave promise of having most long-run value to the store.

---

[1] The names of all individuals have been disguised.

After considering both Moran and Anthony for the promotion and consulting with White, Costilli, and other store employees, Ridgeway awarded the full-time position to Anthony, who held least seniority among the three part-time clerks. The three managers had generally agreed that Anthony was superior to Moran in handling his duties around the store. Costilli had commented that in observing both Moran and Anthony stocking shelves, Anthony was consistently quicker, neater, and more conscientious in handling his aisles. The head checker had told Ridgeway that Anthony was usually "much quicker" in coming to the check-out counter to assist in bagging, to report prices on unmarked items, and to assist customers, and that Anthony was more efficient, helpful, and friendly than Moran. Ridgeway also took into consideration several customer comments he had received in March and April of 1975 complaining of Moran's "lack of friendliness." Ridgeway had discussed those complaints with Moran, and Moran's behavior had improved somewhat following that meeting. Ridgeway concluded, however, that Anthony was more interested in his work and in the store, and that he was the best man available for the promotion. Anthony was given the full-time position in mid-June 1975.

Following Anthony's appointment, Moran filed a grievance with the union on June 23, 1975 complaining that a part-time employee of lower seniority had been hired to the full-time position without first offering the job to him. On June 25, 1975 Virgil Neickhorn, president of Local 896, sent a letter to the company, the relevant part of which stated:

> This is to advise that James Moran has filed a grievance with this office contesting the Company's action of hiring a less senior employee for a full-time job. Mr. Moran was not offered the full-time job opening.
>
> We feel this is in violation of the Agreement: Article 9—Seniority[2]

The company and the union failed to resolve their differences in the first three steps of the grievance procedure. The two parties submitted the following issue to an arbitrator on October 9, 1975:

> Did the Company violate the Agreement when it offered a full-time clerk's position to part-time employee John Anthony rather than offering the position to James Moran, another part-time employee who had about two months seniority over Mr. Anthony?

---

[2] See Appendix.

POSITION OF THE UNION

Counsel for the union interrogated store manager Ridgeway at great length during the arbitration hearing. Ridgeway related the considerations involved in promoting Anthony to the full-time position including the consultations he had had with other personnel in the store and his own observations which led him to conclude that Anthony was superior to Moran in his work and the "best man" for the full-time position. Ridgeway testified that he wanted the "best man" regardless of his seniority, and that his decision rested largely on the person's ability to do the job. He noted that in the past that the company's policy of promoting the "best man" had provided the basis for promoting lower seniority part-time employees instead of Robert Sharp into full-time positions. He also stated that he regarded a full-time position as a promotion from a part-time status.

As a result of analysis of work performance, Ridgeway stated that the results had shown Anthony's work aisle was consistently in "much better shape, neater, and had less back stock" than did Moran's. Under questioning, Ridgeway also testified that he had discussed with Moran several customer complaints regarding Moran's friendliness, but had never given him any written reprimand or report to help improve his performance. The company had an "Employee Corrective Action Notice" form to be used to note for an employee any deficiencies, but Moran had never been given one of these reports. Ridgeway stated that he considered Moran to be a "satisfactory employee" but that there were significant differences between that and an "excellent" employee.

Union president Virgil Neickhorn then testified that Article 9, Section A of the contract had remained the same throughout the past 12 years, during which he had first been a business agent for the union and, for the last two years, president of the local. He stated that at no time during that period had there been a similar grievance filed by any union member.

In the course of his testimony in his own behalf, Moran related that he was presently working approximately 24 hours per week and was being paid about $3.10 per hour. He stated that he "did not remember" anyone in management ever criticizing his work, nor did he recall ever being advised by Ridgeway concerning his lack of friendliness toward customers. He stated that he performed essentially the same work as Anthony. He pointed out, however, that Anthony's aisles were located closer to the check-out stations than his own, and that this probably explained why it took him longer than Anthony to respond to requests for help from the checkers.

In summary arguments, the union contended that a change from part-time to full-time employment status did not constitute a promotion, but rather a straight seniority claim to additional hours of work. The union noted that under Article 9, Section A seniority was defined as "the length of continuous employment within the bargaining unit" and that "all circumstances being reasonably equal, length of service shall be the controlling factor." The union noted that Moran had seniority over Anthony, and that the company manager admitted Moran was capable of performing the clerk's work. Moran had never been formally counseled or reprimanded, and from this it must be concluded that Moran was fully capable of performing the clerk's tasks. The union cited several arbitration decisions holding that in situations in which an employee had the ability to do a job and was a satisfactory employee, seniority should be the controlling factor in determining advancement.

The union argued that despite the fact that Article 9, Section A did not expressly state that a senior part-time employee who was satisfactory should be offered a full-time position in preference to a lower seniority part-time worker, the provision should be interpreted in that manner. It maintained that the spirit of the agreement implicitly led to that interpretation, and that the company should have followed that guide. Ability to do the job should have been the criterion for selecting the full-time clerk. As shown by the testimony, Moran was satisfactory in his work, and the "best man" criterion should not have entered into management's consideration. The union argued that the company's admitted general disregard for seniority in choosing a part-time employee for a full-time position was in violation of the agreement.

Counsel for the union requested that the grievance be sustained. As a remedy, counsel for the union suggested the following: (1) The grievant, James Moran, should be assigned to a 40-hour work week schedule; (2) he should be made whole for the difference in pay that he would have received having worked a 40-hour schedule since approximately June 23, 1975 to the present time; (3) the number of additional hours that he should have been employed as a full-time employee should be credited appropriately and payments made correspondingly to the pension fund; and (4) he should have full-time seniority status effective as of June 23, 1975.

POSITION OF THE COMPANY

The company referred to the testimony provided by store manager Ridgeway during interrogation by the union counsel and cross-examination by company counsel concerning the criteria employed by the company in deciding to promote Anthony instead of Sharp and Moran. The company emphasized its long-standing policy and practice of hiring full-time employees who indicated that they possessed outstanding ability and a very good attitude. For example, in September 1974 and again in April 1975 management promoted less senior part-time men to full-time clerk positions over Sharp. In 1971 management hired a full-time clerk "off the street" bypassing all the part-time clerks who had been considered unqualified to fill the full-time position.

Frank Costilli, the assistant manager, testified that he had been employed at the store for six years, and that he had been the assistant manager for the last 18 months, though he still retained membership in Local 896. As assistant manager his job involved supervising and directing stock work by the clerks. He stated that, based on numerous observations, Anthony was consistently quicker, neater, and more efficient in his stocking work than was Moran. In fact, on average, Anthony stocked 35–40 cases per hour, while Moran stocked 20–25 cases per hour. This was true despite the fact that Moran stocked the "glass aisles," traditionally easier and quicker than the cereal, coffee, and tea aisles handled by Anthony, which required stock rotation, facing out, and other special operations. Anthony was also willing to "look for other jobs when he was done with his aisle" while Moran would only "just do his aisle."

Costilli stated that he never discussed Moran's poorer performance with him, because he felt that the employees might consider his observations to be "spying." He noted, too, that the "Employee Corrective Action Notice" form for employee evaluation had been introduced in the store in May 1975, only a month before the incident in question.

Raymond White, co-owner of the store, testified that he maintained a philosophy of management that full-time employees should be the best employees, and that such persons must be "the most conscientious people who have the store's best interests at heart and who seek a future in the business." He noted management's previous disregard of Sharp's seniority and hiring of people "off the street" as evidence of its consistent policy of hiring the "best person" for full-time positions.

White related the decision of management to employ another full-time clerk in June, 1975. He testified that he normally was in the store two or three days each week, and that he took the place of one of the managers who was on vacation. During those times he was able to make comparative observations of the work of Anthony and Moran. He stated that it was his "considered opinion" that Anthony was "head and shoulders above Moran" in all aspects of work performance. When Ridgeway recommended Anthony for the full-time position, White fully concurred that he was the best man for the job, regardless of his seniority position.

In its closing arguments, the company contended that its selection from among the three highest seniority part-time employees was proof of its concern for seniority, even if it had not promoted the most senior person. The company noted that Section 9 of the agreement only required that the company "give consideration" to part-time employees in selecting full-time personnel, and that it was not required to promote the most senior part-time employee. Since the company was not prohibited by the agreement from hiring someone "off the street," the company should not be more severely constrained in considering part-time personnel than it was in hiring outsiders to full-time positions. The company maintained that the provisions of Section A of Article 9 only required the management to follow seniority in instances of layoffs and rehiring.

The company stated that it regarded the move to full-time status as a "promotion" because of health and benefit provisions and additional available hours of work. It refuted the union assertion that Anthony's new position was merely an increase in hours which should have been given to the part-time employee of highest seniority. Management also stated that the matter was not a disciplinary action requiring it to give notice to Moran of his deficiencies in order to provide him with full opportunity to improve his performance. The company maintained that having given consideration to seniority, it had the right to choose the person whom it considered best suited for the position.

Counsel for the company requested that the grievance be denied.

APPENDIX

Relevant Provisions of the Agreement

ARTICLE 9. SENIORITY

A. In layoffs and rehiring the principle of seniority shall apply. Seniority shall be defined as the length of continuous employment within the bargaining unit, with regard to an employee's experience and ability to perform the work. All circumstances being reasonably equal, length of service shall be the controlling factor. In the event a layoff, not in accordance with length of service is contemplated, the Employer shall first contact the Union and an attempt shall be made to arrive at a mutual solution. Part-time or casual employees shall not accumulate seniority over full-time employees. It is further agreed that part-time employees shall be given consideration for full-time job vacancies. Seniority shall prevail among employees in each store and shall apply to part-time and full-time employees respectively. In the event of transfer it is agreed that store seniority shall prevail. Any employee so transferred shall retain his seniority previously accumulated from the store from which he was transferred for a period of one (1) year. In the matter of promotions or transfers from one type of work to the other or from one store to the other, the Employer shall have the right to exercise his final judgment after giving due regard to seniority. Agreed upon seniority lists shall be established and maintained and such records shall be available to the Union at all times.

QUESTIONS

1. Evaluate the union contention that a change from part-time to full-time employment status was not a promotion, but rather a straight seniority claim to additional hours of work.
2. Even though employee Moran was not the "best man" for the full-time position, should the fact that he was a "satisfactory" employee entitle him to the full-time position because of his seniority? Discuss.
3. To what degree is the company's claim of previous practice persuasive in support of its position?
4. To what degree is the fact that the union had never grieved this particular type of situation a relevant factor?
5. Evaluate the provisions of the agreement which require the company to "give consideration" in moving employees from part-time to full-time status and to "give regard to seniority" in promotions or transfers.

58. TOO MUCH TELEPHONE TIME?

COMPANY: *County Sanitation Districts of Los Angeles County, Los Angeles, California*

UNION: *Los Angeles County Employees Association, Local 660*

BACKGROUND

Leo Harris[1] had been employed as a draftsman for the County Sanitation Districts of Los Angeles County since 1968. When Harris began working for the districts, employees were not represented by any type of collective-bargaining organization. However, in the fall of 1972 Los Angeles County Employees Association, Local 660, initiated a drive to obtain representational rights for the employees of the districts. In February 1973 Harris was made a union shop steward for Local 660, and in May 1973 the association was recognized as exclusive bargaining agent for represented employees of the Districts in a "Professional Employees Representative Unit." In August 1973 a "Memorandum of Understanding" was executed between the districts and the association which covered various aspects of employer-employee relations.

Harris, who was working as a senior engineering assistant in the Sewer Design Section at the time of the execution of the memorandum, had no direct involvement with that instrument's negotiations or drafting. However, later that year, he was elected as one of two representatives of the Professional Unit to serve as a negotiator for the association at "meet and confer" sessions being held with the districts for the purpose of drafting a successor memorandum of understanding. These sessions began in March 1974 and were held during work hours. However, internal meetings of the union negotiators during these sessions were only held outside of regular work hours. Harris fully participated in all of these meetings as a union negotiator.

---

[1] The names of all individuals have been disguised.

367

On May 4, 1974 while the "meet and confer" sessions were still uncompleted, Harris was assigned as a draftsman to a major project, Joint Outfall "F." At the time of his assignment, Harris was advised of the importance of the project and the necessity that the work be completed as scheduled.

For several years, the districts had maintained a policy "prohibiting any personal telephone calls on County phones," and had published several notices to that effect. However, although all employees were aware of it, management still had difficulty enforcing the policy. Management felt that Harris was particularly guilty of violation of the policy, and he had been warned on several occasions by his supervisors regarding his excessive use of the telephones.

On May 16, 1974 Assistant Section Head James Herd spoke to Harris, warning him that he was spending so much time on telephone calls of long duration that it was interfering with the drafting work necessary to keep Joint Outfall "F" on schedule. Later that same day, Herd prepared a memorandum to serve as a record of his warning to Harris. The memo stated:

This is to make record of my counseling Leo Harris on May 16, 1974 relative to excessive use of the telephone for what appeared to be personal business during working hours.

I felt that Harris was spending so much time on telephone calls of long duration that it was interfering with accomplishment of the necessary drafting of Joint Outfall "F," Unit 3B Relief Section 3, on schedule, and I told him so.

I counseled him that he was setting a bad example for other employees of the section in his use of the telephone on District time and that it should not continue.

I instructed Harris to take as much as one minute to tell incoming callers that he is busy and he will be able to talk after hours.

Through conscientious pursuit of their work, other draftsmen in the section of equal and lower salary than Harris out-produce him. The quality of his work is high and his understanding of our work is high. The problem is application.

When the memorandum came to the attention of Section Head Timothy McIntyre, he called Harris into his office and informed him that the document was to be inserted into his personnel file. Harris objected and immediately filed a grievance protesting the insertion of the memo into his file.

While involved in the grievance action, Harris scheduled an appointment with union attorneys concerning presentation of his complaint. On June 3 he advised Herd that he would be leaving work one-half hour early that day in order to discuss his grievance, and he was given permission to do so by Herd. However, management reserved the right of payment for that half-hour, and later charged Harris one-half hour of compensatory time. Harris then filed a second grievance seeking compensation for those lost wages, alleging that management had violated Paragraph 3 of Article XXIV of the Memorandum of Understanding (see Appendix).

The districts and union could not reach an agreement, and elected to submit the question to arbitration. Both parties agreed that there were three primary issues involved in the arbitration:

1. Was the County Sanitation Districts of Los Angeles County in violation of the Memorandum of Understanding effective September 12, 1973 when it placed a warning memorandum dated May 16, 1974 in the personnel file of Leo Harris?

2. Was the County Sanitation Districts of Los Angeles County in violation of the Memorandum of Understanding when it charged Leo Harris one-half hour of compensatory time on June 3, 1974?

3. If the answer to either or both of the foregoing inquiries is in the affirmative, what is the proper remedy?

POSITION OF THE UNION

The union claimed that the time Harris spent on the phone was an activity protected by Paragraph 3 of Article XXIV of the Memorandum of Understanding. It noted that the conversations in question occurred while negotiations were in progress and contended that Harris had a frequent need to call the Local 660 office for advice and guidance. The union also claimed that Harris had to respond to several telephone inquiries of fellow employees concerning the progress of contract negotiations. Prior to this, Harris had never been informed by management of any proscriptions in his exercise of the office of steward, including restrictions on phone calls.

Concerning Harris' second grievance, the union maintained that Harris was processing a grievance, albeit his own, but as a steward, he was entitled to do so "without loss of pay or benefits of any kind," as provided by Paragraph 3 of Article XXIV. It further maintained that Harris had satisfied the other requirements of informing his supervisor as required by Article XXIV, and he should not have been docked for the time spent in processing his grievance.

The union requested that the memorandum of May 16, 1974 be removed from Harris' file and he be made whole for the one-half hour's wages improperly denied him on June 3, 1974.

POSITION OF THE DISTRICTS

The districts maintained that the memorandum from Herd should be retained in Harris' file, since he had been warned on several previous occasions concerning his use of phones for private conversations. The districts claimed that Harris was thus on notice that he would be required to obtain the permission of a supervisor to use the phone for any purpose other than business of the districts; yet he continually failed to do so.

The districts further contended that no provision of the Memorandum of Understanding or other applicable law or agreement permitted the use of work time for the conduct of activities related to "meet and confer" sessions. Rather, the districts maintained that Article XXIV was the only applicable provision, and it was specifically restricted in application to stewards engaged in formal grievance actions.

In response to Harris' second grievance, the districts asserted that Article XXIV was not intended to afford stewards a right to compensation or benefits while involved in processing their own grievances. The districts requested that both grievances be denied.

APPENDIX

Relevant Provisions of the Memorandum of Understanding

ARTICLE X
NON-DISCRIMINATION

The parties mutually recognize and agree fully to protect the rights of all employees covered hereby to join and participate in the activities of Local 660 and all other rights of employees provided in Government Code.

The provisions of this Memorandum of Understanding shall be applied equally to all employees covered hereby without favor or discrimination because of race, color, sex, age, national origin, political or religious opinions or affiliations.

ARTICLE XXIV
STEWARDS

It is agreed and understood by the parties of this Memorandum of Understanding that there shall not be more than (8) stewards for this unit.

Local 660 shall give to the Personnel Manager six (6) copies of a written list of the names of employees selected as stewards, which list shall be kept current by Local 660.

Local 660 stewards may spend a reasonable amount of time to promptly and expeditously investigate and process formal grievances without loss of pay or benefits of any kind. Local 660 agrees, whenever processing of formal grievances is to be transacted during working hours, only that amount of time necessary to bring about a prompt disposition of the matter will be utilized. Stewards, when leaving their work locations to process formal grievances, shall first obtain permission from their immediate supervisor and inform him of the nature of the business. Permission to leave will be granted within a reasonable time unless such absence would cause an undue interruption of work. If such permission cannot be granted when requested, the steward will be informed when time will be made available. Such time will not be more than 24 hours, excluding Saturday, Sunday, and legal holidays, after the time requested by the steward, unless otherwise mutually agreed to.

Upon entering other work locations, the steward shall inform the cognizant supervisor of the nature of his business. Permission to leave the job will be granted to the employee involved unless such absence would cause an undue interruption of work. If the employee cannot be made available, the steward will be informed when the employee will be made available. Such time will not be more than 24 hours, excluding Saturday, Sunday, and legal holidays, after the time requested by the steward, unless otherwise mutually agreed to. Denial of permission for a steward to leave his work location or for an employee to meet with the steward will automatically constitute an extension of time equal to the delay.

Local 660 agrees that a steward shall not log compensatory time or premium pay time for time spent performing any function of a steward.

Except as provided in Article VI (Work Schedules), Section 5 (Emergencies), Management will not transfer a steward to a different work location without approval of the steward or Local 660 unless there no longer is work for the steward in his classification at his work location.

ARTICLE XXXIII
PROVISIONS OF LAW

It is understood and agreed that this Memorandum of Understanding is subject to all current and future applicable laws and Federal and State regulations. If any part or provision of this Memorandum of Understanding is in conflict or inconsistent with such applicable laws and regulations, or is otherwise held to be invalid or unenforceable by any tribunal of competent jurisdiction, such part or provision shall be suspended and superseded by such applicable laws or regulations, and the remainder of this Memorandum of Understanding shall not be affected thereby.

QUESTIONS

1. Was the time that the shop steward spent on the phone protected activity within the meaning of the Memorandum of Understanding? Why, or why not?
2. Did Article XXIV include the right of a shop steward to spend time in processing his own grievance? Discuss.
3. Would it be desirable for a company and union to negotiate specific time limits which a shop steward or union officer could spend on union business? Why, or why not?

59. THE RELUCTANT INSPECTOR

COMPANY: Dayton Tire and Rubber Company, Dayton, Ohio

UNION: United Rubber, Cork, Linoleum and Plastic Workers of America, Local 178

Earl Royce[1] was hired by the company on April 22, 1963 and was assigned to the Tire Inspection Department on April 29, 1964. He worked as a truck tire inspector in that department continuously from that date.

On July 20, 1973 Royce was temporarily assigned to the passenger tire production line as an inspector. This job required him to inspect each tire as it passed his station and stamp it so that all subsequent workers on the line would note that it had been examined and approved. Tires which were not stamped were rejected. Royce informed his supervisor prior to the transfer that he did not feel qualified to inspect passenger tires because all of his previous experience had been on the truck tire line. The company insisted, however, that he transfer to the passenger position on July 20. On that day, Royce's supervisor noticed that he was not stamping tires which were obviously satisfactory. The supervisor questioned Royce about his failure to examine and stamp the tires. Royce again informed management that he did not feel qualified to approve passenger tires. He told his supervisor that he was afraid, because of his inexperience in inspecting passenger tires, that he would pass a bad tire and would be disciplined for doing so.

The company subsequently suspended Royce on that day, July 20, pursuant to Rule 32(a) of the Shop Rules and Regulations established by the company which stated:

Insubordination; (a) Unexpressed refusal to comply with expressed instructions.

That evening the union initiated a strike relative to a disagreement

---

1 The names of all individuals have been disguised.

on the Pension and Insurance Contract, which lasted for ten days. On the first day on which the union returned to work, July 30, 1973, Royce was called to the office and given a three-day disciplinary layoff consisting of July 20, July 30, and July 31, based on violation of Shop Rule 32(a). Royce disagreed with their action and again informed management that he was not qualified as a passenger tire inspector.

The union filed the following "STATEMENT OF PROTEST" in Royce's behalf:

I do hereby protest my layoff by the Company as being unjust, and demand to be reinstated with full seniority rights, and back pay for all time lost from the job.

No satisfactory settlement was reached and the question was appealed to arbitration on November 12, 1973. The issue submitted by the parties was stated as follows:

Did the Company have just cause to impose a three day disciplinary layoff on the grievant Earl Royce, for an alleged violation of Shop Rule 32(a), and if not, to what remedy, if any, is the grievant entitled?

POSITION OF THE UNION

In the arbitration proceedings, the union argued that on several occasions prior to his transfer to the passenger line, Royce had informed his supervisors that he was not qualified to perform the passenger tire inspection, and that he had again brought this to the attention of his supervisors when they questioned his failure to stamp tires on July 20, 1973. His supervisor had warned him that he would be disciplined if he did not accept the transfer to the passenger tire line. Royce had felt trapped by the company: he would be disciplined if, through inexperience, he passed bad tires, and he would be disciplined if he refused to inspect and approve them.

The union contended that it was unsafe and unfair for the company to force an employee to leave his own job classification to which he was entitled under seniority provisions in order to work another job on a temporary assignment. It maintained that in such instances the company should take into consideration that some mistakes would occur.

The union also argued that Royce's failure to stamp the tires did not damage them in any way and did not cause the company any loss. Unstamped tires were returned for reinspection.

The union requested that the arbitrator order the company to pay

Royce for his three days of lost time and remove the reprimand from his record.

POSITION OF THE COMPANY

The company witnesses testified that Royce was temporarily transferred from truck tire inspection to the passenger line. Although they acknowledged there was a slight difference in inspection procedures between the two types, they explained that the jobs were similar, since inspectors searched for identical defects. The company contended that truck tire inspection required a more qualified individual. Management stated that Royce was expressly instructed to inspect and stamp those tires which he approved, and yet he refused to do so, even after such express directions.

The company maintained that Royce's refusal to obey the supervisor's instructions constituted insubordination in violation of Shop Rule 32(a) and that his suspension was justified. Management concluded that leniency was exercised in the issuance of a disciplinary lay-off, because Royce's offense could have been considered "express" insubordination, which is subject to more severe disciplinary measures.

QUESTIONS

1. Was the employee insubordinate within the meaning of the agreement and based on the circumstances of the case? Discuss.
2. Is an employee obligated to carry out an instruction of a supervisor which the employee believes is not safe?
3. If employee Royce had passed a bad passenger tire in this case situation, would he have been subject to discipline as he feared? Discuss.
4. Were there other alternatives open to the employee in this situation than the one which he chose to take?

60. THE "NO SPOUSE" RULE

COMPANY: *Dover Corporation, Norris Division, Tulsa, Oklahoma*

UNION: *United Steelworkers of America, Local 4430*

In the spring of 1974 while her husband was serving in the U.S. Army, Sally Jones[1] applied for a job at the Dover Corporation in Tulsa, Oklahoma. Her husband, Dave, had been employed at this plant prior to his induction into the service, and he was on a military leave of absence from his job. In making her application, Sally noted that she was the wife of Dave and that he was then stationed in Texas, as well as the fact that her father had also been an employee at the plant for several years, and was still so employed.

On April 15, 1974 Sally was hired by Dover as a warehouse carton maker, and her one month probationary period of employment began on that date. On May 15, 1974, the final day of the probationary term, John Allen, the company's Director of Industrial Relations, learned that Sally was married to Dave, and that he was on military leave of absence from the firm. He recognized that a potential problem might arise if Dave sought reinstatement to his old job with Dover. Federal law required that employers rehire employees inducted into military service if they so requested. However, if Dave sought reemployment upon his discharge, while Sally was still employed at the plant, a conflict would be created with the company's established policy of not employing spouses.

Because it was the end of her probationary period, Allen called Sally into his office that day to explain the potential conflict between her continued employment and the reinstatement of her husband. In arranging the meeting, Allen also asked Sally's father, Douglas Adams, and the local union president, Edward Smith, both of whom worked in the Dover plant, to attend. Adams was present, but Smith declined, saying that until the probationary period had ended, the union was

---

[1] The names of all individuals are disguised.

not in a position to alter any decision the company might make concerning Sally's employment.

At the meeting, Allen explained the "no spouse" policy and potential problem to Sally, and informed her that unless she agreed to voluntarily resign if her husband elected to return, a violation of the policy would occur. Sally said she understood the policy and its implications if her husband sought reemployment. She was then allowed to return to her job in the plant. No information was ever formally conveyed to the union concerning the proceedings of this meeting.

In July 1974, Dave Jones was discharged from the Army and returned to Dover seeking reinstatement to his former position. The company's personnel department then requested Sally's resignation, prior to her husband's return. However, Sally refused to tender her resignation. She was then terminated by the company at the end of the week prior to Dave Jones' return to his job. Sally immediately filed a grievance through the union alleging a violation of Article XXIV of the agreement (see Appendix) and seeking reinstatement and compensation for lost wages. The company denied the grievance charge, and the matter was submitted to arbitration. In coming before the arbitrator both parties essentially agreed that the issue in dispute was whether the termination of Sally Jones was for just cause, and if not, what was the proper remedy?

POSITION OF THE UNION

Sally Jones acknowledged that she had been made aware of the company's "no spouse rule" and its implications at the meeting with John Allen on May 15. She did understand that if her husband were reemployed at the plant, one of them could not remain with the company. However, she denied ever having agreed to voluntarily resign from her job if Dave sought reinstatement upon his discharge from the military service.

In arguing for Sally's reinstatement, the union contended that there was not just cause for Sally's termination. It denied any knowledge of the "no spouse rule," but contended that even if it had knowledge, it would be of no consequence in this case. The union agreed that it did not have any right or discretionary power in hiring practices or policies established by the company, as such were not covered in the collective bargaining agreement. However, it claimed that once an individual had been employed, and particularly after the probationary period, the employment decision of the company was of union concern and subject to the grievance procedure.

The union further argued that by allowing Sally to remain with the firm after becoming aware of her marital status and the potential conflict it presented, the company was precluded from dismissing her at some later date for violation of the "no spouse rule." The union thus contended there was insufficient just cause for Sally's dismissal.

POSITION OF THE COMPANY

John Allen testified that he had explicitly explained the "no spouse rule" to Sally Jones at the May 15, 1974 meeting. He had suggested that the most reasonable solution to the potential problem of a violation of the rule was for Sally to give her assurance to him that in the event her husband elected to return to his job, she would voluntarily resign. He testified that at the end of this meeting, he was convinced there would be no problem if such a situation arose, as he felt assured by Sally that she would tender her resignation and avoid any conflict. Allen stated that he allowed Sally to continue in her position, beyond the probationary period, based on that assurance.

The company contended the "no spouse rule" was a realistic rule which had been consistently applied. The rule was developed for good and sufficient business reasons and was a long-standing policy. Concerning Sally Jones, the rule became operative not when she was hired nor when she had the meeting with the Director of Industrial Relations, but rather at the time her husband sought his old job back. The company claimed her refusal to resign was just cause for the company to terminate her, because continued employment was contrary to an established policy of which she was fully aware.

The company argued that the union's attempt to have Sally reinstated to her position was tantamount to usurpation of management's rights to establish hiring rules and procedures, which were outside of the labor agreement. The union grievance should be denied.

APPENDIX

Relevant Provisions of the Agreement

ARTICLE XXIV
MANAGEMENT RIGHTS

The management of an Employer's business and the direction of the working force, including the right to hire, suspend or discharge for cause, or to transfer, to promote or demote, and the right to relieve employees from duty because of lack of work, (except as provided specifically in the Agreement) or for other legitimate reasons, is vested exclusively in the Employer; provided, however, that none of the powers herein reserved to the Employer shall be used for the purpose of discrimination because of an employee's membership in the Union.

QUESTIONS

1. Was the "no spouse" rule of the company a proper regulation under the sole jurisdiction of the company? Discuss.
2. Evaluate the union's role in not participating in the discussion which the employee had with company management while she was still a probationary employee.
3. Why do many companies have rules involving spouses and relatives such as the one in this case? Are such rules desirable from both a company and employee standpoint?
4. To what degree might a "no spouse" rule possibly be in violation of equal opportunity employment laws? Discuss.
5. Did the company's termination of the employee meet the requirements of just cause for discharge under the agreement? Discuss.

61. THE DISABLED BLOWER MOTOR

COMPANY: *Goodyear Atomic Corporation, Piketon, Ohio*

UNION: *Oil, Chemical and Atomic Workers International Union, Local 3–689*

On Monday, January 26, 1976 one of the three 50-horsepower electric motors powering high-pressure blowers developed a short circuit and required rewinding. The chief engineer estimated that 32 man-hours would be required to rewind the motor. The company sent the motor to an outside contractor, The National Coil Company, for repair. No standby motor was available while the repairs were made.

Before the motor was sent out, union steward Hugh Benfield[1] questioned the company's decision to have the work performed by an outside contractor rather than by employees of Department 711, Electrical Maintenance. He called the new contract language to the attention of the line foreman, George Lemson. He also told him that the union would file a grievance charging violation of Article XVI, Section 12,[2] if the work was not performed in Department 711.

The union's grievance was rejected by the company through all three steps of the grievance procedure. The company's reply to the union at the third step read as follows:

This grievance challenges the Company's interpretation of new contract language, Article XVI, Section 12.

The Union's position is that "fully utilized" as used in Section 12 means the use of overtime on all work which could be performed on plant-site that meets the criteria established in Section 12, rather than contracting out.

The Company does not agree that it negotiated any such concept in regard to Section 12. No member of the Company Negotiating Team can recall any conversation between the parties which could lead to such a conclusion.

---

[1] The names of all individuals are disguised.

[2] See Appendix.

As reviewed at the hearing, the Company notes reflect the following: "... Union representatives asked if the Company's opinion of offering as much work as possible to Goodyear Atomic Corporation employees is 40 hours a week." The notes further reflect that the Union representatives at one point stated, "... they wanted full utilization of employees plus some overtime."

As stated in Section 12, the Company will give "full consideration to using bargaining unit employees whenever possible."

The union and the company agreed that the issue to be submitted to the arbitrator should be, "Did the company violate Article XVI, Section 12, when it contracted out the rewinding of the electric motor in question?"

NEGOTIATING BACKGROUND

The company and union negotiated a new collective agreement in May 1975. In its original proposal on April 15 the union suggested the following language for the contracting-out provision:

The Company reserves the right to sub-contract work specifically, but without limitation, for new construction, installation and structural repair thereto. They will not, however, subcontract normal maintenance normally performed by the bargaining unit.

The company countered on April 24, 1975 with the following proposal:

The Company recognizes the desirability of full utilization of bargaining unit employees where sufficient qualified personnel are present, where time limits for job completion will permit, and where resources are available.

In response, the union resubmitted its original proposal on April 25, 1975, with a slight change in the second sentence as follows:

They will not, however, subcontract work normally performed by the bargaining unit.

The company countered on April 27, 1975, with the following proposal:

The Company reserves the right to subcontract, except that it will not subcontract work normally performed by the bargaining unit, for the express purpose of causing a reduction in force.

The company on the following day offered the provision which was adopted by both parties as the current Article XVI, Section 12.

While Article XVI, Section 12, is silent on the question of overtime, the parties briefly discussed overtime during their negotiations on April 23, 1975:

Henry Jenkins (company representative): I am not adverse to overtime to get a portion of the work done rather than let it out to contractors.

John Robertson (union representative): Our objective is to maintain our work even on an overtime basis as long as no law is violated.

Henry Jenkins (company representative): Hiring more people and adding them to the payroll for short periods of time to handle peak work loads and then laying them off could be a headache to both sides.

POSITION OF THE UNION

The union contended that employees of the electrical maintenance department daily and routinely rewound motors; that no special fixture for holding the motor was needed; and that the department possessed the space, equipment, and tools for doing the work.

The union pointed out that there were 135 to 140 electricians in the department, and that none was working overtime. The union argued that these employees, while working overtime, could have completed the repairs to the motor as quickly as the outside contractor. In fact, the disabled motor remained on the shop floor for two days before the outside contractor picked it up.

The union further contended that this case involved only one motor. The work did not require a large amount of extra work extending over a long period of time.

Finally, the union pointed out that the company, on occasions in the past, had assigned work on an overtime basis to electricians in cases such as this one. The contract anticipated that employees would be called upon to work overtime from time to time, as provided in Article X, Section 3(h) (see Appendix).

The union petitioned that those electricians in Department 711 who would have been assigned the rewinding of the blower motor be reimbursed for 32 hours work at the overtime rate of time and one-half.

POSITION OF THE COMPANY

The company replied that none of the electricians in Department 711 was on layoff and that all were working a full 40-hour week.

Under terms of the contract, this constituted the customary work week and represented "full utilization" of all personnel.

All qualified electricians were at that time assigned priority rewinding jobs, utilizing all rewinding stands and equipment. It was not desirable to delay any of the priority work, nor was it possible to delay the repairs to the blower motor. For these reasons, the company made the decision to send the motor to an outside contractor for rewinding.

The company argued that while Article XVI, Section 12, permitted the company to utilize overtime in order to avoid contracting out work, the company was not required to do so in order to keep the work within Department 711. The company cited Article IV of the contract to support its right.

Finally, the company argued that it contracted out the work in good faith and that its actions were reasonable under all the circumstances. It urged that the grievance be denied.

APPENDIX

Relevant Provisions of the Agreement

ARTICLE XVI
Section 12   (Utilization of Workforce)

The Company recognizes a responsibility to fully utilize all its employees; and will not subcontract work without giving full consideration to using bargaining unit employees whenever possible where time limits for job completion will permit, where sufficient qualified personnel are present and where resources are available.

ARTICLE IV
(Management Rights)

. . . The direction of the workforce, the establishment of plant policies, the determination of the processes and means of manufacture, the units of personnel required to perform such processes, and other responsibilities incidental to the operation of the plant are vested in the Company. . . . The exercise of such authority shall not conflict with the rights of the Union under the terms of this Contract.

ARTICLE X
Section 3(h)   (Hours of Work)

. . . The provisions of this Contract shall not be considered as a guarantee by the Company of a minimum number of hours per day or per week or pay in lieu thereof, nor a limitation on the maximum hours per day or per week which may be required to meet operating conditions.

QUESTIONS

1. To what degree is the negotiating background information surrounding Article XVI, Section 12, germane to the arbitration issue?

2. What is meant by the term "fully utilize" within Article XVI, Section 12? Does this provision require the company to work bargaining unit personnel on an overtime basis, rather than to subcontract?

3. Different arbitrators have utilized varying standards in applying provisions such as Article XVI, Section 12. What types of standards might be appropriate for interpreting this and similar clauses?

4. Compare the circumstances of this case with the case of "Subcontracted Heaters" case [Case No. 62 following].

62. THE SUBCONTRACTED HEATERS

COMPANY: *Tecumseh Products Company, Somerset Compressor Division, Somerset, Kentucky*

UNION: *International Brotherhood of Electrical Workers, Local 2360*

On November 22, 1974 twenty-nine employees of Tecumseh Products Company filed the following griveance:

The Company is in direct violation of Article XIX Paragraph 138 of the current labor agreement. Adjustment desired—maintenance dept. employees be paid for all hours worked by outside plumbing contractors; and electrical employees be paid for all hours worked by outside electrical contractors. Plus this action be stopped immediately.

The company denied the grievance, charging that it had not been properly filed because part of the work identified in the grievance had not been contracted out until after the grievance had been filed. It also argued that, even if the grievance had been properly filed, the company was within its rights to contract out the work under terms of the contract.

BACKGROUND

The Compressor Division manufactures small compressors for air conditioners, water coolers, and dehumidifiers. The company engaged two subcontractors in November 1974 to perform certain plumbing and electrical work in the plant. One of them, Brown Brothers, was engaged to install two industrial-type wash basins in the washroom (each basin is about six feet in diameter and can serve about ten persons simultaneously). It also contracted to install a new restroom for truckers and a drinking fountain and waste disposal basin in the cafeteria.

The second subcontractor, Whitaker Electric Company, completed the installation of large high-voltage, industrial-type electric heating units in the heating ducts servicing the office area.

The union protested that all of this work should have been performed by the Maintenance Department employees and should not have been subcontracted.

TIMELINESS OF THE GRIEVANCE

Position of the Company

The company argued that the union's grievance referred to work that had not been contracted out at the time the grievance was filed on November 22, 1974. The company offered in evidence a copy of purchase order No. SA18845, dated December 13, 1974. This purchase order completed the contract between Whitaker Electric and the company to install electric heaters. The company cited Paragraph 31 of the contract which stated in part:

All grievances must be presented at this step within five (5) days of occurrence, otherwise it shall be deemed not to exist and shall have no merit.

Position of the Union

The union argued that various employees had observed preparations to perform certain plumbing and electrical work about the middle of November. One employee, Ronald Blanton,[1] working on the second shift, asked his foreman about the preparations. His foreman told him that the work was being subcontracted to Whitaker. At that point, the union filed a grievance. The union claimed that it would be unrealistic to expect it to undertake a complete study of the company's records and then make a legal determination of when a contract had been agreed upon before filing a grievance. The union requested that the filing date of the grievance be ruled timely, and that the grievance apply to all the plumbing and electrical work described above.

THE RIGHT TO CONTRACT OUT WORK

Position of the Union

The union contended that maintenance employees were qualified to perform the plumbing and electrical work contracted out. They

---

[1] The names of all individuals are disguised.

had on prior occasions performed such work, and had already completed some of the work in question before the subcontractors came in and took over the jobs. They had, in fact, redone some of the work on both the electrical and plumbing contracts after the outside contractors left.

The union also maintained that if the company had originally assigned the work to the maintenance employees, they could have completed it within the company's time requirements, especially if they had been assigned the work on an overtime basis. The company could have completed both projects at less cost employing maintenance employees on an overtime basis then by contracting out the work.

The union further argued that the company violated Article XIX, Paragraph 138, which restricts Article III, Paragraphs 17 and 18 (see Appendix).

The union asked that the 29 employees signing the grievance be reimbursed for all hours worked by outside contractors and that such subcontracting cease.

Position of the Company

The company argued that the work performed by the subcontractors was not "standard production work regularly performed by Bargaining Unit employees."

The company further argued that the necessary manpower was not "readily available" to complete the work "within the projected time limits" (see Appendix, Article XIX, Paragraph 138). The normal work of the maintenance employees was first and foremost to maintain the production machinery. If any time were left, it might be utilized on other projects including those of the type performed by these two subcontractors.

The company pointed out that the plumbing work was done to satisfy employee complaints that the washroom facilities were inadequate. The work had been scheduled to be performed by maintenance employees, but it did not progress fast enough because top priority was always given to the maintenance of production machinery and equipment. As the end of the budget year, December 31, approached, it became urgent to finish the job. Such installations could not be characterized as "regular" because there are not that many commodes and wash basins to be installed in a plant.

The installation of the heaters was urgent as the winter season approached. The two old gas heaters which had previously provided heat for the offices had failed. The work had to be performed after the regular office hours because of the noise in the heating ducts.

To have taken maintenance men from their regular work to finish these two projects would have resulted in down time on production lines because of failure to do necessary maintenance and repair work on production machinery.

The company further pointed out that there were no maintenance employees on layoff, and that all were working at least 40 hours per week and some were working overtime during the period the subcontractors were working.

Finally, the company contended that no provision required the company to provide any specific amount of overtime to any employees. The three employees best qualified to perform the subcontracted work all had refused or been unavailable for overtime assignment to the work in question. The first, a licensed plumber, had regularly refused overtime assignments; the second had other outside employment on Saturdays when much of the work was performed; the third regularly worked overtime in the plant repairing machines during the time they were shut down.

The company requested that in the event the arbitrator ruled the grievance was timely, the grievance should be denied as to its merits.

APPENDIX

The Bargaining Unit as defined by the National Labor Relations Board, Certification of Representation:

All production and maintenance employees at the Employer's Somerset, Kentucky location, excluding all office clerical employees, professional employees, guards and supervisors as defined in the Act.

Relevant Provisions of the Contract

ARTICLE I
RECOGNITION

Paragraph 1. The Company recognizes the Union as the exclusive representative for its employees as defined in Paragraph 2 below for the purpose of collective bargaining with respect to wages, hours, or other conditions of employment in the bargaining unit which they have been so certified by the National Labor Relations Board in accordance with the provisions of the applicable state and federal laws.

Paragraph 2. For the purpose of this Agreement, the term "employee" shall include factory employees employed at the Company's Compressor Division located in Somerset, Kentucky, excluding all salaried employees, office and clerical employees, plant protection employees, supervisory employees, foremen, assistant foremen, foreladies, professional employees, sales and engineering employees and lab technicians.

ARTICLE III
MANAGEMENT RIGHTS AND RESPONSIBILITIES

Paragraph 17. Except as expressly and specifically limited to or restricted by a provision of this Agreement, the Company has and shall retain the full right of management and direction of the plant and its operations. Such rights of management include the right to plan, direct, control, increase, or decrease operations; to determine the products to be manufactured; to shift products manufactured, processes, or types of work or methods in and out of the plant; to subcontract work, except as in Paragraph 138, to change machinery, methods, and facilities, or introduce new methods, techniques and/or machines and products; to establish and enforce rules and regulations; to discipline and discharge employees for just causes; to assign, change, add to or reduce the number of shifts, the schedules to be worked and the work force; to determine who it shall hire, the number of employees it shall employ at any time and the qualifications necessary for any jobs; to determine policies affecting the selection and training of new employees; to assign work duties, transfer employees; to set reasonable standards in accordance with its determination of the needs of the job and the operation. The Company reserves the right to move, sell, close, liquidate, or consolidate the plant in whole or in part.

It is expressly understood and agreed that all rights heretofore exercised by the Company or inherent in the Company as the owner of the business or as an incident to the management not expressly contracted away by specific provisions of this Agreement are retained solely by the Company. Any rights granted to or acquired by the employees or the Union under this Agreement or during its life shall have no application beyond the term of this Agreement or any renewal thereof.

Paragraph 18. It is agreed that the reserved management rights as set forth in this Agreement, including the foregoing paragraph, shall not be subject to arbitration or impairment by an arbitration award under this Agreement unless expressly contracted away or modified by a specific provision of this Agreement.

ARTICLE IV

Paragraph 29. For the purpose of this Agreement, the term "grievance" shall be limited to any dispute between the Company and the Union or between the Company and an employee concerning the application or violation of the provisions of this Agreement.

ARTICLE VI

Paragraph 37. The arbitrator so selected shall schedule a prompt hearing at which time he shall have the power to make determinations of fact on the questions submitted to him and apply them to the provisions of the Agreement alleged to have been violated so long as the grievance is submitted to him in accordance with the provisions, limitations, and procedures specified in this Agreement. No arbitrator shall have the jurisdiction or authority to add to, take from, nullify, or modify any of the terms of this Agreement, or to impair any of the rights reserved to Management under the terms hereof, either directly or indirectly, under the guise of interpretation; nor shall he have the power to substitute his discretion for that of Management in any manner where the Management has not contracted away its right to exercise discretion.

The arbitrator shall be bound by the facts and evidence submitted to him and may not go beyond the terms of this Agreement in rendering his decision. No such decision may include or deal with any issue or matter which is not expressly made subject to the terms of this Agreement. The decision of the arbitrator shall be in writing and shall be final and binding upon the parties when rendered upon a matter within the authority of the arbitrator.

ARTICLE XIX

Paragraph 138. It is the Company policy that standard production work regularly performed by Bargaining Unit employees will not be contracted to a source outside of the Tecumseh Products Company, provided that the necessary manpower, equipment and facilities are readily available and the work can be performed in an efficient, economic and competitive manner as related to quality, quantity, cost and performance within the projected time limits necessary to complete the work involved.

QUESTIONS

1. Was the grievance a timely grievance which was appropriately placed before the arbitrator? Why, or why not?
2. Evaluate Article XIX in comparison to Article III. Which Article is superior in nature?
3. Was the plumbing work standard production work regularly performed by bargaining unit employees? Discuss.
4. Compare the circumstances of this case with the subcontracting issue involved in the "Disabled Blower Motor" case [Case No. 61, preceding].

63. A LUMP ON THE LEG

COMPANY: *Orgill Brothers and Company, Memphis, Tennessee*

UNION: *United Steelworkers of America, Local 2360*

At about 10:45 a.m. on August 20, 1975 a security guard, Alice Mulvey,[1] stationed near a high-security area of the company warehouse noticed a box-shaped bulge on the back of the left leg below the knee of employee George Porter. The bulge measured approximately three inches by five inches and was about one inch high. This high-security area contained small items such as tools, watches, fishing reels, and appliances. The guard suspected that Porter might be attempting to pilfer some of these goods, and reported what she had observed to her supervisor at approximately 11:25 a.m. Immediately the supervisor informed the assistant warehouse manager, Henry Caldwell. Caldwell decided to search Porter's person and, with Nick Fox, the stock operations manager, overtook Porter in the parking lot as he was leaving for lunch at 11:30 a.m. Porter had punched out on the time clock and was on his way to have lunch with his wife who was waiting in a car in the lot. Caldwell asked Porter what he had hidden in the left leg of his pants and requested that he raise his pantleg. Porter denied having anything concealed, and protested that he had submitted to a search once before but would not do so again. He then proceeded to his car and left with his wife. Upon returning from lunch, Porter invited the union president and several other employees to examine his left leg, and nothing was found in his boot or sock.

On August 22, 1975 Porter was terminated by the company for refusal to submit to the search when ordered to do so by Caldwell. Porter immediately filed a grievance which stated:

August 22, 1975

I the undersigned am seeking reinstatement with full restitution for being fired without proper cause. On 8–20–75 I was told to stop and let

---

[1] The names of all individuals have been disguised.

Nicholas Fox and Henry Caldwell search me. This has happened before, so when they told me to stop, I stopped, but I didn't let them search me. I was fired on 8–22–75 for alleged theft and disobeying a direct order.

Ultimately the grievance was submitted to arbitration, where the issue in question was whether the company had just cause and had acted reasonably in discharging Porter for his refusal to submit to the search. (See Appendix for Article III, Section 4 of the agreement.)

BACKGROUND

Orgill Brothers was a wholesale hardware distributor dealing in many types of products. The company maintained inventories of many small items such as watches, pocket calculators, lighters, fishing reels, and other goods which are particularly susceptible to theft. In recent years, the company had suffered severe theft problems from its warehouse facilities, and estimated annual theft losses in 1974 were over $250,000. In an attempt to rectify this problem, the company established high-security areas in which small items were kept under lock and key. Guards were stationed in the warehouse; security boxes were used for filling orders; metal detectors were installed; undercover agents employed; and a $300 reward offered to anyone presenting evidence of theft. The company also adopted a strict policy prohibiting lunch boxes, packages, and purses in the warehouse area, and instituting inspection by guards of all such items leaving the facility. Management personnel also required anyone suspected of stealing to submit to a search.

The union had cooperated with the company in its efforts to stop the thefts, and agreed that an employee might be searched if "probable cause" existed and discharged for theft.

Porter had been searched once prior to August 20, 1975 and subsequently filed a grievance for what he alleged was an unwarranted search of his person.

POSITION OF THE UNION

The union based its argument against Porter's discharge on several points:

1. Although concurring that the company may require an employee to submit to a search, the union argued that the company must have "probable cause" for such an action. In this instance, the union contended that management did not have probable cause for subject-

ing Porter to a search. The union president testified that it was only the size of the bulge which gave rise to "reasonableness" and "probable cause." In this instance, Porter stated that he kept a package of cigarettes on the side of his left leg. Thus, the union argued, the company did not have a reasonable and probable cause to suspect theft.

2.   The union contended that Caldwell's accosting of Porter in the parking lot in front of his wife and other employees was demeaning and embarrassing and totally unreasonable under the circumstances. Porter testified that he felt harassed at being subjected to a second search, and he was embarrassed at being confronted in a public place. He also noted that at the time of Caldwell's request he was outside of the warehouse and on his lunch break.

3.   The union argued that the company violated the collective bargaining agreement by attempting to search Porter without a union representative being present. The union cited Section 2 which is the recognition clause of the collective bargaining agreement, and Section 6, the "adjustment of a grievance" clause, which states ". . . or should any local trouble of any kind arise in the plant there shall be no suspension of work on account of such differences, but an earnest effort shall be made to settle such differences in the following manner . . ." A stipulation follows that in any such local trouble, a "union representative shall be present during the efforts to resolve the problem."

4.   The union contended that the company had never before discharged employees who refused to be searched, and that the penalty of discharge was too severe and violated past practice. The union presented as evidence several letters from the company to various employees, written in 1970, warning them that if they again refused to be searched they would be discharged. This was only Porter's first refusal to be searched, and he had submitted to a search previously.

POSITION OF THE COMPANY

Management maintained that it had acted properly and reasonably in discharging Porter for his refusal to be searched. It based its arguments on several points:

1.   The company contended that it was a long-standing past practice to conduct searches based on probable cause, and that the union had concurred in such actions. It cited previous acceptance and approval by the union of management searches. It also countered the

union presentation of the warning letters of 1970 by explaining that at that time the company had an established system of conducting random searches of employees, but since that time had changed to a policy of searching only in cases of "probable cause."

2. The company argued that in Porter's case, Caldwell did have reasonable and probable cause to conduct a search. Management contended that a person of reasonable caution who observed a box-shaped bulge on someone's leg could logically conclude that a theft was being perpetrated and take appropriate action. In this case, it would not be extraordinary procedure or harassment to request Porter to submit to a search in light of the extensive and established security program in the warehouse.

3. Porter made no attempt to explain what he was carrying nor to discuss it with management. If he did have a pack of cigarettes on the side of his left leg, it would have taken little effort to disprove Caldwell's suspicions. Porter did not request to have a union representative present, but simply walked to his car and departed.

4. The discharge was reasonable and warranted under the circumstances. The company argued that for its security policies to be effective, refusal to submit to a search must be considered serious enough to warrant dismissal. Refusal to submit to a search indicated complete lack of cooperation and disloyalty to the employer, and that the employee had something to hide. If an employee was caught with stolen goods, he would be discharged. If lesser penalties were established for failure to submit to a search, thieves, caught in the act, could avoid termination by refusing to comply with the search request.

The company requested that its discharge action be sustained, and the union grievance denied.

APPENDIX

Relevant Provisions of the Agreement

ARTICLE III—SENIORITY

Sec. 4. An employee shall lose his seniority rights and his employment is terminated:

A. If he quits or is discharged for just cause.

QUESTIONS

1. Did the company have reasonable and probable cause to request the employee to subject himself to a personal search? Discuss.

2. Was the employee within his rights to refuse to be searched?

3. What other alternatives were open to employee Porter given the circumstances of the ultimatum given to him by the company?

4. To what degree is the issue of past practice an important consideration in both the union and company positions? Discuss.

5. Why does a case involving suspected or actual theft pose a difficult dilemma for a labor union in representing a grievant who is accused of such behavior?

64. THE CAR POOL AND THE OVERTIME REFUSAL

COMPANY: *American Can Company, New Orleans, Louisiana*

UNION: *International Association of Machinists and Aerospace Workers, Crescent City Lodge No. 37*

BACKGROUND

Harold Franklin[1] began working at the New Orleans plant on August 10, 1966, as a maintenance helper on the 11:30 p.m.–7:30 a.m. shift. At the time of this case in 1974, he was working as a millwright on the 3:30 p.m.–11:30 p.m. shift. He lived in Picayune, Mississippi, a small town 55 miles from New Orleans.

In March 1974, during the course of a national energy crisis precipitated by a boycott initiated by the Oil Producing Exporting Countries (OPEC), the company posted a notice which read:

Car Pool—With the objective in mind of bringing together those persons who may, because of the present circumstances, be interested in joining or forming a car pool, we wish to offer the services of the Personnel Department.

Those interested please contact the Personnel Department where a form is available. These forms will be reviewed by the Personnel Department and persons living in similar regions of the city will be supplied with information to assist in forming a car pool.

On April 9, 1974 Franklin told his foreman, John Brodie, that he could not work four hours overtime because he was in a car pool. Franklin refused overtime assignments on six other occasions during April, May, June, and July. Each time he gave car pooling as his reason, and each time Brodie advised him that car pooling was not an acceptable reason for refusing to work overtime, although he was

---

[1] The names of all individuals have been disguised.

not required to work overtime in any of those instances. On Monday, August 12, 1974 when Franklin again refused overtime, he was given a three-day suspension.

In giving the suspension, the company cited Article 4, Section 4, "Overtime Notice," from the agreement, which reads as follows:

Local Management will give notice of daily overtime assignments as far in advance as practicable, and, to the extent customer demands are known, will give notice of weekend overtime assignments in accordance with present practices but in no event later than the end of the employee's shift on the preceding Thursday.

Local Management will consider any reasonable request of an employee to be excused from overtime work, but in any event will excuse an employee from overtime on occasions where the working of overtime would cause the employee hardship or serious inconvenience.

The union filed a grievance on behalf of Harold Franklin, contending that the company violated Article 4, Section 4, of the agreement. The union requested that the company remove records pertaining to the suspension from Franklin's file and reimburse him for 24 hours pay.

POSITION OF THE UNION

The union claimed that the company's actions during the April–August [1974] period were designed to place Franklin under heavy duress. It claimed that the most recent incident of August 12 arose when foreman Brodie asked Franklin to stay overtime, since millwright Paul Renaldi would not be in on the third shift because of illness. Franklin refused to work overtime because of car pooling. Brodie then asked the senior millwright, Henry Vaccaro, who reluctantly agreed to work. This incident could have been avoided, according to the union, had Brodie followed the standard procedure of offering overtime to the senior employee first. Furthermore, since the foreman knew of the overtime assignment before the end of the first shift at 3:30 p.m., and since the work could have been performed at any time during the second shift, he could have asked one of the millwrights who was working on the first shift, 7:30 a.m.–3:30 p.m., to stay over an extra four hours. Alternatively, Brodie could have called in a third shift millwright who worked the 11:30 p.m.–7:30 a.m. shift to start four hours early.

The union cited other incidents which it contended were designed to place Franklin under extreme pressure:

1.   On April 30 Franklin was asked to work overtime. He refused because of car pooling. The foreman then asked George Chapin, the senior employee, to work. Chapin, as the senior employee, should have been asked first.

2.   On May 14 the foreman wanted Franklin to work on equipment outside his normal work area. Only after he declined did the foreman ask Vaccaro, the senior millwright in that area, to work.

3.   On May 21 Franklin was asked to work overtime in case Paul Renaldi, a third shift millwright, would be unable to work. The foreman could have avoided the entire problem by telephoning Renaldi who was able to come to work and who did so.

4.   On three other occasions, June 10, June 27, and July 8, Franklin refused overtime because of car pooling. On each occasion senior employees were asked to stay over and did so upon request. No work time was lost because of his refusal to work overtime.

The union argued that Franklin began car pooling at the suggestion of the company, who looked upon it as a means for conserving natural energy resources and lessening travel costs for employees. The company encouraged Franklin to car pool. Now that he had done it, he should not be penalized by the company, which must have anticipated the potential conflict between working overtime and car pooling.

The union maintained that Franklin always worked scheduled overtime when he really was needed by the company. However, it further contended that under Article 4, Section 4, Franklin could refuse overtime work when it could cause him "hardship or serious inconvenience." Missing a ride home, especially when home is 55 miles away, would certainly cause hardship or serious inconvenience.

Finally, this clause had been in the contract only one year, and this was the first grievance that had arisen under it. Both company and union representatives have had difficulty in interpreting it. Franklin should, in any event, be given the benefit of the doubt.

POSITION OF THE COMPANY

The company countered the union's contention that employees could have been called in for overtime work from either the first or second shift on August 12. According to the company, there was only one millwright on the third shift; he had already been called in early and was working when Franklin was asked to stay over. Thus, there was no one to call in from the third shift. Similarly, employees who had worked the first shift had already worked eight hours during the day. To recall them for four hours would require that they work from 11:30 p.m. to 3:30 a.m., thereby effectively eliminating their sleep for that night. In four more hours they would have to report for their regular shift at 7:30 a.m. The company maintained that it had acted reasonably in asking Franklin to work.

The company stated that foreman Brodie asked Franklin to work overtime only after the senior millwright, Paul Vaccaro, had been asked and had declined. Vacarro finally agreed to work after Franklin adamantly refused to do so. The company followed the standard and accepted procedure in assigning overtime work in this and all previous assignments. The union had attempted to inject the issue of discrimination into a situation where none existed.

It was the company's position that it complied with Article 4, Section 4, in asking Franklin to work overtime. Foreman Brodie considered Franklin's request to be excused from working overtime by soliciting Paul Vaccaro to work. A company representative stated, "We believe very strongly that the excuse offered by Franklin, under all the circumstances present here, does not justify his being excused from overtime on the grounds that it would cause him hardship or serious inconvenience within the meaning of Article 4, Section 4."

The company expressed the belief that it had the right to expect employees to work a reasonable amount of overtime, and that employees had a corresponding obligation to do so. It further expressed the belief that employees should not be compelled to work overtime unless it was necessary. On a number of occasions prior to August 12, Franklin had been excused from overtime to accommodate his car pooling. On each of these occasions, however, he was told that since he was the junior millwright, it was very likely that he would be required to work overtime in the future and must make some arrangements to provide for this.

The company pointed out that Franklin admitted to having been told at least three times, and possibly more often prior to August 12, that car pooling would not be accepted as a reason for refusing overtime, and that he would face disciplinary action if he refused on that basis. He consulted with the union on each of these occasions. The union erroneously informed him that he did not have to work overtime. The company argued that employees who disregarded the company's instructions and relied upon the union's interpretation of the contract did so at their own risk. They could not later take refuge in the argument that they were never notified that the company considered their actions cause for discipline.

The company denied that it encouraged Franklin to car pool and thus was prohibited from disciplining him for having acted upon that suggestion. Franklin was car pooling with three other employees from Picayune prior to the memorandum issued by the company, and he was not influenced by the memorandum. In addition, the company contended that the letter neither encouraged nor discouraged car pooling. It was an offer to assist those employees who wished to car pool. The decision to car pool or not car pool was an individual one. Any employee electing to participate in a car pool had to consider the obligation to work overtime when making that decision. In Franklin's case, the company repeatedly advised him to make alternate arrangements for those rather limited occasions when he might be required to work overtime.

The company noted that many of its employees car pooled, but they also worked a reasonable amount of overtime when requested. Franklin was the only employee who had found this to be a problem. Employees may live wherever they wish and they may make whatever travel arrangements they find most convenient. But, in exercising these choices they cannot negate the company's right to expect a reasonable amount of overtime and they cannot invoke Article 4, Section 4 to avoid their responsibility to work overtime. This article does not mean that Franklin had a right to be excused from working overtime.

The company claimed that its three-day disciplinary suspension meted upon Harold Franklin was reasonable under the circumstances and maintained that the union grievance should be dismissed.

QUESTIONS

1. Was the car pool an acceptable reason for the employee to refuse to work overtime given the circumstances of this case? Why, or why not?

2. Evaluate the meaning of the term "hardship or serious inconvenience" within Article 4, Section 4. Why would company and union representatives be likely to disagree in interpreting this provision?

3. Does a company normally have the right to expect employees to work overtime unless specifically prohibited by a labor agreement? Discuss.

4. Why would the union tell the employee that he did not have to work overtime? Should an employee be disciplined for following the instructions of the union leadership? Why, or why not?

5. Some companies have adopted flexible work scheduling which permits employees to choose their starting and ending times within certain limits. Would such arrangements mean that a company could not require an employee to work overtime?

65. THE DISPUTED HOLIDAY PAY

COMPANY: *Rheem Manufacturing Company, Fort Smith, Arkansas*

UNION: *United Steelworkers of America, Local 7893*

BACKGROUND

David Koss[1] was an assembler in the Utility Department of Rheem's heating and air-conditioning equipment manufacturing plant located at Fort Smith, Arkansas. In accordance with the provisions of the collective agreement between the union and the company, the plant closed down Thursday and Friday, November 22–23, 1973 for the Thanksgiving holiday. Koss was scheduled to return to work on Monday, November 26.

However, on Sunday evening, November 25, Koss became very ill with diarrhea and nausea. His wife, that evening, telephoned the family physician who prescribed medication and treatment. While his condition improved, he was unable to report back to work on Monday the 26th. Mrs. Koss attempted to contact the personnel director early that morning to inform him of her husband's illness. The party line was very busy, however, and she was unable to reach the personnel office until almost 11:00 a.m. She was finally able to contact Ms. Elizabeth Jackson, a nurse in the department and inform her that Koss would be absent from work that day because of illness. At the same time she inquired about the effect that his absence would have on his right to receive payment for the previous Thursday and Friday, both of which were designated in the collective agreement as paid holidays. Jackson informed her that his foreman might request a "doctor's slip" to substantiate his claim for missing work on Monday.

Jackson then transferred her to Charles Bigham, assistant personnel director, to provide more precise information about the conditions for receiving holiday pay. Bigham informed her that according to

---

[1] The names of all individuals have been disguised.

Article XIII, Paragraph 2(c) of the agreement,[2] an employee was required to work both the last work day before and the first work day following a paid holiday in order to be eligible to receive the pay benefits. Thus, he informed her that Koss would have to work that day, Monday, to be eligible for the holiday pay for the previous Thursday and Friday. She informed her husband of Bigham's explanation, but he was unable to report to work until Tuesday, November 27, 1973.

Upon reporting to his job on Tuesday, Koss explained his Monday absence to his supervisor, Henry Ryan, and inquired about his holiday pay. Ryan told him that his only hope for receiving holiday pay lay in presenting a "doctor's excuse." He then sent Koss to the personnel office, where Bigham informed him that he would not receive payment for the two holidays because he did not work on the next scheduled work day following the holiday. Koss, nevertheless, following his supervisor's recommendation, submitted a physician's statement concerning his illness to the personnel department on Thursday, November 29. This note stated:

> To whom it may concern: This is to signify that David Koss was under my care from November 25 through November 26.

After receiving the physician's statement, Bigham again told Koss that he was ineligible for holiday pay due to the company's strict interpretation of Article XIII, Paragraph 2(c) of the agreement.

While discussing the loss of his holiday pay later that week with Dale Edie, another employee in Koss's division, Koss learned that Edie had received holiday pay for the Thanksgiving holidays, despite the fact that he had worked only a few hours on Monday, November 26. Edie related that he had called in sick on Monday morning and was told that he was required to work that day in order to receive holiday pay. He then reported to work. He was unable to complete the shift and went home after a few hours. Koss felt that he, too, had a case for receiving the holiday pay, and on December 5, 1973 the union filed the following grievance:

> This grievance is pertaining to Mr. Koss not receiving holiday pay for November 22 and 23, 1973.
>
> On November 26, 1973, D. Koss missed work due to being under doctor's care, the 26th during the next working day after the holiday in question. The settlement requested is that Mr. Koss be paid his holiday pay.

---

[2] See Appendix.

Included on the grievance form was a union allegation that the company had also violated Article XIII, Paragraph 2(g) of the agreement.[3]

The company made the following reply to the union's grievance:

Mr. Koss did not request, nor was he granted sick leave. In order to qualify for holiday pay due to sickness, the sick leave must be approved by the Company and the holiday must fall within the thirty calendar days of the approved sick leave.

The parties were not able to resolve their differences and the grievance was submitted to arbitration.

POSITION OF THE UNION

The union stated that David Koss was actually ill on Monday, November 26, 1973, and submitted the physician's statement as verification of such. The company did not contest this assertion.

Koss had been employed at the Rheem plant since the fall of 1970. He had a good employment record during these three years. He was a good worker; he had never been disciplined for any reason; and he had been absent for only a few days because of illness during that period.

The union contended that the company had not been consistent in requiring employees to work on the scheduled work day following a holiday in order to receive holiday pay. It cited the case of Dale Edie's receipt of holiday pay while having worked only a few hours on Monday, November 26. The union also noted a similar incident involving Loretta Smith, who had received full holiday pay even though she had been permitted to leave work early on Monday, November 26, to attend to a family problem regarding relatives who had arrived in town but could not find her home. The union mentioned that situations such as the two cited indicated that the company administered its holiday pay policy inconsistently. The administration of policies such as this one should not be left to the sole discretion of management; the interests of employees should be protected and the circumstances surrounding each situation should be considered, thus ensuring a more equitable decision-making process.

The union maintained that holiday pay is an "earned benefit" to which employees are entitled. It argued that as an "earned benefit" the provisions of Article XIII, Paragraph 2(g) should govern the

---

3 See Appendix.

employee's right to receive the benefit. The union contended that if an employee were actually sick and could provide a physician's statement verifying his or her illness, the employee should be considered qualified for sick leave under Article XIII, Paragraph 2(g) and be given the benefits commensurate with such leave. This was based on the contention that a physician, rather than the company, is most properly qualified to determine whether or not an employee is too ill to work. An employee who is sick should be provided the benefits specified under the sick leave provisions. Thus, under Article XIII, Paragraph 2(g), Koss would be entitled to holiday pay since a physician had verified his illness and that paragraph provides for an employee to be paid for holidays falling within the first thirty days of sick leave. The union maintained that to allow the company sole discretion to grant or withhold holiday pay without considering a physician's opinion provided it with too great an opportunity to apply the policy in a discriminatory manner.

In support of its claim that the company had not followed customary practices in handling Koss's case, the union noted that this was the first grievance of this type which it had filed. The union claimed that if management had consistently refused to grant claims such as Koss's, there would have been many more grievances since the current agreement was enacted on August 1, 1971.

In a posthearing brief, the union submitted the essence of its argument as follows:

It does not seem ethical that we would negotiate language where illness and injury for work on a holiday would be reasons for receiving holiday pay—when the purpose and intent is that the holiday be a day of rest—and make qualifications stronger where no holiday work was required.

The purpose and intent of [Paragraph 2–g] is very clear and broad;—in fact this provision is one of the most liberal clauses for receiving holiday pay (for sickness) in the Steelworkers Union. At the same time if the Company so requests, they may require a technical reason from a doctor before granting holiday pay.

If this section was construed to mean or be used only for long term illness, an employee would be foolish to return to work after a one (1) day illness when he or she could remain at home under a doctor's care and receive holiday pay plus sickness and accident benefits. As we agreed in negotiations, only one person can determine whether or not one should be on a sick leave and that must be a qualified physician, not the Company.

The union requested full pay for Koss for the holidays of Thursday and Friday, November 22 and 23, 1973.

POSITION OF THE COMPANY

The company justified its denial of holiday pay to Koss on several bases. In a brief submitted at the arbitration hearing, the company outlined three major points in its argument:

1. Mr. Koss was not entitled to holiday pay because he was absent on the first scheduled workday after the Thanksgiving holiday and he was not on approved sick leave. The contract clearly defined the eligibility requirements in Article XIII, Paragraph 2(c) and 2(g) of the labor agreement.

2. It had never been the practice of the company to authorize holiday pay to employees who were absent on the scheduled workday before or after a holiday due to illnesses of short duration. The purpose and intent of Paragraph 2(g) under Article XIII had never been interpreted or applied to include occasional sickness of only a few days duration. In the past, employees had been approved for sick leave only in cases where an extended period of illness was anticipated and upon recommendation by a qualified physician. Since the Company received no recommendation for sick leave from a physician regarding Mr. Koss, and since he was not absent from work for an extended period of time, the company did not believe that holiday pay was justified.

3. Mr. Koss returned to work after being absent for only one scheduled workday. The fact that Mr. Koss was sick that day is not questioned by the company. The key factor was that there was no provision in the contract that employees who were absent for a few days due to sickness in conjunction with a holiday were to be paid holiday pay.

At the hearing, Charles Koenig, director of personnel at the Rheem plant, read the above arbitration brief points and presented several further arguments. He testified that the company had consistently maintained that sick leave must be of more than one day's duration in order for Article XIII, Paragraph 2(g) of the agreement to apply. He conceded that there was no place in the agreement that "sick leave" was explicitly defined, but he argued that it implicitly referred to a period longer than just one day. In support of this argument, he presented a "sick leave list" dated November 23, 1973 which showed 15 employees who were on approved sick leave over the Thanksgiving holidays and who received holiday pay for such. Koenig noted that to be eligible for sick leave, the employee must apply for it and have it approved by the company. He further noted that benefits do not begin until the eighth day of illness and that employees may receive no more than $50 per week for 26 weeks. He again stated that sick leaves were considered to be longer term situations and had never been construed to include single day absences.

The company next contended that it had maintained a consistent program of administering the holiday pay program since its inception. Koenig testified that, to his knowledge, every employee had always been required to work at least part of the day before and day after a holiday in order to be eligible for the holiday pay. He noted that this policy explained the receipt of holiday pay by Edie and Smith, because both had worked part of the Monday following Thanksgiving. Charles Bigham, the assistant personnel director, testified that he had explained the company's application of this policy to Mrs. Koss in his conversation with her on Monday, November 26.

The company also detailed the history behind Article XIII, Paragraph 2(c). The provision had been negotiated as a very "tight" provision, with a specific requirement that employees must work on the day immediately preceding and following holidays. The purpose of this provision was to prevent excessive absenteeism around the holidays. Koenig noted that such absenteeism before and after holidays had been a serious problem at the company's plant in Kalamazoo, Michigan following its adoption of a holiday pay provision in the agreement. Koenig testified that this was the reason for the company's consistent requirement that an employee work at least part of the day before and after a holiday in order to be eligible for holiday pay. He stated that the company was not discriminating against Koss in denying him holiday benefits, but only enforcing a long-standing past administrative policy consistent with the terms of the agreement.

Koenig further testified that the company recognized only one exception to the requirements of Paragraph 2(c), namely, Paragraph 2(g) which provides for sick leave. Koss, however, had not been on sick leave. Mr. Koenig reiterated that sick leave required company approval, that a doctor's certificate was insufficient, and that one day absences had never been construed to be sick leaves. He argued finally that both the language of the agreement and past practice clearly indicated that Paragraph 2(c) was intended to be interpreted strictly, as the company had applied it in this case.

The company requested that the grievance be denied.

APPENDIX

Relevant Provisions of the Agreement

Article XIII, Paragraph 2(c). To be eligible for holiday pay, an employee must work his last scheduled workday prior to and his first scheduled workday after a holiday.

*   *   *   *   *

Article XIII, Paragraph 2(g). An employee who is granted sick leave shall be paid for holidays falling within the first thirty (30) calendar days of his approved sick leave. Such payment would be made upon the employee's return to work, provided the employee returns to work on the first scheduled day following termination of the sick leave.

QUESTIONS

1. Evaluate the union's arguments that the company had been inconsistent, and that administration of policies such as the one in this case should not be left to sole management discretion.
2. Is holiday pay an earned benefit, or is it subject to the restrictions of a labor agreement? Discuss.
3. Should a one-day sickness be considered as a sick leave within the meaning of the agreement?
4. Was the company's policy in regard to holiday pay fair and uniformly applied?
5. If the arbitrator would rule in favor of the employee, what would be the ramifications of such a decision?